BARBARISM AND RELIGION
Volume One
The Enlightenments of Edward Gibbon, 1737–1764

'Barbarism and Religion' – Edward Gibbon's own phrase – is the title of a sequence of works by John Pocock designed to situate Gibbon, and his *Decline and Fall of the Roman Empire*, in a series of contexts in the history of eighteenth-century Europe. This is a major intervention from one of the world's leading historians of ideas, challenging the notion of any one 'Enlightenment' and positing instead a plurality of enlightenments, of which the English was one. Professor Pocock argues that the English Enlightenment of which Gibbon was part was an ecclesiastical as well as a secular phenomenon, one of several Protestant Enlightenments distinct from that of the Parisian *philosophes*, and an aspect of the reconstitution of Europe after the wars against Louis XIV.

In this first volume in the sequence, *The Enlightenments of Edward Gibbon*, John Pocock follows Gibbon through his youthful exile in Switzerland and his criticisms of the *Encyclopédie*, and traces the growth of his historical interests down to the conception of the *Decline and Fall* itself.

Born in London and brought up in Christchurch, New Zealand, J. G. A. POCOCK was educated at the Universities of Canterbury and Cambridge, and is now Harry C. Black Emeritus Professor of History at the Johns Hopkins University. His many seminal works on intellectual history include *The Ancient Constitution and the Feudal Law* (1957, second edition 1987), *Politics, Language and Time* (1971), *The Machiavellian Moment* (1975), and *Virtue, Commerce and History* (1985). He has also edited *The Political Works of James Harrington* (1977) and Burke's *Reflections on the Revolution in France* (1987), as well as the collaborative study *The Varieties of British Political Thought* (1995). A Corresponding Fellow of the British Academy and of the Royal Historical Society, Professor Pocock is also a member of the American Academy of Arts and Sciences and of the American Philosophical Society.

BARBARISM AND RELIGION
Volume One
The Enlightenments of Edward Gibbon, 1737–1764

J. G. A. POCOCK

CAMBRIDGE
UNIVERSITY PRESS

PUBLISHED BY THE PRESS SYNDICATE OF THE UNIVERSITY OF CAMBRIDGE
The Pitt Building, Trumpington Street, Cambridge CB2 1RP, United Kingdom

CAMBRIDGE UNIVERSITY PRESS
The Edinburgh Building, Cambridge CB2 2RU, United Kingdom
40 West 20th Street, New York, NY 10011-4211, USA
10 Stamford Road, Oakleigh, Melbourne 3166, Australia

First published 1999

Printed in the United Kingdom at the University Press, Cambridge

Typeset in Baskerville 11/12.5 pt [VN]

A catalogue record for this book is available from the British Library

Library of Congress cataloguing in publication data

Pocock, J. G. A. (John Greville Agard), 1924–
Barbarism and religion / J. G. A. Pocock.
v. 1 ; cm.
Includes bibliographical references and index.
Contents: v. 1. The enlightenments of Edward Gibbon, 1737–1764.
ISBN 0 521 63345 1
1. Gibbon, Edward, 1737–1794. History of the decline and fall of the Roman empire.
2. Rome – History – Empire, 30 B.C.–476 A.D. – Historiography. 3. Great Britain – Intellectual
life – 18th century. 4. Enlightenment – Great Britain. I. Title.
DG311.G6P63 1999   937'.06'092—dc21   98–41114   CIP

ISBN 0 521 63345 1 hardback

alla memoria di Franco Venturi

Contents

Acknowledgements

These volumes have been a long time in the making, and the list of those who have helped them is long in proportion. The first place must be given to the Department of History of the Johns Hopkins University, which has sustained me in every way for over twenty years, during and after my career in active teaching. Its faculty, graduate students, under-graduates and administrative staff have been true makers of my books, and it has borne the greater part of the costs of producing the typescript.

I am indebted to the American Academy of Arts and Sciences and to the Enciclopedia Italiana for the conference which saw the gestation of this project; to the Woodrow Wilson International Center for Scholars for a six months' fellowship in 1982, during which a great deal of the basic reading was done; to the University of Canterbury for a Canter-bury Fellowship, and the Tanner Foundation for Human Values for an invitation to lecture at Yale, on both of which occasions I was able to elaborate a group of three lectures serving to pilot my major themes; to the Andrew Mellon Foundation and Tulane University, for a visiting professorship in 1996, which gave me much time for writing; and to many other universities in Australia, Italy, Japan and the United States, for the opportunity to develop my ideas. David Womersley organised a conference at Jesus College, Oxford, in June 1994, which brought most of those active in Gibbon scholarship in contact with one another. I am further indebted to the President and Fellows of Corpus Christi College, Oxford, for their hospitality in the Michaelmas Term of 1997.

The research for this project has been carried out at many institutions to which I owe thanks, notably the Library of Congress and the Folger Shakespeare Library in Washington, DC, and the Milton S. Eisen-hower, George W. Peabody and John Work Garret Libraries of Johns Hopkins University; also the Charles W. Tilton Library of Tulane University. The help and kindness of the human staffs of these institutions did much to outweigh the alienation and frustration caused by compulsory computerisation.

The list of fellow scholars on whom I have relied for guidance, help and the exchange of ideas is very long and far above my deserving. I must name first a group of specialists in the study of Gibbon: Patricia Craddock of Florida, Gibbon's biographer, who has saved me from many errors chronological and textual; Michel Baridon of Dijon; Giuseppe Giarrizzo of Catania; and David Womersley of Oxford, who has given us the first critical edition of the *Decline and Fall of the Roman Empire*. To these must be added the names of two giants of Italian historiography: the late Arnaldo Momigliano, who had seen many cities and knew them all, and the late Franco Venturi, unrivalled master of Enlightenment studies. Next come those with whom I have conversed or corresponded, and whose generosity I have exploited. A special place belongs to Wilda Anderson and Orest Ranum of Johns Hopkins, for their unstinted help and guidance through the intricacies of the French *ancien régime* and Enlightenment, and to Nicholas Phillipson of Edinburgh, my pilot in the Scottish Enlightenment and a friendly critic of these volumes as they took shape. Thereafter, I name my guides alphabetically, adding the warning that they are not responsible for the use I have made of them: Guido Abbatista, Silvia Berti, Dena Goodman, Margaret C. Jacob, Alan C. Kors, Joseph M. Levine, Rolando Minuti, James Moore, Maria Luisa Pesante, Mark S. Phillips, Melvin Richter, John Robertson, Anthony Strugnell, Paul Turnbull, Robert Wokler. My colleagues for many years at the Folger Institute Center for the History of British Political Thought, Lena C. Orlin, Gordon J. Schochet, Lois G. Schwoerer, and Linda Levy Peck, have had more to do with this project than they may have noticed at our often talkative meetings.

In another category, many of the doctoral candidates with whom I have worked, at Washington University, Johns Hopkins University and elsewhere, have played parts in shaping this enterprise of which they may not be aware. I name them in chronological order, with my thanks: Arthur H. Williamson, Michael J. Mendle, Harold A. Ellis, Jack Fruchtman, Lionel A. McKenzie, William Craig Diamond, Lawrence E. Klein, John C. Laursen, Peter J. Diamond, James P. Murray, William E. Klein, Deborah Stephan, Cornelius Lettinga, Fred W. Conrad, Philip S. Hicks, John W. Marshall, Wyger R. E. Velema, Chong Son Yu, Eliga H. Gould, David L. Cohen, Zhizhong Zhang, Edith Bershadsky, Lenore Ealy, Robert Mankin, Anne McLaren, James Marino,

Katherine Clark and Mary Catherine Moran. My footnotes and list of references name not a few of these; to the others my debt is not less real.

This book was written, for the most part in blue ink, with a cartridge pen held firmly in the left hand. However, since it is no longer a convention of our civilisation that human handwriting can be read for technological or industrial purposes, my manuscript has been typed and processed, with efficiency and good humour, by Sharon Widomski, Sarah Springer, David Mene, Kate Turney, Catherine Cardno and Ellen Pearson. Elaine Frantz Parsons undertook the index. Felicity Pocock read the entire manuscript aloud while we checked the proofs. I thank them all.

At the Cambridge University Press, my debt is above all to Richard Fisher for his courage, imagination, patience and unfailing support. My late sister Penelope Wheeler, for many years an editor with the Historical Publications Branch of the New Zealand Department of Internal Affairs, helped me with some valuable suggestions. And in a category altogether their own, Felicity, Stephen and Hugh Pocock know things about the rise and progress of this project that nobody else does.

Note on references, quotations and translations

References to the *Decline and Fall* will be in the first instance to the original volume and chapter; in the second, by volume and page to the critical edition carried out by David Womersley (London: Allen Lane, the Penguin Press, 1994). This supersedes the previous modern edition, that by J. B. Bury (1896), on which scholars have been obliged to rely, short of consulting the first printings, for the last hundred years. However, since the edition by Bury is still in many libraries as an object of deserved respect, references will here be given in the third instance to the revision of 1909, reprinted by the AMS Press of New York in 1974. Womersley's edition is unique in paying attention to both the original divisions between volumes, and the changes wrought by Gibbon in printing and revising his own text. References to Gibbon's autobiographical writings are similarly given in two forms: in the first place to Georges Bonnard's *Edward Gibbon: Memoirs of my Life* (cited as *Memoirs*), which is convenient but not exhaustive, and in the second place to John Murray's *The Autobiographies of Edward Gibbon* (cited as *A*), which prints all Gibbon's drafts in full but has not been reprinted since 1897. The bibliographical situation which has made this procedure necessary is less than satisfactory. References to Gibbon's other writings, including his letters, are given to modern critical editions, and where these are lacking to the 1814 edition of the *Miscellaneous Works* by Lord Sheffield. All references are given in what has been found the most compendious bibliographical form.

This volume, like its successor, quotes liberally from Gibbon himself and from texts which supply the contexts illustrating his own. Where these quotations are in languages other than English, the original has been allowed to stand and a translation appended to it. When Gibbon himself wrote in French, it has seemed ridiculous to give a modern English version priority over his own words, and this principle has been extended to his peers writing in the main languages of European culture. Since he was himself cosmopolitan and polyglot, we need more than one language in which to read him and his age. Where a passage in French is cited from an eighteenth-century edition or manuscript, I have followed eighteenth-century spelling and accentuation, which often differs from the modern. Where a twentieth-century edition has been used, modernisation has usually occurred and is silently followed.

The translations supplied are from eighteenth-century English versions wherever these can be found, on the principle that these permit us to hear the voice of the age even where they leave something to be desired. Where such translations are lacking, accredited twentieth-century versions have been used; and only in the last resort have I ventured to supply my own translations. To avoid as far as possible any break in the reader's pursuit of continuity, all translations have been situated as close to the passages they render as modern technology can place them.

It may conveniently be inserted at this point that '*Decline and Fall*' in italic refers to the work, 'Decline and Fall' in roman to the phenomenon, and 'decline and fall' without initial capitals to the concept.

Abbreviations

A	*The Autobiographies of Edward Gibbon, printed verbatim from hitherto unpublished MSS., with an introduction by the Earl of Sheffield*; edited by John Murray. London, 1897
Bury	J. B. Bury (ed.), *The History of the Decline and Fall of the Roman Empire, by Edward Gibbon. With introduction, notes and appendices.* In seven volumes. London: Methuen and Co., 1909
Discours	Jean le Rond d'Alembert, 'Discours Préliminaire des Editeurs', *Encyclopédie ou Dictionnaire Raisonnée des Sciences, des Arts et des Métiers. Discours préliminaire à l'Encyclopédie.* Paris, 1751
EGLH	Patricia B. Craddock, *Edward Gibbon: Luminous Historian: 1772–1794.* Baltimore: The Johns Hopkins University Press, 1989
English Essays	Patricia B. Craddock (ed.), *The English Essays of Edward Gibbon.* Oxford: at the Clarendon Press, 1972
Histoire	*Histoire de l'Académie des Inscriptions et Belles Lettres.* The Hague, subsequently Amsterdam, 1718–
Journal A	D. M. Low (ed.), *Gibbon's Journal to January 28th, 1763: My Journal, I, II and III, and Ephemerides.* With introductory essays. London, Chatto and Windus; New York: W. W. Norton, 1929
Journal B	Georges A. Bonnard (ed.), *Le Journal de Gibbon à Lausanne, 17 Août 1763–19 Avril 1764.* Lausanne: Librairie de l'Université, 1945
Journal C	Georges A. Bonnard (ed.), *Gibbon's Journey from Geneva to Rome: His Journal from 20 April to 2 October 1764.* London and New York: Thomas Nelson and Sons, 1961
Letters	J. E. Norton (ed.), *The Letters of Edward Gibbon.* In three volumes. London: Cassell and Company, 1956

Library	Geoffrey Keynes (ed.), *The Library of Edward Gibbon.* Second edition. N.P.: St Paul's Bibliographies, 1980
Low	D. M. Low, *Edward Gibbon, 1737–1794.* London: Chatto and Windus; New York: Random House, 1937
Memoirs	Georges A. Bonnard (ed.), *Edward Gibbon: Memoirs of My Life.* New York: Funk and Wagnall, 1969
Mémoires	*Mémoires de Littérature tirés des Registres de l'Académie Royale des Inscriptions et Belles-Lettres.* The Hague, 1719–24; Amsterdam, 1724–
MG	Gavin R. de Beer, Georges A. Bonnard and Louis Junod (eds.), *Miscellanea Gibboniana.* Lausanne: Librairie de l'Université, 1952
MW	Lord Sheffield (ed.), *The Miscellaneous Works of Edward Gibbon, Esq. With Memoirs of his Life and Writings, Composed by Himself: illustrated from his Letters, with Occasional Notes and Narrative.* A new edition, with considerable additions, in five volumes; London: John Murray, 1814
Womersley	David Womersley (ed.), *Edward Gibbon: The History of the Decline and Fall of the Roman Empire.* In three volumes. London: Allen Lane, The Penguin Press, 1994
YEG	Patricia B. Craddock, *Young Edward Gibbon: Gentleman of Letters.* Baltimore and London: The Johns Hopkins University Press, 1982

Introduction

This volume, and its successor, are the first of a number of studies which I hope to publish with Edward Gibbon's *Decline and Fall of the Roman Empire* at their centre. At times (though not in this volume) my focus will be on the text of that great work, and at others on texts to which it makes allusion that supply contexts in which passages of the *Decline and Fall* may usefully be read. This widening of focus is intended to lead to a portrayal of the writing of history and other intellectual activities in the setting of the eighteenth century, in which larger context both Gibbon's history and his life as a historian may be situated, so that we understand the *Decline and Fall* as an artefact of its age and culture. At the end of the twentieth century, there are still specialists in some of the many fields which Gibbon studied who can examine and even evaluate his performances in them, treating him as a contemporary and equal who may be paid the compliment of criticism;[1] but the work I am presenting here has the different objective stated in the preceding sentence. *Barbarism and Religion* is not a contribution to the historiography of the Roman empire, but to that of European culture in the eighteenth century.

It has been a long time in the making, and I wish to summarise its history here, partly because to do so will enable me to begin discharging many debts of gratitude, but more because it may help the reader to understand the character of the work presented. It was in the Piazza Paganica at Rome, in the month of January 1976, that the idea of writing a book with the present title first started to my mind. I had been invited to a conference[2] sponsored by the American Academy of Arts and Sciences and the Enciclopedia Italiana, to mark both the bicentennial of Gibbon's first volume – 1976 was a year of many bicentennials – and the sesquimillennial of the deposition of Romulus Augustulus, last

[1] McKitterick and Quinault, 1997.
[2] Its proceedings were published as Bowersock, Clive and Graubard, 1977; see also Rovigatti, 1980.

Emperor of the western empire. We had begun our conference at the head of the Capitol steps, where Gibbon may or may not have sat musing on 15 October, 1764, and adjourned it to the Piazza Paganica and the offices of the Enciclopedia Italiana. I had recently published a book called *The Machiavellian Moment: Florentine Political Thought and the Atlantic Republican Tradition*,[3] which is concerned with the survival into the early modern world of the ancient ideal of civic and military virtue, and its response to the challenge, in the eighteenth century, of the new ideals, and realities, of commercial and civil society; and it occurred to me, at one of the sessions of the 1976 conference, that a study of the *Decline and Fall* would make a valuable counterpiece. I could see, and made it part of the paper I then presented, that Gibbon accepted the thesis of the decline of ancient virtue as largely explaining the collapse of the ancient world, but denied that the process would repeat itself under the conditions of modern society (Rousseau, Raynal and Diderot were among many who by no means shared that confidence). This theme has figured in all that I have since written about the *Decline and Fall*, and will be found in the volume I am here introducing.

The title *Barbarism and Religion*, however, came into my mind at this moment of conception and has been that under which I have planned, re-planned and presented the succession or collection of volumes of which it is now the overall title. It indicates an awareness, dawning then and larger since, that there is far more to the *Decline and Fall* than the tensions between virtue and commerce, ancient and modern, or even, in a sense, than Decline and Fall itself. When Gibbon in his concluding pages remarks 'I have described the triumph of barbarism and religion,'[4] he may be conceding that what set out as a history of the end of the Roman empire has become a great deal more than that. The Gothic, Lombard, Frankish and Saxon barbarians replaced the western empire with systems in whose barbarism may be found the seeds of European liberty; this is declared near the outset of the *Decline and Fall*, though by the end of the work Gibbon has turned away from the west to pursue the less rewarding question of with what (if anything) Slav and Turkish barbarians have replaced the empire in the east. Thus far the theme of barbarism; under the head of religion, we face as Gibbon did the knowledge that the replacement of empire by church as the governing principle of European civilisation is a far greater matter than the secondary question of how far Christianity was a cause of the Decline

---

[3] Pocock, 1975.   [4] Womersley, III, p. 1068; Bury, VII, p. 321.

and Fall. It was already a historiographic commonplace that the end of empire led to the rise of the papacy; Gibbon explored it in depth, but recognised that this theme, however great, was limited to the Latin west and that the challenge of councils, bishops and patriarchs to imperial authority was a history to be told in Greek and led to the world-altering displacement of Greek and Syrian culture by Arabic and Islamic. From this perception he went on to the strangest of his decisions, one perplexing even to him: the decision to leave the history of the medieval and modern Latin west to those who had written it already, and pursue instead the history of Byzantium and its Islamic, barbaric and Latin invaders. It was a decision which he was to find extremely challenging, and how far he met the challenge is still debated.

The *Decline and Fall*, then, is a great deal more than its first volume, that of 1776; a great deal more than the account of ancient civilisation in its last flowering, capped by two famously disrespectful chapters about Christian culture at its first appearance, which it is taken to be in textbook history and cultural tradition. If the first volume recounts the decline and fall of the Antonine monarchy in the second and third centuries of the Christian era, the remaining five recount the full history – ending in decline and fall after eleven centuries of continuous existence – of the Constantinean and Christian monarchy that replaced it, from the foundation of a new Rome by the first Constantine to the death of the last in the taking of his city by the Turks. Far from being a history of the ancient world and its coming to an end, the work as a whole is a history of late antiquity and the middle ages, carried out on a scale unlike anything else in the eighteenth century. We have to consider what led Gibbon to plan and execute such a project, and there is evidence suggesting both that he intended it from the beginning and that he did not quite know in what difficulties his undertaking would involve him. During the twelve or more years in which he wrote six volumes with a span of thirteen centuries, 'decline and fall' became 'the triumph of barbarism and religion', and the *Decline and Fall* became many things both within and exceeding his original intentions.

What had once been intended as a history of the city of Rome became a history of its empire, invaded by barbarians and transformed by the church. Under the heading 'barbarism', Gibbon's initial concern with the Gothic and Germanic invaders who sacked the city and settled the western provinces expanded to become a history of the nomadic and pastoral peoples of Europe's steppe frontier, and a history of Eurasia as far as China, whose relations with Turkic and Mongol peoples he saw to be crucial to what was happening in the Roman and post-Roman west of the continent. Here he drew on Jesuit and Russian scholarship, and on the conjectural history constructed by European jurists, notably those of the Scottish Enlightenment, to explain how human society had passed through a sequence of stages including the pastoral. The *Decline and Fall* grew until it became a world history written on a Eurasian though not on a Euro-American scale, one of a number of such histories characterising the period of Enlightenment. But the jurists' history of human society was more than a means of explaining the role of nomad invaders in the history of the Eurasian civilisations, or the prevalence of hunter-gatherer 'savagery' in the American and Antipodean worlds being conquered and settled by Europeans (a history of which Gibbon took notice when it came his way). It was intended as a deep background to the central theme of Enlightened history. The history of civil society and its morality underlay the history of the system of states through which Europeans had recaptured control of their civil affairs after the long night of 'barbarism and religion', a phrase as old as the renaissance of letters and used to denote the 'Christian millennium' of feudal and ecclesiastical control of a submerged civilisation, which could be dated from Constantine to Charles V or from Charlemagne to Louis XIV. Gibbon once remarked that ancient history was a history of civil authority, modern that of ecclesiastical;[5] and though he was now living in and writing a history 'modern' in the further sense that it had overcome the ecclesiastical and restored the primacy of civil society, one thing which made him a 'modern' as that term was used in the eighteenth century was his command of a critical scholarship that made it possible to return to the ancients and claim to understand them better than they had themselves. It joined with the techniques of historical understanding developed by the great jurists of the age – German, French and Scottish – to form a systematised civil morality meant to enable Europeans to live in their own world, if not without religion then without ecclesiastical disturbance or domination. Enlightened historiography is, almost without exception, the execution of this purpose.

   The Enlightened historians – Voltaire, Hume, Robertson – are concerned with the exit from the Christian millennium into a Europe of state power and civil society; the *Decline and Fall* is exceptional in confining itself to the way into that millennium. If we consider Gibbon as sharing the intentions of this historiography – of which there is every

---

[5] Womersley, III, p. 109; Bury, v, p. 286.

reason to think that he was aware – we must suppose him intent on conquering by its methods the world of late antiquity, in which the system it was formed to overcome had taken shape: on studying, in depth and detail, 'the triumph of barbarism and religion'. It took him time to form this intention and to realise its implications for his work. What had set out to be a history of the fall of the empire became a history of the rise of the church, and alone among the great Enlightened historians Gibbon became an ecclesiastical historian – the best, in the regretful judgment of Cardinal Newman, who had ever practised in England – a historian of theology, and a historian of the philosophy that underlay it: of the Platonic, neo-Platonic and scholastic philosophy which it had long been an aim of Enlightenment to expel from the European mind. Gibbon wrote its history with that end in view; but unlike Voltaire, he wrote its history as that of an active self-understanding force, not of a mere darkness and absurdity which rendered historical thought impossible. Though an unbeliever, he wrote like a great clerical historian, and to understand this aspect of his life and thought we must travel back into a world where Enlightenment was a product of religious debate and not merely a rebellion against it.

Here we have reached the point from which the present volume takes its rise. I have depicted the *Decline and Fall* as involving Gibbon in various historiographic enterprises to which the adjective 'Enlightened' may be applied, and I have used the noun 'Enlightenment' as denoting a process at work in European culture. We have to remember, however, that the terms 'Enlightenment', and still more 'The Enlightenment', entered anglophone usage at a time later than that of the phenomena they are employed to present, and we have to consider the historiographic effects of using them as we do. They are not mere fictions; there were intellectual enterprises at work from the later seventeenth century which they have long been used to isolate and identify. Those engaged in these enterprises were aware in their own terms of what they and their colleagues and competitors were doing – aware even of their historical significance, to a degree itself new in European culture – and the metaphor of light (*lumière, lume, Aufklärung*) is strongly present in their writings. There was something, or a number of things, going on, and there is a good case for employing the words 'Enlightened' and 'Enlightenment' in attempting to write about it. But the active intellectuals of the period did not use the term 'The Enlightenment', or employ it as we do to unify and reify their activities, isolating them in history by means of a definition which includes those whom it should include and excludes those

whom it should not. It is at this point that I enter into debate with the
shade of the great historian to whose memory this book is dedicated.
Franco Venturi, delivering the Trevelyan Lectures at Cambridge in
1969, spoke of Gibbon as 'the English giant of the Enlightenment', but
went on to say that as England, unlike Scotland, could not be seen as
taking part in the phenomenon of 'Enlightenment' as the term was used,
Gibbon must be thought of as an exile from Enlightenment and a
solitary figure in his own country.[6] It was a reading to which Gibbon's
bilingualism, and the division of his life and loyalties between England
and the Pays de Vaud, lent a certain support; but there remained
something unsatisfactory about it. Gibbon ceased to write in French,
and developed a powerful and unique style of English prose, in order to
write the *Decline and Fall*; he became a member of parliament, involved if
not active in the major crisis of the American Revolution, while he was
writing it; and at many points in its text he can be seen carrying out
enterprises of an English resonance and susceptible of an English explanation. The proposition that he must be either not English or not
Enlightened will not quite do; I suspect that Venturi was in search of a
way past it, though I will not attempt to determine whether he ever
found one.

How the problem arose may be seen from the pages of his *Utopia and
Reform in the Enlightenment*, read as a prelude to the volumes of his *Settecento
Riformatore*.[7] Venturi was defining 'The Enlightenment' by the presence
or absence of *philosophes* (alternatively, *gens de lettres*): self-appointed secular intellectuals, offering a criticism of society and putting themselves forward as its guides towards modernity and reform. He rightly
saw that such *philosophes* were not to be met with in England – at least
before the untypical advent of Bentham and the Philosophic Radicals –
and on that ground excluded England from 'The Enlightenment';
though he thought that Scotland might be included in it, by supposing
that Smith, Ferguson and Millar were the equivalents of Genovesi and
Filangieri, the *philosophes* of a major provincial culture guiding Scotland,
as they had guided Naples, towards membership of the European
settecento riformatore. Venturi did not mean by this to consign England to
outer darkness; 'in England', he observed, 'the rhythm was different';
but just what this meant it may be that he never fully explored.

In the present volume I shall attempt to show that Gibbon cannot be
fitted into the paradigm of an Enlightenment defined as the activity of

[6] Venturi, 1971, pp. 132–3; below, pp. 293–4.   [7] Venturi, 1969, 1976, 1979, 1984.

philosophes (whether the Moderate literati of Edinburgh and Glasgow are to be accounted *philosophes* is a further question, to be considered elsewhere). Gibbon is not a *philosophe* in exile, for the reason that from his first and very early encounter with the *gens de lettres* of Paris and their *Encyclopédie* he rejected their enterprise, and continued to do so in terms that were to lead him to Burkean conclusions. However, this is not to be accounted a rejection of Enlightenment; I argue that Burke himself was an Enlightened figure, who saw himself defending Enlightened Europe against the *gens de lettres* and their revolutionary successors, and that he stands for Counter-Enlightenment, in Isaiah Berlin's phrase, only in the sense that his is one kind of Enlightenment in conflict with another. Applied to Gibbon, the programme this implies – that of pluralising Enlightenment into a number of movements in both harmony and conflict with each other – will lead me to argue that there were aspects of Enlightenment which neither required nor produced the presence of *philosophes*, and that this presence, though a widely distributed and deeply important phenomenon, occurs within a context larger than itself. I intend to argue that Enlightenment may be characterised in two ways:[8] first, as the emergence of a system of states, founded in civil and commercial society and culture, which might enable Europe to escape from the wars of religion without falling under the hegemony of a single monarchy; second, as a series of programmes for reducing the power of either churches or congregations to disturb the peace of civil society by challenging its authority. Enlightenment in the latter sense was a programme in which ecclesiastics of many confessions might and did join, but it was capable of leading to a general assault on the central traditions of Christian theology as conveying the notion that divine spirit was present in the world and exercising authority in it; and at this point *philosophes* might appear and conduct anti-Christian and anti-religious programmes of many kinds, linked often but not necessarily with programmes of modernisation and reform. The fifteenth and sixteenth chapters of the *Decline and Fall* earned Gibbon the name of a *philosophe* of the irreligious sort; but these chapters need to be considered in the setting of the *Decline and Fall* as a whole. They offer one among several keys to the question of how Enlightenment led Gibbon to write a great and extraordinary history.

In close but extremely various relations with an indictment of Nicene theology – and ultimately of the central doctrines of the Incarnation, the

---

[8] For earlier statements of this view, see Pocock, 1985b and 1989a.

Atonement and the Trinity – as encouraging the belief that a kingdom not of this world might nevertheless be exercised in it, there went a series of programmes for developing a culture of the mind, founded on method and manners, letters and law, and the critical capacity of reading the texts of European civilisation, which should enable it to function independently of Christian theology and anchor the life of the mind in the life of civil society. This repudiation of theology is, however, intimately related with the theology it repudiates and varies in character as it appears in, and attempts to substitute itself for, cultures enduringly Catholic or Protestant, Anglican, Calvinist or Lutheran. Since Enlightenment cannot be understood apart from theology, it sometimes appears – even in its most viciously anti-Christian expressions – as a tissue of theological statements; and this may help to explain the character of the *Decline and Fall* as a great Enlightened history of Christian theology. By studying Gibbon's early adult life in both its English and its Swiss settings, there can be made to appear a number of ways in which he had occasion to be Enlightened, to find himself involved in conflicts which were those of Enlightenment, and to proceed towards the writing of the *Decline and Fall* as a major work of Enlightened historiography; ways which did not necessitate the presence of *philosophes*, and were compatible with his partial yet real rejection of the Parisian *philosophes* at the time of his first becoming aware of them. Out of the life of the mind in civil society there arose a history of mind and society together.

By this point we shall have established the presence in England of a species of Enlightenment, and shall have escaped from the English exceptionalism imposed by a rigid application of the *philosophe* paradigm. Enlightenment in England was of course intimately bound up with the special, indeed unique character of the Church of England, the key as I see it to early modern English history; but this church (and the young Gibbon with it) became involved in a process of Protestant Enlightenment which appears crucial to the understanding of both the *Decline and Fall* and its author. Here I follow H. R. Trevor-Roper, who in a series of essays[9] contended that the origins of Enlightenment in the Netherlands, England and western Protestantism generally were Grotian, Arminian and Erasmian; the Church of England became involved in this Enlightenment on its Calvinist face, the other remaining Catholic. The concept of a Protestant Enlightenment is crucial to the understanding of Gibbon in both his English and his Lausannais ex-

---

[9] Trevor-Roper, 1968, 1988, 1992.

perience, since his intellectual allegiances remained heavily focused on that *république des lettres* which had flourished in the Netherlands, among Dutch Remonstrants, Huguenot exiles and Genevan and Lausannais refugees from strict Calvinism, in the generation preceding his own birth; we shall see that it was his defence of an erudition very largely theirs, against the philosophic criticism of d'Alembert in the *Discours Préliminaire à l'Encyclopédie*, that led towards the construction of his historiography.

The volume I am here presenting may therefore be considered as an attempt to reshape the geography and definition of Enlightenment, in such a way as to find a place in it for Venturi's 'English giant of the Enlightenment'. Gibbon is at its centre only in the sense that its definitions constantly recur to his position in it; there are of course many aspects of Enlightenment not considered here, for the reason that they are not relevant to him nor he to them, but their absence carries no message that they are not important. If there is a single target of my criticism it is the concept of 'The Enlightenment', as a unified phenomenon with a single history and definition, but the criticism is directed more against the article than against the noun. I have no quarrel with the concept of Enlightenment; I merely contend that it occurred in too many forms to be comprised within a single definition and history, and that we do better to think of a family of Enlightenments, displaying both family resemblances and family quarrels (some of them bitter and even bloody). To insist on bringing them all within a single formula – which excludes those it cannot be made to fit – is, I think, more the expression of one's loyalties than of one's historical insight. Since we are all liberal agnostics, we write whig histories of liberal agnosticism; Gibbon, however, did not write history like that.

This volume, then, traces *The Enlightenments of Edward Gibbon*, following the trajectory of his earlier life through a series of contexts to which the term 'Enlightenment' can in various ways be applied, until we reach his return from Rome to England in the early months of 1765. By that time – though his full encounter with Scottish Enlightenment had still to occur – he was well on the way towards the formation of a concept of historiography as he intended to practise it, and he would have us believe that the conception of the *Decline and Fall* had already occurred, though its gestation was to take another ten years – a proposition by no means unproblematic. We can say, however, that the formation of Gibbon's historiography – even, perhaps, his philosophy of history – was intimately connected with his responses to the various

Enlightenments he had encountered: English, Arminian and Parisian, with Scottish to come. It was connected also with the place he desired to find for himself in European literary and critical scholarship, which is a larger question; but scholarship, we may say, was his Enlightenment.

A second volume will present the grand historiography of Enlightenment as it stood when Gibbon published his first volume in 1776, and will consider the character of the *Decline and Fall* as it appears in this great company. Other volumes may follow under the series title of *Barbarism and Religion*, but their reading should not be subordinated to their place in the series. Each, that is to say, will be designed, as this is, to be read as a single study, rounded out to the point where its contribution to Gibbon studies is defined and delimited; the reader is desired only to remember that others will come. They will provide a series of contexts in which Gibbon's life and the *Decline and Fall* may be situated; I intend neither an intellectual biography nor in the narrative sense an intellectual history, so much as the depiction of a historical world – a *peinture*, as it would have been put in the eighteenth century, rather than a *récit*. Of these contexts, some will be aspects of the intellectual history of the times, while others will be formed by major texts with which Gibbon's writings interacted. I shall study some of these in greater depth than is dictated by their direct relation with the *Decline and Fall*; the latter is a great text inhabiting a world of great texts which existed independently of it as well as in relation to it. It has been put to me that I am attempting an ecology rather than an etiology of the *Decline and Fall*; a study of the world in which it existed, not confined to its genesis in that world. An enquiry of that order begins in the volume which I here deliver to the curiosity and candour of the public.

PART I

England and Switzerland, 1737–1763

CHAPTER I

Putney, Oxford and the question of English Enlightenment

THE GIBBON FAMILY AND THE CRISIS IN CHURCH AND STATE

The purpose of this volume will be to effect a series of contextualisations: to situate Gibbon's life in a succession of settings, in which his creation of the text of the *Decline and Fall* may be usefully understood. It will be observed that I take him to have been the author of that text, and believe the text to be intelligible as the product of his activity.[1] At the same time, that activity was carried on in a number of contexts, of some of which he may occasionally have been more aware than of others, while some may not have preoccupied his attention at any time at all; the possibility that some of the contexts which will be distinguished operated to form his text indirectly, subconsciously or unconsciously, is not ruled out before it occurs. Of these contexts some will be national, or regional, and cultural: English, since Gibbon was born in England, spent much of his life there, and wrote his greatest work in English; Lausannais, since he spent crucial years of his life and completed the *Decline and Fall* there, and first wrote history in the French which he acquired in the Pays de Vaud; and it will be necessary to pay attention to the intellectual climates of Amsterdam, Paris, and Edinburgh, where he did not reside but which were important to him. He must also be considered as a 'citizen', that is a reader and correspondent, of several *républiques des lettres* and scholarly connections; and we shall also be thinking of him as an associate of several 'enlightenments', since it is a premise of this book that we can no longer write satisfactorily of 'The Enlightenment' as a unified and universal intellectual movement. Finally, Gibbon and his book will be situated in contexts formed by a number of continuous patterns of discourse, humanist, philosophical, juridical, theological and controversial, which joined with the discourse of historiography proper to con-

---

[1] A bibliography of the extensive literature by those who deny the reality of authors and the readability of texts will not be included in this book.

stitute the great personal discourse of the text and author of the *Decline and Fall of the Roman Empire*, and offer – once again – a series of contexts in which it can be interpreted. For the duration at least of this chapter, however, that which is being contextualised will be the biography of the author,[2] as Gibbon's life moved towards the point at which composition of the *Decline and Fall* began.

Edward Gibbon was born on 27 April, 1737 – one-third of the way through the reign of George II of Great Britain and Hanover (1727–60), and towards the end of the ministry of Sir Robert Walpole (1721–42) – into a family then resident at Putney, with connections in both the City of London and the counties of Surrey and Hampshire. In later years Horace Walpole, who was not free from the snobbishness of a radical-chic aristocrat, wrote of him as 'the son of a foolish alderman',[3] but he was not sprung from the urban patriciates – not very common in England – to whom the term *bourgeoisie* is properly applied, and his paternal lineages move, in ways typical of the lesser English gentry, from land to commerce and back again to land. It is relevant, however, that his grandfather, to whom we may refer as Edward Gibbon I, had grown wealthy as a contractor supplying the armies of William III and Marlborough; that his father, Edward Gibbon II, attempted feverishly and without success to convert land into a source of personal income; and that the historian himself, Edward Gibbon III, in the clear knowledge that he would remain childless, did much better – with the advice of the well-informed man of business Lord Sheffield – at making landed property the source of an income off which he lived as an expatriate man of letters at Lausanne. None of these facts is irrelevant to the *Decline and Fall*, which is deeply preoccupied, from beginning to end, with the conversion of Europe into that leisured, polite, aristocratically governed commercial civilisation which we have chosen to call the *ancien régime*.[4]

It would be an error, nevertheless, to think of the England into which Gibbon was born as Augustan, stable and complacent, progressing

[2] The authoritative biography, other than Gibbon's *Memoirs* themselves, is now to be found in the two volumes by Patricia B. Craddock, hereafter referred to as *YEG* and *EGLH*. See also Low, 1937. The major studies by Giarrizzo, 1954, and Baridon, 1975, to which extensive reference will be made, are intellectual histories of the formation of Gibbon's mind and work, not quite the same as biographies.

[3] Low, pp. 23, 250. Cf. Craddock, *EGLH*, p. 173, where Gibbon's aldermanic birth becomes Walpole's explanation of his willingness to serve North's government. For Gibbon's view of Walpole, 'that ingenious trifler', see *English Essays*, pp. 122–3.

[4] For the questions of how far Hanoverian Britain may be termed an *ancien régime*, and whether the term itself is currently being used coherently, compare, contrast and reconcile J. C. D. Clark, 1986, Brewer, 1989 and Langford, 1989.

sedately towards liberty, prosperity and empire. It attained all three of these things, but it bought them at a high price in dynastic and religious instability, financial and political turmoil. The salient facts in Gibbon family history are that Edward Gibbon I had been a director of the South Sea Company, a Tory financial project set up to counter the Whig giants of the Bank of England and the East India Company, and on its collapse had been fined of most of his possessions by a vengeful parliament; that Edward Gibbon II had been a closet, a futile but not an inactive Jacobite at least as late as 1745;[5] that Edward Gibbon III grew up in a religiously divided ambience, and that the first crucial occurrence of his career was a conversion to Catholicism as an undergraduate of sixteen. These events are by no means unconnected, and the effects of the last of them can be traced to the closing pages of the *Decline and Fall*. They are all phenomena of the rapidly growing but deeply divided England into which Gibbon came to see that he had been born, and if he succeeded in writing history in a spirit of serene scepticism – which is by no means certain – the roads by which he came to it were not serene at all. We can trace Gibbon's initial progress towards the point at which he became a historian by viewing it in the context of English history after 1688.

The revolution (for so it was called)[6] of that and the following year had been undertaken in an England recently re-Anglicanised, where nobility, gentry and clergy were convinced that the restoration and maintenance of the authority of a royally governed church offered the only way to bury the memory of the calamitous breakdown of sovereignty and governing order in the years of civil war and interregnum. This conviction had not been quite enough to clarify the character of the restored Church of England, or to re-cement its relations with the crown that was its supreme governor; and James II had been overthrown in consequence of the perceived destabilisation of the church brought about by his determination to promote Catholics (with the support of Dissenters) to the high offices from which they were excluded by the Test and Corporation Acts. It had been part of this perception that James could only effect his ends by the exercise of authority known as 'arbitrary' and 'absolute', which would threaten the security of property (including office) under law, itself one of the principal

---

[5] For his doings, such as they were, see Turnbull, 1987.
[6] For recent interpretations of that event, see Jones, 1973; Speck, 1989; Beddard, 1991; Israel, 1991; Schwoerer, 1992; Jones, 1992; Hoak and Feingold, 1996.

meanings evoked by the use of the word 'liberty';[7] but the Church of England, committed to the principle that kingly authority was divinely appointed and might not be resisted, believed itself to have done what was necessary to check James's policies with the passive resistance, and subsequent acquittal by the law, of the Seven Bishops in June and July of 1688. This Anglican triumph,[8] however, coincided with the birth of a male heir to James II and his queen, raising the threat that his policies would be kept up by a line of Catholic successors. His Protestant daughters, Mary of Orange and Anne of Denmark, were involved in the pretence which instantly grew up that the child's birth was an imposture, and Mary's husband, William, was invited to England in an expedition in preparation for which he had already fitted out a powerful armada. It was this Dutch and English initiative that placed on the church stresses which it found difficulty in bearing, and which may be found affecting the politics, and the religious and historical culture, of England during the next century.

   William's intentions – whenever they came to be formed – were dynastic and military; he determined to make his wife and himself sovereigns of England, Scotland and Ireland, and to commit all three kingdoms to the 'grand alliance' he was building against the 'universal monarchy' of Louis XIV. He would have found much greater difficulty in attaining either objective if James II had stood and fought him, instead of escaping to France and placing himself under Louis's protection. By this action James removed the likelihood of civil war in England to the distance at which it remained[9] for the next sixty to seventy years, while at the same time he condemned England to a future of involvement in great European wars. The dynastic and ecclesiastical struggle in England became an issue which could only be settled by the outcome of the wars between France and the grand alliance. During the years (1688–97) of what is variously known as the War of the League of Augsburg, the War of the English Succession, King William's War (the American term) and the Nine Years War, English troops fought in Ireland and Flanders to ensure their own revolution, their position in Britain and the Atlantic archipelago, and the maintenance of William III's struggle against France; and during this war English military and financial organisation underwent the revolutionary changes known by

---

[7] Nenner, 1991.   [8] Goldie, 1991.
[9] It is a matter of controversy among historians how great this distance was. For the recent literature on Jacobitism see Cruickshanks, 1979 and 1982; Lenman, 1980; Colley, 1982; Szechi, 1984; McLynn, 1985; Monod, 1989.

the names of 'the standing army', 'the national debt' and 'public credit', which were to make Great Britain capable of acting as a major power in Europe and America, but at the same time to produce profound new tensions within English political society and transform the English and Scottish perception of history and the place of Britain within it. The tensions generated by this *novus ordo seclorum* were to interact in highly complex ways with those produced by the dynastic and ecclesiastical insecurities of the Revolution Settlement.

This state of affairs lies behind the predicaments in which all three generations of Gibbons at different times found themselves. The Jacobitism of Edward Gibbon II, in particular, can be understood if we address ourselves to the dynastic and ecclesiastical consequences of the Revolution. The replacement of James II by his daughters, Mary and then Anne, was a dynastic failure, since both died without progeny, with the result that even after the Act of Settlement in 1700, which enjoined a Protestant succession, and the enthronement of the Hanoverians in 1714, which supplied it, there was no reigning Stuart line to challenge the claims of the exiled branch to legitimacy. This claim was formidable because of the difficulty which the Church of England long felt in reconciling itself to the changes of dynasty imposed in 1688 and 1714; even after a majority of the clergy had taken the oaths to obey William and Mary as lawful sovereigns, and even after new appointments had rendered the episcopate and upper hierarchy increasingly whig and latitudinarian, there persisted a widespread sentiment that the Revolutionary and Hanoverian monarchy was at best *de facto*, and that something remained to be done before there could be a regime truly *de jure*. The church knew well enough that James II had fallen because the unity of church and crown was defective, but it found difficulty, before and after the reign of Anne, in believing that that unity had been restored. The history of the period constantly persuades us that if the Stuart exiles had thought Westminster worth a Test – as Henri IV had legendarily decided that *Paris vaut bien une messe* – they would have been triumphantly restored; but they never conformed to the church of which they were by law supreme governors until it was too late (if even then).[10] Hanoverian insecurity, however, the result of imperfect legitimation, persisted – in the judgment of Edward Gibbon III – until the accession of George III in 1760; and historians have told us at what a price that

---

[10] The allusion is to Prince Charles Edward's reported visit to London in disguise, and reception into the Church of England, in 1750.

prince bought the support of the country gentry to whom Gibbon belonged.

The Hanoverian succession occurred after the kingdoms of Britain (brought to a closer union in 1707) had taken a leading part in two great wars – those of 1688 to 1697 and 1702 to 1713 – fought by a grand alliance against France. These wars had been marked by the victories of Marlborough and by the establishment of Britain as a significant power on the European mainland, but had altered the English and Scottish ruling structures in ways that were widely resented. They were seen as entailing the growth of new governing elites, made up of army officers, army contractors (even those as Jacobitically inclined as Edward Gibbon I may have been),[11] powerful speculators in the new structures of public credit – some of whom were Huguenot, Dutch and Sephardic aliens – and the mainly Whig and sometimes Dissenting politicians who built on their support. It has been much studied how new political ideologies took shape, first to denounce and then to defend this new system of rule, and we shall have to examine their growth if we are to understand the text of the *Decline and Fall*. For the present, however, it is important to stress how readily discontent with the regime of continental war and high finance became discontent with the imperfectly legitimised Revolution Settlement, and took a high-church and near-Jacobite form. Britain was withdrawn from the grand alliance and played a leading role in making peace at the compromise Treaty of Utrecht, as a result of the massive Tory political victories which ushered in the 'four last years of the Queen'[12] (1710–14); but this spectacular if temporary collapse of the Whig control of politics was in many ways a high Anglican backlash, which took a disconcertingly popular form.[13] The regime was disliked; the Whigs and Dissenters were blamed for it; a reunion of crown and church was hoped for, as a means of ending war, taxation and instability; a basic legitimism in popular culture declared itself.[14] As Anne's life neared its end, a Stuart restoration appeared likely, but the peril of civil war re-emerged as it had so often done in late-Stuart politics. The Tory leaders failed to confront it, fell as dramatically as they had risen and the Hanoverian line was brought in to

---

[11] '…even his opinions were subordinate to his interest and I find him in Flanders cloathing King William's troops; while he would have contracted with more pleasure, though not perhaps at a cheaper rate, for the service of King James' (*Memoirs*, p. 12; *A*, pp. 10–11, Memoir F). Craddock (*YEG*, p. 4) points out that Edward Gibbon I – born in 1675, not as his grandson believed 1666 – was aged seventeen when his career as a contractor began, and we know nothing of his political sympathies at this time. Edward Gibbon III displays a certain ambivalence regarding this family tradition.   [12] Swift, 1758 (Davis, 1951).   [13] Holmes, 1973.   [14] Monod, 1989.

guarantee the Protestant succession. Given the visceral anti-Catholicism of the English masses, the best possible testimony to their equally visceral legitimism is the striking unpopularity of the only available Protestant line, which had to establish its power by a series of highly repressive measures – among them the Septennial Act of 1716, by which a sitting parliament prolonged its own life from three years to seven. This was the parliament confronted by the financial crisis of 1720, which fined Edward Gibbon I of much of his estate and fortune, and of this incident his grandson observed:

> Such bold oppression can scarcely be shielded by the omnipotence of Parliament: and yet, it may be seriously questioned whether the Judges of the South Sea Directors were the true and legal representatives of their country. The first Parliament of George I had been chosen (1715) for three years: the term was elapsed: their trust was expired; and the four additional years (1718–1722) during which they continued to sit, were derived not from the people, but from themselves; from the strong measure of the septennial bill, which can only be paralleled by *il serrar di Consiglio* of the Venetian history. Yet candour will own that to the same Parliament every Englishman is deeply indebted: the septennial act, so vicious in its origin, has been sanctioned by time, experience and the national consent: its first operation secured the house of Hanover on the throne, and its permanent influence maintains the peace and stability of Government. As often as a repeal has been moved in the house of Commons, I have given in its defence a clear and conscientious vote.[15]

The historian is inserting his family history and his autobiography into the framework provided by the progress from illegitimacy to legitimacy of what he certainly saw as a Whig and Venetian oligarchy. In a later chapter we shall consider at what point he supposed that legitimation to have been consummated. What requires to be noted here is that discontent with the Hanoverian succession, like discontent with the Revolution Settlement before it, took not only a dynastic but an ecclesiological and theological form, and that this is crucial to the understanding of Gibbon's early life and its crisis, and of the structure of the *Decline and Fall*.

The inherited predicament[16] which the Church of England derived from the Henrician Reformation was the need to reconcile its status as an apostolic church and member of Christ's body with its acceptance of

---

[15] *Memoirs*, p. 15; *A*, pp. 14–15, Memoir F. Jacob Sawbridge, also the grandfather of a historian – in this case the republican Catharine Macaulay – was another South Sea director who suffered at the same hands. His descendant was less tolerant of the Septennial Act. See Hill, 1992, pp. 5–7.

[16] A full-length history of Anglican political ecclesiology from the 1530s to the 1830s has not yet been attempted.

the sovereignty of the crown, whose wearer for the time being was its supreme head and governor. The political regime in which the crown was the sovereign found itself required to insist that the church must be a sacred and apostolic body, so that the crown might itself claim a sacred and indefeasible authority exercised *jure divino*; but must be on guard against any suggestion that the church's authority was itself of a divine origin that rendered it independent of the crown. This could carry with it the charge of a crypto-papalism in the Church of England, which had done much to bring about the Civil War of 1642 and conduct Archbishop Laud to the scaffold;[17] but the church restored between 1660 and 1662 had been obliged to assert both its sacred character and that of the crown, and had promoted the cult of Charles I as its king and martyr. Without a monarchy sacred, irresistible and even hereditary by divine right, it would be hard for the church to maintain its own sacred and apostolic character, or as we shall see the view of Christ's mission and person that such a church professed. But the ironies of history were such that, either side of the century from 1660 to 1760, the Church of England found only three supreme heads and governors – Charles I, Anne and George III – on whom it could feel that it relied. The sons of Charles I had been most unsatisfactory governors and professors of the church of which their father was held a martyr; both had issued Declarations of Indulgence which compromised the church's status in the kingdom, Charles II had been received into the Roman Catholic Church on his deathbed, and James II – whom the Church of England had accepted as its head despite his professed Catholicism – had pushed the policy of Indulgence so far as to place the church itself in danger.[18] For this reason the church had reluctantly accepted the Revolution aimed at his Catholic heir, and had welcomed the Act of Settlement which imposed the Protestant Succession; but both William III, a Dutch Calvinist by upbringing if not conviction, and the first two Hanoverians, German Lutherans by birth and baptism, owed their supreme governorship of the Church of England to dubiously legitimate parliamentary actions in which the church itself had been little consulted. Even under Anne, 'the Church of England's glory', the very being of the Anglican church-state had been formally if not actually terminated when 'England' had been merged in 'Britain', a single state with two national churches, and the supreme governor of the episcopal Church of

---

[17] Lamont, 1963; Hibbard, 1983; Tyacke, 1987.   [18] J. Miller, 1973, 1989.

England had found herself obliged to uphold a presbyterian and finally disestablish an episcopal Kirk of Scotland.

Unsure of its head and of its identity with the realm of which it was supposed to be the ecclesiastical aspect, the Church of England could not but experience uncertainty regarding its character as a church of Christ.[19] When five bishops and a number of other clergy had accepted deprivation of their benefices rather than subscribe the oaths of obedience to William and Mary, the hierarchy which replaced these 'non-jurors' had been drawn largely from those known as 'latitudinarians' – a term none too exactly denoting, at its first appearance, those who had held ecclesiastical offices and benefices under the Protectorate and had conformed to the episcopal church after its restoration. Suspected of affinities with the Nonconformists or dissenters who had left their benefices in 1662, these conformists and their successors were often strong upholders of the authority of church and state both before and after the Revolution; but it was open to them to hold, or to be suspected of holding, views of the church's nature which emphasised its social, practical and moral rather than its consecrated and spiritual character – views which could entail revaluations of what consecration itself was, and what Christ's actions, mission and even person had been. At the other end of the spectrum, the non-jurors had to choose between regarding themselves as a scrupulous minority accepting sufferings rather than compromise their tender consciences, or as a true church in exile from a church rendered false by its subjection to an illegitimate head and governor – a choice not unlike that which had faced Nonconformists in 1662, except that the latter, less irrevocably committed to the unity of church and state, had been better placed to regard the governing power as itself indifferent to salvation and so not rendered illegitimate by its support of the church they had left. The non-jurors, less exposed to institutionalised persecution than the Nonconformists (for whom the Toleration Act of 1689 had been followed by the Schism Act of 1714), were attracted both by Jacobitism – since a Stuart restoration was the obvious solution to their difficulties – and by schism, or regarding the official church as itself schismatic or apostate; an option some of them adopted when they consecrated their own successors without royal or hierarchical authorisation.

Accusations both of schism and of heresy therefore went back and forth after both the Revolution and the Hanoverian succession, and the

---

[19]　G. V. Bennett, 1975; Kenyon, 1977; J. C. D. Clark, 1986.

politics of the period put strains upon the formulation of Christian belief. Some non-jurors, as we have seen, moved from a strong doctrine of the unity of church and king to declaring that the church retained its apostolic character even under a false king and therefore enjoyed it independently of any king at all. This predictably aroused the slumbering wrath of English Erastianism, which was sometimes turned against the pretensions of even the conformist clergy to authorise the regime as legitimate.[20] Those who denied that the Church of England possessed authority to do this sometimes denied that it was an apostolic communion deriving spiritual authority from Christ himself; it was no more than a voluntary, or a lawfully imposed, association of those professing common opinions and beliefs about him. From this point it was possible to proceed to the discussion of Christ's person, and to find oneself denying that he had been a divine being capable of founding a church which was a mystical extension of his person. There was a politics of Christology in Stuart and post-Stuart England, and beliefs both ancient and modern which modified or subverted the orthodox understanding of Trinity and Incarnation were much discussed and sometimes professed; the *Decline and Fall* itself is largely a study of their history. An extreme form came to be known as deism, which affirmed the being of a God but denied that Christ was part of his substance or any religion a uniquely valid expression of his nature; there were several kinds of deism, displaying their own rationalism and their own mysticism, since they included both philosophical reductions of theistic doctrine to rational theology, and expressions of the belief that the whole universe was pervaded by spirit.

Heterodoxies of several kinds were therefore scattered across the face of an England dynastically and ecclesiastically divided. Even Tories and Jacobites, if they came to hold that the Church of England had in some real sense been disestablished after 1688, might now and then lapse from their ingrained high-churchmanship into positions radical in both church and state. At the height of its aggressive and intolerant power in the last years of Queen Anne, the Tory party was led by an ex-presbyterian, Robert Harley Earl of Oxford, and an acknowledged deist, Henry St John, Viscount Bolingbroke.[21] At microcosmic level, the Gibbon family's circle at Putney reflected this pattern of religious

---

[20] Stephens, 1696, pp. 10 ff. The attack is mainly against those churchmen willing to recognise William III's authority *de facto*, and Stephens is both joining in the attack himself and explaining the attractions which deism may exert over those who launch it.

[21] MacInnes, 1970; Dickinson, 1970.

ambivalence, since it included both the formidable non-juror and pietist mystic William Law[22] – spiritual director of the historian's aunt Hester, a circumstance which later deepened Gibbon's Protestant and *philosophe* mistrust of the influence of confessors over women – and as neighbours the outspoken deists David and Lucy Mallet,[23] soon to be notorious for their posthumous publication (1754) of Bolingbroke's more flagrantly anti-Christian writings. Edward Gibbon III became an infant prodigy of learning among family libraries – though he remembered best that of his mother's father – formed in a none too simple religious environment, and the chronological studies which absorbed his childhood ('the dynasties of Assyria and Egypt were my top and cricket ball')[24] reflected clerical as well as gentlemanly learning.

But the event of his youth which in its small yet momentous way most clearly displays the background of a divided England is of course his undergraduate conversion to Catholicism, and to understand how this came about, and what enduring meanings it had for him, we must revert to the basic dilemmas confronting the Church of England. As we have seen, these arose from the central difficulties of maintaining both its apostolic and its statutory foundations, of reconciling the spirit with the law, grace with works, revelation with social reason. A church independent of the crown threatened papalism; a church wholly subordinate to the crown threatened desacralisation; church and crown alike were deeply averse to both; but the formulae of reconciliation were hard to articulate and perpetually at risk (as is the fate of orthodoxy itself). From the great crises of the civil wars and interregnum, when the Church of England had been disestablished, had nearly disappeared and had been swiftly and unexpectedly restored, the Anglican communion had

[22] Gibbon's account of Law may be found in *Memoirs*, pp. 20–3 (*A*, pp. 23–7, Memoir F); a modern one in Rupp, 1986, pp. 218–42. See also Baridon, 1975, I, pp. 24–7, who holds that both Law and Hester Gibbon broke with the family at Putney because the spirit of Bolingbroke had come to dominate the lifestyle of Edward Gibbon II. Low, p. 45, gives evidence suggesting a later date for their withdrawal.

[23] *Dictionary of National Biography* (hereafter *DNB*), *sub nomine*. It was Mrs Mallet who approached David Hume at a party with the declaration 'we deists should know one another better', to be crushed by the reply, 'Madam, I am no deist; I disclaim the title.' Her identity may also be suspected in the couplet from Dr Johnson's *London: A Poem*: 'Here falling houses thunder on your head/And there a female atheist talks you dead.'

[24] *Memoirs*, p. 43 (*A*, p. 59, Memoir F). On pp. 36–7 (*A*, pp. 48–9, Memoir F), Gibbon recalls the year spent in the library left behind at Putney by his grandfather James Porten, when he fled his creditors in 1748 (after Judith Gibbon's death), and the encouragement given by his aunt Catherine, 'who indulged herself in moral and religious speculation' (its nature unrecorded). At pp. 96–7 (*A*, p. 164, Memoir B), he remarks on Law's contribution to the high-church component of Edward Gibbon II's library at Buriton, where he began to read on his return to England in 1758.

emerged with the perception of a double threat: on the one hand, that of
Rome, interpreting Christ's consecration of the bread and wine at the
Last Supper so as to make the church which administered the transsub-
stantiated elements an authority independent of any earthly ruler; on
the other, that of the independent and sometimes revolutionary sects –
whose brief military dictatorship after 1647 was remembered with
peculiar vividness – interpreting the gift of tongues on the Day of Pen-
tecost so as to invest the congregations in whom the Holy Spirit moved
with independence from all governing authority and sometimes all
social and even moral discipline. Claims on behalf of both the Second
and the Third persons of the Trinity were being advanced along lines
fatal to the Church of England's always imperilled position, and must be
met without compromising the doctrine of the Trinity itself; this proved
difficult and for some not possible.[25] From the perception of a dual
threat to established English Protestantism there arose a two-edged
polemic against the 'superstition' of Rome, which held Christ to be
physically present in the sacraments, and the 'enthusiasm' of the sects,
which held the Spirit to be immediately present in the congregation or
even the individual. Because this was a polemic about the ways in which
spirit could be present in matter, it came to be crucial in the formation of
English and Enlightened philosophy; because it was concerned with the
Spirit's action in human society and in respect of human authority, it
came to be crucial in the writing of history and the construction of the
Decline and Fall.[26] Future chapters of this book will deal with Gibbon's
philosophical and historical development; for the moment we are concerned only with his undergraduate crisis as an expression of the
Anglican[27] predicament.

   The Church of England that took shape after the Restoration of 1660
was a not always easy alliance between so-called 'high churchmen' and
so-called 'latitudinarians', who had found it possible to conform both
before and after 1660. The former had insisted that a sacred monarchy
was necessary to the being of the Church as by law established; the latter
appeared inclined to the belief that forms of government were indifferent to religious experience, which was consequently capable of or-

---

[25] It is valuable here to contrast and reconcile J. C. D. Clark, 1986, who stresses the continued
hegemony of Trinitarian doctrine, with Gascoigne, 1990, who stresses the continued existence of
a Socinian minority within the church – itself acknowledged by Clark, pp. 311–15, 317–20. See
further Champion, 1992.   [26] Pocock, 1982, 1995.

[27] Tyacke, 1987, p. vii, remarks that the term 'Anglican(ism)' does not appear before the nineteenth
century and warns against its over-specific use. It is here employed adjectivally, or as a term of
convenience, where the words 'Church of England' fit awkwardly into the sentence.

ganising itself in subordination to any of them. But it is not possible to reconstruct the two streams of opinion as sharply opposed alternatives. The 'high churchmen' saw their king and supreme governor as a sacred but not a priestly figure, holy because the natural and social order were holy, possessing divine right but not special spiritual gifts; the roots of their thinking were in Hooker, Erasmus and remotely Aquinas. When they looked back to the 'Laudian' and 'Arminian' milieux in which most of them had been formed, they could see the liberation of human sociability and natural authority from the absolute decrees of Calvinist grace, quite as clearly as the swing towards baroque ritualism and ecumenical respect for even the Pope's authority which had briefly characterised 'Arminianism' in England more than elsewhere. Their veneration for apostolic origins drew them towards a history of the primitive church which did not emphasise the Petrine supremacy and presented the rise of the papacy as a late development, and they could follow Erasmus, Grotius and their own ecclesiastical historians in reconciling apostolical Christianity with a historical context. There was nothing here which need set 'high' and 'latitudinarian' churchmen at odds, while on the level of philosophy – where the intellect confronted the problems of the presence of spirit in matter – both groups were equally responsive to Cambridge Platonism, which considered a divinely implanted reason the proper antidote to self-deluded enthusiasm,[28] and to the Baconianism found with other positions in the Royal Society, which, while sharply critical of Platonism as itself enthusiastic, was working its way towards a view of God as creating matter and giving it laws, while remaining distinct from and in no way immanent in it.[29] The distinction between high-church and latitudinarian Anglicanism, therefore, does not itself impede the argument that the origins of Enlightenment in England lie in the maintenance by the church of its Erasmian, Arminian and Grotian traditions.[30]

But the religious and political tensions of Restoration England, rendered acute if seldom edifying by the unstable relations of the crown with the church, gave rise to a new and militant kind of low churchmanship, sometimes brutal and sometimes philosophically subtle, originating in the determination that spiritual authority must never

[28] The best selection and account is Patrides, 1969. See also Cragg, 1968; Ealy, 1997.
[29] For the alliance between Anglicanism and natural philosophy, see M. C. Jacob, 1976; J. R. Jacob, 1978; Gascoigne, 1990.
[30] Trevor-Roper, 1968, 1988, 1992. Concerning the concept of 'latitudinarian(ism)' and the role of 'latitude-men' in English intellectual history see Kroll, Ashcraft and Zagorin, 1992.

again be allowed to challenge the supremacy of magistracy and the social order, from doing which it was in any case precluded by its nature. This determination could be directed against papalism, rigorous Anglicanism or presbyterianism as occasion required, while even the libertinism of Buckingham and the materialism of Hobbes[31] were suspected of preparing the way for a return of spiritual claims under the pretence of exiling spirit from the universe – an enterprise of course disastrous in itself. There arose a systematic and resolute identification of the religious with the social, equally compatible with liberal and with absolutist views of the political authority by which society was governed; the distinction was of secondary importance compared with the paramount need to maintain that the spirit manifested itself, and even became incarnate, only through social channels, reasonable, humane, and obedient to authority, and never in ways subversive of the human and sociable order.[32] Christ as saviour had been king as well as priest and prophet, and the Christian was enjoined to an unconditional subjection to the higher powers; Christ's role as saviour had been to add supernatural sanction to the natural authority of common social morality, through which, rather than through any mystery of atonement, the individual was to be saved.[33] Doctrines of this kind were advanced in ecclesiastical as well as secular circles, but might reach a point at which the central tradition of Christianity began to be challenged. For if Christ came only to reinforce the law, in what ways did the function and the person of the Son differ from those of the Father? And if that law were the universal law of nature rather than a Mosaic covenant, what became of the Father's special relationship with either the first Israel or the second which was the church? The former query reached to the verge of Socinianism[34] or Unitarianism, the latter to that of deism; but an orthodox Anglican concerned with defining his Church's position might find himself framing either. The suspicion of doing so rested particularly on 'latitudinarians', but there were grounds for suspicion irrespective of nomenclature. Anglicans as well as Noncon-

---

[31] Tuck, 1988; Shapin and Schaffer, 1985; J. R. Jacob, 1983; Pocock, 1990b; Mintz, 1962.
[32] Diamond, 1982; Murray, 1986.
[33] Marshall, 1990, 1994, studies this development in its relation to Locke.
[34] A 'Socinian' in the precise sense meant one who affirmed that Christ was a being divine in mission but not in nature; or, under pressure, that he was not co-eternal with the godhead. The term seems often to have been used loosely, to designate anyone who seemed to diminish Christ's divinity or to leave it discussible, but not to denote any specific heresy regarding his nature; these would be known by their controversial names. See further MacLachlan, 1951; Marshall, forthcoming. It is important, if difficult, to distinguish between the technically correct and the colloquial uses of the term 'Socinian'.

formists moved in a 'Socinian' direction, and while the benefits of the
Toleration Act of 1689 were expressly withheld from those who denied
the Trinity, from this time we have to recognise those who remained
within the Church of England while privately holding, or at least
privately discussing, opinions which were certainly not Trinitarian.[35]
John Locke was one such, and Isaac Newton was another.[36] The fact
that their anti-Trinitarianism arose as much from a desire to maintain,
as to destabilise, the authority of the civil magistrate no doubt helped
them to avoid critical confrontation; but the civil magistrate would
never accept support offered him on terms such as those of Thomas
Hobbes. What manner of person was Leviathan to be, and what
manner of person Christ?

Problems of this order were in the making before the revolution of
1688, but were aggravated by the implications of that event and all that
followed. There came to be an explicit, if only an occasional, association
between strong support of the Revolution and Hanoverian succession,
an ecclesiology which reduced the Church of England to a civil association, an epistemology which reduced the knowledge of God to the
holding of opinions, and a theology which reduced Christ to something
less than a co-equal and co-eternal person of the Trinity. From time to
time there emanated from low-church ecclesiastical circles accounts of
the Christian communion which deprived it of spiritual as well as civil
authority and reduced it to a voluntary association of like-minded
believers, to which the civil power might or might not require subscription as a matter of civil policy. One such was the widespread 'Bangorian
controversy' of 1716, named for its initiator Benjamin Hoadly, Bishop of
Bangor; there were the Trinitarian controversies arising when Arian
and Socinian doctrines invaded the Anglican (1690, 1712)[37] and Presbyterian (1719) communions; and the young Gibbon at Oxford found
himself dismayed by the repercussions of another, in character significantly historical: that is to say, Conyers Middleton's account of the
primitive church. The culture in which he grew up was clerical, no
doubt pious, but less devout than historical; engaged in debate over the
sources of authority.

---

[35] Their history is pursued through the eighteenth century by Gascoigne, 1990.
[36] Marshall, 1990, 1994; Manuel, 1963, 1974.   [37] Rupp, 1986, pp. 88–101, 253–6.

THE VISIT TO STOURHEAD AND THE VENTURE INTO ANGLICAN
HISTORIOGRAPHY

Before we further consider Gibbon's juvenile progress towards a religious crisis, then, we must inspect how at the same time he moved
towards becoming a historian. We are the more obliged to consider the
latter progress because Gibbon in his *Memoirs* leaves us a detailed
account of this vocation and dates it from his childhood. These reminis-
cences, however, have not the status of direct evidence. They were
composed, and left unfinished, long afterwards, on either side of the
year 1789,[38] when the revolution in France and the vehement English
reaction against it were bringing Gibbon's scepticism and unbelief
under intensified attack, and he found himself classed with Voltaire as
an author of the revolutionary crisis. In these circumstances he might
have represented himself as having been closer to religious conformity,
and his scepticism as of a kind less dangerous to orthodox belief, than
had in fact been the case; and there exists the possibility that the *Memoirs*
convey a representation of his early life, to be read as an artefact of 1789.
The statements such a reading contained would need to be supported by
further evidence; but even if we do not regard the *Memoirs* as representation, they cannot in themselves be other than recollection, and an
ageing man's recollections of his early life are more likely to be interpretations than assemblages of verifiable data. Where we cannot – as we
sometimes can – check Gibbon's statements in these texts against evidence existing independently of them, we have to decide how to treat
them; and a possible interpretative strategy is to say that they constitute
attempts by a major historian to present his own life as history and
situate it in history as he understood it. On this reading it is possible for
us, where we cannot test the veracity of his statements, to consider the
hypothetical effects of accepting them: to consider to what interpretations of his life they will lead us if we adopt them, and in what ways we
may integrate them with interpretations of our own.

    According to the recollections of his older self, then, the fifteen-year-
old Gibbon 'arrived at Oxford', in 1752, 'with a stock of erudition that
might have puzzled a Doctor, and a degree of ignorance of which a
school boy would have been ashamed'.[39] By the latter statement he
means that ill health had kept him from regular school attendance, and
so from a normal grammar-school training in Latin, let alone Greek – a

---

[38] Craddock, *EGLH*, pp. 272–91, dates the various drafts between 1788 and 1791. Cf. *Memoirs*, pp.
xv–xxxi.   [39] *Memoirs*, p. 43 (*A*, p. 59, Memoir F).

training whose range, depth and severity defy the modern imagination, and which Gibbon was always to miss to some extent.[40] But if he never became 'a well-flogged Critic', he grew at home into a prodigy of uncontrolled reading; and he says:

My indiscriminate appetite subsided by degrees in the *Historic* line: and, since Philosophy has exploded all innate ideas and natural propensities –

Gibbon was not sure he believed this –[41]

I must ascribe this choice to the assiduous perusal of the Universal history as the octavo Volumes successively appeared.[42]

He details the readings in ancient and modern history to which the *Universal History* led him, and which made him, so he tells us, an object of astonishment to his father's friends. But:

My first introduction to the Historic scenes, which have since engaged so many years of my life, must be ascribed to an accident. In the summer of 1751 I accompanied my father on a visit to Mr. Hoare's in Wiltshire: but I was less delighted with the beauties of Stourhead, than with discovering in the library a common book, the continuation of Echard's Roman history which is indeed executed with more skill and taste than the praevious work: to me the reigns of the successors of Constantine were absolutely new; and I was immersed in the passage of the Goths over the Danube when the summons of the dinner-bell reluctantly dragged me from my intellectual feast. This transient glance served rather to irritate than to appease my curiosity, and no sooner was I returned to Bath, than I procured the second and third volumes of Howell's history of the World, which exhibit the Byzantine period on a larger scale. Mahomet and his Saracens soon fixed my attention: and some instinct of criticism directed me to the genuine sources. Simon Ockley, an original in every sense, first opened my eyes, and I was led from one book to another till I had ranged round the circle of Oriental history. Before I was sixteen I had exhausted all that could be learned in English, of the Arabs and Persians, the Tartars and the Turks, and the same ardour urged me to guess at the French of d'Herbelot, and to construe the barbarous Latin of Pocock's *Abulpharagius*.[43]

---

[40] For Gibbon's views on school life and learning, see *Memoirs*, pp. 32–3, 38–9, 39–40, 43–5 (*A*, pp. 43–4, 51–3, 59–61; all Memoir F).   [41] *Memoirs*, p. 119 (*A*, p. 193, Memoir B).

[42] *An Universal History from the Earliest Account of Time to the Present, compiled from Original Authors* appeared in folio at London between 1736 and 1744, in octavo between 1747 and 1748. This became *The Ancient Part* when *The Modern Part of an Universal History* ... appeared in both folio and octavo between 1759 and 1766. See Ricuperati, 1981; Abbatista, 1981. In his journal of 1763–4 Gibbon recollected reading the *Ancient Part* on Macedonian history when aged fourteen in 1751; *Journal B*, p. 166, reference cited in *YEG*, p. 43 and n. The *Universal History* does not occur in the catalogue of Gibbon's own library. He can have read only *The Ancient Part* and is unlikely to have read its volumes on their first appearance in octavo.   [43] *Memoirs*, pp. 42–3 (*A*, pp. 57–8, Memoir F).

Here we embark upon the first of many excursions into contexts furnished by texts other than Gibbon's but indicated by him. The memoirist in his fifties is describing how his fourteen-year-old self encountered reading which was to be crucial to the *Decline and Fall*; and whether or not the experience occurred as described, the recollection of the works listed tells us something about Gibbon's relation to his own work. There is a certain amount of corroborative evidence. In his journal of 1763 Gibbon recalled a passage from the *Universal History* as one which he had read in Bath in 1751, when he was fourteen.[44] It is reported that he bought Barthélemy d'Herbelot's *Bibliothèque orientale* on credit soon after matriculating at Oxford in the following year,[45] and there are letters which indicate that he left his copy in England when sent to Lausanne in 1753, and was trying to recover it three years later.[46] Echard alone excepted, all the works mentioned in the passage quoted are catalogued in his library in early editions,[47] though we may question whether the fourteen-year-old was able to buy folios and octavos or persuade others to buy them for him; perhaps these too are purchases by the gentleman-commoner of Magdalen. We may proceed to conflate what he says of these texts with what they say in themselves, and the first thing we learn is that they were readings in late antiquity, 'the successors of Constantine', 'the Byzantine period' and 'the circle of Oriental history'. More than five-sixths of the *Decline and Fall* was to be devoted to these matters, and we are never to think of Gibbon as a single-minded classical humanist with his mind fixed on the glory that was Greece, the grandeur that was Rome and the elegiacs of the ancient world. At Stourhead in 1751, so he tells us, he discovered an unknown universe, that of late antiquity and Byzantine history, and if we study the works he names as its sources we find that he also discovered a historiography that had treated of this universe.

Echard, he tells us, led him to Howell, and there is a point at which the later work acknowledges its debt to the earlier.[48] Laurence Echard was a country archdeacon who made an income out of works on both Roman and English history, 'common' in the sense that he acknowledged being neither a university scholar nor a statesman writing at his

---

[44] *Journal B*, p. 166.   [45] *Letters*, I, pp. 13, 25.   [46] *Letters*, I, pp. 13, 25.

[47] *Library*, pp. 63 ('Bar Hebraeus', i.e. Pococke, 1663), 148 (d'Herbelot), 155 (Howell, 1680–5), 209 (Ockley, 1708).

[48] Echard, 1713, III, 'the Author's Preface', sig. A4c: 'Nor must I omit the great Helps I receive'd from Monsieur *Le Seur* and Doctor *Howell*, who at least directed me in my Enquiries, and often help'd me out in my Method and Observation.' Howel[l] had died in 1683.

leisure.[49] The third, fourth and fifth volumes of his *Roman History*, first published in 1695, appeared in 1713; they are as Gibbon says by another hand, allegedly unknown to Echard himself; the latter had reached the reign of Constantine and decided to go no further.[50] That reign, with the adoption of Christianity as the imperial religion and the removal of the capital to the new city on the Bosphorus, was generally held to mark the end of Roman history as classically conceived: the end of republic and principate, of pagan philosophy and literature. It is the point reached by the fourteenth chapter, and before the end of the first volume, of the *Decline and Fall*, and Gibbon like his predecessors faced the problem of continuing past this turning-point a history which must still be called Roman. The predecessors identified in the *Memoirs* are neither Renaissance humanists like Biondo or Machiavelli, nor Enlightened philosophers like Montesquieu, but English churchmen, concerned with ecclesiastical history as Gibbon was to be. The continuator of Echard gives his reasons for carrying the story past Constantine.

To leave it with the Second Volume look'd, in my Opinion, like a Ceremony too much in practice amongst some Men, who stick fast to their Friends in their Prosperity, but drop 'em with the first Opportunity, when once Fortune has forsaken 'em. The Roman Greatness appear'd too Majestick, even in its Ruins, not to require our Attention; for Great Men, as whilst living they are gaz'd upon with Admiration, so when dead are they usually attended with a solemn Reverence to their Graves:

the language is humanist, but at the same time that which a client uses of his patron. Gibbon does not write in quite this tone.

But another more prevailing Motive made me wish a Continuation of this History. The Enemies of Christianity have imputed the Downfall of the *Roman* Empire to the Principles of our Religion, as if it choak'd in its Professors the Courage, Vigour and Generosity of their Fore-fathers, and taught 'em to be sluggish, unactive, and no otherwise than passively Valiant; that it was inconsistent with that Greatness of Mind, which so eminently distinguish'd the ancient *Romans* from the rest of their Cotemporaries, and introduc'd a Poorness of Spirit, that made 'em careless and insensible of their ancient Glory.

This was not only glanc'd at by the Heathen Writers of those Times, but is too frequently insisted on in common Discourse by some Men of this Age, who think themselves wiser than the rest of Mankind, and assume a Privilege of condemning the sense of all those whose Reason won't suffer 'em to concur with them in their airy Fancies and ill-grounded Imaginations. The Reader, on

---

[49] There are notices of Echard, mainly in his character as English historian, in Stephan, 1989; Okie, 1991, pp. 32–40; Hicks, 1996, pp. 102–9.
[50] Echard, 1713, III, sig. A3: 'Mr Echard's Preface.'

a Perusal of the following Sheets, will find the Fallacy of these Insinuations, and that the Downfall of the *Roman* Empire was owing to other Causes than what has been suggested by these Men; and that both Principles and practices, very opposite to those enjoin'd by the Gospel, occasion'd its Ruin.[51]

Gibbon was to be accused of this kind of infidelity, and certainly needed to consider whether the Decline and Fall was the result of the decay of ancient virtue or of its replacement by a Christian ethos. The tension between the ancient citizen and warrior, and the Christian confessor and martyr, was ineradicably ingrained in European culture, and the charge outlined by the continuator may be traced back to Machiavelli. He does not identify his contemporary adversaries, but they may well have been deists of a republican inclination, like Toland or Molesworth.[52] In these passages, he signals the central fact that Gibbon in the *Memoirs* does not mention: that from Constantine onwards Roman history was that of the church as well as the empire. This was the turning-point in all civil history written by Christians: the moment at which the history of the Spirit became joined with that of the civil order. The continuator of Echard was not committed to sacred but to civil history; a history of Rome, now organised around the sacred monarchy created by Constantine. He therefore produced three volumes, subtitled respectively

from the Removal of the Imperial Seat by *Constantine* the Great, to the Total Failure of THE WESTERN EMPIRE in AUGUSTULUS, Containing the Space of 146 Years,

from the Total Failure of the WESTERN EMPIRE in AUGUSTULUS, to the restitution of the same by CHARLES the Great, Containing the Space of 324 Years,

and

from the Restitution of the EMPIRE by Charles the Great, to the Taking of *Constantinople* by the *Turks*, Containing the Space of 653 Years.[53]

The young Gibbon – if we follow the *Memoirs* – was being led by this reading not only into late antique and Byzantine history, but into the 'space' the *Decline and Fall* was to occupy. Like him, the continuator of the *Roman History* pressed on as far as 1453, and had difficulty in periodising and organising his material. His fourth and fifth volumes are

---

[51] Echard, 1713, III, sig. A4–A4b.   [52] For these figures see Venturi, 1971 and M. C. Jacob, 1981.
[53] Echard, 1713, the title pages of volumes III, IV, V.

divided into chapters according to the reigns of eastern emperors, so that they constitute a Byzantine history in which the Latin west appears only marginally, marked by such occurrences as the coronation of Charlemagne and the First and Fourth Crusades.[54] Gibbon was to organise the *Decline and Fall* similarly, and in both cases the omission of the Latin middle ages presents a problem. By Gibbon's time, however, it was a problem in Enlightened historiography, since there existed a set of conflicting attitudes towards that period and its dominant culture, which Echard and his continuator were not necessarily obliged to confront. They were writing a Roman history, organised around the successive reigns of Caesars, and these displayed an unbroken succession at Constantinople, not to be found anywhere in the west. The continuator was not unaware that this approach had its problems:

> The reader perhaps may wonder why 'tis still called the *Roman* History, since the people of whom it treats bear so little a Resemblance to those Ancient *Romans*, who were the Subject of the former Volumes: The greatest Reason is that they always call themselves so; their Authors call'd the People *Romans*, and their Princes the *Roman* Emperors, affecting the Title when they had lost the Power, and so were laugh'd at by the rest of the World for their Pains.[55]

No such claims were made by the re-Latinised barbarians of the west, and their history was not, except occasionally, that of a Roman people and its empire. For Protestant clerics like Echard and (probably) his continuator, Latin history was that of Peter's Rome, not Constantine's. There is a long way to go before we understand what its patterns were in Gibbon's case, and they are in no sense anticipated by the *Memoirs'* account of how he discovered the late antique, the Byzantine and the Islamic. The library at Stourhead is a long way from the steps of the Capitol.

From Echard's *Roman History*, the *Memoirs* tell us, the schoolboy student turned back to William Howell or Howel's[56] *History of the World*, and in so doing to high-church scholarship of the previous century. This author had become a fellow of Magdalene College, Cambridge, in 1651, but, perhaps deterred from a priestly career by interregnum conditions, achieved a doctorate in laws, not divinity, and served as chancellor of Lincoln diocese.[57] After the Restoration he produced a number of

---

[54] See the chapter headings of volume v, chapters iii and iv.   [55] Echard, 1713, v, sig. A2.
[56] The former spelling is favoured by the *DNB* and by Gibbon; the latter by the printers of the author's history, carried out with his wife's participation.
[57] *DNB*, under 'Howell, William'; Venn, 1922, vol. I, part ii, p. 418.

historical works,[58] and by his death in 1683 had completed a mammoth *Institution of General History, or the History of the World*, of which a volume published in 1662 had covered the period 'from the Beginning of the World till the Monarchy of Constantine the Great', and a second volume in 1680 continued the story to the Roman empire's 'Ruine and Downfall in the West... And the Erecting of a Kingdom of Barbarians in Italy.' The remaining sections of Howel's work were published in a completed second edition of three volumes in 1685, and it is this which reveals to us his history's true ecclesiastical character. The concluding volume was 'published for the Authors Widdow, by Miles Flesher', and each of the parts into which it is divided carries her dedication to the new King James II. Mary Howel was in collaboration with a powerful group of ecclesiastical sponsors, headed by Henry Compton, Bishop of London, Thomas Sprat, Bishop of Rochester, and Symon Patrick, Dean of Peterborough, who furnished a preface and imprimatur to each part of Howel's posthumous history. Of these the first was headed 'The Church History, or the Ecclesiastical Affairs contemporary with the Constantinopolitan Roman Empire', signifying – as may or may not have dawned on the young Gibbon at Stourhead – that with Constantine Roman history merged with sacred history and must be written in the ecclesiastical genre. The sponsors further, and most significantly, remark

In particular, that *supream Authority* usurped by the *Roman Bishop* is represented, how, and by what means it was first pretended to, but ever rejected by the whole *Catholick church*, which gives to each *Metropolitan* the sole jurisdiction over his own *Flock*, not any *General Commission* to any one whatsoever, for the supervising of *all*, their *Authority* being *equal*, and their *Power* the *same*.[59]

In conjunction with Mary Howel's dedication, the prelates were sending their new king an unequivocal message. We are looking at a tug-of-war between the Anglican clergy and their Gallican-inclined sovereign, each seeking to draw its opponent across a line defined by a somewhat shadowy papal obedience;[60] Howel's adversaries are papalists, where those of Echard's continuator are deists. Since the Laudian

---

[58] *An Introduction to General History, being a Compleat Body thereof, from the Beginning of the World till the Monarchy of Constantine the Great* (London, 1662); *Elementa historiae ab orbe condita usque ad monarchiam Constantini Magni... tironum ad usum* (London, 1670); *An Institution of General History, part 2* (London, 1680); *The Elements of History from the Creation of the World to the Reign of Constantine the Great... Done for the Use of Young Students* (London, 1700). Gibbon, *Decline and Fall*, ch. 17, n. 130 (137 in Bury), calls him 'that learned historian, who is not sufficiently known'.   [59] Howel, 1685, III, sig. A2 b.

[60] It was the late John Kenyon whom I once heard declare that James II was in his own way an Anglican.

rejection of the doctrine that the Pope was Antichrist, with its implication that the history of true religion was the history of an invisible church, Anglican historiography had moved towards presenting the history of the papal usurpation as that of a secular accident rather than a spiritual iniquity, best understood in the context of empire and its disruption.[61] So here; and this imparted to Howel's volumes a strong bias towards regarding the history of eastern empire, Byzantine and Caesaropapal, as the civil and ecclesiastical norm, and the barbarian invasions of the western provinces as the disruption of imperial authority which had made papal pretensions possible. If the young Gibbon was led on by an increasing fascination with late antiquity, he was consciously or otherwise exploring the high-church traditions of his own family; for Jacobites whether English or Scottish were episcopalians more often than they were papalists. The no longer Christian author of the *Memoirs* is in his turn exploring the origins of that commitment to Byzantine history which had weighed on the later volumes of the *Decline and Fall*; we have yet to discover why he resisted this commitment and found it hard to deal with.

Howel's church history follows Eusebius, the late-antique father of ecclesiastical history, and polemicises with the modern Cardinal Baronius, who asserts the Petrine origins of the papal supremacy.[62] But though Howel argues for a church structure composed of equal metropolitans and patriarchs, he does not supply an ongoing history of the church's development in interaction with the secular powers. Like others of this period, his history is a compilation from the works of ancient authors, and this leads to a separation rather than a conflation of the two kinds of history that compose it. Only here and there do we find him confronting those problems in interpretation and generalisation which gave rise to synthetic narrative, as when he anticipates a problem which was to produce Gibbon's crisis at Oxford by remarking of Constantine's vision of a cross in the sky:

neither need we at all to question the Truth of it; For that God made use of Miracles upon extraordinary Occasions, we must not doubt, and such we must confess this to have been, if the extraordinary Condition of the Person, and the vast Consequence be duly considered. That Miracles at this time were not ceased utterly, we may believe from that reason which was even the first Cause of them, and from the Testimony of several Writers who discourse of the first

[61] For this see particularly Peter Heylyn (1600–62), the most active historical writer of the Laudian circle; Heylyn, 1652, 'To the Reader'; Heylyn, 1657, 1681, pp. 26–8.
[62] Howel, 1685, III, part ii, pp. 57 and ff; Pullapilly, 1975.

Plantation of Religion among Barbarous Nations long after this Season, whom it is little less than arrogance to Condemn of Falshood (although perhaps too Credulous in some Particulars) because as extraordinary means seem necessary for the conversion of Later, as were used for the Conviction of former Disciples.[63]

It was no easy matter to determine exactly when miracles had ceased, as all Protestant churches concurred they had. At a much later point Howel broached the grand historical problem of the relations between Christian belief and Hellenic philosophy – around which so much history including Gibbon's was to be written – by observing that

the Reader must not think that the Philosophy of *Aristotle*, which in these later Ages hath obtained the Principality in the Schools, was always of such Reputation as we have seen it in our time. At the beginning of Christianity the Sect of the *Stoicks* much prevailed, but especially, the Opinions of *Plato*, which in the primitive times were of such Repute, that the greatest Rubs, the true Religion met with, were laid by those Prejudices that were thence received. For although much furtherance it received from such Philosophers as were converted, in refuting the Vanities and Impieties of *Paganism*, yet the great Writers against it were all of that Sect, and both Tertullian and *Origen* of old complained, all or most of the Heresies which crept into the Church, took their Original from the Tenets of (this) Philosophy. Long was it e'er the Schools became *Peripatetick*, and Philosophy had ceased to be *Pagan*, e'er she forsook the Academy and the Porch. At length she courted *Aristotle* so much that she made him ample amends for her former Neglects; and here, as formerly she had done much mischief as well as good in the School of *Plato*, so she indeavoured to obtrude the Opinions and Notions of *Aristotle* upon the Christian Faith.[64]

It had long been the orthodox position that the heresies of the patristic age were Platonist in origin; there was in the making a less orthodox and perhaps Enlightened contention that Nicene theology was no less Platonist than its competitors. Howel is capable of the generalisations and figures of speech that frame a history of Christianity and philosophy, but not of developing it into a narrative; such passages as the above are merely digressions. If we look for a narrative structure in his later history, we must find it in some rather fragmentary accounts of how the western empire disintegrated and the eastern survived, and even these are dictated by a humanist concern for the quality of his sources rather than by a pattern of interpretative generalisations. After so firm-seeming an assertion of continuing Byzantine authority as

---

[63] Howel, 1685, III, part ii, p. 2.
[64] Howel, 1685, III, part iv, pp. 31–2. The several parts of this volume are separately paginated.

Rome the *Elder*, being fallen from her ancient Dominion, and now a Captive, the Right of Succession to all her Empire remaining, was devolved upon her Daughter the younger *Rome* or *Constantinople*. And to her fell a very great Inheritance, though vastly short of what her Mother had acquired. For with the Ancient Lady her *Western* Provinces were gone into Captivity . . . But thence Eastward as far as the limit of *Mesopotamia* the *Roman* Empire remained entire to the young Sovereign Mistress; and the Northern Bounds and also the Southern were much the same,[65]

we proceed to a long account of the reign of Justinian, his codifications – Howel was a doctor of laws where Gibbon in his day had to teach himself to be one[66] – and the problems of reading Procopius. But this is to follow:

But see where are we now? What a Prospect doth here present it self. What a vast Empire have we beheld, what large Provinces, what variety of Affairs relating both to Peace and War? Great Armies, great Performances, Strategems and Variety of Accidents, by which the Grandeur and Glory of the *Roman* Empire hath been revived. Behold what a Precipice! We are descending into low, mean and narrow Tracts, and shall find the Empire but short, and our selves straitened; the further we pass, little of Action and less of Performance. Whatever thou wast, the Greatness of Empire, the Glory of Majesty, the Power of Arms, the Efficacy of Laws, the Renown and Splendour of the *Roman* Name, in a measure died and was buried with thee O *Justinian*.[67]

This is as much a lament for the decline of history as of empire. If Heraclius is no Justinian, there is no successor to the outstanding if problematic Procopius; and if the deeds seem petty, it is 'in a measure' because there is no historian able to dignify them. The campaigns of Heraclius, in which he overthrew Chosroes and nearly demolished the Persian monarchy, are or ought to be the equivalent of Justinian's destruction of Gothic Italy, both in their grandeur and in their disastrous consequences; but no one has recorded them worthily, and the personality of Heraclius escapes us without assuming the enigmatic status of Procopius's Justinian. And a modern historian is lacking, as well as an ancient. The reign of Heraclius leads directly to the conquests of the Arab Muslims, the most devastating reverse ever suffered by Greek as well as Roman imperial culture; but of this Howel has no more to say than

that *Heraclius* is blamed, as in a great measure the Authour of this mischief, and is farther taxed upon this account, that busying himself with Opinions and Speculations not proper for him –

[65] Howel, 1685, III, part iii, p. 1.   [66] *Decline and Fall*, III, ch. 44.
[67] Howel, 1685, III, part iii, p. 243.

the allusion is to his involvement with the Monothelite controversy –

> he took no notice of the greatest mischief which ever rose in the East, the greatest Plague that ever happened to *Christendom*, which he might have prevented, and crushed as a Cockatrice in the very Egg. For now at this time *Mahomet* was Captain of the *Saracens*, whose Power he much advanced and instilled into them the venom of a new Religion. He died in the one and twentieth year of *Heraclius* his Reign.
>
> He left for his Successour *Ebubachar* his Kinsman, who taking occasion at the low Estate to which the *Persian* Kingdom was brought, advanced as much as he could the Affairs of the *Saracens*.[68]

Howel goes on to recount the conquests of Abu Bakr and his successors in the khalifat, but gives no account whatever of Islam as a religion and political culture having a founder and a history of its own. We are at the point where the *Memoirs* tell us that Gibbon's interest in Arab history began, but he tells us also that he had to go elsewhere to develop it. Howel has not found, as Ockley was to do, an Arab narrative capable of raising the conquests of early Islam to epic status, but it cannot be said that he has tried very hard to find one; yet Ockley, and Gibbon, inform us that it was not necessary to wait for a *philosophe* historian to recognise Islam as a new force in world history. From his descent of the precipice which he found before him at the end of Justinian's reign, it grows harder to see where Howel perceived his history as taking him. The themes of a diminished east and a disrupted west are maintained throughout the fourth section, which contains

> The Original and Kingdoms of the *Heruli, Goths, Lombards* and *Franks* in *Italy*; the Affairs of *Britain*; the Original of the *Saxons, Angles* and *Jutes*, their Heptarchy; the Monarchy of the *English Saxons*, that of the *Danes*, with its end in restoring of the *English Saxon* Line down to that of *William* the *Norman*, with the *Polity, customs, Laws* and *Language* then in Use.

AND ALSO

> That of the *Constantinopolitan Roman Empire*, from the Promotion of *Nicephorus* to the Death of *Constantine Ducas* XII, A.D. MLXVII, being the Year after the Conquest of this Nation by Duke *William* the *Norman*.[69]

But it is hard to find any thread binding eastern and western history together, or providing western history with any pattern of its own. A shadowy outline does emerge. We hear how

> Not long after this, *Leo* the Emperour and *Gregory* the Bishop of *Rome* falling out

---

[68] *Ibid.*, p. 280.   [69] Howel, 1685, III, part iv, title page.

about the Worship of Images, the Bishop excommunicated the Prince, absolved all his Subjects of *Italy* from their Allegiance, and commanded them neither to pay him Tribute nor any other Testimony of Duty or Allegiance. Hereupon the *Romans, Campanians,* and those of *Ravenna* and *Pentapolis* revolted, and rising in great Tumults laid hands upon their Governours.[70]

The extinction of imperial authority in Italy leads to the rise of the Lombard kingdom, against which the popes turn to the Franks and encourage the Carolingian house to replace the Merovingian kings and then to intervene in Italy. In 800 Charlemagne is proclaimed emperor in Rome, and Howel has this to say:

If he were an Emperour (take the word as one possessing or reigning over divers Kingdoms) yet could he be called by any other addition, better than that of *Roman.* The *Roman* Empire was now almost quite extinct in the West, little or nothing left except a few Islands in the Mediterranean, and perchance a few Maritime Towns lying towards Sicily. The Emperour had been beaten out of this Countrey by the *Lombards,* who having made a Prey at last of the Exarchate, became themselves a Prey to victorious *Charles,* and the Exarchate, by what right soever was challenged as the Churches Patrimony. Grant then that the *Romans* had Power to name him Emperour, to confer that Title on him or any other, a worthless empty title must it be, signifying a Sovereignty over the City of *Rome,* and the small territory of the Exarchate (the rest was quite alienated). [S]uch a Dominion they had at the Banishment of their Kings, the name of one of which would more have fitted him, as *Servius, Tarquinius,* or the like, than that of *Caesar.* That they could give any thing of the Eastern Empire to him or any other, we cannot believe, after that *Constantinople* had been by Imperial Authority made a second Rome, and all Co-equal Majesty and Privileges conferred upon it. *Rome* of late had lost the Imperial Title, been a Captive to Barbarians, a Member of a Kingdom, being though restored to her Liberty afterward, yet it was by the Help and Assistance of her Daughter, and all along truckled under her, and acknowledged the Sovereignty of her Princes, and submitted to the Government of a Duke; till under shew of Religion, she became disloyal, and advanced her Bishops from the Episcopal Chair to the Princely Throne.[71]

This in a sense is the climax of Howel's Decline and Fall. Anglicans of his persuasion were never Ghibellines; the imperial authority in the west was as illegitimate as the papal usurpation which had exalted itself by pretending to confer it, and only the eastern emperors had enjoyed the authority of Constantine. Whether any Christian king could claim to have inherited or replicated it was another question. The king of France could not have inherited it from Charlemagne, who did not possess it,

---

[70] *Ibid.,* p. 58.   [71] *Ibid.,* p. 81.

and Howel's history of that kingdom becomes a history of the French language, culminating with an invective against the design of Richelieu and his Academy to make it the universal language of Europe.[72] Nor is it clear how James II, as Catholic or as Anglican, is to understand his kingship of England; a second Constantine, like his grandfather,[73] he does not appear to be, and Howel's English history culminates with an account of Anglo-Saxon kingship and Norman conquest in which Sir Henry Spelman is much cited and we look, apparently in vain, for the fingerprints of Robert Brady.[74] The history of the barbarian kingdoms seems minimally connected with that of the papacy, though if Howel had lived to write more, he might have continued past Constantine Ducas and the Conquest to recount the Seljuk inroads, the Crusades, the Gregorian papacy and the war of the Investitures, which were to be considered the turning-point of western history in anti-papal eyes. As it is, we seem to have the seed of Gibbon's 'triumph of barbarism and religion', but it is a seed that requires a great deal of watering. By Gibbon's time it had grown into an account of medieval Latin history so strong and ramifying as to relegate Byzantium to the outer horizon of historical understanding; but it is not clear how many of the threads leading to that perception start from the works he is said to have encountered at Stourhead in 1751. How many, it is worth asking, were spun by philosophic historians, how many by Anglican or Gallican clerics?

With 'the circle of Oriental history',[75] the author of the *Memoirs* presents his young self as embarking on an enquiry which was to lead the writer of the *Decline and Fall* far beyond the frontiers of Roman history; and there is evidence to support him, since we know that Gibbon acquired d'Herbelot's *Bibliothèque orientale* within a year of the date given in the *Memoirs*. In struggling with its language, he further made his first encounter with the rich world of French academic erudition, to which so much of his intellectual allegiance was to be given; but, d'Herbelot excepted, his exploration of Arab and Islamic history was one more encounter with English clerical learning. The study of these fields in the seventeenth century had been an Anglican enterprise, instigated by such impeccable churchmen as Lancelot Andrewes, James Ussher and William Laud, as well as by the more suspect figure of John

---

[72] Howel, 1685, III, part iii, pp. 424–47.
[73] For James VI and I in the role of Constantine, see Williamson, 1979.
[74] Pocock, 1987b, chs. v and viii. Brady was a leading figure at Cambridge and in historical polemics about 1680, and the two men should have known one another.   [75] Above, p. 29.

Selden, whom the *Decline and Fall* manages to present as a crabbed presbyterian,[76] and it is possible to trace in it the concerns characteristic of Laudian 'Arminianism'. A principal reason for mastering Arabic and other eastern languages had been patristic, the need to ground Church of England orthodoxy in a learning not under the control of Rome; and there are hints of an aspiration towards a re-union of the English and Greek churches, which would have fortified that ecclesiology of equal metropolitans and patriarchs of which we read in Heylyn and Howel.[77] Edward Pococke,[78] the father of Oxford Arabism, had been encouraged and promoted by Laud before the latter's downfall, and the work to whose 'barbarous Latin' Gibbon refers is an edition of a *Historia compendiosa dynastiarum*, translated from the Arabic of the thirteenth-century Christian chronicler Abu'l Faraj,[79] which situates Muslim khalifs and Mongol khans in a context traceable back to Old Testament patriarchs. This contextualisation of Islam had the effect of reducing Muhammad to the status of an impostor and heresiarch, but equally presented his religion as more than merely diabolical. As Pococke translated Abu'l Faraj into Latin, he also produced an Arabic translation of Hugo Grotius's *De veritate religionis Christianae*,[80] and here we are on the cusp of that transition from Arminianism to ecumenism which paradoxically links high Anglicanism with Anglican Enlightenment. Grotius – who maintained that the truths of natural law would stand even if, *per impossibile*, God did not exist – was in search of statements of Christian belief acceptable to those of all confessions, and Pococke's rendering of him into Latin was intended to reach eastern Christians; but it might also extend to reflective Jews and Muslims in the less confessionally riven world of the Ottoman empire. There was the risk that religion might be reduced to philosophy; but Pococke translated from Hebrew and Arabic the twelfth-century fable of Hayy ibn Yaqzan, the Self-taught Philosopher, who arrived at natural religion through growing up on a desert island, to which he returned after a series of encounters with the religions of the world.[81] It is clear that Pococke was no deist, but he may have been in search of a religion beyond controversy, which he found in the *falasifa*.

Deeply though this fable appealed to Enlightened minds, we are here

---

[76] *Decline and Fall*, v, chapter 51, n. 13.   [77] Toomer, 1996, pp. 15, 218, 282.

[78] This spelling of the name is preferred by Toomer and the *DNB* (Toomer, 1996, p. 116n.); in seventeenth and eighteenth-century spellings the terminal 'e' is a variable.

[79] Pococke, 1663. He insists on Abu'l Faraj's Christian, not Jewish identity; Gibbon continued to catalogue him as 'Bar Hebraeus'.   [80] Toomer, 1996, pp. 145–6, 215–18.

[81] *Ibid.*, pp. 218–25.

concerned with a Christian translation; and the point is that if there could be Muslim philosophers, Islam was less a blasphemy than a heresy, and might be accessible to Christian reason – whatever might be the effects of this upon Christian doctrine and belief. The way was now open for the inexhaustible curiosity of humanists, philologists and other erudites to begin the exploration of Muslim as well as Jewish and Christian Arab texts, language and history. Arabic scholarship at Oxford and Cambridge survived the fall of Laud, and persisted through the Commonwealth and Protectorate – when such enterprises as Brian Walton's Polyglot Bible were means by which the Anglican intellect kept itself alive during the dark days of disestablishment[82] – to a renewed flowering under the Restoration. By the end of Pococke's life in 1691, its energy was fading; but Simon Ockley, taking up the cause at Cambridge in the next two decades, visited the Bodleian to consult

an invaluable collection given by that incomparable prelate and martyr of blessed memory, Archbishop Laud,[83]

in which he found the history of al-Wakidi and wished he knew Turkish and could consult that of al-Tabari, whom Gibbon follows him in describing as 'the Livy of the Arabians'.[84] These works enabled Ockley to escape the limitations of Greek narrations of the Muslim conquests and recount Arab history in a style both heroic and philosophical – for he emphasises that the great deeds of the conquerors were those of men 'who were all humorists, bigots and enthusiasts' and cannot without falsification of their true character be recounted 'as becomes the sedateness and gravity of the Greeks and Romans'.[85] Though by this time Islam was beginning to be exploited for heterodox purposes by such questionable figures as Henry Stubbe, John Toland and Henri de Boulainvilliers,[86] Ockley was writing at a point where Laudian Arminianism expanded into a Christian humanism and curiosity, capable of pursuing or avoiding its unorthodox implications. This was the scholarship that led the young Gibbon, so his older self remembered, to 'the circle of Oriental history', growing out of the 'absolutely new' spectacle of late antiquity.

[82] *Ibid.*, pp. 202–10.   [83] Ockley, 1708–18, reprint, p. xviii.
[84] *Ibid.*, p. xxvi. *Decline and Fall*, v, ch. 51, n. 11.   [85] Ockley, 1708–18, reprint, p. xxxii.
[86] For Stubbe and Toland, see J. R. Jacob, 1983, pp. 64–77, 154–60, and Sullivan, 1982. Boulainvilliers, 1730 (Gibbon owned a copy; *Library*, p. 77).

GIBBON AT OXFORD: A CRISIS IN AUTHORITY

There is then a strong clerical component to the juvenile erudition with which Gibbon arrived at Oxford in 1752; the 'Doctor' whom it might have puzzled is a Doctor of Divinity. The *Memoirs* comment on the clerical character of English as compared with European universities,[87] and when Gibbon (so he tells us) suggested to his first tutor that he might study Arabic, he could have known – and Dr Waldegrave probably knew – that 'oriental' learning at Oxford was a Laudian foundation. Waldegrave no doubt replied that his pupil had better master Latin and Greek first,[88] but even this enterprise was interrupted by the crisis which soon followed.

When the writer of the *Memoirs* comments on the unconcealed Jacobitism of Oxford in the 1750s,[89] he is stigmatising a mentality which had been found in his own family; and when he depicts the ecclesiastical character of Oxford learning, and denounces the fellows and tutors for being too lazy to pursue it,[90] he may be recalling a juvenile disappointment at finding the high-church and non-juror clerical learning, which had been the glory of Oxford, in abeyance and no longer expected of him. The university could have made another Warburton out of the young Gibbon, and the mature historian was still bitter at its failure to do so. He had moved into very different paths of learning, and these constitute his greatness; he could think of himself as a humanist and philosophical historian, and of his youth as dominated by a 'blind and boyish taste for the pursuit of exotic history';[91] but his juvenile essay on 'the Age of Sesostris' – though he later thought its title suggested by Voltaire's *Siècle de Louis XIV* – was clearly an essay in chronology, that favourite pursuit of ecclesiastical learning, undertaken in the society of Sir John Marsham and Sir Isaac Newton.[92] It was not a preference for exotic over ecclesiastical history which was to drive Gibbon away from Oxford, but a crisis in the interpretation of the history of the Church of Christ.

When he claims that Magdalen College neglected his religious education and omitted to ensure that he subscribed to the Thirty-Nine

---

[87] *Memoirs*, p. 46 (*A*, p. 62, Memoir F).

[88] *Memoirs*, p. 55 (*A*, p. 79, Memoir F). 'His prudence discouraged this childish fancy; but he neglected the fair occasion of directing the ardour of a curious mind.' This is Thomas Waldegrave (1721–84); Craddock, *YEG*, p. 315, n. 5.   [89] *Memoirs*, p. 53 (*A*, p. 76, Memoir F).

[90] *Memoirs*, pp. 47–55 (*A*, pp. 64–78, Memoir F).   [91] *Memoirs*, p. 55 (*A*, p. 79).

[92] *Memoirs*, pp. 55–6 (*A*, pp. 79–81, Memoir F). Marsham was the author of *Canon chronicus aegyptiacus, ebraicus, graecus* (London, 1672); Newton of *The Chronology of Ancient Kingdoms Amended* (London, 1728).

Articles of the Church of England,[93] he is in fact not reliable, since his written subscription happens to have survived.[94] But it is more important to note that he is not casting himself as a youthful Socinian or Arian, finding difficulty like many others in subscribing the militantly 'Athanasian' articles in which the church required a declaration of the strongest Trinitarian convictions. William Chillingworth, something of a hero to the Gibbon of the *Memoirs*, had on returning like him from a brief conversion to Rome found these articles a stumbling-block, and his final subscription had been delayed and perhaps not without reservations. But the *Memoirs* on the face of it complain that the young Gibbon should have been required to subscribe and instructed in orthodox doctrine, and – if it were not for the Mallets – one would expect a Tory family background to have imposed high-church and Athanasian requirements. Magdalen's failure with Gibbon was a Tory failure; he blames Oxford for driving him away from the Church of England, and does not thank it because he never returned in spirit to that communion. Perhaps by 1790 he was defending himself against Anglican charges of infidelity; but there are deeper meanings than that.

In the circumstances of an adolescence recollected nearly forty years afterwards, Gibbon became involved in the recurrent eighteenth-century debate over the historical and philosophical actuality of miracles. It is important to understand why this debate was a crucial one. The belief in miracles was not a residue of archaic superstition or neo-Platonist magic – though it came to be perceived as both – but a serious assertion of Christ's divinity and the church's derivation of authority from his person. Its significance was if anything underlined by the post-Puritan emphasis on the ethical and social character of Christ's mission as saviour; for the more it was insisted that he came to add supernatural sanctions and the promise of eternal life to the injunctions of a natural morality already known to man, the more important it became that the character of these sanctions should be explicit and specific. If he had been a divine being possessed of divine powers, these must have been exercised to reinforce and even transcend his verbal preaching of morality, so that miracles were necessary signs of his divine character, intelligible to the reflective and the vulgar alike. If he had left behind him a church which was not merely an association of those who believed in his teachings, but a communion of those believers with his person in and beyond time, it was important that his power to work signs and

---

[93] *Memoirs*, pp. 57–8 (*A*, p. 83, Memoir F).   [94] Low, p. 40.

wonders should have been continued in the church which was an extension of his person. It was common ground to nearly all churches that the apostles – whom scripture declared to have received the gift of tongues, to have healed the sick and raised the dead, and most of whom tradition declared to have undergone martyrdom – had by both their actions and their sufferings borne witness to the truth and positively communicated it through signs working on the mind and spirit of beholders. But among Protestants it was generally held that miracles of this kind had ceased at some point after the lifetimes of the apostles, and been replaced by the faith that went with the hearing of the Word of God; while Catholics, uncomplicatedly willing to affirm that their church was still exactly what it had been when Christ left it among the apostles, were prepared to assert that miraculous powers had been given to it and might to this day be manifest in the lives and deaths of specially holy persons. This was part of the claim that the Roman Catholic Church possessed a unique authority as the direct extension of Christ's person, a claim which Protestant communions desired to repudiate in the case of Rome without necessarily asserting it of themselves. To a church like that of England, claiming to be both Protestant and apostolic, it was therefore highly important to determine by what stages the miraculous powers given to the apostles had ceased and by what spiritual gifts it could be said they had been replaced; this was part of the process of determining in what sense and to what extent such a church enjoyed spiritual authority, questions we have seen to be crucial in the ecclesiology of the Church of England. If miraculous powers had ceased, it was important to supply the history of the process; but such a history must encounter the sort of history Catholics were prepared to write, according to which they had not ceased at all and history was simply the record of their and the Church's continuity.

In the new year of 1749, three years before Gibbon's matriculation at Oxford, Conyers Middleton, a Cambridge divine, had published *A Free Inquiry into the Miraculous Powers Which are Supposed to have Subsisted in the Christian Church, from the Earliest Ages through Several Successive Centuries: By Which it is Shewn that We have no Sufficient Reason to Believe, upon the Authority of the Primitive Fathers, that any Such Powers were Continued to the Church, after the Days of the Apostles.*[95] This work had occasioned scandal, as it was meant to, and Oxford had conferred honorary degrees on two of Middleton's opponents. It is important to understand why Gibbon remembered it as

---

[95] Wellek, 1976, is a modern facsimile edition.

deeply disturbing to him in youth. Middleton had been at pains to affirm the veracity of the miracles performed by the Saviour and his apostles, and had denied only that miracles had been performed after their lifetimes. But this was enough to restrict miraculous energy to an effect of Christ's divine nature, possessed by him in person and conferred by him upon the apostles in person, but not communicated to the institutional church in such a way as to make it a mystical extension of his person. Middleton began to appear an extreme low-churchman, intent to deny the church the character of a spiritual communion and reduce it to an association of those who accepted Christ's teaching and believed in his divinity. However, it was not possible to stop there; Christ and his church were so intimately connected that if the latter were not a divine communion it became hard to believe that the former was a divine person, and Middleton was open to the suspicion of Socinianism if not deism. Leslie Stephen, the agnostic author of the entry concerning him in the *Dictionary of National Biography*, thought he would have done better to resign his orders than to remain as librarian of Trinity College.[96] These impressions were reinforced by the vehemence of his language regarding the post-apostolic fathers and martyrs, whom he condemned as fanatics, enthusiasts and impostors, proclaiming the existence of spiritual powers within themselves instead of attending to 'the calm and sober precepts of the Gospel', whatever Middleton thought these were.[97]

These, however, are not the characteristics of the *Free Inquiry* – though he notes that its 'bold criticism... approaches the precipice of infidelity'[98] – which the mature Gibbon recalled as precipitating the crisis of his youth. As he tells it, he read the *Inquiry* as a problem in the transmission of authority; we have to remember that this term denotes not merely that which may constrain the intellect, but that which authorises the exercise of spiritual power. Miracles were not only the exercise of such power, but the signs of its presence, authenticity and efficacy; and without a continuous exercise of miracles, it was doubtful if there was any continuously authoritative church – doubtful, therefore, if there was a divine person whose spiritual power any church exercised.

[96] *DNB*, under 'Middleton, Conyers', signed 'L.S.'
[97] Wellek, 1976, preface, pp. xxxi–xxxiii; pp. 26–71, section III, *passim*; 82–3, 88, 96, 98, 109, 116–18, 135–6, 157–60, 185–7. The words quoted are at p. 205.
[98] *Memoirs*, p. 58 (*A*, p. 84, Memoir F). Gibbon's *Vindication of Some Passages in the Fifteenth and Sixteenth Chapters of the History of the Decline and Fall of the Roman Empire* (London, 1779) adds that Middleton 'rose to the highest pitch of scepticism, in any wise consistent with Religion' (Womersley, III, p. 1151).

Gibbon says that his younger self therefore repudiated Middleton's assaults on the miraculous powers and the personal characters of the post-apostolic fathers, saints and martyrs, but found the authority thus reconstituted carried on into later ages of the formation of Catholic practice and doctrine.[99] In this he was confirmed by reading English translations of two works by Jacques Benigne Bossuet, Bishop of Meaux; evidently the *Exposition de la doctrine de l'église catholique* and the *Histoire des variations des églises protestantes*.[100] It was not merely Bossuet's vindication of the primitive character of Catholic usages that swayed the young Gibbon, but his monolithic solution of the problem of authority: what the church was it had been from the beginning, and if miraculous powers had been given to the apostles as signs of their authority, the powers, the signs and the authority persisted in the church to this day. The diversities of the Protestant churches were a sufficient proof that they lacked any true link with Christ.

Gibbon, we can now see, was behaving as nervous young men at Oxford have behaved from time to time since the reign of Henry VIII and have not ceased behaving to this day. Having selected authority as the sign of a true church, he was deciding that the only true church possible must be the one whose claim to authority was absolute, uncompromising, unmediated and unmodified, and which affirmed its institutional continuity as unbroken since the days of Christ and the apostles. This decision was to drive him out of the Church of England, which could make no such claims without modifying them, and his retreat from Catholicism was to lead him back to a history not unlike that which Anglicans could write of themselves, though never back to more than a nominal membership in the Anglican communion. He was to write a history of the church nearer to Middleton's than to Bossuet's, yet on the last pages of the *Decline and Fall* to display some unexpected benignities towards historical Catholicism. The story of his juvenile conversion has encouraged one modern interpreter to conclude that his life and writings were governed by the hopeless search for an absolute and undivided authority which escaped him when he failed to remain a Catholic.[101] It is easier to suppose that Gibbon embraced a pluralist and ironist view of existence and was tolerably happy with it.[102] But his

---

[99] *Memoirs*, p. 59 (*A*, p. 85, Memoir F). In his preface (Wellek, 1976, pp. ii–v) Middleton had cited Locke's *Third Letter on Toleration* to the effect that the believer in miracles on the authority of the church historians must either 'go no further than the Apostles' time, or else, not to stop at Constantine's'. [100] *Memoirs*, p. 264 (Bonnard's note identifying the English translations).
[101] Gossman, 1981.
[102] Gossman indeed aims (p. 120) at a critical study of irony as 'an ingredient of the liberal temper'.

Oxford conversion was certainly moved by the search for an undivided authority, and the sources leave us unclear as to where this need came from. In his reading – it is unlikely to have been in conversations with his aunts[103] – he must have encountered some extremely rigorous assertions of high-church principles; but he does not tell us of any such experience, and seems rather to blame Oxford for not providing it. What can be affirmed is that Middleton's work, and Gibbon's Oxford experience, are not intelligible without that background of a divided England to which we have been paying attention – and if a boy of sixteen knew only so much of the issues that moved his conversion, the historian he became studied them until he knew far more than he believed.

On learning of this episode five years later – and five years too late – Thomas Waldegrave, who had left Oxford by the time it occurred, wrote to Gibbon that had he known of the latter's crisis, 'I should immediately have put you upon reading Mr Chillingworth's Religion of Protestants; any one page of which is worth a library of Swiss divinity.'[104] It was a very English response, and very Anglican. Whatever his un-soundness on the Trinity, William Chillingworth had supplied, in his *The Religion of Protestants a Safe Way to Salvation* (1634), the acknowledged Anglican remedy for cases of Gibbon's kind. It might well have been effective, in which case we might never have had the *Decline and Fall*. What 'Swiss divinity' did for Gibbon we shall learn in the next chapter. Meanwhile, his bitterness against Oxford, in part a bitterness with its failure to help him in the way Waldegrave described but had not prescribed, could be further directed against his half high-church, half deist family at Putney, who received the news of his conversion with fury and consternation. What Edward Gibbon III had just done, in getting himself received into the Church of Rome, constituted an offence at law; and if the law was not much enforced, Edward Gibbon II was still trying to live down the memory of his Jacobite activities before 1745. What is noteworthy, and of vast importance to the patterns of Gibbon's future life, is that no attempt seems to have been made to reclaim their prodigal for the Church of England.[105] No stern preceptor of the stamp of William Law, no prudential reconciliator of the stamp of William Chillingworth, was called in; instead, he was removed from Oxford, placed for a few days in the care of the Mallets of all people, 'by whose

---

[103] Catherine Porten was an intelligent but not a trained reader; with Hester Gibbon, certainly a high-church doctrinaire, he did not much converse.   [104] *MW*, II, p. 137.

[105] Low, p. 45, enquires into the Mallets' possible role in this omission.

philosophy I was rather scandalised than reclaimed',[106] and then dispatched to Lausanne, a city of which the Gibbons knew little,[107] to be placed in the tutelage of the pastor Daniel Pavillard, of whom they can hardly have heard. The family's actions suggest more panic than consideration; they wanted their remittance man out of England at all costs; yet, probably without knowing it, they had played the liberal rather than the Tory card, and had exposed the errant Gibbon to a religious, scholarly and philosophical culture more diverse than Putney and Oxford, Law and Mallet, Middleton and Bossuet, could have provided – one, nevertheless, in which Gibbon's juvenile concerns could be refined and developed.

[106] *Memoirs*, p. 68 (*A*, p. 130, Memoir B). See Baridon, 1975, I, pp. 39–40.
[107] The suggestion seems to have come from Edward Eliot (*Memoirs*, p. 68; *A*, p. 130), later Gibbon's parliamentary patron, who had sojourned at Lausanne in 1746 in the company of Philip Stanhope, natural son of Lord Chesterfield. De Beer (*MG*, 70–2) gives details of their connections with the Deyverdun and Bochat families and quotes Chesterfield's letters as evidence of what the English were expected to learn from Swiss travel.

CHAPTER 2

Lausanne and the Arminian Enlightenment

The disgraced adolescent who arrived in Lausanne in June 1753 was entering on a new historical scene, of great importance to his future writing of history and our understanding of it. The religious tensions inherent in English culture had brought him to Catholic conversion and exile to the Pays de Vaud; those inherent in Swiss Calvinist culture were to restore him to Protestantism but in the end to scepticism, and to intensify his involvement in the clerical erudition that underlay all religious debate, taking him in directions which we can recognise as those of Enlightenment, but of a Protestant Enlightenment active in all the Calvinist or partly Calvinist cultures of western Europe. Of these England, with its Puritan past and the revulsion against it, was or had been one, and Scotland, whose civil and historical philosophy was not yet of the importance to Gibbon it would assume later, was another. In Lausanne, a territory subject to the ruling city of Berne, which had imposed a strictly Calvinist formula upon it a generation before his arrival, Gibbon found himself exposed to all the tensions afflicting a network of Calvinist churches reaching from Geneva to Amsterdam, and these introduced him to new and powerful forms of erudition operating in Christian culture, to a view of theological debate as itself deeply historical, and to an understanding of post-classical European history as driven by that debate.

Lausanne and the Pays de Vaud deeply affected Gibbon. In the years beginning in 1753 he absorbed Franco-Swiss culture to the point where he almost forgot English and ceased to be an Englishman;[1] he was to return to Lausanne at a series of important moments in his future life, and might have ended his days there but for a sudden decision in 1793 to revisit England and there to undergo the surgery of which he died. If he

---

[1] *Memoirs*, pp. 69–71, 86, 105–7 (*A*, pp. 131, 152, 175–7, Memoir B). See his letter of February 1755 to Catherine Porten (*Letters*, I, pp. 3–5) as evidence of what could happen to his English.

is a significant – and to Venturi an enigmatic – figure in the history of Enlightened culture in England, there is also a place to be sought for him in that of French-speaking Switzerland and Protestant France; perhaps in that revival of liberal and post-Jacobin historiography which connects Germaine de Staël, whose parents were his close friends if they were not hers, with François Guizot, who translated the *Decline and Fall* into French and thought of European history in ways owing much to Gibbon even if their historical personalities were profoundly different.[2] These are figures, and their lives are phenomena, in the history of Protestant culture; and to understand what had happened to Gibbon at Oxford and was about to happen to him at Lausanne, it is necessary to survey important aspects of the history of Protestantism in the seventeenth century, with their centres in the Netherlands and England, the Swiss cities and France.

   The chain of developments may be said to begin in the deeply though partially Calvinist culture of the independent Netherlands. About 1610 the theologian Jacobus Arminius put forward a group of propositions which amounted to a challenge to the absolute decrees of grace, at the centre of the Calvinist doctrine of predestination. Though highly technical in character, the 'Arminian' position was seen as questioning whether the individual's salvation was due to divine grace alone, and so opening the prospect that he might be saved by his own works or virtues, his own reasonable and social nature. The political implications of this were rapidly perceived. Strict Calvinism was clericalist in character, since in giving undivided power to God's grace it gave unchallengeable authority to the ministers who preached God's word; whereas the Arminian position diluted clerical power by emphasising the salvific capacity of those human attributes which might come under the authority of the civil magistrate. At the Synod of Dordrecht in 1614, where international Calvinism dealt with what was perceived as the Arminian crisis, the ruling patriciates of many Dutch cities supported the Arminian faction, while the princes of Orange, backed by James VI and I of Great Britain, allied themselves with the clergy against their political rivals. In the political crisis that ensued, there were laid down the lines of the three-sided crises that occurred in Dutch politics in 1650, 1672 and as late as 1747, while clergy and academics became divided into those who opposed and supported the Remonstrance which defined the Arminian position. Since toleration was a political strategy followed by the patri-

---

[2] Fontana, 1991; Thom, 1995; Siedentop, 1997.

ciates and regents who recurrently held power in the Netherlands, 'Remonstrant' churches and congregations survived and followed up the implications of Arminianism.

These tended to reinforce the authority both of the secular magistrate – if he was not too inextricably allied with an autonomous clergy – and of the individual as social being, since he could now see his salvation as activated by his works and his intelligence, his sociability and his rationality; *gratia non tollit naturam sed perficit*. When the two found themselves in alliance, 'Arminianism' could be Enlightened in a socially conservative sense, though it might also operate at a level on which the individual's spiritual experience, conceived as an 'inner light' and allied or identified with what some called 'the great spirit reason', appeared an abounding and amazing grace not predestined by any absolute decree. 'Arminian' traces are to be found among some of the most radical seeds appearing at the short-lived English revolutionary moment[3] – we are dealing with phenomena that appeared in all Calvinist cultures – but their antinomian tendencies must be understood within, not against, the emphasis laid on human experience, society and history. In the Netherlands, and elsewhere, Arminian theology became associated with Erasmian humanism, and the latter's study of textual and other evidence regarding the history of Christian belief encouraged the perception of dogma itself as a species of human behaviour, in accordance with the doctrine that it was through their works, carried out in society and in time, that human beings might or might not be saved. The great jurist and scholar Hugo Grotius was an Arminian, whose studies of religious doctrine and its history encouraged him, and others, in ecumenical hopes for a reunion of the warring churches, and the Remonstrant community at Amsterdam was to make that city the centre of an enlightened Protestant network entertaining visions which looked beyond religious conflict. This, however, was the point at which 'Arminianism' – an increasingly collective and imprecise term – became open to the suspicion, and at times the reality, that it was relying less on rationalism than on a liberal scepticism, and that the latter might end in a voluntary submission to an authority which was not that of God's word. To the Englishman Richard Baxter, Grotius's ecumenism looked suspiciously like crypto-papalism, and there were Catholic intellectuals who exploited the connections between scepticism, faith and submission to authority in precisely the way feared by Baxter and many others. The

---

[3] Lamont, 1979, ch. 3, makes this point while portraying Richard Baxter's struggles to escape Arminianism, which he feared for its ecumenical tendencies.

crucial turn towards Enlightenment came only when liberal scepticism became the ally of civil society, rather than the civil magistrate or the spiritual authority.

In England, wrote Venturi, 'the rhythm was different', for the reason that the Church of England, half apostolic and half Erastian, was at the same time half Catholic and half Calvinist, so that the 'Arminian' attack against Calvinism was carried on by those among the higher clergy deeply committed to what they saw as a sacred monarchy and desired to exalt as the imperial power in a sacred and apostolic church; while at the same time their insistence on the apostolic origins of their own or-dination was seen by their enemies as a crypto-papal assault on that monarchy's sovereign authority. Nowhere else in Protestant Europe was the Arminian movement within Calvinism so visibly associated with a return to Catholic though not Roman ecclesiology, and a baroque ritualism within Protestantism itself; and the politics of this paradox were to reinforce the deep confusions which characterised if they did not cause the civil war in England. In the Laudian and high-church posi-tions that became enduring within Anglicanism, we may trace both an Arminian ecumenism, which made those such as Howel willing to consider the Pope no Antichrist but a patriarch who had succumbed to the temptations of civil history, and a rigorous orthodoxy insistent that the apostolic church and the imperial monarchy which was part of it represented Christ's presence among men. There is Enlightenment which flows from these positions as well as Enlightenment which reacts against them and attempts to destroy them; and a crucial role is played by that latitudinarian Anglicanism which carried the doctrine that Christ's message was wholly compatible with civil order towards the point where Christ might be no more than the divine messenger of civil morality. Conyers Middleton, reaching and probably passing that point, had been the occasion of Gibbon's crisis at Oxford.

In broader and not only English terms, we have reached the point where 'Arminianism' could be accused of 'Socinianism', and the two thought of as sequential. That is to say, the doctrine that humans might be saved through the exercise of human capacity became enlarged to include the exercise of intellectual capacity for criticism and debate, not excluding though not limited to the kind of scepticism which might lead to fideism and submission; but in another direction than this, the road lay open to a substitution of discussion for communion, in which the theological and philosophical debate over Christ's person replaced any actual contact with him and the primary duty of the Christian became that of being reasonable about Christ. Established churches, wishing to avoid the extremes of papal submission and congregational enthusiasm, might welcome this development, until it was seen as subverting their own relation to Christ and the authority it conveyed. Arminian thinking was seen as opening the door to a purely rational view of Christ's nature, and so to the doctrines of Lelio and Fausto Sozzini, whose intellectual conviction of the divine unity had led them to opine that Christ was a being divine in mission and even origin but not at one with the divine nature, not unlike that messenger of morality to whom reasonable Anglicanism found itself in danger of reducing him. The latter Sozzini, latinised as Faustus Socinus, had removed to Poland and founded the Unitarian congregation of the Rakovian Catechism, some of whose members, driven into exile, had been charitably welcomed by Amsterdam Remonstrants, some of whom in turn certainly shared their convictions. This was far from the only incident endowing Socinianism with a universal significance. William Chillingworth's Jesuit antagonist, in the debate producing the work belatedly recommended to Gibbon by Waldegrave, had insisted that if there were no infallible church the only alternative would be Socinianism, since Christ would then possess no spiritual body present after his ascension. And to continue the debate over his nature was no neutral act, since a body forever discussed is an idea but never a presence. Chillingworth himself, developing a probabilism not unlike scepticism, had found it difficult to subscribe the more Trinitarian of the Thirty-Nine Articles.

In Huguenot France, the great academies which trained ministers for the Protestant congregations divided; Sedan leaning towards the rigorous Dordrecht position, Saumur prepared to experiment with such Arminian or Remonstrant theses as that saving grace might be for all sinners and not the elect merely, or that it might operate on them through the reason which all possessed, and not exclusively through direct conversion or illumination.[4] Any step away from the absolute decrees and the rigid separation of sheep from goats, elect from reprobate, admitted human reason and the social virtues to take part in the work of human salvation, enhancing the authority of society in whatever form it took but enhancing also the proposition that it was through their social nature and under social authority that humans knew Christ. The mother church of Geneva, lying outside France but deeply committed to the flow of French students whom its academy derived income from

---

[4] Armstrong, 1969.

training, experienced the same divisions, apparent both within the *compagnie* of the clergy and between the patrician families from whom both ruling magistrates and pastors were drawn: Tronchin, Mestrezat and Chouet against Turrettini and the latter's rigorist allies.[5] This became among other things a division between the Protestant scholasticism favoured by rigorists, and the new, often Cartesian, philosophy to which the 'Arminians' or 'Salmurians' were drawn by their interest in the covenant of works and reason. But when the rigorist party, headed by François Turrettini, framed the *Consensus Helveticus* in 1675, it was as the name shows an appeal to the Protestant cities of the Swiss confederation to which Geneva did not yet fully belong: to Zwinglian Zurich as well as to Calvinist Berne, which controlled Lausanne and the Pays de Vaud. The politics of theology were soon to be complicated by the growing persecution of the Protestants in France and by Geneva's agonisingly exposed position between its enemy Savoy, its protector France and its ally Berne, none of whom it trusted further than it had to.[6] Turrettini's defiant proclamation of the autonomy of grace was found repressive, as well as imprudent, by the powerful minority of clergy and magistrates who held that they could manage both the city they governed and its relations with Louis XIV by means of civil reason and reason of state. The idea that religious and civil liberty protects the sovereignty of the civil order was taking shape in the paradoxical context of a peaceful response, bordering on collaboration, to the violent and massive intolerance to which reason of state and Gallican convictions were leading the king of France.

We may follow the complexities of this story, and the history of Protestant Enlightenment, by following the careers of individuals who did more than most to shape the intellectual world in which Gibbon was living at the end of his sojourn in Lausanne seventy to eighty years later. Jean Le Clerc,[7] of a Genevan clerical family with Salmurian leanings, was teaching at Saumur in the early 1680s; he had come under a variety of Arminian influences and should probably not have subscribed the more rigorously Calvinist clauses of the *Consensus*, much as Gibbon came to see that he should not have (and believe that in fact he had not) subscribed the Athanasian clauses of the Thirty-Nine Articles. From these widely separate deviations the two non-contemporary men were to arrive at comparable positions. At Saumur Le Clerc published, pseudonymously and with a collaborator, a work of an obviously

[5] Heyd, 1982.   [6] Fatio and Martin-van Berchem, 1985, pp. 159–311.
[7] No study of him appears to have replaced Barnes, 1938.

heterodox character,[8] in which the post-Arminian position that men were to be saved through their reasonable natures grew towards the assertion that reason must be free to apply itself to all questions of religious belief, some of which might turn out under that scrutiny to have been absurdities. He was summoned to answer for it, and after a painful encounter with François Turrettini left Geneva and Saumur forever.[9] He did so at a time of gathering Catholic persecution, when the academy at Sedan had already been closed by royal decree, that at Saumur was to follow, and Geneva itself was unsure of its own future; but he was a refugee from Calvinism, not Catholicism. He spent some time in France – where he moved in Catholic circles and became interested in the writings of Richard Simon – and in England, where he hoped for an appointment as preacher in one of the French churches set up in London;[10] but through the unstinted generosity of Philippus van Limborch was welcomed and maintained by the Remonstrant community in Amsterdam, where he spent the rest of his life.

Le Clerc's trajectory here intersects with that of others notable in the history of Protestant Enlightenment. He arrived in September 1683, the month in which John Locke reached the Netherlands as a refugee conspirator fleeing the vengeance of his King.[11] The tensions between the Church of England, its ex-presbyterian opponents, and the monarchy which it could not trust to act as its head, had reached a point where there was a perceived danger that the crown might seek a road towards re-Catholicisation – a prospect by no means welcomed at Rome, where the Pope had one Gallican sovereign on his hands already, and no desire for another – but the church was obliged to support the monarchy against the greater danger of a renewal of civil war. Locke was in exile because of his involvement in the failed policies of the Whigs, perhaps including his authorship of the *Treatises of Government*, still in manuscript but capable of being read as an incitement to rebellion.[12] His genius as a philosopher had yet to declare itself to the world, but during the next five years in Amsterdam he was to revise his theology by means of a close scrutiny of Trinitarian and Socinian doctrines, and his philosophy by writing the *Essay on Human Understanding*, the work which made him a leader of European Enlightenment and had radical im-

---

[8] Barnes, 1938, pp. 59–62; it was *Liberii de sancto-amore epistolae theologicae, in quibus varii scholasticorum errores castigantur. Irenopoli, 1679* (actually Saumur, 1681). The collaborator was Henry Desbordes.
[9] For the complicated story of these proceedings, and the involvement of Limborch and others, see Barnes, 1938, pp. 63–87.
[10] Some of these journeyings preceded Le Clerc's final exit from Geneva; Barnes, 1938.
[11] Cranston, 1957, p. 230.   [12] Laslett, 1960; Ashcraft, 1986; Marshall, 1994.

plications for theological and historical understanding. He did this while in a close association with Limborch, and also with Le Clerc; the Amsterdam years, however, situate him at the turning-point at which currents previously existing became what we may term the Protestant Enlightenment.

Le Clerc reached Amsterdam in time to encounter his associates and rivals in co-ordinating the movements we denote by that name. The persecution of Huguenots in France was mounting towards the Revocation of the Edict of Nantes in 1685, and a gathering of exiles was forming in Rotterdam and Amsterdam; Pierre Jurieu and Pierre Bayle had arrived in the former city in 1681 and Jacques Basnage was to join them in 1685. With Jurieu as a partial exception, all were major actors in forming the climate of the Protestant Enlightenment – which was the climate Gibbon found in Lausanne seventy years afterwards – and in shaping the species of erudition that became a principal object of his intellectual allegiance. One of the crucial contexts in which Gibbon must be situated was shaped by French-speaking Protestants who were contemporaries of his grandfather.

The politics, ecclesiology and philosophy of the Huguenot *réfugiés* – with whom the Genevan Le Clerc was associated but should not be identified – has always proved hard for anglophone historians to deal with, if only because it was a revolt against Calvinist rigour as well as against Catholic persecution. Guy H. Dodge's *The Political Theory of the Huguenots of the Dispersion*, still the main work on the subject available in English, was begun before and published after the Second World War,[13] and written in the mighty shadows of Figgis and McIlwain. It accordingly focuses on the figure of Jurieu, and presents him, justly enough, as an exponent of seventeenth-century resistance theory, proclaiming a right of rebellion against religious persecution while falling short of any doctrine of religious toleration, in which Jurieu certainly did not believe. But there are several reasons – which Dodge perceived but perhaps could not accept fully – why we are obliged to see Jurieu as a figure of the century that was ending, rather than of that which was to come. He preached resistance to Louis XIV, urged his brethren to rebel in alliance with William III and the anti-French coalition of the Nine Years War, and in the turbulent mainstream of the older Protestantism engaged in apocalyptic calculations and prophecies presaging the downfall of the Babylon of Versailles. What complicates the story, in the first place, is

[13] Dodge, 1947. See now Laursen, 1995.

that Bayle and Basnage took a line against Jurieu which can be mistaken for that of sceptics and deists, and in the second place that it is important to avoid making that confusion. Enlightenment, it has long been recognised, consists in part in the rejection of Jurieu and what he stood for; but the nature of that rejection needs to be carefully defined.

The Revocation of the Edict of Nantes, coinciding as it did with the accession of James II in England and leading in a few years towards the revolution of 1688 and the outbreak of the War of the League of Augsburg (or Nine Years War), seemed at first sight to give that conflict the character of a war of religion. What appears to us an impolitic lurch towards persecution seemed to contemporaries – by no means committed as yet to toleration as a principle – simply a resumption of the offensive of international Catholicism against international Protestantism. The proceedings of James II and VII in all three of his kingdoms, his overthrow by William of Orange's expedition first to England and then to Ireland – where Huguenot exiles in the Dutch service played their part in completing the English Protestant conquest – and on the other hand the French devastation of the Protestant Palatinate, all strongly indicated the possibility that the great confessions were at war once more, and the alliances of the House of Orange with Catholic Spain, Savoy and the Emperor merely suggested that the complicated diplomacy of the older wars of religion was being resumed. Clearly this was how Pierre Jurieu saw matters, with his vigorous apologies for William III and his programmes for Huguenot rebellion to be supported by the adversaries of the French monarchy; his writings therefore form a continuation of an earlier age. But among his colleagues and friends of the *Refuge* he was to encounter vehement opposition, and Huguenot writers were to aim at the conversion of another war of religion into an international system of contending yet co-existing states, each practising as much religious toleration as could be exacted from it. *Raison d'état* was to prevail over confessional warfare – perhaps at bottom this was a Grotian programme – and the theological implications of such a politics were to provide an important component of what we mean by Enlightenment.

Since the destruction by Richelieu of their independent military power within the kingdom of France, the Huguenots had increasingly emphasised their loyalty to the king and the absolute and irresistible character of the latter's authority, from which they expected the toleration and protection that should reward their fidelity. But toleration necessarily raised difficult questions of political ecclesiology: what was the sacred character of a monarchy which recognised two religions and might perhaps be identified with neither, and what manner of church, and of Christ's presence, would such a monarchy assert to exist in its realm? The campaigns (at times semi-military) of repression waged against the Huguenots between 1678 and 1685 constituted the monarchy's rejection of the allegiance offered it on terms which implied toleration, lessening the king's status as elder son of the Church and infringing the principle of *un roi une foi*. Jurieu drew the resistant's conclusion: protection had been withdrawn, and the contract of subjection was at an end (which was not to say that it might not, in favourable circumstances, be renewed). In Pierre Bayle and Jacques Basnage, however, his former friends and pupils, he met adversaries who steadfastly counselled the Huguenots they had left behind in France to passive obedience and non-resistance – if these Anglican terms may be admitted to a rendering of Huguenot discourse. Bayle was the author of that two-faced work, the *Avis important aux réfugiés* (1690); Basnage urged the Church of the Desert to give up both its prophesyings and its arms, and submit first to its pastors and afterwards to its king.[14] The naked fear which any clergy felt of self-propelled congregational enthusiasm of course played its part here; what happened when a few Camisard prophets made their way to London is an episode of itself in English religious history.[15] But Bayle and Basnage were not the French king's quislings; while counselling faith in the renewal of his protection, they conducted a lifelong polemic against what his apologists and theologians were saying in support of his persecutions, and we have to see the scepticism and the scholarship of these Huguenot publicists in the context of a common strategy, aimed against the renewed Catholicism of Maimbourg and Bossuet but also against the older Calvinism of Jurieu.

There is, that is to say, a link between their war on two fronts, against persecution and against rebellion, and the scepticism which they displayed towards authority in all forms and the allegations of fact – usually sacred – on which it was based. That their scepticism might end in counsels of submission does not diminish its erosion of the bases of authority; they were vesting it in history, while paradoxically making the authority of history consist in the fact that it was hard to know with finality. This is the political thrust of the scepticism of Bayle's *Dictionnaire*, but the question which has to be determined is that of the meaning of

[14] The major studies of Bayle are those of Labrousse, 1963–4, Dibon, 1959 and Rex, 1966. For Basnage see Cerny, 1987.   [15] Schwartz, 1980.

the term; there could be many varieties of scepticism directed at different propositions in theology and philosophy, leading to a variety of consequences.[16] It is easy to see that one variety could be Arminian, or more strictly a consequence of Arminianism; from a respect for the endeavours of Christians to contribute to their own salvation and a belief that reason played its part in the operations of grace, there could arise a respect for the operations of reason and a tolerance exhibited when these led to diverse conclusions. It could be affirmed – as it had been more than once at Saumur[17] – that reason must be applied to the preaching of gospel and doctrine, and that the preacher must have liberty to employ reason at all points; and given the premise that reason was not infallible, religion could be seen as an affair of sincere and fallible men doing what they could with the instrument given them by God and nature. When the Amsterdam Remonstrants charitably welcomed the Polish Unitarians, it could have been with the intention of disputing with them rather than agreeing with them. But the issues on which this debate must turn – the nature of Christ's divinity, the Incarnation, the Atonement, the Trinity – were precisely those on which debate itself could never be a neutral concept. If Christ were present among men only in the form of a series of propositions over which faith and reason held intellectual debate, he was present only as an idea, at a time when the status of ideas was itself coming to be debatable. He was not present in the structure of any visible church, no church contained either ministrants or exponents authorised to convey his presence to others, and the Church of Christ was reduced to a series of debating societies, whose deep and undoubted sincerity and seriousness would not mask their fundamental if sometimes fideist scepticism. There were many who earnestly desired such a result, and saw it as by no means incompatible with the strong civil authority of magistracies and even clerisies. These would be happy to see the Remonstrant College as just such a debating society, an international research centre in which the study of religion replaced religion in the institutional or even personal sense, and to see it as an instrument in the enterprise of replacing both persecuting Catholicism and rebellious Protestantism by the operations of states which were tolerant because they no longer saw Christ acting directly or institutionally in the structure of human societies. But peace and toleration were being bought at a high price, nothing

[16] For this see the writings of Richard H. Popkin, in particular Popkin, 1979; Laursen, 1992.
[17] For the stages by which Saumur turned away from the Dordrecht Calvinist position, see Barnes, 1938, pp. 55–6, and Armstrong, 1969, generally.

less than the divinity of Christ as it had been defined in the centuries of the church's existence, and this was why Arminians had constantly to defend themselves against the charge of Socinianism – a charge often but not always unfounded.

However, the evaluation of the debates occurring among the Huguenot *réfugiés* is immeasurably complicated by the circumstance that the principal adversaries of Jurieu were not in any sense Arminians. Like Jurieu himself – all three had been friends – Pierre Bayle and Jacques Basnage were affiliated with predestinationist Sedan rather than universalist Saumur, and with Geneva under the ascendancy of François Turrettini. The debate among them took place in the precincts of the Walloon Church at Rotterdam rather than the Remonstrant College at Amsterdam; and Bayle's differences, first with Jurieu, and then with Le Clerc, came to be based, not on any large-minded Arminianism leading him towards Socinianism, but on his fierce scepticism regarding the powers of the intellect in matters of religion, which led him – as Elisabeth Labrousse has magisterially examined – towards pyrrhonism in one direction and fideism in another. Bayle's, we are now told, was in fact a very Calvinist scepticism, rigorously separating reason from grace; and from Rotterdam to Amsterdam came to be a longer journey than from Sedan to Saumur. Bayle and Le Clerc were seldom friends, soon rivals and in the end enemies,[18] and their later controversies turned on Bayle's conviction that Le Clerc had become a Christian rationalist, who thought it possible to ground religion in natural law and natural reason. Bayle would have none of this; he thought the problems of theodicy, of reconciling God's goodness with God's omnipotence, insoluble by human reason and susceptible only of a solution by faith, in whose absence one must accept authority but authority would be well advised to impose toleration.

Not everyone understood or accepted the fideist component in Bayle's scepticism, and it is not likely that Gibbon, in whom fideism is hard to trace,[19] was one who did. The thrust of scepticism, where not directed against patristic or scholastic authority, was coming to be increasingly aimed at Nicene and Trinitarian orthodoxy, and here the views of Bayle command attention. There is no article on Arminius or Arminianism in Bayle's mighty *Dictionnaire historique et critique*, but there is one on Simon Episcopius (1583–1643), who had been Arminius's im-

---

[18] Barnes, 1938, ch. VII ('La rèpublique des lettres; querelles'), pp. 228–37; Labrousse, 1963, I, pp. 259–65. For an account of Bayle differing from hers, see Popkin, 1979.

[19] Turnbull, 1982.

mediate successor, and here a lengthy footnote[20] aligns Bayle with Le Clerc, who has confuted Jurieu's attempt to charge Episcopius with Socinianism. Bayle cannot resist remarking that Le Clerc has been instructed to do this by his superiors, the Amsterdam Remonstrants, but he applauds him for carrying out the task, and remarks that while Jurieu deserves credit for remaining silent in the face of Le Clerc's rebuttal, he would have done better still to withdraw his charges and confess himself mistaken. Jurieu could make his enemies one another's allies, and the charge that Arminians necessarily became Socinians was the kind of thing Bayle enjoyed dismantling; but he had no particular commitment to the defence of Arminian doctrine, and the significance of these pages in the *Dictionnaire* is that they show us how easily all roads could lead to the spectre of Socinianism. In the article on Socinus himself, Bayle alludes to a widespread belief that several powerful European princes would introduce Socinianism if only they dared, but adds that since the Socinian sect disapproves of both war and magistracy this is hardly likely to happen, and that the fantasy that the sect is secretly multiplying everywhere may be dismissed. He goes on to a lengthy confutation of a charge of crypto-Socinianism brought against Arnauld and the *école de Port Royal* in general, to whom he was certainly no closer than he was to Episcopius and the Remonstrants of Amsterdam.[21] This is all very Baylean, but he is testifying to the existence of a widespread concern with Socinianism which, however much it fantasised about underground conspiracies based on the Rakovian Catechism, arose from the recognition that something of a Socinian nature lay in the political logic of much that was happening in Latin[22] Europe. It was not the activities of the Socinian confession that mattered. Everywhere the peace seemed to be menaced, and the authority of the civil sovereign challenged, by the spiritual claims of church and sect, revived by the disastrous proceedings of Louis XIV; and a revision of the divinity ascribed to Jesus Christ might follow from the response to these claims. If the Spirit had not been incarnate in the Flesh, there was no one in the world who could claim authority from the Spirit; in the last analysis it was as simple as that. If Jesus had been simply a man, social authority had nothing to fear from him; if the claim that he had been more than a man was such that only social reason could discuss it, the outcome of the debate was predetermined. The counter-offensive against the decrees of grace had opened up such a debate within Calvinist and quasi-Calvinist Protestan-

---

[20] Bayle, 1696, pp. 1056–7 (footnote 14).   [21] *Ibid.*, pp. 1065 (text), 1070–4 (footnote M).
[22] By 'Latin' is meant that Europe whose history derives from the problems of Latin Christianity.

tism, and this was one reason why Arminians found themselves constantly accused of Socinianism; but the accusation had increasingly less to do with the confession formulated in Poland than with the recognition that the termination of the Wars of Religion and the substitution of enlightened reason of state were not possible without a renewed debate about the divinity of Christ, in which not all wanted to admit themselves engaged. Bayle was something far more complex than a Socinian, but he understood the place of that term in the history going on about him.

Scepticism, and the forms of authority which it attacked, alike rested, in that clerical culture, on erudition and the interpretation of texts; but there was a point at which scepticism became more than doubt – a way of life and even a way of, or substituting for, religion itself. This is among the significances of the *république des lettres*, as the phenomenon which the words denote was shaped by the activities of the men we are considering. Humanist in origin, the term was established in Latin and the vernaculars[23] and denoted first a journalistic activity of collecting and publishing correspondence, book notices and reviews reflecting the intellectual doings of learned men (and now and then women), all over Europe, and secondly a supposed international community of the learned men themselves, defined as members of the *république* by their activity in contributing to its published proceedings. It had become a phenomenon of the print culture whose centre was in the Netherlands, and in the decades following the Revocation such energies as those of Le Clerc in Amsterdam and Bayle in Rotterdam[24] combined with those of the Dutch printing houses to give it so strongly Huguenot a character that its name became nearly synonymous with the *Refuge*.[25] Though open to debate on all sides – there were Jesuit journals as well as Huguenot and Remonstrant – its very openness became a weapon, in rendering all things debatable and substituting the authority of debate for that of dogma; if critical method and scholarly caution kept the

---

[23] For a survey of this term and its uses, see Waquet, 1989. Those commenting on the figure often remark that this republic has no government but is under the sovereignty of reason alone. This seems one source for its use to denote the cosmopolis of free-thinkers described by Bayle in the *Dictionnaire*, article 'Catius' (Waquet, 1989, p. 484). Waquet cautiously endorses Koselleck's view that the *république* signifies the community of intellectuals excluded from power by absolute monarchy; the interpretation in this chapter is rather different.

[24] Bayle edited the *Nouvelles de la république des lettres* from 1684 to 1687; Le Clerc the *Bibliothèque universelle et historique* from 1686 to 1693, the *Bibliothèque choisie* from 1703 to 1713, and the *Bibliothèque ancienne et moderne* from 1714 to 1726.

[25] Goldgar, 1995, studies the scholarly culture of the *république*, unhappily to the exclusion of its intellectual and polemical vitality.

debate inconclusive, it was still an act of authority to do so. Humanist in origin, textual criticism was a largely philological technique applied to, and shaped in, the study of Europe's classical origins; but since the days of Erasmus and Valla, it had been understood that it could be no less applied to church antiquity and sacred origins, and that the consequences of doing so were commonly heterodox, less because they led to heretical conclusions than because they historised orthodoxy and heterodoxy alike by reducing them to particular judgments by particular men in particular circumstances. Le Clerc and others saw the *république* not simply as an international learned society but as a kind of alternative church, a Christian communion based on the scholarly and amicable discussion of the various possibilities of theology past and present. At the end of the road, of course, lay Socinianism, to which the very logic of discussion seemed to point; but there were many stopping-places along the way, and the value of discussion was always that it might remain inconclusive, with Christian charity or enlightened good taste taking the place of final commitment. The *république des lettres* was therefore the international clearing house of the *esprit de méthode*. Those engaged in it regarded themselves as *journalistes* or *nouvellistes*, and Bayle's great *Dictionnaire* is an outgrowth and companion of his *Nouvelles de la république des lettres*. Its later volumes in particular contained more about people than about ideas, and more about moderns than about ancients. Bayle, as a *nouvelliste*, was more interested in how people said things than in the things they said;[26] and increasingly, when he and others after him described themselves as *philosophes*, this was what they meant by philosophy. In the *querelles* then going on, in France, England and the republic of letters generally, the 'moderns' remained fascinated by classical and sacred literature, but they were replacing the authority inherent in the text by the study of the human mind or minds that had produced it. This was an important move in Enlightenment, but at least in the Netherlands-centred print culture being built by the Remonstrants and the *réfugiés*, it was a Protestant move before it was a philosophic.

Gibbon in his generation at Lausanne became exposed to this growth of critical study. He came to admire both Le Clerc and (with reservations) Bayle, and he made use of the former's *bibliothèques* and other journals succeeding them to acquaint himself with what was going on in the world of ancient literature and modern scholarship. A decade later,

---

[26] For the relation of *journaliste* to *historien*, see Labrousse, 1964, II, pp. 27–38.

we even find him trying his hand at being a *journaliste* himself.[27] But there was a tendency then, as there is now, for the critical enterprise to substitute itself for the texts it studied, and in this tendency – it was known as pyrrhonism – Gibbon would have no part; he looked on texts as evidence of an ancient actuality which moderns might seek to recapture, and he more than once criticised Bayle, as he many times criticised Voltaire, for allowing his own critical cleverness to get between him and the texts he should have mastered.[28] This is not an attitude easily observed in the displaced undergraduate at Lausanne; but what he found there was not only a culture stamped by Arminian Protestantism, but strong traces of the *république des lettres* and its turn towards erudition. By the end of his first five years in the Swiss city, he knew what Le Clerc and Bayle stood for and aligned himself with their critical scholarship; but though he steeped himself in Le Clerc's *bibliothèques*, the works of Protestant scholarship he ended by taking as his guides were major ecclesiastical histories as well as essays in critical reading. If we accept what evidence there is to support his account of the Stourhead experience, we accept Gibbon's intimation that his mind turned in childhood towards histories written in the grand manner, and that these belonged more in the category of ecclesiastical history than the prose of the *Memoirs* may indicate. Histories of this kind had been among the products of the Huguenot diaspora.

The great Catholic offensive against the *religion pretendue réformée*, at its height around 1683, had been waged in part by the production of major works of historiography, upholding the undivided and continuous authority of the church and exhorting the schismatic to submission: Louis Maimbourg's histories of Calvinism and Lutheranism, Bossuet's *Exposition de la doctrine de l'église catholique* and *Histoire des variations des églises protestantes* – the works that later proved fatal to Gibbon at Oxford – to say nothing of his *Histoire universelle*. To these the *réfugiés* produced replies: Bayle's *Critique générale de l'histoire du calvinisme de M. Maimbourg* (1682), Basnage's *Histoire de la religion des églises réformées* (1690) and *Histoire de l'église chrétienne* (1699 and 1721), Le Clerc's *Historia ecclesiastica duorum primorum saeculorum* (1716); and even Jurieu produced an *Histoire critique des dogmes et des cultes* (1704), in which he answered Bossuet by declaring – as his Calvinism alone might predispose him to do – that there had existed no continuously visible church possessing a monopoly of orthodoxy and authority, but that the centuries of early Christianity had been an age of

---

[27] In the *Mémoires littéraires de la Grande Bretagne*, edited by Gibbon and Deyverdun in 1766.
[28] *Decline and Fall*, I, ch. 25, n. 45 (47 in Bury); V, ch. 50, n. 110 (118 in Bury); ch. 52, n. 25 (27 in Bury).

controversy, contestation and the struggle for self-definition.[29] Here the Calvinist scepticism regarding works and the Arminian scepticism regarding absolute decrees – whether or not reinforced by the even deeper scepticism of Bayle – met to produce an openness towards history as the way to study ecclesiology. The attack on the monolithic authority of Rome was extending itself backwards to the age of the councils and the definition of orthodoxy. The intention was less to vindicate the heresies than to enquire into the authority that had defined them as such; but the effect was to depict heresy and orthodoxy alike as products of the human intelligence, not of extraneous authority. How far the young Gibbon at Lausanne was reading histories of this kind cannot be determined; but twenty years later, in the *Decline and Fall*'s first volume, he cited among his guides to early Church history the writings of Le Clerc, Basnage (including his *Histoire des Juifs*, published in 1716) and the *Histoire de Manichée et du Manichéisme* published in 1734 by another Huguenot of the *Refuge*, Isaac de Beausobre. The interest in heresy had grown into an interest in the extra-Christian.

It was at Lausanne that Gibbon encountered the strategy, and the culture, of that liberal Protestantism that was seeking to ally belief with criticism and faith with scepticism, and was moving irreversibly towards the identification of religion with freedom of religion; and we may take it that in his mind critical freedom, and the freedom to write history, at some point substituted themselves for belief altogether. How and when this substitution occurred is a further question, but for the present it seems desirable to consider the impact of Protestant Enlightenment on the English culture which he had left but to which he was to return, and on the Lausannais culture which he was to find comfortable as an alternative home. If we revisit the account of Anglican culture in which the latitudinarian impulse alone could lead towards heterodoxy and deism, we find it reinforced and complicated by the history of John Locke. After five years in Amsterdam, that philosopher returned to England in the wake of the Orange invasion, where he published his *Treatises of Government* and *Letter on Toleration* without putting his name to them, and in the same year published and acknowledged the *Essay on Human Understanding* which was to make him a figure of Enlightenment in Europe. This he did in an England where the struggle against Calvinism was virtually over, and the question was that of the terms on which the established church was to rule and the Nonconformist con-

---

[29] These works are considered in Perry, 1973.

gregations were to survive. The *Second Treatise on Government*, translated as it soon was into French by the Huguenot Daniel Mazel,[30] might by its advocacy of resistance seem to place its anonymous author in the camp of Jurieu, as the translator probably intended; Locke in England could not own it as his because there was strong official denial that the revolution of 1688 had been an act of resistance or dissolution of government. The toleration extended to Nonconformists by the statute of 1689 was an act of leniency by the regime of which the established church was part, not a confession that the foundations of belief lay in decision after debate. It was a clear indication of the tensions which might emerge from such a concession that the benefits of toleration were specifically denied to congregations professing an open disbelief in the Trinity, since that was the direction in which the re-establishment of doctrine as debate commonly led. Locke himself is hard to convict of a decisive adoption of Socinian doctrine, but his continued insistence on keeping the question open had essentially the same effect; he was regularly accused of Socinianism,[31] and from his time it seems possible to trace a 'Socinian' or Unitarian undercurrent within the Church of England, content with the closet status of private discussion until it came out and requested relief from the Thirty-Nine Articles in the 1770s. When this happened, a Lockean view of religion and its relation to civil government was perceived as a theory having revolutionary conse-quences,[32] and a bitter encounter between Gibbon and Joseph Priestley formed part of the Christian and clerical reception of the *Decline and Fall*. Gibbon, who had by then no beliefs shared with the Church of England, did not therefore desire to disestablish it, and scented fanaticism and enthusiasm in those who did. His brand of Enlightenment, like Bayle's with which it was not quite identical, was directed against religious rebellion as much as religious authority.

The *Essay on Human Understanding*, which we shall find Gibbon put to read at Lausanne, may be thought of as Locke's European classic, read everywhere as a historic contribution to philosophy. It was read as a training in method, an education in how the mind worked, and in its demonstration that the mind might form but could not validate ideas lying outside its experience had the largely conservative purpose of setting limits to the human propensity to formulate systems of belief. As a treatise at once anti-papal, anti-Platonist, and (in its later recension) anti-enthusiastic, it was welcomed in many Church of England circles

---

[30] Mastellone, 1988.   [31] Marshall, 1994, and forthcoming.
[32] Haakonssen, 1996b; Pocock, 1985, ch. 9.

which did not fear the 'Socinian' implications perceived in it by others; and 'the great Mr Locke' was an object of Anglican veneration until the rise of Rational Dissent.[33] As a treatise on method, the *Essay* encouraged the study of how the mind both should and should not – but nevertheless did – proceed in the generation of ideas and systems of belief, and thus contributed – though Locke himself was not a historian – to that conversion of theology into the history of theology which supported the presentation of laws and customs, opinions and ideas, as effects of what were called *les progrès de l'esprit humain*. This furnished Enlightened historiography with philosophic foundations, so far as these were needed, but at the same time had more radical implications than were welcomed by all Enlightened minds; for if the mind was limited to the study of what it could produce, might it not follow that the mind produced everything and was its own object of study? The philosophical implications of this might be cosmic.

As Locke was preparing his *The Reasonableness of Christianity* (1695), he found it necessary to distance himself from John Toland's *Christianity Not Mysterious* (1696); and the so-called 'English deists' – Toland, Collins, Blount, Bolingbroke as edited by David Mallet – are often presented, as they were by Venturi in his first analysis,[34] as England's chief contribution to Enlightenment as a unitary phenomenon. But this is to overlook their radical separateness from that sober, even if Socinian, subordination of religion to the civil order which made Anglican clergy able to accept Locke; and it is also to disregard the various forms which 'deism' was capable of taking. This word came into play when philosophical theology became independent of Christ and Christianity, thus going farther than Socinians were willing to travel. It might take the form of a 'natural religion', involving a deity who had no need to enter into covenant with the Jews or take on flesh as Christ; or it might take the more radically dangerous form of a 'religion of nature', in which the universe as perceived by reason took on many of the attributes of God and did not require those which it did not assume.[35] Toland was willing to experiment with deism in both these forms, but when he took the latter path he became identified with Spinoza – and in antiquity with Epicurus and Lucretius – as the authors of a pantheism in which creator and creation, mind and matter, were one because the mind was part of what it perceived and could be considered the universe grown conscious of itself.[36] Hume, and probably Gibbon, were never deists in either the

---

[33] Young, 1998b.   [34] Venturi, 1971, pp. 5–7.   [35] M. C. Jacob, 1981.
[36] For Toland see M. C. Jacob, 1976, 1981; Sullivan, 1982; Iofrida, 1983; Daniel, 1985.

former or the latter sense; they were sceptics; and in them the Enlightenment which tried to set limits to the human mind confronted an
Enlightenment which made the mind the object of its own self-worship.
It was a new form of enthusiasm; where the mind had once thought itself
inspired or possessed by God, it now thought itself to be God, or part of
what God had been conceived as being. Even Locke had been interested
in the possibility that matter might think,[37] and materialism was a
possible source of enthusiasm.

These possibilities were not unknown in the England Gibbon had left
behind; but there is no sign that the Mallets had been breathing them
into his infant ear, and it would be some time before he encountered
them in the reading he began at Lausanne. In that city, however, he did
encounter the continuing shock waves of the collision between Calvinist
and Arminian doctrine, and he could have encountered – though apparently he did not – Protestant mysticisms of a kind which were to
concern him in the *Decline and Fall.* Forty years after the event, Lausanne
was still reacting to the imposition in 1716, by the ruling city of Berne, of
a strictly Calvinist *Formula Consensus,* one of several such confessions
drawn up at Geneva in the days of François Turrettini. The Bernese
purposes had certainly included the repression of Arminian tendencies
and their feared Socinian consequences, and this had been an issue in
Franco-German Calvinist Switzerland since the Huguenot refugees of
the 1680s had included some nearer to Saumur than to Sedan, and to
Jean Le Clerc than to Turrettini. In consequence there had occurred
some significant intellectual displacements, several of which were effective in shaping Gibbon's conceptual equipment. Jean Barbeyrac, a
philosophic jurist of Huguenot descent, had judged the time proper to
give up his rectorship of the academy of Lausanne and accept a
professorship at the university of Groningen in the Netherlands.[38] Here
he continued his work as an advocate of Locke's philosophy and an
editor, translator and publicist of the treatises of Samuel Pufendorf on
natural jurisprudence. It was largely through Barbeyrac's labours in the
république des lettres that Pufendorf's works made their way into the
universities of Scotland, where they played an important part in that
replacement of Calvinist theology by civil morality which is so major an
engine in bringing about the Scottish engagement in those processes
which we term Enlightenment.[39] For a time he was joined at Groningen
by his fellow Lausannais Jean Pierre de Crousaz, who had succeeded

---

[37] Yolton, 1983.   [38] Vuilleumier, 1927–33, III, pp. 640–2, 659–61.
[39] For Barbeyrac's role in Scotland, see Moore, 1989; Haakonssen, 1996a, pp. 58–9.

him as rector and figured none too heroically in the imposition of the *Formula* by Berne;[40] but Crousaz returned to Lausanne and republished his system of logic,[41] which Gibbon's tutor Pavillard prescribed for his retraining in Protestantism. The *affaire du consensus* was in fact far from inaugurating a Calvinist age of ice at Lausanne; it seems more than anything a symbolic re-assertion of Bernese authority over the Pays de Vaud, and led in practice to an era of mutual accommodation, in which Berne imposed its rule at the price of toleration and the theology of both Berne and Lausanne became increasingly liberal and undogmatic once the *Formula* was accepted. The development was akin to that at Geneva, where the *Consensus Helveticus* devised by Francois Turrettini was converted into a liberal and scholarly teaching of natural religion by his son Jean-Alphonse, whom Jean Le Clerc not surprisingly welcomed as a spiritual son of his own.[42] The Swiss Protestant cities were falling under the sway of rational theology, and the question was how far this could be restrained from the Socinianism inherent in it, or the deism which the *Encylopédistes* affected to discover at Geneva.

In the opinion of Henri Vuilleumier, however, the magisterial historian of Protestantism in the Pays de Vaud, the action of 1716 had been motivated by Bernese fears of pietism no less than of Socinianism, and pietisms of several sorts had made their appearance or been heard of in German-speaking Berne. Vuilleumier lists them: German, Swiss, Netherland, French, English, ranging from the Catholic pietism of Antoinette Bourignon to the Camisard prophets in London and the Christadelphian sect founded by Jane Leade and Christopher Pordage;[43] and it is evident that the direct enjoyment of Christ against which so much Enlightenment was a reaction was becoming paradoxically intermingled with the rational attenuation of his person that characterised it. This is a development of no small importance, since it shows how easily the reason that was the mind's instrument could still become an indwelling principle in which the mind took part, and how readily the name and therefore the person of Christ could become attached to reason in this sense. When this happened the prophetic language of millennium and apocalypse which foretold Christ's return could cross borders and pervade the language of reasonable religion; the Dutch Collegiants, to

[40] Vuilleumier, 1927–33, III, pp. 582, 678, 685, 689–91.
[41] Crousaz, 1724. His other works are listed in Vuilleumier's index.
[42] Vuilleumier, 1927–33, III, ch. III, section i; Heyd, 1982, pp. 198–202; Barnes, 1938, pp. 196–201.
[43] A very full account, from a Lausannais perspective, is given by Vuilleumier, III, chapter ii, pp. 183–550, covering both the European sources and the Vaudois varieties of pietism. ('Vaudois' refers to the Pays de Vaud, rather than the surviving Waldensian communities.)

give one example, contrived to be both Socinians and millenarians,[44] and Gibbon was to detect precisely the same combination in Priestley. Reason, even the reason of Enlightenment, could beget its own form of enthusiasm, and could adopt – or be adopted by – the language of Christian enthusiasm and its offshoots. The names of Fatio de Duillier and Isaac Newton himself[45] remind us that the most powerful of scientific intellects could still engage with the systems of prophecy, typology and symbolism that offered to reveal signs in the world. Vuilleumier records a number of Lausannais notables of whom this seems to have been true.[46] There is no indication that Gibbon knew of them, and the presence of pietism appears neither in his letters from Lausanne nor in his recollections of his time there; but the *Decline and Fall* is full of references to the phenomenon for which they stood – ranging from chapter 13, where we hear that the Alexandrian neo-Platonists 'by a very singular revolution, converted the study of philosophy into that of magic', to chapter 54, where the origins of Protestantism are connected with Manicheans, Bogomils and Albigensians, and a savage footnote about Priestley occurs at the end.[47] Gibbon came to understand well enough how the pursuit of a rational interpretation of scripture could lead back to symbol, system and immanent meaning, and if he did not study these matters at Lausanne, that city was his first introduction – unless we look back to William Law, Behmenist and non-juror – to the world in which such things were possible. Pietism in Lausanne, Rational Dissent in England twenty years later, both pointed to the margins on which Arminian and Anglican Enlightenment turned back upon itself, and the spectre of enthusiasm was re-awakened; an enduring problem in the history of philosophy, and for philosophy itself.

---

[44] Fix, 1990.
[45] For Fatio, Vuilleumier, III, pp. 212–13; Schwartz, 1980. For Newton, with whom he was closely associated, Manuel, 1974.
[46] Vuilleumier, III, pp. 267–321, 385–90, 407, 491–519, for close studies of these men.
[47] *Decline and Fall*, III, ch. 54, n. 42 (49 in Bury).

CHAPTER 3

The re-education of young Gibbon: method, unbelief and the turn towards history

Early in the five years Gibbon spent at Lausanne,[1] he was restored to Protestantism, and there is the question of what part the Swiss experience generally played in his movement away first from orthodox, and then from any, Christian belief. He also resumed under tutorial direction, the progress of his studies, venturing into classical scholarship both ancient and modern. There was nothing un-Christian in such studies, yet once the step away from authority had been taken, erudition might become *philosophe* and substitute itself for theology and sacred history; and we have set up a framework through which it was possible to proceed from Arminian and Remonstrant learning to critical scepticism and a choice between fideist submission and further rejections of belief. In this progress, once embarked upon, erudition might play a part; and we desire to know whether, or how far, Gibbon followed such paths during his Lausanne years. Here we are confronted by the account given in his *Memoirs*, and by the problem of what evidence there may be to confirm them or to support other answers to our question; and we remind ourselves that if such evidence is lacking, the *Memoirs* tell us how Gibbon remembered, or chose to present, his early experience, and we can consider only the consequences of accepting or rejecting such interpretations.

His formal restoration to Protestant communion occurred on Christmas Day 1754, some eighteen months after he arrived in Lausanne. We have only the pastor Pavillard's letters to tell us what passed between them during this period,[2] but in a letter to his aunt announcing his reconversion, the seventeen-year-old recounted how, after

---

[1] 'Four years, ten months and fifteen days'; *Memoirs*, p. 88 (*A*, p. 154, Memoir B).
[2] Pavillard's letters to Edward Gibbon II (*Memoirs*, appendix, pp. 214–27) reveal that he also thought it his function to wean Gibbon from his persisting Jacobitism (p. 217); Baridon, 1975 (p. 45) observes that this must have been received with mixed feelings at Putney.

wavering long time between the two systems and at last fixed for the protestant, when that conflict was over I had still another difficulty; brought up with all the ideas of the Church of England, I could scarce resolve to communion with Presbyterians as all the people of this country are. I at last got over it in considering that whatever difference there may be between their churches and ours, in the government and discipline [,][3] they still regard us as brethren and profess the same faith as us.[4]

We are rightly warned[5] against reading into this passage the irony of Gibbon's mature writings, which both signals his rejection of belief and forms his substitute for it. However, he might have reflected at some point on the oddity that it was his Tory family with their non-juring associations who had despatched him to the non-episcopal environment of the Pays de Vaud, and there is a touch of ecumenism about his return to Protestantism; if any difficulty occurred about his taking communion in the Church of England when restored to that country, nothing seems to record it. The tone is very different thirty-five years later, when the *Memoirs* remark of the act of communion at Christmas

It was here that I suspended my Religious enquiries, acquiescing with implicit belief in the tenets and mysteries which are [*or* were] adopted by the general consent of Catholics and Protestants [*or* of the Christian world].[6]

There is irony here. Apart from the ambiguity of 'implicit belief' – which if it was not explicit could not be unreserved – 'the tenets adopted by general consent' include the entire fabric of Nicene theology, of whose fiercely contested formation and imposition the *Decline and Fall* had by the time of the *Memoirs* supplied an anything but acquiescent history. If the young Gibbon took the road leading through doubt to submissive belief, the mature historian is indicating that his acquiescence was to a 'general consent' about which he knew more than he is allowing to appear in his text; and the words 'suspended my Religious enquiries' look beyond the ecumenical to the Enlightened message that such enquiries defy the human intellect and should end in doubt since they cannot end in faith. The step beyond faith to renewed scepticism was the essential Enlightened step, and could lead to the replacement of the pursuit by the history of theology. Gibbon at some point took that step; we look for evidence on whether it was in the making, or was taken, during his first sojourn at Lausanne, and whether the climate of Arminian Protestantism had anything to do with it.

The *Memoirs* indicate that his re-education at Lausanne was con-

---

[3] For the insertion of this comma, see Norton's note 2, next reference.   [4] *Letters*, I, p. 3.
[5] Low, p. 51; *YEG*, pp. 59–60.   [6] *Memoirs*, p. 74, with nn. 2 and 3 (*A*, p. 137, Memoir B).

ducted in conversational French, which once he had learned it became his preferred language of study and even of thought; that it involved a return to classical studies, in which he improved his Latin and began his Greek; that it further involved – a fact of both cultural and biographical significance – some study of 'modern' history and geography; but that it possessed a philosophical dimension relevant to the Protestantism of its time and place. We are told that Pavillard – who despite Gibbon's remark that he was not 'eminent for genius or learning' had been at least a candidate for a chair in polemical theology – encouraged him less immediately to read theology than classical literature and critical method.

As soon as we began to understand each other, he gently led me into the path of instruction; I consented with pleasure that a portion of the morning-hours should be consecrated to a plan of modern history and Geography, and to the critical perusal of the French and Latin Classics, and at each step I felt myself invigorated by the habits of application and method. The principles of philosophy were associated with the examples of taste, and by a singular chance the book as well as the man[7] which contributed the most effectually to my education, has a stronger claim on my gratitude than on my admiration. Mr. De Crousaz the adversary of Bayle and Pope is not distinguished by lively fancy or profound reflection, and even in his own country at the end of a few years, his name and writings are almost obliterated. But his philosophy had been formed in the school of Locke, his Divinity in that of Limborch and Le Clerc; in a long and laborious life several generations of pupils were taught to think and even to write, his lessons rescued the Academy of Lausanne from Calvinistic prejudice, and he had the rare merit of diffusing a more liberal spirit among the clergy and people of the Pays de Vaud.[8] His System of logic which in the last editions has swelled to six tedious and prolix volumes, may be praised as a clear and methodical abridgement of the art of reasoning from our simple ideas to the most complex operations of the human understanding. This system I studied, and meditated and abstracted, till I [have[9]] obtained the free command of an universal instrument which I soon presumed to exercise on my catholic opinions.[10]

This recollection is endorsed by a letter written to his father on 10 January 1756, a year after his reception as a Protestant, in which he reports in part on

Ma Philosophie. J'ai achevé la Logique de Monsieur de Crousaz laquelle est

---

[7] Crousaz died in 1750, and Gibbon therefore did not meet him.
[8] This is a just account of the intention and even the effect of Crousaz's teachings, but the reader of Vuilleumier will not think he played a single-handed role in achieving these results.
[9] Omitted in one manuscript; the text seems better without it.
[10] *Memoirs*, pp. 72–3 (*A*, pp. 135–6, Memoir B).

fort estimée dans de pays-ci en partie avec Mons: Pavillard et en parti dans mon Particulier. Je vais lire pour la seconde fois l'Entendement Humain, et aussitot que je l'aurai fini je commencerai l'Algebre que vous me recommandez tant.

And there is a further reference to 'ce même Locke dont vous me conseilliez tant la Lecture'.[11] In the same letter Gibbon informs his father of the progress of his French – in that language – though the involvement of Edward Gibbon II in his son's education may legitimately be questioned. Under whatever guidance, the re-Protestantisation of the Oxford apostate was still proceeding, and the master texts he read included several by luminaries of the *république des lettres* – Locke the associate of Limborch, Crousaz the disciple of Locke, Limborch and Le Clerc, as well as of Barbeyrac. From both Gibbon was receiving a training in method which was at the same time a training in how the human mind worked and in how to observe it at work, and there can be little doubt that Pavillard knew very well what effect this 'universal instrument' would 'exercise on my catholic opinions'. To study how the mind formed 'simple ideas' and proceeded to 'the most complex operations' was the approved antidote to the errors of transubstantiation and the belief that it could apprehend the presence of real substances, and it remained for the historian to decide how the Platonic, patristic, and scholastic intellects had nevertheless arrived at these erroneous convictions. The way lay open to the critical history of Christian theology and philosophy, but there is no indication that Gibbon in 1756 was being led in this direction. The passage quoted is embedded in a report on his progress in French, Latin and at last Greek, and in the accomplishments of a gentleman – dancing and drawing, of which there is little to say.

The training in method which had such clear implications for religious belief could also serve as an instrument in the critical reading of texts, in so many ways a calculus of probabilities, and it was not a great distance to the study of algebra. Since we know, independently of the *Memoirs*, that Gibbon at Lausanne was set to read Locke and Crousaz, we may take up the retrospective account which the *Memoirs* give following their introduction in the narrative, and find it to be an account of both erudition and scepticism. 'The principles of philosophy were associated with the examples of taste'; this crucial sentence introduces the subject of Crousaz and his logic. 'Taste' in the enlightened vocabulary meant more than aesthetic discrimination, and more than a

---

[11] *Letters*, I, pp. 12–13. For a translation see *YEG*, p. 63.

preference for humane over sacred literature; it meant logic and method, pursued less as abstract sciences than in the practice of reading polite letters. Gibbon says that he learned both philosophy and taste from Pavillard and Crousaz, whatever their shortcomings, and he means that he learned both to read a text and to examine the operations of his own mind in doing so. But a mind intent on examining itself while reading a text said to be the Word of God is not in communication with the Spirit behind the Word, and this of course was precisely the objective with which the philosophy of taste and method had been introduced. A little later in the *Memoirs* Gibbon recalled how he set out to study Greek at last, and how

> the lessons of Pavillard again contributed to smooth the entrance of the way, the Greek Alphabet, the grammar and the pronunciation according to the French accent. As he possessed only such a stock as was requisite for an Ecclesiastic, our first book was St John's Gospel, and [we] should probably have construed the whole of the new testament had I not represented the absurdity of adhering to the corrupt dialect of the Hellenist Jews. At my earnest request we presumed to open the Iliad; and I had the pleasure of beholding, though darkly and through a glass, the true image of Homer whom I had long since admired in an English dress[12] –

Pope's, no doubt.[13] One hardly knows what to make of the portrait of Gibbon reading Homeric Greek with the darkened eye of the Pauline flesh, but it is the rejection of the Johannine Gospel that claims attention here. It had long been a stumbling block for humanist scholars that the evangelists and apostles had written an impure provincial dialect, neither Greek nor Hebrew, and under the growing dictatorship of taste and polite letters the style mattered more than the Logos. The text here repudiated, however, is that one of all the New Testament scriptures which proclaims that the Logos has been made Flesh, and which is central to the authority of Incarnation; the debate with ancient Arians and modern Socinians invariably turned on it.[14] Gibbon in this passage reminds us how humanist grammar, Lockean method, and polite critical taste combined to move the mind in a 'Socinian' and anti-Trinitarian direction.

This does not mean that theological and ecclesiological debate were omitted from Gibbon's retraining. Dr Waldegrave's remark, quoted

---

[12] *Memoirs*, p. 77 (*A*, p. 141, Memoir B).
[13] Gibbon owned this translation in editions of 1760 and 1771 (*Library*, p. 152).
[14] Levine, 1997, for the controversy among scholars over the Johannine text – in the Epistles, not the Gospel – on the Three Witnesses.

earlier, that one page of Chillingworth was 'worth a library of Swiss divinity'[15] is answered by Gibbon's verdict that

the intermixture of sects has rendered the Swiss Clergy acute and learned on the topics of controversy[16]

which had after all been Pavillard's chosen field of study. But the outcome of Gibbon's re-Protestantisation is known to us only as recollected in the *Memoirs*, and these record the progress of a scepticism which may have required more years than those spent at Lausanne, though springing from roots laid down there. In recounting his Oxford conversion they align him with two figures briefly reconciled with Catholicism, Chillingworth and Bayle.[17] Neither had followed the Remonstrant route; Chillingworth's crisis, recounted and pursued in his *The Religion of Protestants a Safe Way to Salvation* (1634) – the book which Waldegrave thought would have been sufficient in Gibbon's case – turned on a dispute with an English Jesuit, Fisher alias Knott, who sternly maintained that if there was not a single infallible church the only alternative was Socinianism, since Christ would have been deprived of his mystical body and therefore of his divine nature.[18] Chillingworth was close to agreeing; even after his return to the Church of England he had difficulty accepting the Trinitarian articles of the Thirty-Nine, and (says Gibbon in the *Memoirs*)

soon deviated from his own subscription; as he more deeply scrutinized the article of the Trinity, neither Scripture nor the primitive fathers could long uphold his orthodox belief, 'and he could not but confess that the doctrine of Arius is either a truth, or at least no damnable heresy'. From this middle region of the air, the descent of his reason would naturally rest on the firmer ground of the Socinians; and, if we may credit a doubtful story, and the popular opinion, his anxious enquiries at last subsided in Philosophic indifference. So conspicuous however were the candour of his Nature, and the innocence of his heart, that this apparent levity did not affect the reputation of Chillingworth. His frequent changes proceeded from too nice an inquisition into truth. His doubts grew out of himself, he assisted them with all the strength of his reason: he was then too hard for himself: but finding as little quiet and repose in those victories, he quickly recovered by a new appeal to his own judgment; so that in all his sallies and retreats, he was, in fact, his own convert.[19]

How comfortable this would have left Dr Waldegrave is matter for conjecture. Gibbon was sending out a strong hint that his own

[15] Above, p. 48, n. 104.   [16] *Memoirs*, p. 73 (*A*, p. 136, Memoir B).
[17] *Memoirs*, pp. 61–5 (*A*, pp. 89–93, Memoir F).   [18] Chillingworth, 1742, pp. 13–15.
[19] *Memoirs*, p. 63 (*A*, pp. 90–1, Memoir F).

philosophic indifference seemed to him in retrospect to have grown along a route leading through and beyond Socinianism, in which the mind turned from its own doubts into itself, as Hume turned from philosophy to play backgammon. Chillingworth's pursuit of his re-iterated self cuts him off – as Gibbon sees it – from any search for God. A similar tale is told of Bayle.

> In reviewing the controversies of the times, he turned against each other the arguments of the disputants: successively wielding the arms of the Catholics and protestants, he proves that neither the way of authority, nor the way of examination can afford the multitude any test of Religious truth; and dex-trously concludes, that custom and education must be the sole grounds of popular belief.[20]

There is no hint here that Bayle's scepticism, or Gibbon's, rested on a foundation (or attained a pinnacle) of fideism; and if part of the moti-vation is the desire to protect the multitude from persecution by the magistrate, another is the desire to deny them any capacity to examine doctrine for themselves. This can best be done by indicating that even the learned find such questions unexaminable, and are left reflectively examining the workings of their own minds. Thus Gibbon towards the end of his life, and it is possible that the reading of Locke and Crousaz had led the young mind of 1753–8 to similar conclusions. There were minds at Lausanne moving the same way, if with less pyrrhonist rigour; and Gibbon seems to present the only philosophical intellect with whom he recalls corresponding during these years, that of François Louis Allamand, in the role of a lesser Bayle.

> Mr Allamand had exposed himself to much scandal and reproach by an anonymous letter (1745) to the Protestants of France; in which he labours to persuade them that *public* worship is the exclusive right and duty of the State, and that their numerous assemblies of dissenters and rebels are not authorized by the law or the Gospel. His style is animated, his arguments are specious; and if the papist may seem to lurk under the mask of a protestant, the philosopher is concealed under the disguise of a papist.

It was more than half a century since the *Avis important aux réfugiés*, but the tolerationist strategy of subverting both ecclesiastical authority and congregational independence continued unabated.

---

[20] *Memoirs*, p. 64 (*A*, p. 92, Memoir F).

Our correspondence in his absence [from Lausanne][21] chiefly turned on Locke's Metaphysics which he attacked and I defended, the origin of ideas, the principles of evidence, and the doctrine of liberty.

And found no end, in wandering mazes lost.

By fencing with so skillful a master, I acquired some dexterity in the use of my philosophic weapons: but I was still the slave of education and prejudice; he had some measures to keep; and I much suspect that he never shewed me the true colours of his secret scepticism.[22]

There is some deviousness in this passage.[23] Gibbon does not quite conceal that it was Allamand who defended, and Gibbon who attacked the doctrine of innate ideas assailed by Locke; and Vuilleumier points out that Allamand in writings then and thereafter animatedly defended the Christian religion against Voltaire, Diderot and Holbach, a formidable series of adversaries.[24] Gibbon does not mention these writings and did not own them, though he did at a later date purchase and may have used the translation of Addison's *Essay on the Truth of the Christian Religion* published in 1771 by the Lausannais Seigneux de Correvon.[25] If Allamand entertained a 'secret scepticism' – which is not certain – it is more likely to have been the extent of his Socinianism, rather than deism or infidelity, which like Locke he chose not to admit in public.[26] A Socinian could remain a Christian, while redefining or choosing not to define the nature of Christ.

We have, then, not much more than the *Memoirs*' account of how Gibbon's early reading at Lausanne was connected with his turn away from the search for authority to ironic scepticism. This account convincingly links his studies in method with his later positions, but the link is a long one and we are not sure when or by what stages he made the traverse of which we have only his recollection. There is enough, however, to justify the assertion that Gibbon's unbelief, when arrived at, was fundamentally ironic. It was not based on an account of God, or the world without God, alternative or opposed to the Christian – Gibbon, like Hume, was neither a deist nor an atheist, but a sceptic – but on a conviction that the human mind was incapable of arriving at such

---

[21] They conversed on a number of occasions when Allamand was in town. He was a country pastor in the village of Bex. Gibbon's letters to him are lost, but Allamand's replies survive in *MW*, I, pp. 436–55.   [22] *Memoirs*, p. 82 (*A*, pp. 147–8, Memoir B). My italics.   [23] Turnbull, 1991.

[24] Vuilleumier devotes a sub-chapter to Allamand; IV, ch. III, section XI, pp. 237–300.

[25] For him see Vuilleumier, 1927–33, IV, pp. 260–2, 266–73. *Library*, p. 45.

[26] For Voltaire, at Les Délices, corresponding with Allamand, clearly hoping that the latter would endorse his belief that Swiss Calvinism in general was becoming Socinian, see Adams, 1991, pp. 135–41.

accounts (called 'systems') and that attempts to do so might be morally sincere but were intellectually dishonest. This conviction was arrived at as much through criticism as through what we should term philosophy, though criticism tended to use the latter word after annexing it to itself. Locke and Crousaz showed the mind operating in the world of objects, but Gibbon studied its operations in the world of texts, where he could see how every system designed to organise the universe was the product of the mind and its limitations. Hence irony: the contemplation of the gap between what it envisaged and what it achieved. There is a significant passage in the *Memoirs* when Gibbon

cannot forbear to mention three particular books, since they may have remotely contributed to form the historian of the Roman Empire. 1. From the provincial letters of Pascal which, almost every year I have perused with new pleasure, I learned to manage the weapon of grave and temperate irony even on subjects of Ecclesiastical solemnity. 2. The life of Julian by the Abbé de la Bléterie, first introduced me to the man and the times; and I should be glad to recover my first essay on the truth of the miracle which stopped the rebuilding of the temple of Jerusalem. 3. In Giannone's Civil history of Naples, I observed with a critical eye the progress and abuse of Sacerdotal power, and the Revolutions of Italy in the darker ages.[27]

In this passage – where no Protestant is named – the author of the *Decline and Fall* gives first place to a training in irony among his recollections of that work's formation. A reader of Pascal might question whether 'temperate' is the *mot juste* for that impassioned Jansenist, and whether Gibbon is not enrolling him in a scepticism which tempers one's respect for all religious positions whatever. It may be more important to ask, however, whether there is a recognition here that irony has become the chief mode in all Gibbon's perception of history. In the remainder of this passage – it might be replied – texts and narratives – in themselves anti-miraculous and anti-sacerdotal – move back to the centre of attention, and we ask how far they too are to be read ironically. There remained the question of the historical artefacts which texts, including the Gospels, were now seen to be; and here there arose, for minds in the first half of the eighteenth century, the problem of pyrrhonism: did texts tell us anything more than that certain minds, more or less unreliable, had constructed them? Gibbon presents his young self at Stourhead as discovering new past worlds, contained in the texts of great narratives.

The progress of Gibbon's erudition during his years at Lausanne can

---

[27] *Memoirs*, p. 79 (*A*, p. 143, Memoir B).

be connected with his training in method; there was a logic of probability, governing human perceptions of the world, applicable to the critical reading of texts. Here we possess a great deal more evidence independent of the *Memoirs* than is the case regarding the progress of his scepticism, for in addition to what his letters tell us – which is not much – Gibbon at this time began keeping records of his studies in a programmatic and self-critical form. The *Memoirs* continue:

> This various reading which I now conducted with [skill and] discretion was digested according to the precept and model of Mr. Locke into a large Commonplace book, a practice however which I do not strenuously recommend,[28]

meaning that he came to prefer abstracting to excerpting the books he read. This commonplace book survives[29] and has been intensively studied by Patricia Craddock, Gibbon's biographer.[30] It is the predecessor of a series of journals in which Gibbon intermittently recorded, in French or in English, his doings, while reviewing his readings, writing dissertations on points of interest great or small, and critically inspecting both his authors and his own progress, down to his arrival at Rome in October 1764.[31] In his Lausanne records – beginning in 1755, his eighteenth year – we see him remedying the ignorance of which a schoolboy would have been ashamed, while improving the erudition which might have puzzled a Doctor. That is to say, while pursuing a serious mastery of Latin and Greek – never perfect in the latter case – as well as of French, he set himself an ambitious programme of classical studies, conducted according to critical principles which had been those of the Moderns in the Battle of the Books,[32] and were now usurping the name of philosophy. The foundations of learning were in classical scholarship; Gibbon aimed to read the ancient poets, orators and – placed at the head in a category of their own – historians, from Homer to Tacitus; but the methods of study were modern,[33] and so in a related measure was the history he began to study. He excerpted and annotated the Abbé de la Bléterie's life of Julian the Apostate,[34] of whom he would

---

[28] *Memoirs, ibid.*   [29] British Library (BL) Add. MSS 34880, fols. 2v–82v; *YEG*, p. 318 n. 18.
[30] *YEG*, pp. 65–79, 89–95, 305–7.   [31] *Journal A*; *Journal B*; *Journal C*.
[32] Levine, 1991. The *Memoirs* (p. 75; *A*, pp. 138–9) contain a listing of the moderns he then studied; they include Conyers Middleton's life of Cicero, 'which I then appreciated above its true value'. Cf. Giarrizzo, 1954, pp. 52–3.
[33] Craddock (*YEG*, pp. 66–7) notes, however, that his use of the Abbé Banier's *Mythologie et les fables expliqués par l'histoire* is concerned only with the problem of historical evidence, not yet with the study of mythology and ancient religion.   [34] *YEG*, pp. 72–5.

have read in Howel and Echard, and this venture into late antiquity introduced him to the figure towards whom he came to feel an enduring interest and exasperated affection. The Arabic dimension of the Stourhead reading was not forgotten; it is in the January 1756 letter to his father that he asks for his copy of d'Herbelot, and Craddock has found him citing Ockley in a way which suggests it was from memory.[35] Moving into the history of the Christian middle ages, he read the Abbé le Sueur's *Histoire de l'eglise et de l'empire*,[36] to which Echard's continuator had been indebted, and Voltaire's *Annales de l'empire* as well as his *Abrégé de l'histoire universelle*.[37] Here, he remarks, he was receiving training in French literary and historical thought,[38] and it was in French translation that he now read Pietro Giannone's *Istoria civile del Regno di Napoli*.[39] In all these works he was encountering the relations between church, empire and kingdoms which had been the master theme of Anglican as it was to be that of Enlightened historiography; and the time he spent studying the Lausannais Loys de Bochat's *Mémoires sur l'ancienne histoire de la Suisse*[40] prefigures the projected history of the Swiss republic which was long to engage his interest in modern history. Loys de Bochat, the lately deceased uncle of Gibbon's friend Georges Deyverdun, had completed a French translation of Gottfried Arnold's *Unparteyische Kirchen und Ketzer-historie*, but had been advised not to publish it. Gibbon seems not to have known of this pietist classic, but it is an intriguing thought that the translation was probably lying in the Villa de la Grotte, where he was later to live for many years.[41] Enthusiasm was never far away.

With such names as Giannone and Voltaire we come in sight for the first time of the great names normally associated with Enlightenment. Voltaire was living at Les Délices during these years, and Gibbon attended performances of tragedy in the poet's private theatre; he found them tedious and unconvincing, but admits that they altered his theatrical taste in a neo-classical rather than a Shakespearean direction.[42] He was also beginning to read Voltaire's historical works, but it may be asked whether these were of cardinal importance to him, or whether this was his Enlightenment. After reminding us that it was at his father's wish[43] that he attended lectures in algebra and geometry, the *Memoirs* say:

---

[35] *YEG*, p. 71.   [36] Printed in three volumes at Geneva in 1684, in eight volumes in 1719.
[37] *YEG*, pp. 66, 75.   [38] *Memoirs*, p. 71 (*A*, p. 134).   [39] *YEG*, pp. 68–71.   [40] *YEG*, pp. 76–8.
[41] Vuilleumier, 1927–33, III, pp. 322–4. Bochat also left unpublished an essay on *La Réformation et son influence sur la société civile*; Baridon, 1975, I, p. 44.
[42] *Memoirs*, pp. 82–4 (*A*, pp. 148–9, Memoir B).
[43] 'From a blind idea of the usefullness of such abstract studies' (*Memoirs*, p. 77; *A*, p. 141).

as soon as I understood the principles, I relinquished for ever the pursuit of the Mathematics; nor can I lament that I desisted before my mind was hardened by the habit of rigid demonstration so destructive of the finer feelings of moral evidence which must however determine the actions and opinions of our lives. I listened with more pleasure to the proposal of studying the law of Nature and Nations, which was taught in the Academy of Lausanne by Mr Vicat a professor of some learning and reputation. But instead of attending his public or private course, I preferred, in my closet, the lessons of his masters and my own reason. Without being disgusted by the pedantry of Grotius or the prolixity of Pufendorf, I studied in their writing the duties of a man, the rights of a Citizen, the theory of Justice (it is alas! a theory) and the laws of peace and war which have had some influence on the practise of modern Europe. My fatigues were alleviated by the good sense of their commentator Barbeyrac: Locke's treatise of Government instructed me in the knowledge of Whig principles, which are rather founded in reason than experience; but my delight was in the frequent perusal of Montesquieu whose energy of style, and boldness of hypothesis were powerful to awaken and stimulate the Genius of the Age.[44]

This is, until the last sentence, an account of Protestant Enlightenment: the study of natural jurisprudence replacing Calvinist doctrine without proceeding to geometrical extremes, and even so better read in gentlemanly privacy than heard in the schools. We have to do with a personality never at ease with public speech, who probably preferred reading neo-classical tragedy to hearing it declaimed from a stage. When the *Memoirs* were written, Gibbon had some reason to play down his association with Voltaire, much insisted on by his clerical and evangelical enemies, but it is really not likely that the above passage masks an early or a continuing Voltairean inspiration. Relations between the *Essai sur les moeurs* and the *Decline and Fall* are complex and need to be studied, but the latter, complete and published by the time of the *Memoirs*, is replete with allusions to Voltaire which express the opinion which Gibbon soon formed: that his genius was flawed by an easy scepticism which made him inattentive to facts and contemptuous of erudition. At another extreme – not yet visible – it is important to distinguish Gibbon from Adam Smith and the Scottish school, for whom history was an offshoot of legal and moral philosophy. He was primarily a humanist and man of letters, committed to grand historical narratives which he read through the lenses of philosophy and jurisprudence in order to understand them better. It is this which must be kept

---

[44] *Memoirs*, p. 78 (*A*, p. 142, Memoir B). Note the use of the singular in mentioning Locke on government. There had been a new edition of *Du gouvernement civil, par M. Locke*, in which Mazel's translation was augmented by Rousset de Missy, published at the Hague in 1755. See M. C. Jacob, 1985, and 1991, pp. 110–16.

in mind as we examine the question raised by the concluding sentence just quoted: what was this 'Genius of the Age' which Montesquieu awoke – specifically, according to another draft of the *Memoirs*,[45] by his authorship of the *Esprit des lois*?

Giuseppe Giarrizzo's *Edward Gibbon e la cultura europea del settecento*, which may be said to have originated the modern study of Gibbon, was written in Naples, at the Istituto Italiano per gli Studi Storici, in the mighty shadows of Croce and Meinecke. It is suffused with their perception of historicism – *lo storicismo, der historismus* – as growing out of natural jurisprudence and in the end replacing it; and in his first chapter, entitled 'La Conversione alla Storia', Giarrizzo set out to situate Gibbon's Lausanne years in a moment of this process, choosing the passage just quoted from the *Memoirs* as the kernel of his argument, and concluding: 'Bayle, Grozio, Locke, Montesquieu; la coscienza europea scopre finalmente la Storia.'[46] He quoted Barbeyrac's introduction to one of his translations of Pufendorf:

Il ne faut presque pas sortir de soi-même, ni consulter d'autre maître que son propre Cœur. L'expérience la plus commune de la Vie, et un peu de réflexion sur soi-même et sur les objets qui nous environnent de toutes parts, suffisent pour fournir aux personnes les plus simples, les idées générales de la Loi Naturelle, et les vrais fondemens de tous nos Devoirs.[47]

[One should hardly ever go beyond one's self, or consult another teacher than one's own heart. The everyday experience of life, and a little reflection on one's self and the objects which surround us on every side, should suffice to furnish the simplest among us with the necessary ideas of the law of nature, and the true foundation of all our obligations.][48]

Such formulae were to strike the next century as profoundly anti-historicist, because they depicted the laws of the mind, which produced ideas, as simple, unchanging, and having no history. Giarrizzo, however, seized upon Barbeyrac's 'il ne faut pas sortir de soi-même' as a starting-point for historicism, since if everything was done by the human mind it was done by that mind where it happened to be and as the conditions of its time and place obliged or allowed it to operate. 'La conversione alla storia' was therefore a European process, in which Gibbon at Lausanne took part through the reading of the great works mentioned in the *Memoirs* and by Giarrizzo; and the latter came close to

---

[45] *A*, p. 234, Memoir C.   [46] Giarrizzo, 1954, p. 35.

[47] Quoted by Giarrizzo, 1954, pp. 32–3. It is from Barbeyrac's preface to his translation of Pufendorf's *De jure naturae et gentium* (*Le droit de la nature et des gens*, Amsterdam, 1734).

[48] Translation JGAP.

claiming that Gibbon had become a *philosophe* disciple of Montesquieu[49] by the time he left Lausanne in 1758. A generation after Giarrizzo, David Womersley began investigating the thesis that Gibbon began the *Decline and Fall* in a spirit of 'pragmatic, philosophic historiography', in framing which the *philosophes* saw Montesquieu as their leader, but then moved on to a more complex vision.[50]

There is substance to this interpretation. The move from methodization to historicization can be seen taking place, though the reader of the *Memoirs* is enjoined that no 'conversione alla storia' was needed in Gibbon's case, and Giarrizzo recognised the tension between narrative and philosophy in Gibbon's mind.[51] To what extent it was necessary to pass through a phase of belief in a fixed human nature governed by unvarying causal laws is a further question. As for the role of Montesquieu, Gibbon's Lausanne papers display his presence in essays on Sallust and Caesar;[52] but here it is the *Considérations sur les causes de la grandeur des romains et de leur décadence* that we encounter, and the strong links between the *Considérations* and the *Decline and Fall* must turn our thoughts towards historiography before philosophy. The evidence for Montesquieu's importance in shaping Gibbon's work at Lausanne is strong but internal, and rests largely on two important essays completed after his departure. The *Essai sur l'étude de la littérature*, begun in 1758 and published in 1762, is strongly Montesquieuan in argument and much more so in style – as the *Memoirs* self-critically observe[53] – and the same may be said for the *Lettre sur le gouvernement de Berne*, which Giarrizzo dated to 1758, but may be more probably assigned to Gibbon's second sojourn at Lausanne in 1763–4.[54] The question to be resolved is that of how far Montesquieu's role was decisive in drawing Gibbon into a mainstream of European intellectual history running through Enlightenment to historicism.

Here we have to do with a paradigm: a fixed and authoritative set of assumptions which have identified Enlightenment with a sequence of great texts, whose history consists in their serial relations with one another, so that it becomes the history of 'The Enlightenment' and all meanings of the term are to be found within it. Even the social and cultural contexts within which this process is said to have taken place are

---

[49] Giarrizzo, 1954, p. 35: 'da ora in poi egli farà di Montesquieu la luce dei suoi problemi'.
[50] Womersley, 1988, e.g. p. 5; cf. Womersley, I, e.g. p. lxvi.
[51] Giarrizzo, 1954, pp. 41, 66, 69.
[52] *MW*, IV, pp. 399–434; Giarrizzo, 1954, pp. 65–70; *YEG*, pp. 89–94.
[53] *Memoirs*, p. 103 (*A*, pp. 172–3, Memoir B).
[54] Giarrizzo, 1954, p. 35 and n. 67; *YEG*, pp. 187–9.

defined and constrained by being grouped around it, so that it conditions them as much as they do it. This paradigm is not purely an
invention, inasmuch as it was invented by the actors in the process and
not only by historians after them, so that the activities we call 'Enlightenment' need only to be redefined as 'the invention of Enlightenment'. The texts constituting the sequence, and the activities contextual
to their production, can to a large degree be located in and around
Paris, in the course of the reconstruction after 1714 of the great intellectual and artistic institutions which had empowered Louis XIV's France
to claim, and come close to exercising, cultural as well as political
hegemony in western and central Europe. When Voltaire came to write
the history of Enlightenment as he understood it, he presented it as the
continuation – by no means a simple one – of the *siècle de Louis XIV*.
There is a further narrative of cultural hegemony, in which the activities
of the *philosophes*, the *Encyclopédistes* and the *salonnières* can be seen annexing the term *république des lettres* from the Netherlands-based oper-
ators who had formerly conducted it, and making it identical with 'the
business of Enlightenment'[55] and, in due course, with the *settecento
riformatore*, so that a complex of Paris-based activities became the gener-
ators of ideas and practices to which a Europe-wide public looked as its
centre. All this can be seen taking place, explicitly recognised by those
involved in it; but it is a corollary that it was preceded by an earlier
république des lettres, Protestant and Arminian, Dutch and Huguenot, to
which the name and vocabulary of Enlightenment may justly be applied, but which was culturally and historically distinct and not a mere
precursor of the Enlightenment of Paris.

    Gibbon's Lausanne belonged to this Protestant network, and we have
uncovered the roles of Bayle, Le Clerc, Basnage and Barbeyrac in the
formation of his erudition and his understanding of it. However, the
French-speaking Pays de Vaud could not be untouched by the culture of
les français de France, and as French came to be Gibbon's second if not his
first language, he read not only the *nouvelles* and *bibliothèques* of the
république des lettres, but the *Mémoires* of the Académie des Inscriptions et
Belles Lettres,[56] the great foundation looking back to Colbert and
Richelieu, and based on the unparalleled resources of the Bibliothèque
du Roi, whose erudition was to equal that of the Protestant *république* as
the focus of his intellectual loyalties. The relation between the Parisian
érudits and the Parisian *philosophes* was very soon to become problematic

55 Darnton, 1979; Goodman, 1994; Velema, 1993.
56 For the first notice of these in his reading and writing, see *YEG*, p. 68.

in Gibbon's mind, but we are at the point where he began to encounter the luminaries of Enlightenment in its paradigmatic form. It was of some importance to the young Gibbon that Voltaire was at Les Délices, and he had begun to read his histories; the *Memoirs*, while cautioning that 'I then rated [him] above his real magnitude', describe Voltaire as 'the most extraordinary man of the age',[57] permitting letters and philosophy to define history. It was at this time too that he began to read Montesquieu; the statements in the *Memoirs* that he was much affected by him are supported by internal evidence; and the metaphor of saying that Montesquieu 'awoke the genius of the age' further defines history in terms of intellect, culture and what we cannot but term Enlightenment. This is our metaphor, but it is very close to being Gibbon's.

'The age' possessed a 'genius' for doing what Montesquieu led it in doing; what was that? Vicat, Grotius, Pufendorf, Barbeyrac and Locke introduce it in the passage quoted from the *Memoirs*, and define it as civil morality organised as natural jurisprudence and scrutinised by methodical philosophy; in Protestant cultures it replaces Calvinist theocentrism, and everywhere the passions of theology which disrupt civil society in civil war. But with Montesquieu we are in the culture, Gallican if not Catholic, of the *grande nation*, and the rhythms of Enlightenment are different. What Louis XIV failed to carry through, the intellectual circles of the Regency and the reign of his successor are trying to carry on, and the culture in which they do so is undeniably hegemonic in much of Europe. Gibbon's *Memoirs* summarise a perspective in which the work of the Protestant jurists, Latin, systematic, and even pedantic, is carried on in the reigning language of modern Europe by a *grand seigneur* of polite letters. With extraordinary if unpredictable linguistic virtuosity – Gibbon says he came to regret his fascination by Montesquieu's style[58] – the *président à mortier* sets about, and transforms, the enterprise of surveying the *lois*, or institutions, and the *moeurs*, or values, of civil society and explaining how they arise from the workings of the mind; and because he is a *pittore*[59] as well as a *philosophe*, he does so by setting them in a framework where rhetoric and *belles-lettres* organise all the resources of literary and historical knowledge.

To Gibbon, looking back after completing the *Decline and Fall*, the 'genius of the age' for which Montesquieu stood – we may choose to call it 'Enlightenment' – might well seem to have been this: the 'philosophical' explanation of laws, customs and civil behaviour by

---

[57] Above, p. 82, n. 42.   [58] *Memoirs*, p. 103; *A*, p. 173.
[59] *Esprit des lois*, preface, any edition.

reference not only to a generalised human psychology and the moral law accompanying it, but to the mind's operations under conditions to be reconstructed by late-humanist erudition. In Montesquieu's *Considérations* and his *Esprit des lois*, he would find a series of interpretative structures of importance to the *Decline and Fall*: an account of Roman *grandeur* as the product of military and civic *virtù*, and *décadence* as produced by the corruption of *virtù* under the burdens of the empire it had won; an overall account of European history as the passage from an ancient world of warlike virtue to a modern world of commerce, which refined the passions and transformed *les moeurs*; a typology of forms of government as founded on the *principes* of virtue, honour and fear; an indictment of Ludovican monarchy as despotic, linked with a general theory of despotism as an 'oriental' phenomenon; a scheme, already taking shape in juristic thought, of human society as passing through a succession of stages, hunting, herding, farming and trading; a peculiar concern with the problem of feudal society, as displaying the extremes of violent lawlessness, legality and liberty. All these structures are importantly employed in the *Decline and Fall*. Montesquieu's concerns with contemporary politics – his emphasis on mixed government and the separation of powers – are connected with his understanding of English government, and may be connected with the development of Gibbon's views on the politics of Britain and Berne.

All this must be taken into account when we consider Montesquieu as retrospectively represented in Gibbon's *Memoirs*, written about 1789. It is another matter to reconstruct his impact on the young mind that began reading him between thirty and thirty-five years earlier (he himself died in 1755). Here we have to do with the proposition that he taught Gibbon to think of history and philosophy as primarily a *science des causes*, and that the mature Gibbon moved towards more complex perceptions. The evidence on the first part of this proposition must be sought less in the *Decline and Fall* than in the *Essai sur l'étude de la littérature* and the *Lettre sur le gouvernement de Berne*, both of which, whatever their dating, are closely connected with Gibbon's first sojourn at Lausanne. We cannot consider the former, however, which we know to have been begun early in 1758,[60] without taking account of Gibbon's second well-documented encounter with Enlightenment in its paradigmatic form. This began at Lausanne when he embarked upon an *Essai sur l'étude des belles-lettres* which – changed to '*de la littérature*' – became a reply to Jean le Rond

⁶⁰ *YEG*, p. 116.

d'Alembert's *Discours préliminaire à l'Encyclopédie*, published with the first volume of that undertaking in 1751. Here was an enterprise with which Montesquieu had not been intimately associated, carried out by 'une société de gens de lettres' who vastly respected him but recognised that he had not been one of them, and who included Voltaire, Montesquieu's opponent on all matters having to do with monarchy and feudalism, despotism and orientalism. If all this was 'Enlightenment', there was debate within Enlightenment; and Gibbon contributed to this debate from a standpoint neither Montesquieu's nor Voltaire's. His first move in the paradigmatic history of Enlightenment, then, is seen as having been made as a very young man at Lausanne, and as having been both contentious and complex.

The *Essai sur l'étude de la littérature* is studied at length in a later chapter of this volume, where it will be treated as, if not a major work, yet of major importance for the understanding of Gibbon's place in the history of Enlightenment, of historiography and of Europe in his time and afterwards. It will there be shown to have entailed his defence of, and alignment with, erudition; both that of the Protestant *république* (extending to Anglican church history) and that of the Académie des Inscriptions et Belles Lettres (extending to Gallican). The relation of erudition to Enlightenment will have to be considered, including as an important detail the relation between the progress of Gibbon's erudition and the progress of his scepticism. The *Essai*, however, though begun at Lausanne, was completed after his return to England, published while he was serving as an officer in the Hampshire militia, and remembered in the *Memoirs* as background to his visit to Paris in 1763. The English and Parisian contexts of his career need therefore to be considered as we evaluate the *Essai* and its significance, and it will be studied in the settings they provide. At the point we have now reached, however, it is not inappropriate to examine the *Lettre sur le gouvernement de Berne* and the Montesquieuan elements in its character. Its dating has been contested, but it very probably belongs to Gibbon's second sojourn at Lausanne in 1763–4. On the other hand, it is in a great many ways a commentary on the account of Vaudois culture and politics given in this chapter and its predecessor, and may be considered on these grounds apart from its setting in the later date.

It can also be read as reiterating and expanding a number of points made in a journal of 1755, when the young Gibbon had been taken by the Pavillards on a tour of the chief towns of Switzerland. This journal, a report to his father in England, is an essay in the literature of travel as

the age understood it, and dutifully relates the chief buildings, government, religion and history displayed in turn by the chaotically mixed
sovereignties of the Swiss *ancien régime*.[61] The tone is firmly Protestant,
but not noticeably Anglican; an account of 'notre bon Roi Henri VIII'
simultaneously hanging Catholics and burning Protestants leads to a
notice of the Marian exiles in Zurich and their subsequent influence in
the Church of England.[62] When the party arrives at Berne, the diarist
considers – as Montesquieu had done already[63] – the parallels between
Bernese history and that of early Rome, and suggests that the former
like the latter may be embarking unthinkingly on the road to empire,
neglecting the grievances of its subject allies.

Vous saves le reste, que l'obstination de Rome a les rejetter causa la guerre
Sociale, qui manqua perdre la République, et qui about à faire accorder aux
aliés tout ce qu'ils avoient demandé avant la perte de 300,000 vies. Les Bernois
ont lû l'histoire, pourquoi n'ont-ils point remarqué que les mêmes causes
produisent les mémes effets?[64]

[You know the rest: how Rome's obstinate refusal to accept them caused the
Social War, which nearly destroyed the Republic and ended in the concession
to the allies of all they had demanded before the loss of three hundred thousand
lives. The Bernese have read history; why have they not observed that the same
causes produce the same effects?][65]

On the same page, it is true, we are placed in modern, not ancient
history by a mention of Bernese investment in English South Seas stock,
which has led to a tightening of oligarchy;[66] a point well taken in the
context of Gibbon family history. The language here is both Lausannais
and Montesquieuan, and bridges any gap there may be between 1755
and 1764.

The *Lettre* is certainly Montesquieuan, and is in fact Gibbon's first
essay on empire in the context of European history; there seems a strong
case for assigning its composition to 1764.[67] It suggests that the government of Berne has become unduly oligarchic, on the model of Venice,
and has therefore come to neglect the all-important principle of the
separation of powers; and it depicts the repressive consequences of this
despotic rule as a neglect of the principles of liberty which have sprung

---

[61] Edited by G. R. de Beer and G. A. Bonnard; *MG*, pp. 8–84.   [62] *MG*, pp. 37–8.
[63] *Considérations*, ch. IX; Lowenthal, 1965, p. 94; Richter, 1990, p. 102.   [64] *MG*, p. 53.
[65] Translation JGAP.   [66] *MG*, p. 53 and editors' note.
[67] The text is in *MW*, II, pp. 1–32; Sheffield placed it among Gibbon's correspondence. A critical
    edition is supplied by Louis Junot; *MG*, pp. 108–41. Published in 1952, Junod's preface states the
    case for a 1763–4 dating of this piece. For Giarrizzo's and Craddock's views, see p. 85, n. 54.

up in Europe since the establishment of free tenures in land by the barbarian invaders of the Roman empire.[68] But while this may be read as a criticism of the government of Berne itself, the *Lettre* is written from a standpoint defiantly Vaudois and Lausannais. It points out that the government of subject territories cannot respect the separation of powers and is therefore dangerous to ruling cities which may wish to observe it in governing themselves.[69] Liberty, commerce and the arts have therefore failed to flourish in the Pays de Vaud; but there is also a passage aimed directly at the imposition of the *Formula Consensus*, compatible with a Montesquieuan critique but not included within it.

La partie souveraine de l'état avoit sucé avec le lait, toute la dureté du systême de Calvin, Théologien atrabiliaire, qui aimoit trop la liberté, pour souffrir que les Chrétiens portassent d'autres fers que les siens. D'ailleurs sa conformité avec les idées d'un célèbre philosophe, intéressoit l'honneur du nom Allemand à le soutenir.[70] Comme les sentiments s'étoient adoucis dans le Pays de Vaud, en proportion avec les moeurs, il falloit y envoyer des formulaires, et des inquisiteurs, destinés à faire autant d'hypocrites qu'ils pourroient, non à la vérité par le fer et le feu, mais par les menaces et les privations d'emploi.

En soutenant les droits de l'humanité, je n'outre point les maximes de la tolérance. Je veux bien que le magistrat ne distribue les récompenses du public, qu'à ceux qui enseignent la religion du public. Je ne lui défends pas même de contenir dans le silence ces novateurs trop hardis qui voudroient éclairer le peuple sur certains objets où l'erreur fait son bonheur. Mais que le souverain se prêtant avec chaleur aux minuties théologiques, decide des questions qu'on ne peut décider, assurément il est absurde. Qu'imposant des confessions de foi, il ne laisse à des pasteurs vieillis dans le ministère, et qui ne demandoient qu'à se taire, que le choix du mensonge ou de la mendicité, assurément il est injuste. Mais la persécution cessa. Qui la fit cesser? Un sentiment de honte? les larmes des sujets? ou bien la crainte qu'inspira l'enterprise d'un Davel, enthousiaste il est vrai, mais enthousiaste pour le bien public?[71] Encore même il regne à Lausanne une inquisition sourde. Les noms d'Arminien et de Socinien remplissent encore ces lettres où de très honnêtes gens rendent compte à leurs

---

[68] *MW*, pp. 13, 16–17; *MG*, pp. 125, 129–31.   [69] *MW*, II, pp. 26–7; *MG*, pp. 138–9.

[70] The likeliest candidate for this role is Albrecht von Haller, whom Gibbon had met at Berne in 1755 (*MG*, p. 60); but whether a historian of philosophy would endorse Gibbon's judgment is another question. Louis Junod (*MG*, p. 134, n.4) suggests Leibniz or Wolff. It is worth remembering that the young Gibbon had shown greater interest in the writings of Swiss antiquarians about Berne, Loys de Bochat among them (*MG*, pp. 61–2, 66).

[71] The allusion may be Gibbon's only reference to the history of pietism. It is to Jean-Louis Abraham Davel, a militia officer who proclaimed a one-man rebellion in 1722 and was regretfully but firmly executed by the Bernese authorities; he had in his youth encountered a *belle inconnue* who foretold his future to him and seems not unlikely to have been one of the adolescent prophets wandering from the Church of the Desert, where Camisard apocalypticism was then at its height. Vuilleumier, 1927–33, III, ch. iii, section x, esp. pp. 725–6.

protecteurs des sentiments de leurs concitoyens; et c'est suivant ces indices que les places se distribuent.[72]

[The sovereign element in the state had imbibed at the breast the harshness of the system of Calvin, that atrabilious theologian who loved liberty too much to endure that Christians should wear any fetters but his own. In addition, his doctrine's conformity with the ideas of a celebrated philosopher pledged the honour of the German name to its retention. Since convictions had become more moderate in the Pays de Vaud, proportionably with the refinement of manners, it was thought necessary to send thither formulae and inquisitors, designed to make as many hypocrites as they could, not indeed by the sword and the stake, but by threats and deprivation of employment.

In upholding the rights of humanity, I do not press too far the maxims of toleration. I am content that the magistrate should distribute the public stipend only to those who teach the public religion. I do not forbid him to impose silence on those over-bold innovators who would enlighten the people on certain matters where its happiness depends on error. But that the sovereign should intervene with warmth in the minutiae of theology, and decide questions which can never be decided, is assuredly absurd. That it should impose confessions of faith and leave pastors grown old in the ministry, who desire only to keep their own counsel, with no other choice than that between mendacity and mendicity, is assuredly unjust. Yet this persecution ceased. What made it cease? A sense of shame? the tears of the subjects? the fear produced by such enterprises as that of Davel, an enthusiast indeed but an enthusiast for the public good? And still there reigns at Lausanne a secret and sullen inquisition. The names of Arminian and Socinian abound in those letters in which truly honest men report to their protectors on the sentiments of their fellow citizens; and it is on the basis of such information that offices are distributed.][73]

When he wrote the *Lettre sur le gouvernement de Berne*, Gibbon was well acquainted with the rhetoric of Protestant and perhaps also Voltairean Enlightenment. Theological questions were by their nature insoluble and the sovereign should refrain from imposing solutions to them. If he did not, a culture in which everyone was more or less what the words 'Arminian' and 'Socinian' had come to mean would find itself using these labels to intimidate the honest and outspoken, instead of those theological demagogues who told the public truths it was dangerous for them to know. What these were, over and above the conventional content of 'Arminian' and 'Socinian', Gibbon did not say; but he had clearly passed beyond a conformist degree of scepticism to some other.

At the end of Gibbon's first Lausanne period, then, we are able to observe a Protestant and Arminian Enlightenment and a French and Montesquieuan Enlightenment, together present in his writings, distinct

[72] *MW*, II, pp. 20–2.   [73] Translation JGAP.

in origin but in no way evidently in conflict. The need to subject ecclesiastical to civil authority is more explicit in the former than in the latter components of his discourse, but is nowhere absent or contested. The factor present at all points of his activity is erudition, and while this functioned as an important instrument of what we call Enlightenment, there is little reason to doubt Gibbon's repeated assurances that it functioned independently as the dominant interest of his young and his mature life. We are next to encounter a quarrel with Enlightenment in its *Encyclopédiste* form, which he conducted on the basis that it slighted and undervalued erudition; some deep fissures in Enlightenment will be seen opening up from this point. The *Essai sur l'étude de la littérature*, however, in which Gibbon, still in his early twenties, gave voice to this quarrel as he understood it, is the product of his English as well as his Swiss experience, and it is first necessary to study his return to England and its setting in the Europe of which Enlightenment was the expression.

CHAPTER 4

The Hampshire militia and the problems of modernity

(1)

Gibbon left Lausanne and returned to England early in 1758, travelling at some risk in disguise as a Swiss officer in the Dutch army, in order to pass through France at a time of war with England –

the resentment of the French at our taking their ships without a declaration had rendered that polite nation somewhat peevish and difficult.[1]

He was needed at home; his father had remarried and desired to break the entail, and in good eighteenth-century fashion the son needed to ensure his hopes of the inheritance. Gibbon recognised – at least in recollection – that he needed to leave Lausanne, and separate from Suzanne Curchod,[2] if he was ever to be an Englishman again, and he soon found himself a young country gentleman, dividing his time between the family estate in Buriton, Hampshire – where he worked on the French manuscript of the *Essai sur l'etude de la littérature*[3] – and London, where he found English polite culture a little less than congenial. Lady Hervey figures in the *Memoirs* as the nearest equivalent England had to a *salonnière*, and there are hints of something less than an affinity with Samuel Johnson's Club which he was to join later. It may also be significant that he tells us of this time that he decided against the profession of the law, partly because black-letter was not his kind of scholarship but also because he lacked the gift of eloquence necessary

---

[1] *Memoirs*, p. 87 (*A*, p. 153, Memoir B). These seizures had occurred as far back as August 1755, when Anglo-French hostilities in the Atlantic and America had not yet reached the formal declaration of war in 1756. They are denounced in heated terms by Raynal's *Histoire des deux Indes* (1772, 1780).
[2] For the history of this honourable and sentimental affair, see Gibbon's biographers.
[3] *YEG*, pp. 126–33, 135–6. He also records (*Memoirs*, p. 211; *A*, pp. 249–50, Memoir C) that in late 1759 he made a detailed study of Grotius's *De veritate religionis Christianae*, which did not much reinforce his faith.

for success at the bar.[4] In interpreting Gibbon's life as a gentleman scholar, it is valuable to bear in mind that he found it easy to take his place as a gentleman, difficult and challenging to find his vocation as a scholar, and that this is important not only to his personal history, but to the history of the culture to which he belonged.

In the year following that of his return, he and his father accepted commissions in the Hampshire Grenadiers, a regiment of the new national militia recently created by act of parliament, and though Gibbon never heard a shot fired in action, more of his life than he had bargained for in the next two and a half years was spent under canvas and in the life of the camp. It is known to everyone who has read Gibbon that he wrote of this period:

the Captain of the Hampshire grenadiers (the reader may smile) has not been useless to the historian of the Roman Empire;[5]

but if we explore fully what he says of his militia service in the *Memoirs*, we shall find there some complex historical comment on the changes coming over Britain in his lifetime, and on their place in the history of ancient and modern Europe which he had both written and lived in.

I have already hinted that the publication of my Essay was delayed till I had embraced the military profession. I shall now amuse myself with the recollection of an active scene which bears no affinity to any other period of my studious and social life. From the general idea of a militia I shall descend to the Militia of England in the war before the last;[6] to the state of the Regiment in which I served, and to the influence of that service on my personal situation and character.[7]

It is made plain elsewhere that Gibbon soon gave up any idea of a regular army commission, and that he 'embraced the military profession' in the sense that he was on full-time service for an interlude of two and a half years. Two of his brother historians had served outside the realm in the war preceding his, but he is closer to David Hume, who was a staff officer on a brief expedition (1746) against L'Orient and saw active service abroad,[8] than to Adam Ferguson, who was chaplain to the Black Watch regiment in Flanders (1745) and saw service in the

[4] For this period, see *Memoirs*, pp. 92 (the bar), 94 (Lady Hervey); *A*, pp. 158–9, 160 (Memoir B). The hint regarding Johnson is discussed by Craddock, *YEG*, p. 125.
[5] *Memoirs*, p. 117; *A*, p. 190 (Memoir B).
[6] Gibbon wrote the *Memoirs*, here dealing with the Seven Years War, after the War of the American Revolution and before the outbreak of the war with revolutionary France.
[7] *Memoirs*, p. 107; *A*, pp. 177–8 (Memoir B).
[8] Hume, 1742–, 'My Own Life', (Miller, 1985, pp. xxxiv–xxxv).

field.[9] From this recollection of public service interrupting a life of *otium* and *studium*, he continues:

The defence of the state may be imposed on the body of the people, or it may be delegated to a select number of mercenaries: the exercise of arms may be an occasional duty or a separate trade; and it is this difference which forms the distinction between a militia and a standing army. Since the union of England and Scotland the public safety has never been attacked and has seldom been threatened by a foreign invader; but the sea was long the sole safeguard of our isle. If the reign of the Tudors or the Stuarts was often signalized by the valour of our Soldiers and sailors, they were dismissed at the end of the campaign or the expedition for which they had been levied. The national spirit at home had subsided in the peaceful occupations of trade, manufactures and husbandry, and if the obsolete forms of a militia were preserved, their discipline in the last age was less the object of confidence than of ridicule.[10]

Gibbon proceeds to quote the Tory, Catholic and Jacobite Dryden's satire on the militia,[11] written at a time when a professional army was taking shape under William III, and adds:

The importance of such unworthy soldiers was supplied from the aera of the restoration by the establishment of a body of mercenaries: the conclusion of each war encreased the numbers that were kept on foot, and although their progress was checked by the jealousy of opposition, time and necessity reconciled, or at least accustomed, a free country to the annual perpetuity of a standing army. The zeal of our patriots, both in, and out of, Parliament (I cannot add both in, and out of, office) complained that the sword had been stolen from the hands of the people. They appealed to the victorious example of the Greeks and Romans among whom every citizen was a soldier; and they applauded the happiness and independence of Switzerland which, in the midst of the great monarchies of Europe [,] is sufficiently defended by a constitutional and effective militia. But their enthusiasm overlooked the modern changes in the art of war, and the insuperable difference of government and manners. The liberty of the Swiss is maintained by the concurrence of political causes; the superior discipline of their militia arises from the numerous intermixture of Officers and soldiers whose youth has been trained in foreign service; and the annual exercise of a few days is the sole tax which is imposed on a martial people consisting for the most part of shepherds and husbandmen. In the primitive ages of Greece and Rome, a war was determined by a battle, and a battle was decided by the personal qualities of strength, courage and dexterity which every citizen derived from his domestic education. The public quarrel was his own: he had himself voted in the assembly of the people; and the private

---

[9] There is no full biography of Ferguson. For an account of his earlier life see Sher, 1985. It seems not to be the case that he was present at the battle of Fontenoy.

[10] *Memoirs*, pp. 107–8; *A*, p. 178.   [11] Dryden, *Cymon and Iphigeneia* (1700), lines 399–413.

passions of the majority had pronounced the general decree of the Republic. On the event of the contest each freeman had staked his fortune and family, his liberty and life; and if the enemy prevailed, he must expect to share in the common calamity of the ruin or servitude of his native city. By such irresistible motives were the first Greeks and Romans summoned to the field: but when the art was improved, when the war was protracted, their militia was transformed into a standing army, or their freedom was oppressed by the more regular forces of an ambitious neighbor.[12]

Looking back on his militia years from a time after the completion of the *Decline and Fall*, Gibbon was incorporating in his personal and national history the concepts basic to his history of Rome, which in those years he was learning from Montesquieu and Hume and could have learned from Machiavelli and the writers of antiquity. He was recapitulating the classical and renaissance account of ancient liberty as that of an armed citizenry, which involved the individual in both political and military action through the exercise of his immediate personal qualities, often known as his virtue; and he was indicating both that this state of public life had declined in ancient times, and that its supersession constituted an essential difference between ancient and modern civilisation. The crucial decline in Roman history had occurred when the legions ceased to be citizens and became the professional servants of emperors; in the passage quoted, however, Gibbon does not seem to carry the story beyond the rise of the Macedonian military state, that 'ambitious neighbor' which had overcome the freedom of the Greek cities and obliged the Romans to transform their military system in the process of overcoming it. Even in antiquity, the martial virtue of the citizen had been a primitive phenomenon.

By the time he wrote the *Memoirs*, Gibbon had been for many years involved – as he was in the years when he served in the militia – in the sophisticated historiography of arms, liberty and culture which was to be among the great themes of his age; and he was incorporating what he said of ancient history in the contemporary history of the two modern nations he knew best. Whether or not the Swiss militia had been much discussed in English parliamentary debates about the standing army, Gibbon introduces it as the exception which proves the rule that in modern societies, where individuals are engaged in 'the peaceful oc-cupations of trade, manufactures and husbandry', militias and the martial spirit are not to be expected. Because the Swiss are the exception rather than the rule, he has little to say here about their trading and

---

[12] *Memoirs*, pp. 108–9; *A*, pp. 79–180.

manufacturing cities, preferring to suggest that Swiss mercenaries and
militias alike are drawn from peasant alpine communities where the
economy is still primitive. It was the modern economy which had made
militias obsolete and professional armies possible and therefore necessary, and this was perceived, in Britain and Europe from about the year
1700, as a momentous historical change, among the greatest ever recorded, occurring in contemporary experience. The profound change
which had occurred in ancient history, when the legions became the
armies of the emperors, had now to be understood in the light of a
change in the modern world, signalling Enlightenment to some, corruption to others and the interplay between the two to philosophical
analysts. Without this debate we cannot hope to understand the historiography of the eighteenth century, or the historical world in which it
was situated.

(II)

We may begin by situating English in the context of European military
history, where its position was for a long time anomalous. In the great
continental monarchies, with their unstable landward marches, military
power had contributed to the growth of absolute kingships, but had
taken the form of large mercenary forces contracted for with domestic
or foreign entrepreneurs. It was when funds ran out to pay these – as
frequently happened – that they became masterless hordes living off the
land and engaged in an ongoing guerrilla war with peasant populations.
In England and Wales, however, this rarely happened after the late
fifteenth century, and was passionately resisted when, as in 1628, it was
threatened. The basic military fact, such as it was, remained the locally
raised and officered militia of the shires.[13] The civil war of 1642 began as
a contest between king and parliament for control of these forces,
resulting in a bitter because undesired series of conflicts within the
gentry elites, fought and won in the end by self-taught amateurs of
genius like Oliver Cromwell and many of his officers. Especially in the
southwestern counties, the First Civil War came to be a history of local
self-organisation to resist mainly royalist depredations, and the
politicisation of the encounters between Clubmen and the better-discip-
lined army of Fairfax.[14] The central military experience in English
historical memory came to be neither feudal conflict, nor foreign in-

---

[13] Boynton, 1967.   [14] Fletcher, 1981; Morrill, 1990.

vasion, nor mercenary warlordism, but civil war, regicide and dissolution of the government; an experience as much political as military.
Cromwell's army, the so-called New Model, was not a militia, but a
regimental army; not a mercenary army, because its politicisation made
it insistently disown the title; not a standing army maintained by the
state, because it was forever in search of a state which could either
maintain it or pay it off – a set of imperatives which both made it a
revolutionary force and inhibited it from acting as one.[15]

Two authors of genius appeared, summarising the situation and
offering means of superseding it. Thomas Hobbes produced a masterwork of philosophy, leading to the conclusion that the power of decision,
and the sword which enforced it, must be altogether yielded into the
hands of the sovereign. James Harrington produced a masterwork of
historical analysis, tracing the history of the sword through the warrior
citizenries of antiquity, the professional legions of the Caesars, and the
unstable baronial monarchies of the high middle ages, to what he
thought a restoration of antiquity, in the form of a commonwealth of
freeholders, who could not escape constituting a republic because the
sword was irretrievably in their hands once more. He had however
failed to foresee the state's capacity to maintain its own armies, and once
the New Model had abdicated, new structures took shape in which
ancient hoplites and Gothic freemen must serve as an antithesis and
irrecoverable alternative. The first true standing army in English history
was as Gibbon indicates a product of the Restoration, an attempt to
invest the monarchy with a military power sufficient to ensure that civil
war could never happen again.[16] The parliaments of the Restoration
further settled the issue of 1642 by formally pronouncing the king the
sole authority over the militia, to which the guards and other regiments
were to be a standing reinforcement.[17] In a sense they were adopting
Hobbes's solution to the problem of anarchy; but it was one thing to
surrender the sword into the hands of Leviathan, another to ensure that
Leviathan would not fumble with it and renew civil war by thrusting it
back into the hands of the subject. The restored Stuarts possessed
household regiments, garrison towns and the beginnings of a fiscal and
bureaucratic structure capable of maintaining them in time of peace;
but their subjects mistrusted the standing army as a threat to their
liberties as much as they relied on it as a guarantee against renewed civil
war, and were by no means convinced that the threat of such a renewal

[15] Kishlansky, 1979; Woolrych, 1987; Gentles, 1992. [16] Childs, 1976; Webb, 1979.
[17] Schwoerer, 1975; Western, 1965.

had been removed. Here again it is useful to situate the English wars in a European context wider than that which explains them.

In continental Europe, the function of absolute monarchies and their armies was to put an end to the Wars of Religion, conventionally supposed to have ended with the Peace of Westphalia in 1648.[18] In the previous chapter we have seen that this was by no means finally assured when the Nine Years War began forty years later, but that there was by then a deep-seated determination that wars of religion should not begin again. It helps our perspective to consider the English civil wars, and the Wars of the Three Kingdoms of which they were part, as a separate series of such wars, fought for reasons of religion[19] uniquely English because they centred around the establishment of church and state set up in the Henrician Reformation. The Restoration of 1660, intended to resolve the undesired revolutionary crisis set going in 1642, proved an incomplete restoration of the unity of church and crown, and therefore did not remove the possibility of renewed civil wars which would be also wars of religion. In 1688, a year of which Gibbon significantly says nothing in the passages quoted, James II's alienation of the Church of England led to a crisis threatening England with foreign invasion, a war of succession, and a renewal of civil war. The last did not occur because both James and William of Orange were by now in command of professional standing armies – the latter's supported by the financial power of the province of Holland – and the confrontation between them ended without battle and without any necessity being imposed on the English country elites to draw swords unwillingly against their neighbours. The standing army had begun to perform in England what would soon be seen as its historical function.[20] Nevertheless, again unnoticed in the passage from Gibbon's *Memoirs*, the reign of William III would be seen by contemporaries – and continue to be seen by Jacobite historians like Thomas Carte, writing at the close of the 1740s, and by radical patriot historians like Tobias Smollett and Catharine Macaulay,[21] writing at the advent of George III's reign – as inaugurating a new historical era in which the standing army would dominate civic virtue and corrupt it.[22]

The civil war of 1642 had as its successor the dynastic, commercial and European war of 1688, of which one aspect was a second War of the

---

[18] Marino, 1998.   [19] Morrill, 1991, 1993.   [20] Pocock, 1988, 1994.
[21] Carte, 1747; Smollett, 1757; Macaulay, 1763–83.
[22] Goldie, 'The Political Thought of the Anglican Revolution', in Beddard, 1991, pp. 102–36; cf. Lenman, 'The Scottish Nobility and the Revolution of 1688–90', *ibid.*, pp. 137–62.

Three Kingdoms (1688–91), fought for European as well as for British reasons, in Scotland and Ireland rather than in England. The British kingdoms found themselves committed, as potentially they had been since 1672, to a struggle against a new historical force: the kingdom of France, at once Catholic and anti-Papal in the sense that it was Gallican, whose enormous military power, based on a standing army financed by non-parliamentary taxation and officered by a partly professionalised *noblesse de l'épée*, threatened Europe with what was called universal monarchy or universal empire.[23] This term, crucial to the *Decline and Fall*'s underlying structure, had passed through a number of meanings. It could denote Charles V's or Philip II's apparent attempt to revive universal Christian empire in the Spanish line; it could denote the danger of an oceanic monopoly of the world's commerce, an ambition ascribed first to the Spaniards and after them to the Dutch and even the British. But when the French monarchy arose, as had happened in history before, on the defeat of Imperialist power in Europe; when in 1672 it invaded the Dutch republic with the aim of destroying its independence and annexing its trade; finally when in 1702 it claimed the succession to the Spanish empire in both the Old and New Worlds, it was open to the reproach of aiming at universal monarchy in all the old and several new senses of the term. It was against this apocalyptic or post-apocalyptic historical monster that William of Orange took his new kingdoms to war in 1689, and posthumously in 1702; the question was less whether the war should be waged than how.

Tories – many but by no means all of whom were country gentry of families longer established than the Gibbons – could favour wars against the threat of universal monarchy posed by France, while remaining far from happy about participation in the kind of war conducted by William III and his successors, Anne on the throne and Marlborough in the field.[24] These were wars fought in continental Europe, entailing large British military presences in Flanders, Germany and more confusingly Spain, and, as British financial power increased, massive subventions to continental allies as far away as Peter the Great's Russia. To support first the operations of William's troops in the mid-1690s, and then by degrees the continental system which developed out of them,[25] it was necessary to institute a British, as well as a Dutch, fiscal and financial structure capable of paying the troops and the allies regularly without

---

[23] See Robertson, 1993a, in particular the contributions of Franz Bosbach, Steven A. Pincus and the editor. [24] Charles Davenant's writings are aimed at this audience; Pocock, 1975, pp. 437–46. [25] French historians used to call it *La prépondérance anglaise*; Muret, 1937.

bankrupting the state in the process (as would have been the norm within living or recent memory).[26] This was brought into being by what we know as 'the Financial Revolution',[27] beginning about 1694, which instituted first the Bank of England and in due course the National Debt, and made it possible for England and later Great Britain to act as a continental power on a basis of credit, backed by increased taxation but no longer dependent on the latter's immediate yield. This system, in the long run stable and successful, recurrently seemed to Tories bought at too high a price, and whenever they raised this complaint they had the support of radical Whigs or 'Commonwealthmen', who looked back to Shaftesbury and even to the opposition to Cromwell's Protectorate, and thought the settlement of 1689 had missed an opportunity of setting limits to the power of the crown.[28] As the danger of prerogative faded, these came to contend, a new menace had taken its place: that of the crown's 'influence' or patronage powers, capable of 'corrupting' parliament itself by bringing members of both houses into personal dependence on the executive and its ministers. This 'influence', Tories and Commonwealthmen went on to contend – it is their conjunction that constitutes Gibbon's 'patriots' – had been exponentially increased by the wars of William III; the union of 'public credit' and 'standing armies' had set up a state of a new kind, unknown to Charles I or his opponents, governed by a new class of public creditors (the 'monied interest') who used their power to subsidise a military establishment and engage in new wars, creating new levels of debt and new power for themselves in an unending spiral.[29] The opposition to the American war almost a century later, which was to assail Gibbon personally as he wrote the *Decline and Fall*, was in part conducted by 'patriot' intellectuals who contended that the game against the 'influence of the crown' was all but lost, and that a process which had begun with William III now threatened Britain with despotism.

An early if not the first debate over the historical issues entailed by this perception took place in 1698, when a House of Commons under country party and Tory leadership was forcing William to reduce his armies at the end of the Nine Years War. It obliges us to recognise just how far the problem of the standing army was already perceived in

[26] 'A bank never paid an army, or paying one soon became no bank' – James Harrington in 1658 (Pocock, 1977a, p. 404). The case of the Genoese banking house of Spinola, which both financed and commanded the Spanish armies in the Netherlands, might have been cited in rebuttal.
[27] Dickson, 1967.   [28] Goldie, 1980; and classically, Robbins, 1959.
[29] Pocock, 1975, pp. 446–61; 1985, ch. 6.

terms of the operation of new historical forces; if one wanted to employ the rather worn phrase 'the historical revolution', it could usefully be applied to the polemicists of the 1690s. Andrew Fletcher of Saltoun, participating in an English debate from a distinctively Scottish stand-point, identified liberty with the Roman and Gothic social structures in which arms to be used in a public cause had been the personal property of free men; his *Discourse of Government in its Relation to Militias*[30] is the first classical recital since Harrington of the 'patriot' rhetoric outlined by Gibbon in the *Memoirs*. About the year 1500, Fletcher contended, new discoveries in trade, navigation, culture and war – the compass, printing press and gunpowder identified by Francis Bacon long before him – had made it worth the individual's while to delegate his own defence to mercenaries whom he paid to fight for him. As a result, these huge social goods – Fletcher was an energetic promoter of Scottish commerce and the Darien scheme – had been bought at too high a political and moral price; for once the individual parted with the means of defence, he had parted with the material and moral prerequisites of his own liberty, and was helpless against the increasingly corrupt and powerful governments which paid the soldiers for him and could use them against him. The only remedy Fletcher could propose was the maintenance, in a world dominated by trade and commerce, of political communities that were at the same time militia encampments, and would resemble Swiss cantons rather than the powerful monarchical states taking power in post-1500 Europe.[31] Many aspects of this vision were, as Fletcher very well knew, utopian.

This was to go very far beyond anything which Harley, Foley or Jack Howe wanted in the English House of Commons, but it reveals much about the ideological presuppositions behind them. Not only was Fletcher's political theory a historicism authentically new; it rested on a historical vision richly and consciously ambivalent. The Gothic armed freeholdership which had ruled before 1500 was popish and unen-lightened, feudal and disorderly; yet it had been free, and its evils could not be eliminated without endangering liberty itself. What this reflected in English consciousness – the Scottish was another matter – was that the standing army had come to put an end to civil and religious war, the worst experience which the political community had ever suffered; but

[30] Fletcher, 1697, 1698 (as *A Discourse concerning Militias and Standing Armies*). Fletcher's *Political Works* were first published in 1737; for a modern edition, see Robertson, 1997a, and for comment, Robertson, 1985 and 1993a.
[31] Fletcher, 1704, *An Account of a Conversation...*; Robertson, 1997, pp. 175–215.

that it had achieved this end by putting it out of the community's power
ever to launch a civil war again, and this under inspection was turning
out to mean a loss of personal and political autonomy greater than had
occurred at any time in civil, or perhaps sacred, history. Hobbes's *bellum
omnium contra omnes*, Locke's dissolution of government, the state of
nature itself, were receding from historical immediacy into juridical
fiction, and nobody would have to live through them again; Leviathan
had acquired the power of the sword as a result of structural changes
which ensured that he would never give it back;[32] but with the loss of the
power to precipitate these disasters, the individual had lost that which,
in seventeenth-century theory, made him and his predicaments the
foundation of the being of all governments. This is why Fletcher and
other debaters of 1698 saw the rise of the standing army as a moment of
profound historical change. With the enormous benefits that commerce, enlightenment and the ending of the wars of religion were
bringing him, the individual was losing – and could see that he had been
losing for two hundred years – the personal autonomy which had made
him capable of participating in government while bearing the means of
power in his own two hands. At the end of the eighteenth century, the
French revolutionaries singing 'Aux armes, citoyens!' and the American
revolutionaries enacting that 'the right of the people to keep and bear
arms shall not be abridged', were still trying to restore or to ensure it to
him.

  If liberty, and with it the foundations of government, consisted in the
exercise of property, there must be property in the exercise of arms;
the state of nature and the transition to the state of government depended on this truth. This important, but by modern scholars neglected,
proposition in juristic political theory was reinforced by the ancient
proposition, rooted in the so-called hoplite revolution of pre-classical
antiquity, that it was the capacity to bear arms in a public cause which
made man a citizen. Machiavelli had revived this proposition, but had
denied that gunpowder warfare was putting an end to the conditions
under which it could be maintained as a *verità effettuale*. After one and a
half centuries of religious war conducted by mercenaries, the tech-
nologies of the 'military revolution',[33] backed by the discovery that
armies must be regularly paid by fiscal machinery if they were to be
instruments of *ratio status* and the *ultima ratio regum*, were transferring
arms out of the property of the individual and into the permanent

---

[32] Pocock, 1996.   [33] Parker, 1988.

control, upkeep and possession of the state. This was perceived as a profound crisis of liberty, and the perception led to a rapid and spectacular revision in and increase of historical awareness. Among users of the English language, James Harrington had been a prophet of this change, but had lived and written in the era of the Cromwellian army, before the military and financial revolutions were completed. Andrew Fletcher, revising Baconian and Harringtonian generalisations to provide the new vision with historical foundations, was declaring that the new age had arrived, diagnosing its dangers and asking what remedies were necessary and possible.

Fletcher's equal and adversary in historical insight was the London journalist Daniel Defoe.[34] Writing a defence of standing armies contemporary with Fletcher's critique, but aimed against another pamphleteer,[35] Defoe in effect accepted the contention that it had been the increase of commerce and enlightenment which had induced the individual to give up his monopoly of the bearing of arms, but insisted that it had been prudent, necessary and profitable for him to do so. In societies dominated by personal martial virtue, Defoe began saying, the individual had lived under the domination of the stronger, exercised in feudal baronages or republics on the Polish model. It was a telling argument among Scots, soon to be engaged in repudiating George Buchanan's account of their history in which the public liberty had been maintained by magnates, barons, the chiefs of kindreds and their tenants, retainers and kinsmen.[36] Defoe declared that the individual was more free to pursue wealth, leisure, enlightenment and the enjoyment of rights if he divested himself of the obligation to bear arms and paid others to discharge it for him. At a stroke, the concepts of freedom and virtue were changed; they no longer entailed the individual's immediate participation in the *res publica* of government and self-government, or the definition of the citizen as one who ruled and was ruled, but enjoined him to seek fulfilment in an exchange of money for goods and services including those of the state. He did not defend or assert his own liberty in arms; and if he did not – Machiavelli and Fletcher joined in insisting – he must be content to be governed by those who paid the soldiers. Defoe's solution was that, indirectly rather than directly, he should be one of these himself; he should be represented in a parliament which

[34] Pocock, 1975, pp. 432–5, 453–6. For Defoe's historical vision as a precursor of Enlightenment, see Katherine Clark, 1998.
[35] Trenchard, 1697; Defoe, 1698. For the controversy as a whole, Schwoerer, 1975, ch. VIII.
[36] Kidd, 1993.

held the power of the purse and could grant or refuse the executive the funds with which it maintained the armies which were otherwise in its exclusive control. There must be a government of checks and balances, in which the fiscal and executive branches were clearly separated and – as Edmund Burke was to put it a century later – public virtue was nowhere better displayed than in the management of the public revenue.[37] Virtue was no longer direct and personal, valorous and honourable, except in those specialised cases where the individual found himself involved in the exercise of arms at a higher than mercenary level; it had become indirect and prudential, exercised in the conduct of a system of delegated, monetarised, specialised and in the formal sense alienated relations between personalities never displayed in their wholeness. Liberty was the exemption from this display, the freedom to be many things at different times. The defence of this freedom, or its extension in the wars of commerce, was delegated to low-paid and low-skilled operatives, the military proletarians of the post-classical and post-feudal world.

(III)

There was needed a new ethos, a redefinition of virtue in what could no longer be its Athenian, Roman or Machiavellian sense; but the situation was complicated by the sovereign need of making an end of the wars of religion and the Christian devotion that had made them possible. Ancient and modern virtue challenged one another in the act of offering to replace Catholic, Calvinist and sectarian convictions by an ethos of civil society, and Enlightenment may be characterised as the modern challenged by the ancient. How the new ethos arose may be understood by scrutinising the debate of 1698. Defoe, a London dissenter and failed tradesman who is one of the few authentically bourgeois writers in English history, insisted on the need for commercial probity, honour and willingness to meet commitments without which the level of taxable income necessary to pay the armies could not be maintained, and there could not be the confidence in the government's willingness to meet its obligations that made society willing to bear the national debt.[38] But the system of government Defoe upheld was not conducted from London, but from Westminster, the royal and parliamentary capital where court and country met and the new mercantile and military system was

---

[37] Burke, 1791; Pocock, 1987a, pp. 199–200; Mitchell, 1989, pp. 273–4.
[38] Pocock, 1975, pp. 454–7; 1985, pp. 99–100.

maintained by aristocratic and royal patronage and with the land-holding gentry's none too certain support. In the Spectatorial circles of 'the polite end of town', Addison,[39] more critically Shaftesbury,[40] and a great many others worked out an ethos, largely humanist, courtly and Ciceronian in its origins, whose key terms were 'manners' and 'polite-ness' and which offered the leisured individual, whether his property were real or personal, the means of moving freely, authoritatively and with self-possession, in a world where human capacities were being rapidly diversified by commerce but had not escaped control by a court – Westminster or Versailles – which had preceded the market as the national *entrepot* where service was exchanged for protection and favour. The individual acquired this capacity, of which manners and politeness were the techniques as well as the values, in proportion as he laid down arms and moved instead in a world, a 'town', a '*bon ton*' at once courtly and commercial. The market upheld the court and did not challenge it; and the great centralised monarchies which French theor-ists of this movement called *états policés* – at once polite and policed – were the engines by which modernity replaced the feudal, the barbaric, the ancient and the fanatical.

Manners and politeness, then, were concepts commercial, but con-sciously not bourgeois; the Spectator Club was a point of contact where the country gentleman and the London merchant could meet and polish one another, and in that role had taken over much of the function of the court. There was to be a commerce, a conversation, an intercourse – these words combined economic, social and sexual meanings – linked with Ciceronian *otium et negotium*, aimed at replacing the world of the free arms-bearer who might also be the religious fanatic; a renewal of the humanist enterprise, seeking a victory over barbarism and religion. The cult of 'polite letters' and 'polite learning', so marked in the London we have come to term 'Augustan', was aimed at removing letters from the control of the older clerical elites – the clergy above all, the lawyers, more recently the virtuosi and the antiquaries – and placing them in the hands of an urban and urbane leisured gentry, who would transfer 'philosophy' from the disputation of the schools to the conversation of the drawing-room and the club – Locke, Addison and Shaftesbury all dwelt on this objective[41] – and whose social power was declared by their will to consume culture rather than produce it. Congreve wished Vol-

---

[39] Bloom and Bloom, 1971.
[40] Klein, 1994.
[41] See in particular Klein, 1994, chs. 1 and 5.

taire to meet him as a gentleman rather than a playwright; Gibbon wished to be known as a gentleman who wrote history for his amusement. 'Amusement', indeed, was not merely frivolous; it was the deployment of the powers of taste and science, the powers of the cultivated mind; but an aspect of the Enlightened rejection of fanaticism was its resolute amateurism, its refusal to know so much that the mind became the prisoner of its own knowledge. The Battle of the Books in England was on one level the conflict between the amateur and the pedant; on another, however, it displayed the discovery by the Moderns that the critical capacities they cultivated had opened the way to an erudition and a historical insight beyond what was known to Ancients in the accepted sense.[42] It is crucial to the understanding of Gibbon as an Enlightened figure that he pursued erudition and laboured at it, in defiance of the contempt which the polite and the philosophical sometimes displayed. 'Taste' and 'science', important terms in his vocabulary, meant the exercise of a judgment that called on all the powers of the intellect; and he had to prove that it did against the contentions of others. This conflict, however, was fought out within the shared conviction that politeness and philosophy were necessary merits of the commercial and post-clerical society.

These were aspects of the ethos which society offered the individual in return for the surrender of his arms-bearing capacity (except in the state's service), his capacity for autonomous citizenship (but we have seen that this was most vigorously contested) and his capacity for direct knowledge of things and immediate religious experience. It has been described as the triumph of the social over the political,[43] and perhaps in the end the sociable animal has no being outside his relations with his fellow members of society. But while the process of Enlightenment seems to have entailed the decision that civil society offers better protection than the civil magistrate from the disruptions of religious conflict, this implied no loss of regard for civil government, and all the philosophies of the age laboured to constitute and reinforce it. Civil society must be governed and protected against anarchy; governments must be sovereign in order to define and protect their own jurisdictions. The commerce exchanged between the severally governed societies reinforced their power as states as well as moderating its exercise. There arose a rhetoric whose argument will prove of the greatest importance to the *Decline and Fall*; of Dutch and English origin, but accepted

---

[42] Levine, 1991.   [43] Hannah Arendt is the best-known expositor of this view.

progressively throughout western Europe,[44] it affirmed that an age of conquest – in due course to be identified with antiquity as well as with recent modernity – was being superseded by an age of commerce, and that consequently universal monarchy had lost what historical justification it might have possessed. There was no need of a universal empire to unify and police the now oceanic trade routes of the world; commerce was better conducted by independent states trading with one another under their own governments.[45] This was initially a mercantilist argument, though capable of development in a free-trade direction, and one well suited to the needs of maritime states like those allied under the Stadholder King; it lent itself to the polemic against a territorial monarchy claiming to dominate the European and American land masses, while leaving a little obscure the possibility that great navigational corporations might establish universal empire by dominating the commerce and investment capital of the oceanic world. For the next hundred years, the French whom the argument against universal empire identified as 'Rome' might retaliate by identifying the Dutch or British who used the argument as 'Carthage'.

This was the portrait of 'Europe' which emerged from the War of the Spanish Succession; a Europe often described as a 'republic' but more accurately as a 'confederation' of independent sovereign states, held together in a permanent association by a *jus gentium* which ensured that wars would end in treaties and that some of these *foedera* would be so lasting as to approach the status of public law (it was the exposition of this law that made the Swiss jurist Vattel rank as the successor to Grotius and Pufendorf).[46] This confederation, or polity of states based upon treaties, was further held together by the ties of a common commerce, and by the shared civilisation of 'manners' which flourished in a commercial culture – whether or not it was in the practices of commerce that they originated. At the end of the era during which it was possible to describe 'Europe' in these terms, Edmund Burke may be found proclaiming that manners are more important than laws, and that the new barbarism of Revolution is aimed at destroying them and reversing the course of European civilisation. It is important to understand that Burke spoke as a philosopher of Enlightenment, not of Counter-Enlightenment.

It was claimed that this 'Europe' had been achieved by a treaty, that

---

[44] Haitsma Mulier, 1980. For the advent of this rhetoric in Italy – achieved in part through a reading of Locke's monetary writings – see Venturi, 1969, pp. 479–82.
[45] Hont, 1990; Robertson, 1993b.   [46] Marino, 1998.

of Utrecht in 1713. The war which it terminated had been aimed at the threat of universal monarchy contained in a French acquisition of the Spanish monarchy and its empire, but in its course the policies of the allies, Dutch, British and Austrian, had become so far involved in alternative schemes for a Spanish succession as to raise the thought that there could be more aspirants to universal monarchy than one. An Austrian monarchy was briefly installed in Naples, and the ceilings of Vienna displayed Charles VI gazing through the Pillars of Hercules like Charles V before him. Andrew Fletcher suspected William III of high ambitions for the multiple monarchy he headed, and the Tory gentry, happy to see Britain strong at sea and in trade, wanted to know why they were fighting in Spain for an Austrian succession. Led by Harley and Bolingbroke and offered a dangerous spokesman in Swift, they voiced their revulsion against the military and financial monarchy their state was becoming under the supposed hegemony of Scots, Dissenters and the 'monied interest';[47] but if this was a rebellion against the new order in British politics, they could claim that in recoiling from excessive ambitions on the continent, they were reinforcing the new order of a republic of states in Europe. The system confirmed at Utrecht – a Tory action of which the Whig historian Macaulay approved in the next century[48] – did not need to be so stable as to eliminate wars; it needed only to contain them within *raison d'état*, the law of nations and the civilisation of manners. It was the first attempt to construct a European order, replacing both the wars of religion and the excessive power of Louis XIV; coming after the Anglo-Scottish Union and achieved as an Anglo-French condominium, it was the first 'Europe' in which a British state was a principal member. It may be thought of as the *ancien régime*, once we realise that this order came to an end in the wars of the American and French Revolutions;[49] but we must realise also that the *ancien régime* considered itself to be modern, having superseded the Roman empire, the medieval paparchy, the wars of religion and the universal monarchies. It was the Europe of Enlightenment, and Gibbon, serving in the militia, was both upholding and commenting upon it.

This system of states in due course generated its own historiography. In assessing the process it is important to avoid a cliché now current and abstain from calling them 'nation states'. They were either multiple monarchies, or confederations of diverse sovereignties, Dutch, Swiss or

---

[47] Pocock, 1975, pp. 446–8.   [48] Pocock, 1985, p. 303.
[49] Venturi, 1979, 1984; tr. Litchfield, 1989.

(less clearly perceived) German. The identification of state with nation was not an Enlightened but a Revolutionary achievement. What was presumed about the Enlightened state was the stability of its 'interests', whether those of the reigning family or of more impersonal components in its structure, such as merchants, soldiers or churches; and there existed an extensive literature in which publicists expounded the 'interests' – often amounting to the histories – of the several states constituting 'Europe'. These states, however, whether monarchies or confederations, were further legitimised, in the view of things we consider as Enlightenment, by their capacity to act as commercial and civil societies, and to mobilise and direct those human resources which would free civilisation from its dark post-classical past. There was therefore a need for histories of arts and manners, commerce and civil society itself; we give the name 'philosophical history' to the historiography which attempted to satisfy this need, especially but not necessarily when it based itself on the new, critical and methodical ways of studying the mind and its operations in the world to which the term 'philosophy' is more specifically applied. Debates about the philosophy of history, such as that Gibbon conducted against d'Alembert, can be seen arising at this point; but the structure of Enlightened historiography was often 'philosophical' in senses entailing looser applications of the term.

There arose a grand narrative, which it is possible to explore through a series of studies of the major Enlightened historians, including Gibbon in his maturity. This opposed a system of sovereign civil societies, for the most part monarchies, arising at the end of the fifteenth or of the seventeenth century, to a series of precedent macrohistorical conditions, above all the papacy and empire held to have dominated Europe from the time of Charlemagne to its breakdown in the wars of religion. The monarchy of Louis XIV, claimed Voltaire, had put an end to the last-named condition and instituted an Enlightened Europe; but, argued his opponents, Louis had brought a renewed threat of universal monarchy, and both the Grand Alliance and the Treaty of Utrecht had been needed before a balance of power and a republic of contending but civilised states could replace it. In spite of the emphasis we have laid on Enlightenment as a response to Calvinism, there seems to be no major Enlightened history of the wars of religion outside the British kingdoms, and the great antithesis of these histories came to be the Christian millennium in the Latin provinces: the ascendancy of the papacy and empire, and the French, English and Spanish feudal kingdoms which had replaced them. As the Enlightened Europe of Utrecht was a construct of France and the Maritime Powers, so its scheme of history was both Latin and Atlantic, with little room for German history, less for Central European, and none whatever for that of the successor states to the Greek empire – at least until Petrine Russia claimed a place in this western order and its scheme of history. The prehistory of this Europe was the history of the Roman church and the feudal kingdoms among which it had existed – a history of barbarism and religion. But it was further understood – for reasons lying deep in *philosophe*, Protestant, humanist and Ghibelline perceptions – that the church in turn was a successor to the Roman empire, as that had been a successor to the Roman republic. At this point the prehistory of Enlightenment acquired a new dimension; the wealth of classical literature entered the historical universe; and the states system and its civil society became modern in a double sense, as having superseded the ecclesiastical and the fanatical – beginning to be called the medieval – and as having superseded the ancient and the virtuous, now seen as the chief adversaries of the critical and the commercial. In this grand scheme of Enlightened history, Gibbon in his militia years began searching for a theme and a place.

This historiography had been slow to develop. In England, Boling-broke, who saw himself as the architect of the Treaty of Utrecht, desired greatly to be remembered as a historian writing in the Tacitist neo-classical tradition of Guicciardini, Sarpi and Clarendon, who had recorded in the Greek and Roman manner the vicissitudes of the emergent states of modern Europe. Neither he nor his friend Swift, however, was of the stuff from which great historians are made; and it is part of the long hiatus in English neo-classical historiography that the *Letters on the Study of History* are all we have of the great history of which he seems to have dreamed, and which would have traced the growth of a European states system to its culmination at Utrecht, when he himself would have figured as a second Clarendon, unjustly dismissed from the role of statesman to enter in exile on that of historian.[50] In France, the grand theme had to be developed through the criticism as well as the glorification of Louis XIV, and Gibbon did not have access to Voltaire's *Siècle de Louis XIV* till well after its publication in 1751, or to any version of the *Essai sur les moeurs* till after 1756. Of the Scottish histories of Europe he was to find important, Hume's *History of England* appeared between 1754 and 1762, Robertson's *History of Charles V* in 1769; of Scottish philosophi-

---

[50] Hicks, 1987, 1996.

cal histories of civil society, Adam Ferguson's *Essay on the History of Civil Society* came his way in 1766–7, while the views of Adam Smith became known to him through personal acquaintance before the first volume of the *Decline and Fall* appeared in the same year, 1776, as the *Wealth of Nations*. If the erudition Gibbon most admired was formed in the *république des lettres* and the Académie des Inscriptions before he was born, the grand Enlightened historiography in which he must be situated was a much later growth, and this must have affected his long search for a narrative theme.

There further arise two important considerations. The master works of Enlightenment historiography, just set out, are seen to have been produced and published in the era of the Seven Years War, while the *Decline and Fall* is accompanied by the War of the American Revolution; and it can be argued that in the former as well as the latter of these wars, the Europe of Utrecht which had occasioned that historiography came to an end. Utrecht and its Enlightenment amounted to a compromise between France and Britain to control the consequences of the Spanish succession, and the Europe it sought to stabilise was Alpine and Rhenish, Atlantic and west Mediterranean, as – complicated by empire in America and its demand for African slaves – were the wars ensuing on the Utrecht settlement. In the war of 1756 to 1763, however, that Europe was exploded in two directions; Anglo-French rivalry escalated into a hugely expensive contest for empire in the river systems giving access to North America, and found itself conjoined to a Prussian-Austrian-Russian contest for empire in a central and eastern Europe of which the parties to the Utrecht settlement – even Britain after the Hanoverian succession – had not needed to take much account. 'Europe' found itself enlarged towards Russian Eurasia in one direction, towards the global ocean and the continents beyond it in another. This must be considered if we are to understand the enlargement of European into world history evident in the *Decline and Fall*, as in the great global and American histories of Raynal and Robertson which accompany it; an enlargement, however, prefigured in Voltaire's *Essai sur les moeurs*. Enlightened history remained Eurocentric, but it looked beyond Europe.[51]

In the second place, it is important to remember that while the historiography of Enlightened Europe was 'modern', in the sense that it described the triumph of commerce over ancient virtue as well as over barbarism and religion, the criticism of modern in the name of ancient

---

[51] O'Brien, 1997.

values was already in place and had generated macrohistorical schemes such as Fletcher's revision of the work of Harrington. Montesquieu had explored the tensions between commerce and virtue, and did not think he had brought them to closure, while – to look ahead – not even Hume and Smith were certain that the modernity whose triumph they described and celebrated was going to endure. Earlier in the century, Montesquieu's *Considérations sur les causes de la grandeur des Romains et de leur décadence* had made it clear that the corruption of ancient virtue did explain the fall of the ancient world, and this might be considered either a reassurance or an admonition to the modern. Enlightenment, as the word is used in this chapter, was not sure of itself; not sure whether to preserve the ancient or to abandon it; and this is inherent in the ambiguity of the militia in which Gibbon served, his studies during his service, and his reflections on his service and the moment in history which it occupied.

(IV)

At the end of the Walpole ministry, Britain became involved in a blue-water war with Spain and then in the far more complex European conflict of the War of the Austrian Succession, which reawakened fears of both French universal monarchy and continental involvement through the Hanoverian connection. British troops suffered a reverse at Fontenoy in the Netherlands, and there ensued a Jacobite war in Britain itself, which for lack of a serious French invasion became little more than a raid by some Highland clans. This, however, revealed the military nakedness of both kingdoms, and the Jacobite army reached Derby before regular or Hanoverian troops could be brought against it. This episode is counted as one of the origins of the Scottish Enlightenment, since the Moderate party among Edinburgh clergy took shape with the intention of promoting a Scottish culture better able to defend itself;[52] whether this should take a martial or modern form was a question to be debated. In both kingdoms composing the Union, the events of 1745 led to a revival of interest in forming national militias; but it was only after a decade and a half of party politics, diplomatic revolution and war against France in Europe, America and India – the war on foot when Gibbon returned from Lausanne – that Pitt's ministry took the steps[53] which transformed the character and concept of the

[52] Sher, 1985, is the authoritative account of this development.
[53] For the whole process and its far-reaching consequences, see Gould, 1991, 1992, 1997.

English militia by removing it from country localism and embodying it as a national force under the authority of king-in-parliament. Gibbon recounts the story in his most sustained passage of reflection on the history of his own country and his own time. Following the paragraphs earlier quoted on the ancient and Swiss militias he says:

Two disgraceful events, the progress in the year forty-five of some naked highlanders, the invitation of the Hessians and Hanoverians in fifty six, had betrayed and insulted the weakness of an unarmed people. The country gentlemen of England unanimously demanded the establishment of a militia: a patriot was expected... and the merit of the plan or at least of the execution was assumed by Mr Pitt who was then in the full splendour of his popularity and power. In the new model

(a significant use of words ?)

the choice of the officers was founded on the most constitutional principle since they were all obliged, from the Colonel to the Ensign, to prove a certain qualification, to give a landed security to the country, which entrusted them for her defence with the use of arms. But in the first steps of this institution the legislators of the Militia despaired of initiating the practise of Switzerland. Instead of summoning to the standard *all* the inhabitants of the kingdom who were not disabled by age, or excused by some indispensable avocation, they directed that a moderate proportion should be chosen by lot for the term of three years, at the end of which their places were to be supplied by a new and similar ballot. Every man who was drawn had the option of serving in person, of finding a substitute, or paying ten pounds; and in a country already bur-thened, this honourable duty was degraded into an additional tax...

But the King was invested with the power of calling the Militia into actual service on the event or the danger of rebellion or invasion; and in the year 1759 the British islands were seriously threatened by the armaments of France. At this crisis the national spirit most gloriously disproved the charge of effeminacy which, in a popular Estimate,[54] had been imputed to the times; a martial enthusiasm seemed to have pervaded the land, and a constitutional army was formed under the command of the nobility and gentry of England. After the naval victory of Sir Edward Hawke (November 20th 1759) the danger no longer subsisted; yet instead of disbanding the first regiments of militia, the remainder was embodied the ensuing year, and public unanimity applauded their illegal continuance in the field till the end of the War. In this new mode of service they were subject like the regulars to martial law; they received the same advantages of pay and cloathing, and the families, at least of the principals, were main-tained at the charge of the parish...

With the skill they soon imbibed the spirit of mercenaries, the character of a

---

[54] Brown, 1758, a widely read jeremiad at the unprosperous onset of the Seven Years War (*Library*, p. 80). See Crimmins, 1983, though this is not primarily a study of the *Estimate*.

militia was lost; and, under that specious name, the crown had acquired a second army, more costly and less useful than the first. The most beneficial effect of this institution was to eradicate among the Country gentlemen the relicks of Tory or rather of Jacobite prejudice. The accession of a British King reconciled them to the government and even to the court: but they have been since accused of transferring their passive loyalty from the Stuarts to the family of Brunswick; and I have heard Mr. Burke exclaim in the house of Commons 'They have changed the Idol, but they have preserved the Idolatry!'[55]

There are one or two things Gibbon does not say about this militia: that it was not extended to Scotland, that it provoked widespread popular riots in England; but he has indicated that it was a modern and not an ancient phenomenon, that it was not an embodiment of republican or Gothic civic virtue, though its 'constitutional' character does not seem to be diminished by its 'illegal continuance'. He is saying that it was a Whig as well as a patriot achievement, which transformed what national enthusiasm there was into a second standing army at the Crown's disposal. There is still enough blue-water Toryism in his discourse to make him remark that it ceased to be justifiable after the danger by sea was removed at Quiberon Bay; but he has earlier remarked that 'the sea *was long* the sole safeguard of our isle',[56] and there is a passage in the *Decline and Fall*'s first volume which indicates that it cannot be so for ever.[57] In these ways Gibbon is moving away from any Tory or patriot preferences he may once have had, and in a Whig direction; and his main conclusion about Pitt's militia is that it was the means of reconciling Tory and Jacobite families like his own to the House of Hanover. This reconciliation, in his judgment, came about late and for blue-water reasons; it was not completed until George III ascended to the throne, in the second year of Gibbon's militia service, declaring that he 'gloried in the name of Britain' and was therefore not committed to the interests of Hanover. But the new monarch set himself to get rid of Pitt and conclude a peace which did not give Britain a universal empire of the seas and the Americas; and his breach with powerful Whig factions brought down the charge, by Burke and many others, that he had purchased Tory loyalty at too high a price. Gibbon, a beneficiary of that reconciliation, was to sit in Parliament through the American crisis as a follower of Lord North and to lose both his place and his seat in the political storms of 1780. His judgment on Burke's outburst is studiously withheld. He gives his estimate of what service in

[55] *Memoirs*, pp. 109–11; *A*, pp. 180–2 (Memoir B).   [56] Above, p. 96; my italics.
[57] The account of the overthrow of Allectus; *Decline and Fall*, I, ch. 13; Womersley, I, p. 367; Bury, I, p. 388.

the Hampshire militia did for him, and concludes in the following terms:

> But my principal obligation to the militia was the making me an Englishman and a soldier. After my foreign education, with my reserved temper, I should long have continued a stranger in my native country, had I not been shaken in this various scene of new faces and new friends: had not experience forced me to feel the characters of our leading men, the state of parties, the forms of office, and the operations of our civil and military system. In this peaceful service I imbibed the rudiments of the language and science of tactics, which opened a whole new field of study and observation. I diligently read and meditated the *Mémoires militaires* of Quintus Icilius (Mr Guichardt), the only writer who has united the merits of a professor and a veteran.[58] The discipline and evolutions of a modern battalion gave me a clearer notion of the Phalanx and the Legion, and the Captain of the Hampshire grenadiers (the reader may smile) has not been useless to the historian of the Roman Empire.[59]

This passage from the *Memoirs* elaborates an entry in Gibbon's journal, written at the end of his militia service:

> But what I value most, is the knowledge it has given me of mankind in general, and of my own country in particular. The General system of our government, the methods of our several offices, the departments and powers of their respective officers, our provincial and municipal administration, the view of our several parties, the characters, connections and influence of our principal people, have been impressed in my mind, not by vain theory, but by the indelible lessons of action and experience . . . So that the sum of all is, that I am glad the militia has been, and glad that it is no more.[60]

The militia was the politics of court and country in action and in microcosm. This account of political knowledge gained by experience is written fairly close to the experience itself, and is the work of a young, intensely self-reflective man acutely conscious of what he was and what he might become; and the personality in formation and under inspection included the author of the *Essai sur l'étude de la littérature*, intent on self-shaping as a man of letters and a political being. The captain could do more than instruct the historian in what a regiment was like on the march or the drill-ground (what a battle was like Gibbon never learned from experience); more than impel him to take up the study of a modern military historian writing under a Roman name. The two together had passed through an intensive course of education, not only manly – though Gibbon regretted that life in an officers' mess had taught him to

---

[58] Guichardt, 1760. Gibbon later possessed (*Library*, p.141) his *Mémoires critiques et historiques sur plusieurs points d'antiquités militaires* (4 vol., Berlin, 1774).   [59] *Memoirs*, p.117; *A*, p. 190.
[60] *Journal A*, pp. 194–5.

drink more than was good for him – but political; not a training in ancient virtue,[61] but the education of a young country gentleman in county and national politics perceived through the lenses of military service. It was an education for a Whig and a modern, a reconciliation with the way his country had been going since 1688 and 1714. The *Memoirs* inform us that service in the militia made the historian a participant in history, both that of England and Britain engaged in the transition from ancient to modern values, and that of arms in relation to society, which was the key to the transformation and perhaps the destruction of ancient civilisation and its replacement by medieval and then by modern Europe.

Without this experience he might have remained something of an expatriate, whose preferred literary language was in any case French until the late 1760s. Within weeks of his return to England in 1759, he had resumed his work on his *Essai sur l'étude de la littérature*, which he published in French with a London bookseller two years later.[62] As a defence of the *érudits* against the *encyclopédistes*, this work exhibits the young Gibbon's relation to the Parisian Enlightenment and must be considered in that context; but the manner of its publication as well as composition reminds us that even in England – then as now the least bilingual of west European cultures – the language of the polite letters, and of the culture of manners, was often French. It has even been argued that French culture was so far dominant that some of the origins of English nationalism may be found in the revolt against it.[63] The clatter of wooden shoes, in a hundred English texts since the fifteenth century, should assure us that there was plenty of anti-French cultural chauvinism already; but this was an era of real regard for the ease and polish which the *grande nation* was supposed at the time to exhibit towards strangers. Gibbon indicates that he set about restoring his command of English style by reading the masters of English polite letters:

our English writers since the Revolution: they breathed the spirit of reason and liberty, and they most seasonably contributed to restore the purity of my own language which had been corrupted by the long use of a foreign Idiom. By the judicious advice of Mr Mallet

(with whom and his wife Gibbon had become 'domesticated')

---

[61] 'It was found by experience that the greater part of the men were rather civilized than corrupted by the habits of military subordination'; *Memoirs*, p. 115; *A*, p. 188. The pair 'civilized and corrupted' occurs often enough in the *Decline and Fall* to make it clear that Gibbon is saying that the ancient fate had been avoided in this instance.
[62] *Memoirs*, pp. 99–103; *A*, pp. 167–72 (Memoir B).   [63] Newman, 1987.

I was directed to the writings of Swift and Addison: wit and simplicity are their common attributes: but the style of Swift is supported by manly original vigour; that of Addison is adorned by the female graces of elegance and mildness; and the contrast of too coarse or too thin a texture is visible even in the defects of these celebrated authors.[64]

This reading (as Gibbon recalled it thirty years later) was judiciously directed by Bolingbroke's literary executor towards a blending of Tory and Whig styles, at a time when the two were approaching a new synthesis in both Gibbon family history and the history of English politics after the accession of George III; but it is worth noticing that there were still tensions, expressible in a metaphor of gender. The Tory Swift is too coarse and masculine, the Whig Addison too feminine and thin, and Gibbon goes on to indicate that he found the perfect synthesis in the styles of Robertson and Hume, Scotsmen practising that most masculine of literary activities, the writing of history. Catharine Macaulay, who would in a few years vigorously claim a woman's place in this branch of literature, was less a feminist than a patriot; as a Sawbridge by birth, opposition came to her naturally.

Militia service gave Gibbon what family life and leisure would not have yielded, the sense of belonging to a *patria*; it did not make him a patriot as that term was then used, but a ministerial Whig with Tory undertones. This political culture was to satisfy him for another twenty-five years (1759–83) but not longer; and we have seen that it was, and that he knew it to be, a culture in structural historical change. The movement from civil, religious and dynastic internal war towards enlightenment and power in the community of nations could be represented as the movement of the public self towards the refinement and multiplication of sociable, cultural, commercial and conversational capacities. Gibbon's use of the metaphor of gender at this point reminds us that the movement was seen as a tension, and perhaps a dialectic, rather than a progress. The 'manly' *virtus* of Swift may be too coarse, the 'female' elegance of Addison too refined, and there opens a path down which the refinement of manners may lead to 'effeminacy'. The establishment of the militia repudiated this charge when brought against the English, and it had to be kept in mind that both Gibbon's model writers were involved in the dialectic of virtue and politeness; if Swift was too coarse, Hume could nevertheless call him the first author of polite prose in English. Gender, it needs to be added, was more than a metaphor. The ideology of refined manners and polite conversation offered

---

[64] *Memoirs*, p. 98; *A*, p. 166. For 'domesticated', *A*, p. 160.

women a way out of the separation of *polis* from *oikos* and a role in the *république des lettres* and the urban, national and intellectual network which communicated manners and ideas; but this did not make all articulate women Addisonian Whigs, as we learn from Catharine Macaulay, whose commitment to Roman civic virtue was absolute, austere and republican.[65] It is Gibbon who conveys that the writing of history may unite the masculine and feminine virtues, and there is a faint hint that he found Robertson's style more 'masculine' than that of Hume,[66] the adversary of Catharine Macaulay in displaying the movement of English history from ancient to modern. They all lived in a complex world of opposing and interacting values, where history could not be written as a one-way song.

[65] Macaulay, 1763–71, 1773; Minuti, 1986; Hill, 1992.

[66] *Memoirs*, p. 99 (*A*, p. 164): 'The perfect composition, the nervous language, the well-turned periods of Dr Robertson . . . the calm philosophy, the careless inimitable beauties of his friend and rival.'

CHAPTER 5

Study in the camp: erudition and the search for a narrative

We possess the journal – the first of a series Gibbon kept between 1761 and 1764[1] – which records that his life as a militia officer was also a life of study. It was intended, we gather, to be a daily chronicle of drilling, drinking, reading and reflection, but there are lacunae and passages of retrospection, some filling in periods during which daily entries were not made, others surveying periods of study and even writing. It is partly concurrent with the completion of the *Essai sur l'étude de la littérature*, which is written in French, the language of the *république des lettres*; but this journal, unlike its successors, is kept in English, the language of the militia and the political world to which the writer currently belonged. Its value to us is that it continues the record begun by the Lausanne commonplace book;[2] the record of Gibbon's self-training in classical and modern studies, which never quite equipped him to be a classical scholar – the deficiencies of his schoolboy and undergraduate years were not to be overcome – but enabled him to ground his thinking as a modern in the critical study of antiquity. It was this which made him a historian, the thing he says he always intended to be, and the militia journal shows his self-training as a scholar in harness with his search for a grand historical subject. The capacity to read texts critically, vital as we shall see to the writing of Enlightened history, was also a great part of what the age meant by 'philosophy', and the figure of Gibbon *philosophe* can be seen taking shape in the journal the young officer kept as a man of letters; but at the same time it was what was meant by 'erudition', and we can read this journal as continuing the record of Gibbon's deter-mination to be a scholar and make that role essential to his self-definition as a man of letters, engaged in the *belles-lettres* rather than the *beaux-arts*. This in turn – as we shall see in a later chapter – was crucial to his debate with d'Alembert in the *Essai sur l'étude de la littérature*; and, concurrent with the keeping of the journal and constantly present in it, this was the young Gibbon's statement of what we should term his

[1] *Journal A.*   [2] Above, p. 81.

philosophy of history. There is a great deal going on during the militia years; Gibbon is shaping himself as an Englishman, an officer and a gentleman, and at the same time as a man of letters, meaning both a scholar and a *philosophe* of a particular kind. We are engaged in a search for the cultural sources of both his scholarship and his philosophy, while remembering that the captain and the historian are not to be kept apart.

The journal records an intricate blend of ancient and modern scholarship. Beginning as he remembered even before he left Lausanne, Gibbon was fascinated by the *Mémoires de l'Académie des Inscriptions et Belles-Lettres*, focused largely on imperial and late antique Roman history (the discovery of Stourhead);[3] at the outset of his militia service he was reading La Bléterie upon emperors and La Bastie on their assumption of the title of Pontifex Maximus. But the preceding winter had seen him learning Italian by reading Machiavelli's *Discorsi sopra Tito Livio* and *Istorie Fiorentine*;[4] and Machiavelli, it is notorious and the subject of much mystification,[5] is historian of both the decline of Rome and the rise of medieval and modern Europe. Gibbon records that work on the *Essai* had made him conscious of a need to understand ancient paganism thoroughly, and with this end in view he began reading Cicero's *De natura deorum*, and with it Isaac de Beausobre's *Histoire de Manichéisme*.[6] Here he is studying the interactions of polytheism with philosophy; Cicero's was an ancient classic on that subject, and in Beausobre he says he found

the most ample and candid account of the ancient Philosophical Theology both in itself and as blended with Christianity.

The debate was already ancient as to how far Hellenic theology had anticipated Christian, as the orthodox believed, or had helped to shape it, as maintained by its critics; Gibbon was in contact with the philosophical debate over natural religion, with what was to prove a governing theme of the *Decline and Fall*, and with one of the great works of Huguenot scholarship which he was to take as his guides. At the same time, however, he was looking about for a subject around which to build a major 'historical composition', and the options he considered were one and all drawn from the fifteenth through the seventeenth centuries: the expedition of Charles VIII to Italy,[7] the life of Sir Walter

---

[3] Above, p. 29.   [4] *Journal A*, pp. 10–11.
[5] Strauss, 1969; Mansfield, 1979; Rahe, 1992. For Machiavelli as a pre-modern, see de Grazia, 1989; Parel, 1992; Pocock, 1994.
[6] *Journal A*, pp. 22–3. Cf. p. 44: 'the great philosophical and Theological work of M. de Beausobre' (1734).   [7] First mentioned *Journal A*, p. 24 (April 1761).

Raleigh,[8] the history of the Swiss,[9] the history of Florence.[10] More than a year separates the first pair of choices from the second, and it was during that interval that the *Essai sur l'étude de la littérature* was completed and published. Robertson and Hume, as well as Loys de Bochat and Machiavelli, were in Gibbon's mind and – the third above excepted – figure in the record of his reading; and his interests show in combination – it is too early to speak of a tension – his will to perfect himself as a critical scholar and antiquarian, and his interest in writing a history of the emergence of the European states system from medieval conditions, which we shall later come to term 'the Enlightened narrative'.

Gibbon did not find – indeed he never found – a theme for a history of post-medieval Europe written in the grand manner, though he was in search of one as early as 1761, while he read and studied in camp. The problem he faced here was a humanist and classical commonplace; Scipio and Caesar had studied in their tents; but in a world moving from virtue to politeness it took on an added historical dimension. As a militia officer seeking to be a man of letters he was involved in the movement and came to see it as an aspect of the history of his own country and his own time. He observes at this point in the *Memoirs*:

After his oracle Dr Johnson

– who was no oracle to Gibbon –

my friend Sir Joshua Reynolds denies all original Genius, any natural propensity of the mind to one art or science rather than another. Without engaging in a metaphysical or rather verbal dispute, I *know* by experience that from my early youth, I aspired to the character of an historian.

He may be recalling his schoolboy visit to Stourhead, and the books he found there.

While I served in the Militia, before and after the publication of my Essay, this idea ripened in my mind; nor can I paint in more lively colours the feelings of the moment, than by transcribing some passages, under their respective dates, from a journal which I kept at that time.[11]

The denial of original genius is anti-essentialist enough to be part of that enlightenment which reduced the metaphysical to the verbal; however, Gibbon is asserting the essence of his self by insisting on his involvement in history. The passages in the *Memoirs* transcribed (and

[8] *Journal A*, p. 30 (4 August 1761); clearly written in retrospect.
[9] *Journal A*, p. 103 (26 December 1762).
[10] *Journal A*, p. 104. This is a retrospect of the year 1762.
[11] *Memoirs*, p. 119 (*A*, p. 193, Memoir B). Gibbon presumably claims friendship with Reynolds as a fellow member of the Literary Club.

somewhat adapted) from his journals record his search for a historical subject, and this in turn tells us something about the tensions between values in his culture as it moved through history.

His first choice was Charles VIII's invasion of Italy in 1494, an episode already recognised as inaugurating the rivalry of Valois and Habsburg, and with this bipolarity the 'balance of power' which characterised the modern European states system.[12] Gibbon wrote a treatise of ten pages on Charles VIII's claim to the crown of Naples; rather interestingly it is in French, perhaps because he had been reading in the *Mémoires de l'Académie* on the subject,[13] but perhaps because he was already unsure whether English or French should be his language as a historian. Lord Sheffield, his literary executor, translated it into English,[14] and because Gibbon's writings in French remain uncollected the original survives only among his papers.[15] It is also noteworthy that this treatise is juristic rather than historical, rejecting the *jus conquestus* and enquiring what basis Charles's claim had in *jus gentium* and *jus naturale*. The circumstance is of interest to those who hold that Enlightened historiography originated in a more sophisticated jurisprudence;[16] but it tells us that Gibbon did not yet know how to exploit the opportunity which the episode of 1494 offered for a narrative history in the grand manner. The Valois claim to Naples looked back to the Angevin incursion of 1266, which as Gibbon knew from Giannone had overthrown the Hohenstaufen and ended the wars of the Innocentine papacy against the Germanic empire; and it looked forward to the ages of Charles V and Louis XIV. In the summer of 1761, however, Gibbon rejected the subject

as too remote from us, and rather an introduction to great events than great in itself.[17]

Its history, we may add, had been written by Francesco Guicciardini – with whom Gibbon's interest in Florentine literature would have made him acquainted[18] – and within a few years would be made a central episode in the formation of Europe by William Robertson in his *View of the Progress of Society in Europe* and his *History of Charles V* (1769). Gibbon had already read Robertson's *History of Scotland* and the Tudor and

---

[12] When the present writer was introduced to European history as a freshman in 1942, it was still a point of doctrine that 'modern history' began with this invasion.   [13] *Journal A*, p. 24.
[14] *MW*, III, pp. 206–21.   [15] BL Add. MSS 34880, fols. 163v–174r. *YEG*, pp. 150–1.
[16] Baridon, 1975, pp. 288–91.   [17] *Journal A*, p. 30.
[18] Gibbon at some time bought an edition of the *Storia d'Italia* published in Geneva in 1636, and later the Florentine edition of 1775–6. *Library*, p. 141.

Stuart volumes of Hume's *History of England*,[19] in both of which works the growth of a states system receives emphasis; and he may have recognised that his masters in philosophical history had pre-empted his first choice of a subject. His next move is striking. After considering a succession of romantic figures, chiefly medieval but ranging from Richard I to Montrose, 'I at last fixed upon Sir Walter Raleigh for my hero.'[20] This was an unphilosophical and foredoomed choice; a courtier of the Virgin Queen, dabbler in neo-Platonist magic, and author of a far from Enlightened *History of the World* was not a figure to whom he ought to devote years of his life; but the project caused him to read all six volumes of Hume's *History of England*, in search of Raleigh's place in the reign of James VI and I and the place of that reign in history. Given Gibbon's current interest in chivalric heroes, it is intriguing that he considered Hume's volumes on pre-Conquest and feudal England to be 'ingenious but superficial'.[21] It would be premature to find in the young Gibbon a frustrated medievalist, and he never repudiated the philosophic contempt for that period; but when after a year's reading he recorded his abandonment of the Raleigh project, his language conveys an extensive but not a final rejection of post-medieval history as a subject.

Between August 1761 and July 1762, Gibbon had been studying Hume's *History* and Thomas Birch's life of Raleigh, but the picture emerging from the *Journal* is one of a more intense study of antiquity. He continued reading the *Mémoires de l'Académie*, for the detail they supplied on ancient life and art, and embarked on a complete and exhaustive reading of the *Iliad*.[22] Here no doubt his intention was to improve his command of Greek[23] – we remember that the defects of his education had left him self-taught as a classicist; but he aimed to read ancient poetry as *belles-lettres*, and this meant that he had a commitment to reading Homer as a source of historical information. The text of the *Journal* from 1761–2 has to be read in conjunction with that of the *Essai sur l'étude de la littérature*, considered in a subsequent chapter; and since we know that Gibbon had embarked on Beausobre with a view to understanding the character of ancient paganism, it is of interest to find him remarking that Homer's dialogue between Zeus and Poseidon

gives a clearer idea of the Greek Polytheism than the laborious researches of half our modern critics and divines.[24]

---

[19] *Journal A*, p. 9; referring to the winter of 1759.   [20] *Journal A*, p. 30.
[21] *Journal A*, p. 42.   [22] *Journal A*, pp. 49, 51, 57, 67–71, 82–3, 85–9, 92–6, 107, 109–11, 113–17.
[23] *Journal A*, pp. 52, 68, 134–6.   [24] *Journal A*, pp. 82–3.

On completing his reading of the *Iliad*, Gibbon remarks that as Homer

was not only the Poet, but the Lawgiver, the Theologian, the Historian, and the Philosopher, of the Ancients . . . no writer ever treated such a variety of subjects. As every part of civil, military, or oeconomical life is introduced into his poems, and as the simplicity of his age allowed him to call every thing by its proper name, almost the whole compass of the Greek tongue is comprized in Homer.[25]

It was necessary to repudiate some ancient fanatic who had insisted that Homer was the actual inventor of all the arts and sciences,[26] but Gibbon was seeking to combine command of vocabulary with language as the key to ancient manners, an enterprise begun by the humanists and continued in a different spirit by the *philosophes*. On finishing the collected works of Fontenelle, he noted that 'the *Histoire des Oracles*, tho' excellent, is somewhat superficial',[27] and resolved to embark on the several *Bibliothèques* published by Jean Le Clerc. These continuous *reportages* of the Huguenot *république des lettres* now took their place in his reading beside the *Mémoires de l'Académie*, which they supplemented without supplanting; and in addition to news of the world of modern letters, they drew Gibbon's attention back to the great figures of Protestant scholarship: Grotius, Ussher, Limborch, Leti, Locke and Vossius.[28] During these months he also discovered the works of Guichardt on ancient military history, and found that since their author had seen service in the field they bridged the gap between the captain of the Hampshire militia and the scholar who was not yet the historian of the Roman empire.[29]

All this immersion in antiquity and the most advanced of its modern interpreters went on during the year in which Gibbon was waiting for reviews of the *Essai* and reading for his history of Raleigh. When he recorded his abandonment of that project, he gave as his reasons the discovery that it was satisfactory neither as a biography nor as a chapter of general history, and that

no part of the English history has been so thoroughly studied as the reigns of Elizabeth and James I. Something I might have added but it could have been but little to a subject which has exercised the accurate industry of *Birch*, the lively and curious acuteness of *Walpole*, the critical spirit of *Hurd*, the vigorous

---

[25] *Journal A*, p. 116.   [26] *Journal A*, pp. 173–7.
[27] *Journal A*, p. 79.   [28] *Journal A*, pp. 84–5, 87.
[29] *Journal A*, pp. 71–5: 'So that tho' much inferior to M. Folard and M. Guichardt, who had seen service, I am a much better judge than Salmasius, Casaubon, or Lipsius: mere scholars, who perhaps had never seen a battalion under arms.'

sense of *Mallet* and *Robertson*, and the impartial philosophy of *Hume*. Could I even surmount these obstacles, I should shrink with terror from the modern history of England, where every character is a problem and every reader is a friend or an enemy: where a writer is supposed to hoist a flag of party, and is devoted to damnation by the adverse faction.[30]

We are looking at an account of Gibbon's decision to avoid both the history of England and any subject treated by Robertson or Hume. It was true that the former was dangerous territory; Hume's attempt to write a non-factious history had been greeted with fury by all factions, who had proceeded to classify it as factious according to their own factious lights; and Gibbon, with his Jacobite background and Catholic past, was no man for the arena in which such combats went on. But Hume's was also an attempt to write a philosophical history, geared to the accounts of the movements from fanaticism to rational religion, and from warlike virtue to commercial politeness. Raleigh would be a hard man to fit into any such schema, and nobody outside England could be expected to take an interest in him.[31] The *Memoirs* now cite the *Journals* as isolating two major historical projects, neither of which Gibbon in the end carried out but which provide evidence that he was still looking for a subject in philosophical history which would bring him a European reputation. One was a history of the Swiss wars of independence, the other a history of the decline of the republic of Florence from Cosimo il Vecchio to Cosimo il Granduca:

The one is a poor virtuous state which emerges into glory and liberty, the other a republic rich and corrupt, which, by degrees, loses its independency and sinks into the arms of a master. Both lessons equally usefull... What makes this subject still more precious are two fine *morceaux* for a Philosophical historian, and which are essential parts of it, the Restoration of Learning in Europe by Lorenzo de Medicis and the character and fate of Savonarola. The Medicis (*stirps quasi fataliter nata ad instauranda vel fovenda studia, Lips. Epist. ad German:. et Gall:, Ep. VII*) employed letters to strengthen their power and their enemies opposed them with religion.[32]

In the *Memoirs*, Gibbon modified this to read:

the one a poor, warlike, virtuous Republic which emerges into glory and freedom; the other a Commonwealth, soft, opulent and corrupt, which by just degrees is precipitated from the abuse, to the loss of her liberty; both lessons are

[30] *Journal A*, p.103; transcribed *Memoirs*, p. 121.
[31] *Memoirs*, p. 122 (*A*, p. 196). A portrait of Raleigh hangs by the portrait of Locke in the entry to Monticello; what would be Jefferson's image of the Elizabethan hero?
[32] *Journal A*, p. 104.

perhaps equally instructive... The character and fate of Savonarola, and the revival of the arts and letters in Italy will be essentially connected with the elevation of the family and the fall of the Republic. The Medicis (stirps quasi fataliter nata ad instauranda vel fovenda studia, Lipsius ad Germanos et Gallos. Epist. VII) were illustrated by the patronage of learning, and enthusiasm was the most formidable weapon of their adversaries.[33]

Behind this Plutarchan antithesis of virtue and corruption something else is lurking. Voltaire in the *Siècle de Louis XIV* had grouped the age of Lorenzo de' Medici with those of Pericles, Augustus and Louis as moments at which the arts had flourished under the patronage of a single ruler; it is one of the most monarchical and least republican pronouncements in the historiography of Enlightenment. Gibbon visibly has reservations; he almost certainly has in mind Tacitus's pronouncement that the arts depended on republican liberty and declined under the Augustan principate. The revival of the arts is 'essentially connected with... the fall of the Republic'; were they an instrument of corruption? And the poor, virtuous, and warlike Swiss had neither arts nor manners; Gibbon might have read in one of Hume's essays that the polite and enlightened French considered the deportment of 'a Swiss educated in Holland' as the last word in uncouthness,[34] and he is certainly thinking of Hume when he identifies religious enthusiasm as the last stand of Florentine liberty. Fletcher, like Rousseau after him,[35] had identified the growth of the arts, whether in the late Renaissance (as here) or in primeval antiquity, where Rousseau placed it, as the moment when individuals were tempted to give up their liberty, and it was a problem for all societies moving out of the Gothic into the modern condition to determine whether liberty and politeness could be combined without corruption. Gibbon, trying to be both soldier and scholar in the militia transformed into a second standing army, was in various ways involved in this historical problem and was proposing to study it in the histories he was projecting.

There is a Machiavellian moment – that is, a moment of republican doubt as to the movement of history – implicit in Gibbon's new set of interests, and though nothing was to come of his projected Florentine history, the plan for a Swiss one was not given up until 1767, by which time much had happened in Gibbon's life. It would have been a modern

---

[33] *Memoirs*, pp. 122–3 (*A*, p. 197). The Latin may be translated: 'A stock born as by a fatality to the restoration or the encouragement of learning.' It is Lipsius's and Gibbon's choice of the word *fataliter* which arrests attention; were the arts fatal to liberty?

[34] Hume, 'Of the Rise and Progress of the Arts and Sciences'; *Essays* (Miller, 1985, p. 127).

[35] *Discourse on the Sciences and the Arts* (1750); *Discourse on the Origins of Inequality* (1754).

history; the Swiss confederation, no less than the great monarchies to the west and east of it, was a component of the system of European states; but Gibbon was placing himself on the hinge between ancient virtue and modern commerce, the militia and the standing army, and when a few days later – if the dating of the *Journal* is to be relied on – he

took in hand my friend Voltaire's *Siècle de Louis XIV* [which] will employ some few leisure hours, and will afford me great entertainment,[36]

it was because he had been reading memoirs of the Fronde, and not with the expectation of any transforming experience of philosophical history. Hume and Robertson (at least the latter's *History of Scotland*) were in his hands already, and when he gave his verdict on the *Siècle* it was in the knowledge that Voltaire was an extraordinary man but in the conviction that he was not a substantial historian.

When he treats of a distant period, he is not a man to turn over musty monkish writers to instruct himself.

An antiquarian – especially a modern – was one capable of instructing himself from monkish writers.

He follows some compilation, varnishes it over with the magick of his style, and produces a most agreeable, superficial, inaccurate performance. But there [in the reign of Louis XIV] the information both written and oral lay within his reach, and he seems to have taken great pains to consult it. Without any thing of the majesty of the great historians, he has comprized, in two small volumes, a variety of facts, told in an easy, clear, and lively style. To this merit, he has added that of throwing aside all trivial circumstances, and chusing no events, but such as are either usefull or entertaining. His method (of treating every article in a distinct chapter) I think vicious, as they are all connected in human affairs, and as they are often the cause of each other, why separate them in History? The first Volume is much less interesting than the second; Arts and manners were a subject almost untouched; but so many writers had exhausted the battles and sieges of Lewis XIV's reign, that it was impossible to add anything new, especially in so confined an abridgement. Besides, those detached particulars wanted less that art of narrating, which Voltaire never possessed, with all his other talents.[37]

We may prefer to accord the *Siècle de Louis XIV* more greatness than Gibbon here saw in it; but he was making some serious points. He does not see it as a revolutionary new departure, since he is already aware that classical narrative and the history of manners are hard to combine

---

[36] *Journal A*, pp. 122–3.
[37] *Journal A*, pp. 129–30. Observe the past tense; is he thinking that Voltaire's career is over?

in a single narrative; nor does he think Voltaire a master of narrative of the former kind. It may be the case that Gibbon was identifying the problem which confronted him in his search for a subject: that of finding one which should be both a history of the transformation of manners and capable of being narrated with 'the majesty of the great historians'. He had not found it yet, nor did he ever find it in the emergence of modern manners from medieval barbarism and religion, where Hume, Robertson and Voltaire all found the theme of their histories.

Gibbon continued his immersion in ancient history and modern scholarship;

having finished Voltaire, I returned to Le Clerc (I mean for the amusement of my leisure hours;) and laid aside for some time his *Bibliothèque Universelle*, to look into the *Bibliothèque Choisie*, which is by far the better work.

1st. From the books he speaks of, he is more succinct in regard to the Theological and Polemical spawn which overflowed Europe upon the revocation of the Edict of Nantes; he speaks of no modern books but what deserve it, and often speaks of ancient ones.[38]

Gibbon seems to have been writing with a hangover, but 'spawn' is uncharacteristically harsh language for the Huguenot *république* to which he owed so much; he may have found the mutation of Calvinist theology into critical scholarship at times exhausting to follow. In spite of a swelling in the left testicle,[39] he continued his studies of grammar and rhetoric, and embarked on a reading of Longinus's *De sublimitate*.[40] There was a historical dimension to this; he believed Longinus to have been the counsellor of Zenobia of Palmyra, and both were to be prominent figures in the 1776 volume of the *Decline and Fall*. In 1762 Gibbon was struck by Longinus's apparent insistence that the arts of speech could flourish only where men were free, and wondered how such truth and nobility of sentiment had been possible in the decadence of the late empire. The answer must lie in the character of Zenobia's husband, Odaenathus,

that great man, and of the greater Zenobia, who both (contrary to the other tyrants) proposed less making themselves Roman Emperors, than detaching the East from the Empire, and erecting a new Monarchy upon quite different foundations.[41]

Here is a foretaste of his later work, but his knowledge of Longinus, Odaenathus and Zenobia may have dated from Echard and Howel, and

---

[38] *Journal A*, pp. 130–1.   [39] *Journal A*, p. 136. Gibbon was in the end to die of this malady.
[40] *Journal A*, pp. 138–42, 154–7, 163–6, 169–73. *Library*, p. 182.   [41] *Journal A*, pp. 139–40.

his present studies were focussed upon rhetoric. On completing his reading of Longinus, he began, 'as a natural supplement', an equally attentive reading of Edmund Burke's *Philosophical Enquiry into the Nature of our Ideas of the Sublime and Beautiful*,[42] and while he found the two works very different, it does not appear that he considered them as the product of separate moments in history. His enquiries could be critical without being historical; he was educating himself in taste. It was again under Le Clerc's guidance that he studied the life of Erasmus, and wondered how a man of genius but such ignoble personal character should have become an oracle to all Europe. In language recalling that of d'Alembert, with whom he had taken issue in the *Essai*, Gibbon remarks:

we must say that it was owing to the time when he lived; when the world awakening from a sleep of a thousand years, all orders of men applied themselves to letters with an Enthusiasm which produced in them the highest esteem and veneration for one of their principal restorers.[43]

Enthusiasm could beget fanaticism and even idolatry; but the Renaissance idolatry of ancient texts had been satisfyingly satirised by Erasmus himself in the *Ciceronianus*.[44] One of the giants of critical scholarship – this time a man, unlike Erasmus, utterly devoid of religious scepticism – makes his appearance when Gibbon records that he has been reading Tillemont's *Histoire des empereurs* for more information about Odaenathus and Zenobia, and finds it much better to read the *Historia Augusta* as digested by the great Jansenist

than in the originals, who have neither method, accuracy, eloquence, or Chronology. I think them below the worst monkish Chronicles we have extant,[45]

than which there could be no stronger language. Together with Beausobre and Le Clerc from the Protestant camp, Gibbon had found in the more than Catholic Tillemont[46] another of his enduring intellectual companions, one whom he loved to tease but from whom he could not be parted without serious loss.

Gibbon's record of his studies during his militia years – it is of interest to note when he kept one and when not – is of course the affirmation of a life already dedicated to scholarship, carried on in circumstances that both enriched and distracted it. The *Journal* can also be read as indicating his situation in the changing culture of his time,[47] to which

[42] *Journal A*, pp. 179–81. *Library*, p. 82.   [43] *Journal A*, p. 148. Below, pp. 187–8.
[44] *Journal A*, pp. 151–2.   [45] *Journal A*, p. 161.   [46] Neveu, 1966.
[47] Giarrizzo, 1954, should always be consulted on this.

history the militia was itself a contributing factor. In essence, Gibbon was training himself in the critical method of early Enlightened erudition, which believed itself to differ from the philology of the Renaissance and baroque times in seeing deeper into the workings of the human mind and the structures of laws and manners.[48] Considered as ideology, critical method was a reinforcement of modernity, as understood in the first half of the eighteenth century; it was an intellectual tool which accompanied the growth of that new Europe in which there should be no longer any essences, but only manners, commerce and taste. But as is true of all confrontations between *anciens* and *modernes*, modernity was engrossed in the study of antiquity, and could not live without reinforcing Europe's obsession with its classical past. The enemy was not the primitive but the medieval. We have seen how Gibbon applauded Le Clerc's turn away from 'theological and philosophical spawn' to review more ancient books and fewer modern; the 'modern' being the Christian and the controversial. In his constant return to classical and late antique studies, therefore, we are not necessarily to see any tension between the ancient and the modern, once we use the latter to denote the critical culture which fed upon the classical and was itself a kind of neo-classicism. If there is a tension, it is more apparent to us than it was to Gibbon in 1761–2, and lies in his continuing search for a subject for grand historical narrative situated somewhere in the world after the year 1300; we shall find that all the great Enlightened historians found their subjects there, and we already know that he did not. The self-training in classical and critical culture continued through the years in which he had not found what his subject was to be.

   Gibbon did not abandon the project of Swiss history until late in 1767, three years after the visit to Rome when he tells us the *Decline and Fall* was conceived. There is more here, however, than the need to take part in the Enlightened narrative of how the states of Europe had emerged from their ecclesiastical and feudal past. The passage in the *Journal*, transcribed in the *Memoirs* nearly thirty years later, sets Swiss history in Plutarchan contrast with Florentine, and clearly shows that the problematic relationship between republican liberty, enlightened manners and the arts was on Gibbon's mind as he considered modern and recent history; and since he did not mention it, we may suspect that he was not satisfied by Voltaire's proposal that the arts had flourished only in

---

[48] Kelley, 1990.

interludes of informal and formal monarchy.[49] He preferred to cite Longinus's Tacitean insistence that they only throve in liberty, and to wonder how Longinus had met his own specifications under the Thirty Tyrants or at the court of Palmyra. The problems of liberty and monarchy, virtue and politeness, were on his mind as he considered both modern Europe and the Roman empire, and were to prove crucial in the organisation of the *Decline and Fall*. The *Memoirs* have shown us how he used them in constructing the image of his own life and time, and in what ways his militia experience was both symbolically and practically their expression, placing him between militia and standing army, virtue and politeness, England and France. The dilemma of the age is vividly illustrated by his actions in 1763, as the first journal comes to an end. Within thirty-six days of the disbandment of the militia he was in Paris

to enjoy the society of a polished and amiable people in whose favour I was strongly prejudiced;[50]

to expose himself to the arts and manners of what was universally believed to be the most polite people in all Europe, in whose language he was still disposed to think and write. But though the French might have been peevish with him in 1758, five years later he found the Parisians riding a wave of anglomania, the direct consequence of the British victories over France in the war just ended:

our opinions, our fashions, even our games were adopted in France; a ray of national glory illuminated each individual, and every Englishman was supposed to be born a patriot and a philosopher.[51]

The British succumbed to gallomania because they believed the French to be polite; the French succumbed to anglomania because they believed the English to be free and virtuous; yet the one could be believed corrupt and the other barbarous. It was in this cultural tension, if not contradiction, that history had to be both lived and written. And the war just ended had been more than a moderate contest in reason of state between two rivals and partners in the shared civilisation of post-Utrecht Europe. In North America and India it had been a struggle between Britain and France for empire in other continents, which had

[49] Voltaire took this position at the opening of the *Siècle de Louis XIV*. I shall discuss his historiography in a succeeding volume.
[50] *Memoirs*, pp. 124–5 (*A*, pp. 199–200, Memoir B). The passage clearly states that the opulence of Paris is the effect of absolute monarchy, which has concentrated there and at Versailles the cultural treasures which in Britain are 'scattered from Inverary to Wilton', in the great country houses. [51] *Memoirs*, p. 126 (*A*, p. 200).

left Britain victorious, burdened with debt and diplomatically isolated. In German, Slavic and Ottoman Europe it had been a struggle between military and bureaucratic empires – Austria, Prussia and Russia – for supremacy in wide areas without natural frontiers. The American and French revolutions and the partitions of Poland occurred in consequence of this war, which carried history into regions where much of Gibbon's narrative in the *Decline and Fall* was to be situated, but of whose politics in his own time he was not much aware. The renewed Anglo-French amity of 1763 can be seen as beginning the sunset of the Enlightenment born of the Treaty of Utrecht, of which Gibbon's *Decline and Fall* is very much a product, but during whose *crisi* and *caduta* it was to be published between 1776 and 1789.[52]

That lay in the future. More immediately, Gibbon put the militia behind him and set out to enjoy not only the politeness but the philosophy of Paris, furnishing himself through Lady Hervey and the Mallets with introductions to the Comte de Caylus and Madame Geoffrin.[53] With the culture of the *Encyclopédie* and the *gens de lettres*, however, he was already at odds, having published the *Essai sur l'étude de la littérature*, a sustained critique of d'Alembert and vindication of the scholarship of the Académie des Inscriptions and the Huguenot *république des lettres*, which (when Enlightened and no longer the spawn of Calvinism) was to be so totally his own. He rightly believed that this would not prevent his being affably received at Paris, but it raised questions about his relationship to the Enlightenment he found there. These questions were of importance to the author of the *Essai*, if not much noticed in what reader-response there was to it; and in all we have been noting about Gibbon's record of his studies while in the militia, we have to bear in mind that the *Essai*, completed and published while they were going on, states in response to the *Encyclopédie* the far-reaching if not yet mature philosophy of history that lay behind them. Our next enquiry must be an investigation of the *Essai*, not confined to the context of Gibbon's studies but as conducting them into the contexts of Parisian Enlightenment and European (including insular) historiography in general.

---

[52] Venturi, 1979, 1984; Litchfield, 1989, 1991.   [53] *Journal A*, p. 202.

PART II

The encounter with Paris and the defence of erudition, 1758–1763

CHAPTER 6

The politics of scholarship in French and English Enlightenment

(1)

Two years before Gibbon set out for Paris, and at the mid-point of his militia service, he had published his first printed work, the *Essai sur l'étude de la littérature*. In later years he pronounced himself disappointed by this short treatise, which he presented as a piece of juvenilia, written and published prematurely, and there is no sign that he saw it as laying down a programme followed in his subsequent writings. There is, however, a good deal to be learned from a close study of the *Essai*, and in this section of the present work we shall find that it was a considerable achievement for a man in his early twenties, and that it has much to tell us about Gibbon and his times. We already know that it was begun at Lausanne, where he read d'Alembert's *Discours préliminaire à l'Encyclopédie*; it therefore confronts us, and may be said to have confronted him, with Enlightenment in its paradigmatic form, that laid down by the *philosophes* and *gens de lettres* of Paris when they associated themselves to produce the *Encyclopédie* under the collective signature of 'une sociètè de gens de lettres'. The *Encyclopédie* is said to contain a programme of philosophic Enlightenment, and though we may debate both the character of this programme and the question whether it is all the *Encyclopédie* contains, its presence is hard to deny, if only because it seems to have been widely acknowledged by readers in the second half of the eighteenth century. The work was much reprinted and exported to many areas of France and Europe, by a major effort of the publishing industry, not without producing change in that industry itself;[1] and it had the effect, and may have had the intention, of transforming the meaning of 'la république des lettres',[2] so that the phrase came to denote, first the *sociétés de conversation* at Paris where the *Encyclopédie* was produced, second those all over Europe – the 'Europe' of Utrecht and beyond it – who

[1] Darnton, 1979.   [2] Goodman, 1994.

137

read and responded to it, and third a cosmopolitan culture of print and conversation engaged in disseminating forms of Enlightenment which might be regionally produced in many national cultures, but were characterised by the intensity of their interaction with what originated in Paris and was distributed from that centre.[3] In these ways there came to be recognised, and to exist, what we have come to call 'the' Enlightenment, a movement at once cosmopolitan and Francocentric, with the result that the Paris of the *philosophes* continued to assert the claim to intellectual and cultural leadership in 'Europe' already put forward by the court culture of the *grand siècle* , and European history was written in terms of the transition from *grand siècle* to *siècle des lumières*; the latter both rebelling against and continuing the former. We shall meet both d'Alembert and (later) Voltaire as self-consciously the historians of this transition and of Enlightenment in this sense.

There is no question of the actuality of the processes just described – though it is a question how long it took to recognise and invent them – and there is no doubt that such a cosmopolitan and hegemonic 'Enlightenment', together with the various reactions against it, did come to exist. What is being challenged here is its title to be called 'The Enlightenment'; it is a premise that Gibbon is too massively Enlightened a figure to be either included in it or defined by his exclusion from it; and we are engaged in a search for other 'Enlightenments' with which he may be connected, and consequently for a plurality of Enlightenments which cannot appropriately be grouped together and unified by employment of a definite article. The 'cosmopolitan' and 'European' character of 'Enlightenment' thus pluralised is not being denied – it is an incidental, not an essential effect that some emphasis must fall on 'Enlightenment in national contexts'[4] – but it is being complicated, by an intensification of the patterns of exchange and interaction which it is shown to have contained. Gibbon's early life, with its forced exile and movements between English and Franco-Swiss culture, has enabled us to begin distinguishing between a number of 'Enlightenments', of which some are and others are not to be described in 'national' terms. There has been a Protestant Enlightenment, consisting in significant degree of reaction against Calvinism as well as of resistance to Tridentine and Gallican Catholicism, in whose history England figures both as regional variant and as independent contributor; and on a level exceeding the doctrinal, there has emerged a Utrecht Enlightenment, consisting in a

---

[3] Venturi, 1969, 1971, 1976, 1979, and 1984.   [4] Porter and Teich, 1981; Robertson, 1997b.

reorganisation of the European states system, ideologically aimed at superseding universal monarchy, wars of religion and papal supremacy, in a historical series extending so far back as a supersession of the ancient by the modern and forming the grand narrative of Enlightened historiography including Gibbon's *Decline and Fall*. It is to be added, by way of caution, that on the Protestant front we have not yet considered Scottish Enlightenment and its historiography, and that though we have identified France as an agent in creating the European order shaped by the Treaty of Utrecht, we have not begun to consider the grand and central narrative of how Enlightenment, in the above or any other sense, may be said to have taken shape in Catholic France, other than the Huguenot diaspora.

Whatever the processes which this entailed, the launching of the *Encyclopédie* is now and was soon after it happened recognised as a moment when they came together and became a European phenomenon. The problem of Gibbon's place in the history of Enlightenment may be defined by the circumstances that his response to d'Alembert's *Discours préliminaire* was instantly hostile and that to the *Encyclopédie* as a whole remained dismissive; we need to decide from what he excluded himself by this rejection and with what he may be identified in consequence of it. In the first place it must be pointed out that he began his response to d'Alembert in Lausanne and completed it in England; these two Protestant cultures – and, we may add, what Enlightenment signified in them – play their part in shaping this response, which is in part a declaration of allegiance to the old *république des lettres* against the new. In the second place, however, the *Essai* was written and published in French, though in England at a time of war against France, in which Gibbon was serving as an officer; the hegemony of French letters was both recognised and contested in England, and the *Memoirs* give testimony to the deep ambivalent relationship between French and English culture which existed as late as 1763. In the third place, Gibbon did not look on French culture as a monolith; the *Essai* proclaims an allegiance to the Académie des Inscriptions et Belles-Lettres as strong as that to the Remonstrant-Huguenot *république*, and its character is at the same time profoundly Montesquieuan. The *Memoirs*, we shall find, elaborate a distinction between *académiciens* and *philosophes* which will have to be considered in its proper place; but if Gibbon came, as others did, to attribute to the *Encyclopédie* a philosophic and political programme to which he declared himself opposed, that was not the point at which his criticism of d'Alembert originated. The *Essai* endorses the statement in the *Memoirs* that Gibbon as early as 1758 resented what he thought to be d'Alembert's downgrading to the status of mechanical operation of what was termed 'erudition', and set himself to show that this was both imaginatively and philosophically important. From his 'defence of erudition' important consequences may possibly be deduced.

As we do so, we shall necessarily encounter the concepts of history and historiography. The *Essai* is concerned with the *étude de la littérature*, of which histories formed only one among many genres; it is not a defence of history as a genre outstanding among the others. Gibbon was, while he prepared it for publication, engaged in a quest for the subject of an ambitious historical narrative, but we are not to regard that quest as of central importance to the structure of the *Essai*. It is the case, as we shall see when we anatomise this text, that the concept of erudition that emerges is in a certain sense profoundly historical, and that the same comes to be true of what Gibbon means by 'the study of literature'; but though it was coming to be recognised that the word 'history' could be extended to include the new meanings that the pursuit of erudition was bringing to it, these had not yet been substituted for or synthesised with the older meanings derived from classical and rhetorical historiography. We arrive here at a point where we must consider Arnaldo Momigliano's dictum that the problem of eighteenth-century historiography, which Gibbon triumphantly solved, was the reconciliation of erudite (or 'antiquarian') scholarship, Renaissance and baroque in its origins, with the new 'philosophical' history generated with Enlightenment.[5] To this it is necessary to add that the two, together or apart, had to be reconciled with the narrative historiography whose origins were much older; but we cannot explore this question in detail before we expound both the Momiglianan formula and the various kinds of historiography which were open to, and made demands upon, the eighteenth-century mind. It was towards this problematic that the debate between d'Alembert and Gibbon must be seen moving; but the problems of erudition and literature that concerned them were broader in range and must be considered first.

In his *Memoirs* – written long after – Gibbon defined an aesthetic and philosophical problem with which the triumph of 'philosophy' as defining Enlightenment had confronted him and moved him to compose the *Essai*. The text of the latter is independently available and we

---

[5] Momigliano, 1955, 1966.

may test the *Memoirs* by it. The later work says:

In France, to which my ideas were confined, the learning and language of Greece and Rome were neglected by a philosophic age. The guardian of those studies, the Academy of inscriptions ['et Belles-Lettres', though Gibbon does not give the full title here] was degraded to the lowest rank among the three Royal societies of Paris: the new appellation of *Erudits* was contemptuously applied to the successors of Lipsius and Casaubon; and I was provoked to hear (see Mr D'Alembert's Discours préliminaire à l'Encyclopédie) that the exercise of the memory, their sole merit, had been superseded by the nobler faculties of the imagination and the judgment. I was ambitious of proving by my own example as well as by my precepts that all the faculties of the mind may be exercised by the study of ancient litterature.[6]

Gibbon's problem is humanist; he says he wished to defend the intellectual dignity of the activity in which he was most engaged – the philological and critical study of ancient literature, chiefly classical – against its degradation by the 'philosophy' prevailing in France, the cultural milieu 'to which my ideas were confined' (as if from Lausanne his eyes had been fixed upon France, near yet different). There is a structural confrontation between the Académie des Inscriptions and the *Discours préliminaire*; but the problems afflicting the former are not limited to what d'Alembert has to say about it, which is in fact very little and by no means hostile. The fortunes of erudition in the age of Enlightenment form a complex story, and to understand it properly we must consider what they were, first in France and then in England.

(II)

We begin by exploring the politics of intellect in France since the assumption of his inherited power by Louis XIV, with attention to the place of this process in the history of European historiography. It was a characteristic of what Edmund Burke called 'that ostentatious and not impolitic reign' to organise arts and learning as manifestations and instruments of royal power, and to that end a number of academies had been created, of which the Académie des Inscriptions et Belles Lettres was particularly concerned with scholarship and erudition. Though Gibbon believed the latter term had been coined as one of opprobrium, it has survived and gained currency, so that it may be used here; there is little doubt, however, that some kind of crisis occurred in the early eighteenth century, and of this we have two recent studies: a four-

---

[6] *Memoirs*, p. 99 (*A*, p. 167, Memoir B).

volume work by Blandine Barret-Kriegel, *Les historiens et la monarchie,* and a single volume by Chantal Grell, *L'histoire entre érudition et philosophie,*[7] in both of which titles the link between history and erudition is explicit. Barret-Kriegel's second volume is headed *La défaite de l'érudition.* She studies a series of institutions in which medieval as well as classical documents, texts and inscriptions were subjected to study, and shows how the interests of the monarchy and the church – *le roi, la loi et la foi* – extended scholarship from the Greco-Roman through the Gallo-Roman, Carolingian and Capetian periods. To understand the significance of this fully we must await the reconstruction of the history of historiography; but it is already clear that erudition was associated with the study of history, and that both were exposed in the late seventeenth century to a variety of sceptical attacks, which explain her use of the term *défaite.*

Her first volume, *Jean Mabillon 1632–1717,* brings her in company with Marc Bloch, since Mabillon was the great Benedictine scholar whose *De re diplomatica* (1681) was in Bloch's judgment a victory for the human spirit displayed in critical and historical research.[8] Undertaken in reply to the Jesuit Bollandist scholar Papebroeck, who had adjudged all monastic charters unreliable, Mabillon's treatise indicated the methods by which the authentic might be distinguished from the inauthentic, and in so doing, Bloch declared, took a giant step towards the cardinal principle of historical research: that every document may be made to yield more information than its author meant to put there, which is how we recognise it as the authentic product of its historical milieu. Papebroeck, it is significant to observe, was delighted to see his own scepticism, with its pyrrhonist implications, dispelled and the company of clerical scholars restored to a universe in which the true might be known from the false; criticism reinforced authority by putting it to the test; but Barret-Kriegel goes on to recount the great *querelle* between Mabillon and Rancé, abbot of La Trappe, a *frondeur* turned *dévot,* who held that a monk's business was prayer, discipline and spiritual exercises, and that one who had renounced the world had not time to write a history which could be situated only in it.[9] The challenge has been brought in our own time by Maurice Cowling (a *frondeur* of less devotion) against Dom David Knowles, Regius Professor at Cambridge,[10] and we may find Voltaire, Hume and Gibbon concurring that a monk should not write history, not

---

[7] Barret-Kriegel, 1988–9; Grell, 1993.   [8] Bloch, 1952, pp. 35–8, 64–7.
[9] Barret-Kriegel, 1988–9, I, pp. 87–146, and II, pp. 254–68.
[10] Cowling, 1980, I, part II, ch. 5, pp. 129–55.

because having renounced the world he was above writing history, but because he was beneath it; Gibbon describes Gildas as 'a monk, who in the profound ignorance of human life had presumed to exercise the office of historian'.[11] Here is erudition attacked by Rancé in the name of spirituality; we have some distance to go before we see it attacked by what Momigliano termed – or, to be fair, saw the *érudits* as terming – 'the invasion of the holy precincts of history by a fanatic gang of philosophers who travelled very light'.[12]

To begin our understanding of the process, we return to Barret-Kriegel's account of what happened within *la monarchie*. She studies in turn three great institutions of learning: the Benedictine Congregation of Saint-Maur at Saint-Germain-des-Près,[13] to which Mabillon belonged; the Académie des Inscriptions et Belles-Lettres,[14] of great importance to Gibbon, who complained of its 'degradation' in the passage quoted from his *Memoirs*;[15] and the Cabinet des Chartes,[16] belonging mainly to the second half of the eighteenth century and less closely related to the problems treated here. Though the Congregation of Saint-Maur was not a royal foundation in the same direct sense as the Académie des Inscriptions, it is clear that Mabillon and his brother-scholars were servants of the monarchy as well as of the church. The cast of their minds was in this sense Gallican; the diplomas and charters whose authenticity and inauthenticity they strove to distinguish had been granted in a France where royal authority existed together with abbatial, episcopal and papal; and there is an important sense in which the criticism of charters was a reinforcement of their authority, and of whatever authority had granted them. This meaning lies behind the three very important claims made by Mabillon on behalf of *érudits* like himself: that such a *savant* was 'un historien' (a significantly new assertion coming from one who did not write narrative histories),[17] 'un juge' (let us recall Gibbon's 'nobler faculties of the imagination and the judgment'), and 'une personne publique'.[18] It is the third claim which should detain us. Rancé of La Trappe might ask whether a monk living under the Rule of St Benedict could be 'une personne publique', but Mabillon was saying that an *historien*'s function made him one; he inhabited a public

---

[11] *Decline and Fall*, ch. 38; Womersley, II, p. 196; Bury, IV, p. 159.
[12] Momigliano, 1966, p. 42.   [13] Barret-Kriegel, 1988–9, III, part 1, pp. 23–188.
[14] *Ibid.*, part 2, pp. 171–322.   [15] Above, p. 141.
[16] Barret-Kriegel, 1988–9, IV, part 2, pp. 7–96.
[17] Barret-Kriegel, 1988–9, II, p. 149, quotes Pére Bastide as writing: 'un homme qui n'a jamais écrit l'histoire et qui n'a fait que des préfaces ne doit pas usurper le nom d'historien'.
[18] For these three claims see Barret-Kriegel, 1988–9, II, p. 151.

space constituted by the actions and documents of ecclesiastical and secular authority – not the same thing as a *république des lettres* – and his critical activity was designed to reinforce it by distinguishing its false foundations from its true. The relations between freedom and authority suddenly appear less simple than we may have supposed; and it may be that a historian cannot altogether deny the legitimacy of the social and political structures one studies, and of which one may be a member. It is not altogether a coincidence that Papebroeck, whose sweeping denials of authenticity to charters provoked Mabillon's *De re diplomatica*, was a Jesuit – the Society could be thought both an enemy and an aspirant to secular power – or that the researches of his Bollandist community came under papal condemnation in 1695;[19] Rome did not always find Jesuit activities convenient, nor were they free from ambivalence. We can see, further, that Gallican historical criticism preserved ecclesiastical authority while placing it under institutional and royal scrutiny, leaving its sacred foundations untouched. Those – when any such there were – who regarded all claims to spiritual authority in secular affairs as false might be tempted to reject the researches of Mabillon no less than of Papebroeck, and to echo Rancé's attack upon erudition from a standpoint diametrically opposed to his own.

La défaite de l'érudition, then – whatever exactly may be meant by that term – was a political process involving public persons in a public space; part of the complex politics of Gallicans, Jesuits, Jansenists and freethinkers which characterised Louis XIV's later years and continued under his successors. Barret-Kriegel offers accounts of it 'dans l'église et dans l'opinion publique'.[20] As regards *l'église*, we are offered an account in which the fortunes of Mabillon's Maurist erudition develop before a background formed by increasing ecclesiastical mistrust of Biblical higher criticism – clearly an *érudition* of a very different kind. The publication of Spinoza's *Tractatus theologico-politicus* in 1665 caused an extraordinary shock-wave to run through Netherlands, French, English and German clerical as well as rabbinical culture. Its rigorous questioning of the authenticity of the Mosaic and other sacred books created a scenario in which all religions were both produced and scrutinised by reason under the eye of the magistrate, and it advanced a metaphysics and theology in which creator and creation, spirit and matter, matter and mind, were so far brought into unity as to evoke in orthodox minds a nightmare vision in which atheism and pantheism became one, and

---

[19] *Ibid.*, pp. 255–68.   [20] Barret-Kriegel, 1988–9, II, part 3, pp. 218–79.

the scepticism of the enquiring mind became the enthusiasm of believing itself matter endowed with the power to think. These were the least happy of circumstances[21] for the Oratorian priest Richard Simon to publish in 1678 his *Histoire critique du Vieux Testament,* followed in 1689 by a companion work on the New Testament, works designed with the Catholic purpose of showing that there were enough uncertainties about the text of scripture to make the judgment and therefore the authority of the church absolutely necessary. Once again the relationship between criticism and authority showed itself; but it was equally a concern for the structures of authority which moved Bishop Bossuet to an unrelenting campaign against Simon and his enterprise. To subvert radically the authority of Scripture left the determination of doctrine open to the naked decision of either the civil sovereign or the Pope; and the Gallican Bossuet desired neither a Hobbist nor an Ultramontane solution any more than did a contemporary Anglican. In his mind Simon may have appeared a Papebroeck of Biblical scholarship, but it does not follow that he looked about for a Mabillon. The third danger to which Simon had left the church and monarchy exposed was that of doubt's boundless sea, a state of things in which every enquirer conducted his or her critical enquiry, with the Socinian consequences soon to be apparent to Pierre Bayle; and Bossuet held that it was the structure of the sacred which must at all costs be preserved, as a Mabillon might not have denied but which it was not in a Mabillon's power to ensure. This conviction may have unified all three of the historiographical enterprises in which Bossuet engaged: his polemics against Simon and Fénelon; his composition of the *Histoire universelle,* a synthesis rather than a vindication of sacred history; and his *Variations des églises protestantes,* which together with the responses to it forms the major controversy in ecclesiastical history at the close of the seventeenth century.

So much, then, for the *défaite de l'érudition dans l'église*; it is clear that the issue was less whether textual criticism should erode sacred doctrine, than whether it should substitute its own form of authority for that of the church. *Philosophe* criticism, when it arose, took the form of a revulsion against both kinds of authority, and concerned that of the *érudits* as equally clerical with that of their adversaries. From this we pass to what is termed a *défaite de l'érudition dans l'opinion publique,* and find it to entail the formation of an *esprit philosophique* which in turn modifies our understanding of *opinion publique* itself. The famous *querelle des anciens et modernes*

---

[21] Barret-Kriegel, 1988–9, III, part 3, chs. 1 and 2, pp. 221–54.

here enters the story.[22] It was initially a debate as to whether the classical models of Greek and Roman literature should be contemplated as unattainable or might be imitated; secondly, as to whether they could only be imitated or might be outdone, having been exceeded according to their own standards by the neo-classical perfection of French culture. The latter was the position of the Moderns,[23] and of some *philosophes* like Voltaire; an important component of his understanding of Enlightenment was his conviction that the moderns had completed what the ancients had only begun. Erudition entered the controversy at this point, with its detailed philological researches which revealed that the ancients had lived in a world of their own, and that it could be known in such detail that it could never be imitated. The past was a foreign country, and the moderns were people unlike the ancients, either their barbaric inferiors or engaged in enterprises they had never undertaken. Here was the possibility of a modernism more radical than that of the *querelle*, carrying the implication that each culture lived in its own historical universe; a radical conclusion might be that there had occurred a complete breach with the past, a more conservative one that the processes of historical change were so complex that human action was totally absorbed, and might only be explained, within them.

It is a premise of modern historiography that the *philosophes* of what we call Enlightenment did not go so far, but fell back on the position that all history was produced by the workings of the human mind, and that these workings could be understood independently of the historical settings in which they were engaged, so that the mind could be seen producing these settings and there was a *science de l'homme* to which any *science de l'histoire* was at best ancillary. Gibbon's critique of d'Alembert can, as we shall find, be read as the criticism of such a position; but he was not a nineteenth-century historicist any more than d'Alembert was a nineteenth-century positivist, and the relations between *érudition* and *philosophie*– to give them these names – were complex precisely because the two were not fully disengaged. It can be claimed, then, that the *défaite de l'érudition* was partial but not total, and consisted in the rise of a category of *philosophes* who were indifferent to erudition and sometimes scornful of it, believing that they could understand the phenomena of history without its aid and without allowing it to alter their conclusions. The *Encyclopédistes* may, at the cost of some simplification, be held to

---

[22] Barret-Kriegel, 1988–9, II, part 3, ch. 4, pp. 269–79.
[23] By 'Moderns' I indicate those who took that position in the *querelle*; by 'moderns' those they indicated as writers or artists other than 'ancient'. Similarly with 'Ancients' and 'ancients'.

stand for these *philosophes*. The *érudits* did not cease to exist and it is not clear that the *philosophes* set out to defeat or displace them; it is crucial to understand that they were capable of conducting Enlightenment in their own terms; but their *défaite* consisted in the appearance and self-organisation of a class of *philosophes* who claimed not to need them. The paradox would arise that these *philosophes* proceeded to write history, and could neither do without erudition nor acknowledge their debt to it. Barret-Kriegel ends her four volumes by lamenting this divorce, on the grounds that it inhibited the development in France of a philosophy of the state in its history, which might have anticipated (and in the philosophical sense prevented) Revolution; she has gone on to contend that the state has not been receiving its due.[24] Grell, indicating that the separation of *érudition* and *philosophie* was not absolute, heads one of her chapters 'Fondations et faux-semblants d'une antinomie'.[25]

If we allow these processes to have taken place *dans l'opinion publique*, the question may arise whether this term is neutral or significantly variable. We have seen that the *érudit* might claim to be both a *historien* and a *personne publique*, meaning not only that his office was a public one but that he held a public office, of which his membership of an *académie* might be a sign or a species. *L'opinion publique*, then, might be a tissue of judgments formed among the occupants of public office. There exists, however, the alternative of defining the 'public space' as occupied, and indeed invented and created, by those excluded from public office or choosing not to exercise it, and acting in the capacity either of citizen, the individual acting as public being, or of critic, defining himself as public being through his commentary upon the exercise of office by others. To write history was classically to conflate these two roles; written by citizens, it displayed the actions of public beings, whether citizens or rulers, to be judged by a posterity of citizens; but with the rise of monarchies and states, it had become an activity performed by the holders of an office. The *philosophes* were now tempted to define the *érudits* as office-holders, *personnes publiques* in a restricted version of Mabillon's definitions, and *opinion publique* as the creation of history by those who had no more to do with public office than to evaluate its exercise; so that *érudition* appeared a species of official history, to be dismissed by those who understood the laws of the mind that underlay its workings. The debate between Gibbon and d'Alembert may be read as turning on the question whether such a divorce has taken place, and what will be

[24] Barret-Kriegel, 1989.   [25] Grell, 1993, pp. 19–49.

the consequences if it has. The freely operating critic – one of d'Alembert's *gens de lettres* – may exercise his own kind of power, and it will not be disciplined by the restraints of office.

The *Encyclopédie* was presented by *une société de gens de lettres*, and we shall find that the *Discours préliminaire* offers an account of the history made by the *gens de lettres* no less than of history as viewed by them. How Gibbon thought of himself when he read the *Discours* in Lausanne it is hard to say, but by the time he completed and published his reply in England he was once more a gentleman, a gentleman of letters, or in a phrase he once used of himself 'a gentleman who wrote for his amusement',[26] and the social position signified by such language was very different from that indicated by the French phrase. A gentleman had his property and his position in the country; and however much this was qualified by his need for the favour of the court, the funds of the City, or – though this did not matter to Gibbon – the patronage and interest of great men, it gave him a social role bordering on citizenship and even magistracy, which nothing could take away and which nullified any radical divorce between office and critical intelligence. There was little need of academies, and consequently little need of distinguishing oneself from them; the outcasts of English society – the non-jurors and dissenters, the desperate underworld of the publishing industry – were not outcasts of state. Consequently there might be freethinkers in England, but they were not *philosophes* in the Enlightened sense; and as a further consequence, Gibbon might not understand the *Encyclopédie* as intended to organise the *gens de lettres* 'to act in corps and as a faction in the state',[27] or if like Burke he came to understand it in these terms, he might repudiate it altogether.

Because the structure of English society was as it was, movements akin to those occurring in France, and serving purposes which may be defined as those of Enlightenment, differed from the French in both character and consequences. There was something resembling a *défaite de l'érudition* (the English word for *érudits* was 'antiquaries'), consisting in a movement which employed the term 'polite letters' or 'polite learning' in a claim to take letters away from the older clerical elites and place it in the hands of the leisured and urbane gentries, formed by the new society of commerce at the points where country intersected with commerce and city. Locke, Addison and Shaftesbury aimed at transforming philos-

---

[26] *Memoirs*, p. 126 (*A*, p. 200, Memoir B). The text runs 'a man of letters, or rather a gentleman, who wrote, etc.', and it is of some interest that Sheffield appears to have edited out the central phrase.

[27] Burke, 1791, p. 78.

ophy by removing it from the disputation of the schools to the conversation of the drawing-room. In Oxford, it was felt by the time of Gibbon's
birth that a great age of medieval and ecclesiastical scholarship was
ending under the disdain of a new spirit. The Jacobite antiquary
Thomas Hearne recorded a conversation with a Master of University
College concerning a Dean of Christ Church:

'As for Dr Aldritch', said the Master, 'he was a Despiser of Antiquities.' I told
him that the Dean was a truly learned man . . . 'He was only for polite learning',
said the Master. 'Why', said I, 'that is Antiquity.'[28]

Hearne might feel he was standing in the last ditch, but also that he
had won this exchange. Henry Aldrich had been a leader of the Christ
Church circle who had figured as Ancients in the Battle of the Books,[29]
and the antiquities they despised could only have been medieval and
philological; as Ancients they were committed to the view that classical
literature was of such supreme merit that it could, and must, be studied
and imitated immediately, without the intervention of any critical ap-
paratus. It was the cultivated taste of the polite man which made him an
Ancient. The Modern, by comparison, was not one who held that
English neo-classicism had outdone the ancients at their own game, but
one who believed that there were depths of meaning in ancient literature which only close philological reading could reveal to the imagination. William Wotton, perhaps the most remarkable of this persuasion,
went so far as to claim that there were things to be known about the
ancients which they had not known about themselves,[30] and Richard
Bentley is famous for the (possibly ascribed) remark 'it is a very pretty
poem, Mr Pope, but you must not call it Homer',[31] meaning that
erudition could uncover a Homeric world which imitation could not
discover. If it was Gibbon's claim that erudition both demanded and
enriched imagination, the point had been conceded even by its satirists:

> With sharpened sight pale Antiquaries pore,
> Th' Inscription value, but the Dust adore.
> This the Blue Varnish, that the Green endears,
> The Sacred Rust of twice two hundred Years.[32]

Pope invests the antiquary with magical and alchemical power even
where he is most absurd. It is a pseudo-Popean line which says of
Hearne:

[28] Quoted by Douglas, 1943, p. 247. See ch. XIII, 'The End of an Age', for the topic of 'polite
learning' and its triumph. [29] Levine, 1991. [30] *Ibid.*, p. 41. [31] *Ibid.*, p. 222 and n. 9.
[32] Douglas, 1943, p. 20.

> To future Ages will his Dullness last,
> Who hath preserved the Dullness of the Past.[33]

All the contempt in the world for monkish learning could not conceal the fact that the nature of the Church of England was contested and ecclesiastical history must be studied from the primitive age to the Tudor. The debate was conducted among lay and clerical authors alike, so that they were not separated one from another, but were found on both sides of a party debate; in the Battle of the Books Tories – Aldrich, Boyle, Swift – tried to seize the high ground by expressing a 'polite' disdain for their opponents, while Whigs – Bentley, Wotton – employed 'modern' and critical skills in uncovering complexities of history which underwrote an authority rooted in change. There persisted a high-church Latinity, royalist, patristic and apostolic to its depths;[34] but it persisted in a world where sophisticated historical argument was employed by its allies as well as its opponents.

The paradox before us is that because England was a deeply divided ecclesiastical and clerical culture, party and confession took the place of philosophy. There was no polarisation into clerics and anti-clericals; the latter of course abounded and employed deistic and unbelieving arguments, but as Burke perceived they had no need to organise themselves as 'a faction in the state'. This role as Venturi detected was reserved for Rational Dissent in the 1770s and 1780s. Similarly, because the English state did not maintain academies – the Royal Society and the Society of Antiquaries operated under royal patronage but exercised no royal authority – the politics of intellect, including the 'polite' campaign against clerical learning, were conducted among factious but freely operating lay and clerical elites, and the 'philosophical' campaign against faction – important in Scotland as well as England – went on within rather than against the structures of church and state. Bolingbroke's contempt for antiquarian scholarship is very like Voltaire's or d'Alembert's, and drew on the same currents of feeling; but the *Letters on the Study of History* do not amount to an *Encyclopédie*, and the English deists 'never acted in corps or were known as a faction in the state' because they were never organised as an anti-estate of *gens de lettres*. Swift and Defoe both projected English academies, but it is counter-factual to imagine what their effects might have been.

It was because Enlightenment and ecclesiastical primacy were so intimately associated in English (and, we shall find, in Scottish) culture

---

[33] *Ibid.*, p. 246 and n. 2; Levine, 1991, p. 240. Pope disclaims any reference to Hearne in a footnote.
[34] J. C. D. Clark, 1994, pp. 32–42, 59–87.

that Gibbon became both a philosophical unbeliever and a major
ecclesiastical historian; and this may be found present in embryo at the
bottom of his disagreement with d'Alembert over the place of erudition
in the *république des lettres*. When he was writing his *Essai sur l'étude de la
littérature*, however, he had scarcely resumed thinking as an Englishman,
and the presence of an English ideology in his writings was a recently
fertilised seed; we shall see what it grew into. If he did not yet think as an
Englishman, however, it does not follow that he thought as a
Frenchman. Chantal Grell has written of him encountering the *Encyclopédie* while 'séjournant en France';[35] but Lausanne is not in France, and
it was *au coeur d'une francophonie protestante* that Gibbon encountered the
erudition of the Remonstrant-Huguenot *république* which he defended in
the *Essai*. The prestige of Parisian culture, nevertheless, was enormously
high in both Lausanne and England, and seems if anything to have
increased in Gibbon's mind during his militia service, at the end of
which he set out on a pilgrimage to Paris as a centre of Enlightened
culture. But again, he saw that culture as divided. In the *Memoirs* he tells
us that he resented some kind of downgrading which he thought had
been visited upon the Académie des Inscriptions et Belles Lettres,[36] and
it was the *Mémoires* of that academy which he bought, at no small cost, on
his return to England.[37] He did not buy the volumes of the *Encyclopédie*,
and they are cited rarely and with little approval anywhere in his
writings.[38] In the *Mémoires de l'Académie* he discovered a world of French
erudition which impressed him no less greatly than did that of the
Huguenot diaspora, and was in its own way equally Enlightened. To
what extent he thought he was defending these *érudits* against the
philosophes, and to what extent he might have been justified in thinking
so, are questions yet to be considered; and it is necessary to set the
erudition of the Académie in its proper place – challenged but not
altogether defeated – before proceeding to d'Alembert's *Discours préliminaire* and Gibbon's response to it in his *Essai*.

[35] Grell, 1993, p. 22.   [36] Above, p. 141.   [37] *Memoirs*, p. 97 (*A*, p. 164, Memoir B).
[38] Womersley, III, p. 1214.

CHAPTER 7

Erudition and Enlightenment in the Académie des Inscriptions

Gibbon embarked upon and completed the *Essai sur l'étude de la littérature* in the belief that erudition was under attack from d'Alembert; may we add 'and those whom d'Alembert led and represented'? Neither the *Essai* nor the *Memoirs* is very specific in naming or defining such a group, and what the latter work has to say is better postponed until we consider Gibbon's visit to Paris after the *Essai* was published.[1] We have, however, by now encountered the notion of a separation and perhaps an opposition between 'erudition' and 'philosophy', and the language of the *Memoirs* indicates that Gibbon had come to think that 'a philosophic age'[2] was making light of the detailed textual scholarship he came to associate with the notion of history. If this was in his mind between 1758 and 1762, he may have seen d'Alembert's *Discours préliminaire* and the *Encyclopédie* it introduced as a vast philosophic offensive against values he set out to defend; but we should be cautious in ascribing to Gibbon our perception of the *Encyclopédie* as a grand event, complex but unified, in the history of the European mind. By the time the *Memoirs* were being written – Gibbon left them unfinished and unpublished – Burke (whose presence may be found in them) had characterised 'the vast undertaking of the *Encyclopedia*' as an event 'not a little' important in what he believed 'these gentlemen', the *gens de lettres*, aimed to carry out;[3] Gibbon, however, referred to it simply as 'their immense compilation' and the *Decline and Fall* does not make much of it.[4] We should beware, then, of hypostasising the *Encyclopédie* and setting Gibbon in opposition to all we say it stood for; there is the more challenging hypothesis that it did not mean a great deal to him. He was, in the *Memoirs*, dismissive of his *Essai* written against d'Alembert, and the significances we are going to dis-

---

[1] Below, chapter 10. [2] *Memoirs*, p. 99 (*A*, p. 167). [3] Burke, 1791, p. 97.
[4] Womersley, III, p. 1214, for references to the *Encyclopédie*.

cover in it during the next few chapters were not necessarily apparent to the historian of the Roman empire.

That erudition, and even the materials of erudition, were under attack from the intellects we call 'philosophical' Gibbon did not need the *Encyclopédie* to tell him. In an incomplete essay on Livy written at Lausanne, he remembered having seen it somewhere in Bolingbroke,[5] and this may be an allusion to information or reading supplied by David or Lucy Mallet. In both France and England – Lausanne may have been another story – there is reason to suppose that a language of contempt for *érudits* and antiquaries (we have yet to consider exactly who they were) was so widespread in polite conversation that we do not need very much textual evidence for Gibbon's awareness of it. His encounter with the *Discours préliminaire* may have been no more than a culmination or last straw.

On the other hand, we have found reason to be careful in assessing *la défaite de l'erudition*, which means less that erudition was driven from the field than that it encountered opposition and was prevented from dominating it. The history of intellect, notably in the France of the *académies*, records a politics of hegemony and contestation, and in the *Essai sur l'étude de la littérature* we shall find Gibbon organising a critical history around this fact. It does not follow, however, that there was a *politique à l'outrance*, that the *philosophes* aimed to destroy or even defeat the *érudits*, or that the latter did not share some of the values of the former, which in turn we must be careful not to over-simplify. By the time he wrote the *Memoirs* – which was the time of the revolution – Gibbon was inclined to represent matters in such a light;[6] but he arrived at this position as the result of events, and we must enquire whether the *Essai* can be read as a station on the way to it, bearing in mind that to know the outcome is to risk writing a whig history. For the present it is necessary to emphasise that, as the Remonstrant-Huguenot *république des lettres* stood in Gibbon's mind as one citadel of erudition in which he fortified himself, and found one brand of Enlightenment necessary to his thinking about religion, so there was another, deeply French and Parisian, which had attracted his allegiance by the time he wrote the *Essai* and before he could make any visit to Paris. We must now consider how *l'érudition* survived its *défaite* in the long career of the Académie des

---

[5] *MW*, IV, pp. 427–8; *YEG*, p. 94. Bolingbroke was saying that he would rather have the lost books of Livy than those commentated by scholars; a jest at once Ancient and Enlightened.
[6] Below, pp. 248–51.

Inscriptions et Belles-Lettres,[7] of which Gibbon records that he spent twenty pounds on the twenty volumes of its *Mémoires*, 'which since the year 1759 [have] been doubled in magnitude though not equally in merit'.[8]

It may be that this institution's greatest years ended with the death of Nicolas Freret (1688–1749),[9] who had been its secretary since 1742, but Gibbon's remark that it 'was degraded to the lowest rank among the three royal societies' does not seem to refer to any specific event, and must be set against its reorganisation in 1701, when its province was enlarged from the scrutiny and provision of medals and other inscriptions commemorating *la gloire du roi* to a far more general commission, which made it an assembly of *savants* who might call themselves *historiens* as Mabillon had used the term. This province came to be defined as that of *les belles-lettres*, meaning by that word less the products of contemporary genius – the province of the Académie Française, where the great moderns were free to style themselves Ancients if they so wished – than the literature of antiquity and even the middle ages, in studying which the *érudits* were free to develop the methods of philological and historical reconstruction that qualified them as Moderns. Specialising in the institutional and cultural worlds implicit in Greek and Roman literature, they amassed that rich knowledge of classical and late-classical antiquities which made the *Mémoires de l'Académie des Inscriptions* so invaluable to Gibbon in the formation of his erudition; but this was only one of three great fields of learning which they made their own.

The *érudits* of the Académie were Gallican in the thrust of their ecclesiastical learning, members and allies of the *noblesse de la robe* in their juridical; and in studying the antiquities of the French (and Frankish) church and monarchy they carried on the tradition, both of Etienne Pasquier and the great sixteenth-century jurists and of Mabillon, a member of the Académie, in using critical research to strengthen the edifice of authority by eliminating its weaker pillars. The monarchy was a neo-classical creation laying down foundations in Greco-Roman antiquity, Christian late antiquity and the world of the barbarian invaders whom it claimed to have civilised. Looking further afield, the Académie des Inscriptions expanded its researches into a third field, the study of the 'oriental' civilisations of nearer and further Asia. Through the Jesuit

---

[7] Barret-Kriegel, 1988–9, III, part 2, chs. 1–4; Grell, 1993, *passim*. The best, perhaps the only, study of its culture available in English is that of Gossman, 1968.

[8] *Memoirs*, p. 97 (*A*, p. 164); *Library*, p. 44.

[9] Barret-Kriegel, 1988–9, I, pp. 161–201; Grell, 1993, pp. 84–98.

and other missions, Arabic and Chinese manuscripts and transcripts were flowing into the Bibliothèque du Roi, and there were members of the Académie who included them in their province; Freret in his generation, Joseph de Guignes in Gibbon's, undertook the serious study of Chinese. Since Confucian China was emerging as a great myth of Voltairean deism, there were philosophical and Enlightened, as well as Christian, reasons for engaging in its study, and Arabic and Chinese learning figure both in the debate over the relations of philosophy to erudition, and in the emergence of an Enlightened picture of world history.

There is Enlightenment, of an unmistakable kind, going on in the *Mémoires* and the *Histoire de l'Académie des Inscriptions et Belles-Lettres*. These scholars were *modernes*, less interested in imitating the Ancients than in understanding them, and moving towards the dicta – of central importance in the eighteenth-century perception of history – that

L'histoire d'un peuple consiste moins dans le récit de ce qu'il a fait que dans la peinture de ce qu'il a été[10]

[The history of a people consists less in the narrative of what it has done than in the portrayal of what it has been]

and that the *Académie*'s object was

L'histoire de l'esprit humain et des divers systèmes qu'il a enfantés.[11]

[The history of the human mind and the several systems which it has begotten.]

The distinction between *récit* and *peinture* is worth noting; narrative and context must be differently treated; but the language of the second quotation reminds us that we are approaching the point at which d'Alembert tried to separate *l'histoire de l'esprit humain* from erudition and claimed that *philosophie* could write it better. We have not yet discovered why this happened, but it was not because the *érudits* rejected philosophy or were incapable of presenting one of their own, or because it was impossible for an *érudit* to be a *philosophe* in the more specific senses of the term. The extraordinary personality of Freret shows how it was possible to pass back and forth over the gap which d'Alembert seemed to Gibbon to be intent on widening.

As *érudits* – perhaps also as servants of the monarchy – the members of

---

[10] Gossman, 1968, p. 169; La Curne de Sainte-Palaye's *Discours* on being received into the Académie Française in 1758.

[11] Gossman, 1968, p. 159; Charles Le Beau, secretary to the Académie des Inscriptions, 1768. Translation JGAP.

the Académie des Inscriptions were required to pay attention to the problem of pyrrhonism, and had debated its application to Roman antiquity in a series of contributions, initiated by Levesque de Pouilly, in 1722–4. Pyrrhonism had been crucial in shaping the relation or lack of one between philosophical and historical knowledge ever since Descartes had pointed out that all knowledge based on documents rested on neither sense-perception nor reason, but on the authority one saw fit to ascribe to the document or text and its human or divine author; what Word, it might be asked, was there that could possibly be made Flesh?[12] A vast literature, from the seventeenth to the twentieth century, records the ensuing debate,[13] and had Gibbon been in the full sense a philosopher of history, both he and we should have been obliged to take account of it. By the time of the debate in the Académie, however – which we know he studied attentively – there had taken shape the great response of the learned, which took the name of *la critique*. Mabillon and the Benedictines in France, Bentley and the Moderns in England – to say nothing of Dutch or German scholarship – had in their very different ways shown how it was possible so to read a text as to extract from it meanings which the author need not have intended, and which did not therefore rest upon his questionable authority. Whether the information thus obtained could be verified at a level exceeding that of probability was of course the next question; but so much of what we know as Enlightenment consisted in the substitution of the probable for the metaphysical that any *philosophe* assault on textual information (i.e. *inscriptions et belles lettres*) as merely probable must be a debate within Enlightenment, in which the *philosophe*'s role might prove ambiguous or destructive.

This issue lay behind Gibbon's encounter with d'Alembert, and had earlier lain behind the debate in the Académie des Inscriptions. In both, however, it was the discourse of *la critique* that was employed, with a degree of confidence that necessitated little reference to its epistemological foundations; history was speaking for itself. Anticipating the Huguenot Louis de Beaufort – a figure of some importance to Gibbon, who met him on his way to England many years later – de Pouilly had contended that early Roman history was a tissue of heroic fictions, on which Machiavelli[14] and many another had founded insecure speculations; the Abbé Sallier in reply had argued that it was based on the *fasti* and other pontifical annals, which had to be consistent and to that

---

[12] This problem was most trenchantly explored by Hobbes in *Leviathan*.
[13] For a first sampling, see Popkin, 1979.   [14] *Mémoires*, VIII, p. 22n.

degree reliable because they were the authenticating pasts of central Roman institutions.[15] De Pouilly had countered by drawing attention to the difference between history, which rested on the credibility of named authors, and tradition, authenticated only by the memory and consensus of an anonymous many.[16] Freret, in a contribution of great length, had enlarged the whole problem far beyond the specific case of Roman history, and would have furnished a detailed reply to a fully pyrrhonist argument had one been before him.

In an earlier discussion of the prodigies reported by ancient historians,[17] Freret had declined to take up the common explanation that these were merely ingenious impostures, fabricated by the cunning priests of false – or if one were a deist, of all – religions. Anomalous phenomena, he said, abnormal births and meteorological oddities, intermittently occurred and were reported in modern times, without a class of impostors to fabricate them. What was peculiar to antiquity was a class of historians, culturally conditioned to report striking political and military events and connect them with anomalies viewed as omens. It was useless to blame these historians for doing what was normal in their cultures, or construct elaborate scenarios of falsification. We are listening to the voice of a sophisticated Enlightened sceptic, unwilling to let even his scepticism take control of his intellect, and such a mind would find the blanket dismissals of evidence ascribed to pyrrhonism altogether too suggestive of *système* and not of *méthode*. In his contribution to the volume in which de Pouilly and Sallier had debated, Freret considered what it was like to live in the century after the great

chronologists – Scaliger, Petau, Ussher, Vossius, Marsham, Pezron, Dodwell – in an age when admiration of their learning fell short of idolatry for their authority.[18] They had gone wrong in spending too much energy ascribing degrees of credibility to the ancient authors (sacred and profane?) with whom they had to deal, and then reconstructing the narrative according to these prior judgments; this was not the method appropriate to finding one's way about in a probabilistic universe.

La méthode qui peut nous mener au vrai dans quelque étude que ce soit, est celle qui commence par rassembler des connoissances certaines sur les points particuliers, et qui ne regarde les principes généraux que comme le résultat nécessaire de toutes les propositions particulieres, dont la certitude est déjà

---

[15] *Mémoires*, VIII, pp. 70–1.   [16] *Mémoires*, VIII, pp. 126–39.   [17] *Mémoires*, VI, pp. 108–13.
[18] *Mémoires*, VIII, p. 230.

constante; c'est celle que ne se contente pas de discerner les diverses nuances du certain et de l'incertain en général, mais qui sait encore faire la différence des diverses especes de certitude propres à chaque Science, et à chaque matiere; car il n'en est presque aucune qui n'ait sa Dialectique à part.[19]

[Method, which will lead us to truth in any branch of study, consists in collecting certain facts on particular points and regarding general principles merely as the necessary result of the aggregate of particular propositions already established as certain. It is not content with perceiving the shades of difference between certainty and uncertainty in general, but can distinguish between the various kinds of certainty proper to each science and each subject; for there is none which has not its own peculiar dialectic.][20]

Freret's contrast between *système* and *méthode* is a manifesto growing largely out of this account of the historian as detective, and possesses a historical dimension not unlike that we shall soon encounter in d'Alembert's *Discours préliminaire*; 'cet amour déréglé des Systèmes', he says, 's'est emparé des Sciences depuis longtemps'. The concept is in itself a noble one:

Les Philosophes entendent par ce mot de Système, un assemblage de faits certains, de véritez demonstrées, de propositions évident, qui, liées les unes aux autres par un rapport naturel et nécessaire, forment un seul et même corps, dont toutes les parties se soutiennent, et se prêtent une force et une lumière mutuelle. Ainsi, la bonté d'un Système dépend de la liaison et de la vérité de chacune de ses parties: si une seule se dément, bientôt l'édifice entier s'ébranle, et se renverse de lui-même.[21]

[Philosophers understand by this word 'system' an assemblage of certified facts, demonstrated truths and evident propositions, which, linked together in a natural and necessary relation, form a single body of knowledge, all parts of which support one another and lend each other a reciprocal strength and clarity. Therefore the value of a system depends upon the position and strength of each one of its parts; if any one gives way, the whole edifice will soon crumble and collapse of its own weight.]

This Kuhnian scenario reminds us that geometry seemed to be the perfect *système* because it was incapable of collapse. We now enter a Lockean universe of particularity where *systèmes* are not possible.

Rien au monde n'est plus beau que cette idée: mais les bornes que la Nature a prescrites à notre esprit sont si étroites, que je ne sais si nous devons nous flater de pouvoir jamais ramasser toutes les connoisances nécessaire pour former un

---

[19] *Mémoires*, VIII, pp. 232–3.
[20] Translation JGAP, as are all quotations from Freret in this chapter.
[21] *Mémoires*, VIII, p. 235.

Système général et complet sur quelque matière que ce soit. Nous ne connoissons guere que des veritez particulieres, presque toujours disjointes les unes des autres; et l'expérience ne nous a que trop souvent convaincu de la fausseté de tous ces Systèmes ingenieux, que la Critique, la Politique et la Philosophie ont imaginez dans ces derniers siècles: à quoi ont abouti leurs promesses magnifiques?

[Nothing in the world is more attractive than this idea; but the limits prescribed by Nature to our intelligence are so restricted that I doubt if we should flatter ourselves with the hope of ever accumulating enough knowledge to form a general and complete system on any subject whatsoever. We hardly know anything beyond particular facts, almost always disconnected from each other, and experience has too often persuaded us of the falsity of all those ingenious systems constructed by critics, political theorists and philosophers in recent centuries. What has come in the end of all their magnificent promises?]

One would like to know whether Freret is reckoning 'ces derniers siècles' from the sixteenth century or the thirteenth.

Je ne prétende pas, dans ce que je dis ici, confondre avec l'amour des Systèmes, le caractère d'esprit méthodique, que l'étude des Sciences éxactes a remis à la mode dans notre siècle: on n'en faut point d'autre preuve, que la conduite des deux plus célèbres Compagnies des Philosophes que soient dans l'Europe, la Société Royale de Londres, et l'Académie des Sciences de Paris... L'esprit philosophique est bien différent de l'esprit de Système; autant le premier est nécessaire, autant le second est dangereux.[22]

[I do not mean in what I say here to confuse the love of system with that methodical intelligence which the exact sciences have brought to the fore in our own age. Of this there is no better evidence than the record of the two most renowned philosophical societies in Europe: the Royal Society in London and the Academy of Sciences in Paris... The spirit of philosophy is very different from the spirit of system; the former is as necessary as the latter is dangerous.]

There follows immediately a passage on the Peripatetic and scholastic sources of the *esprit de système*; but 'dans ces derniers siècles', which now seem to be post-scholastic, 'l'amour des Systèmes' has been as dangerous as ever. Descartes, great man as he was, was obliged to overthrow the so-called Aristotelian system – so called by 'les derniers siècles', to add to our confusion – by substituting one of his own, in no way less chimerical for the fact that it was founded on systematic doubt.[23] We learn that doubt can engender *systèmes* of its own, of which pyrrhonism is perceptibly one, when Freret brings the history of the sciences together with the history of textual criticism.

La vraie Critique n'est autre chose, que cet esprit philosophique, appliqué à la

[22] *Mémoires*, VIII, pp. 235–6.   [23] *Mémoires*, VIII, pp. 237–8.

discussion des faits: elle suit dans leur examen, le même procedé que les Philosophes employent dans la recherche des véritez naturelles. La justesse du raisonnement s'applique à toutes sortes de faits; elle n'est point bornée aux seuls phénomenes de la Nature. C'est cette Critique qui fournit à la Philosophie une grande partie de ces faits de Morale et de Physique, sur lesquels elle travaille; c'est elle qui lui donne l'intelligence de ce qu'ont dit et pensé les Grands-hommes qui ont vécu avant nous; par là elle met les Philosophes en état d'augmenter l'étendue de leur esprit, en ajoutant à leurs propres connoissances, celles que les Anciens avoient acquis. Mais d'un autre côté, la Philosophie a éclairé, et a dirigé la Critique; c'est elle qui lui a appris à douter, et à suspendre son jugement; c'est elle qui l'a rendue difficile sur le choix de ses preuves, et sur le degré de leur force. Ainsi la Critique doit aussi, sans doute, beaucoup à la Philosophie. Cependant, comme l'excès des meilleures choses peut devenir dangereux, je ne sai si le Philosophie ne se rend pas quelquefois la Critique trop difficile et trop douteuse: la crédulité étoit le défaut du siècle de nos peres; peut-être celui où nous vivons donne-t-il dans l'extremité opposée. Le caractère de notre siècle semble être, de ramener tout au doute absolu: non seulement on regarde aujourd'hui la suspension, ou l'époque des Académiciens, comme l'état naturel des esprits justes; mais encore on fait gloire de se livrer à cette Philos-ophie dangereuse, dont l'unique but est de toute detruire, sans jamais rien établir.

Il falloit démontrer à nos Peres la fausseté de plusieurs ouvrages manifeste-ment supposez; et l'on est aujourd'hui dans l'obligation de nous prouver la vérité des Histoires les plus indubitables.[24]

[True criticism is nothing other than philosophic enquiry applied to the study of facts; it follows in examining them the same procedures that philosophers employ in research into natural science. Exact reasoning is proper to facts of every kind; it is in no way limited to natural phenomena. Criticism in this sense supplies philosophy with a great many of the moral and physical facts with which it works; it gives it knowledge of what was said and thought by great men who lived before us, and enables philosophers to enlarge their understanding by adding to their information what was acquired by the ancients. But on the other hand, philosophy has enlightened and guided criticism; it has taught it to doubt and to suspend its judgment, and has rendered it scrupulous in choosing standards of proof and assessing their rigour. So criticism owes much to philosophy, and of that there is no doubt. Yet it can be dangerous to have too much of any good thing, and I wonder whether philosophy has not made criticism sometimes too scrupulous and too sceptical. Credulity was the fault of our fathers' age, but perhaps ours has gone to the opposite extreme. The character of this century seems to be to reduce everything to absolute doubt. Not only do we regard suspension of judgment, or the *epoche* of the Academics,[25]

---

[24] Pp. 239–40.
[25] 'Académiciens' here refers to the ancient school of philosophers known by that name. For *epoche* as meaning 'suspension', see Laursen, 1992, pp. 16–17.

as the natural condition of enlightened minds; we glory in abandoning ourselves to that dangerous philosophy which aims to destroy everything and
establish nothing.

It was necessary to convince our fathers of the falsity of several works which
were obviously mythical; today we must struggle to prove to ourselves the
reliability of the most unquestionable histories.]

This train of thought culminates in the observation that Pierre Bayle
was a 'pyrrhoniste le plus outré';[26] but doubt had engendered systems far
less *méthodiques* than the *Dictionnaire*. Freret does not mention the inimitable Hardouin, who had proved that all ancient literature was a
concealed allegory, concocted by medieval monks;[27] but he does pay
attention to the Scottish Newtonian John Craig, who had sought to fix
the date of the Second Coming by establishing the period at which all
faith would have perished, using a calculus of probabilities which
showed exactly when the credibility of all biblical witnesses would have
been reduced to zero.[28] Misplaced *systèmes* were a principal cause of
fanaticism, and pyrrhonism could be a cause of fantasies as well as of
fanaticisms. If they knew this in Paris, they knew it no less well in
London, Amsterdam and Lausanne; but just where it was that historians
learned their way out of it is a larger question.

The contrast of *système* with *méthode* was beginning to take on significance in the field of religion and theology, looking far beyond the
relations of *belles-lettres* with *philosophie*. Could any coherent set of beliefs
about God and his creation – any 'true intellectual system of the
universe', as the Englishman Ralph Cudworth had put it[29] – be founded
on a strictly experimental *méthode*: any, that is, beyond a rigorously
minimal deism? There is another *discours* addressed by Freret to the
Académie, which carries us into the field of comparative religion and
indicates what issues might come to be at stake. *Réflexions sur les principes
généraux de l'art d'écrire, et en particulier sur les fondements de l'écriture Chinoise*
was published in 1731, but bears a marginal date of 1718.[30] Freret saw
Chinese studies as a means for the *Académie* to vindicate itself against its
critics.

La connoissance, au moins historique, des opinions de tous les Peuples de
l'Univers n'est pas moins du ressort de cette Académie, que celle des faits ou des
Langues. Je ne crois pas que nous voulions nous borner à ces deux derniers

---

[26] P. 243 n.   [27] Kors, 1990, pp. 343–4 (n. 69); Momigliano, 1955, p. 89.
[28] *Mémoires*, VII, pp. 294–5. The work by Craig mentioned is *Theologiae Christianae Principia
Mathematica* (London, 1699); *History and Theory*, Beiheft 4 (1965).
[29] His work of that title was published at London in 1678. Ealy, 1997.
[30] *Mémoires*, IX, pp. 328–69. The marginal date is at p. 328.

points, et nous rendre nous-mêmes complices des insultes que l'on fait quelquefois à l'Académie sur ce faux principe.

[To understand, at least historically, the opinions of all people in the world is no
less the province of this Academy than the knowledge of facts or languages. I do
not think we wish to limit ourselves to the two latter, and make ourselves
accomplices in all the insults which have been heaped on the Academy
following this false assumption.]

D'Alembert's criticisms of the *érudits* were not so new as the frame he set
them in.

Les Chinois forment aujourd'hui la plus ancienne Monarchie de l'Univers: ils
ont cultivé les sciences dès les prémiers tems, et subsistent au moins depuis plus
de 4000 ans, avec les mêmes mœurs et les mêmes usages. Ils ne méritent pas
moins notre curiosité que les Grecs, les Latins et les Arabes Commentateurs
d'Aristote, dont on enseigne la Philosophie dans nos Ecoles, ne fût-ce que pour
comparer leurs diverses opinions.[31]

[The Chinese are today the most ancient monarchy in the world. They have
cultivated the sciences since the earliest times, and have maintained the same
customs and usages for at least four thousand years. They deserve our curiosity
no less than the Greek, Latin and Arab commentators on Aristotle whose
philosophy we teach in our schools, were it only to compare their very different
opinions.]

Freret went on to employ the case of Chinese writing to construct an
experiment in the history of language and philosophy. He stated the
difference between an alphabetical script, which depicted sounds, and
one like the Chinese, which depicted ideas, and could therefore communicate across barriers separating peoples who spoke different languages. One could ask, though Freret apparently does not, how ideo-
grammatic writing might have arisen and functioned after the biblical
Confusion of Tongues. There might also be a pictographic script, which
merely depicted things, as the Egyptian hieroglyphics, not yet de-
ciphered, were supposed to have done. But the exciting thought raised
by an 'ideographic' script, in an age when it was agreed that the human
mind received impressions, conceived ideas, and found names for them,
was that there might in principle be such a thing as a 'universal
language', a system of notation which rendered instantly communicable
the experiences of the mind in receiving impressions and forming ideas,
and reduced language to what Enlightened thinking was coming to
mean by the term 'philosophy'. The trouble here, however, was that

[31] *Mémoires*, IX, p. 362.

human communities possessed both 'universal', 'natural' or 'philosophic' histories, dictated simply by the laws to which the workings of the mind might be reduced, and idiosyncratic or 'particular' histories, dictated by experience, tradition, the capacity of the mind to construct artefacts and fictions, imposture, ideology, interest and superstition. The human mind was incurably poetical as well as philosophical.

Dans les Langues parlées, cette raison empêche souvent que l'on ne puisse découvrir la racine commune de deux expressions, dont le son est très voisin, et dont les significations sont très éloignées. Il en est de même des caractères de l'Ecriture Chinoise; les métaphores et les figures ont du y causer une grande irrégularité.

[In spoken languages, this often means that we cannot discover the root common to two expressions of very similar sound and very different meanings. It is the same with the characters of Chinese writing; metaphor and figure must be the cause of the great irregularity we find there.]

After reducing the thousands of characters to a base of two hundred radicals, therefore, Freret abandoned all thought that he might have found a universal system of philosophic notation.

Cette irrégularité est peut-être la plus grande cause de la difficulté que l'on éprouve aujourd'hui en étudiant ces caractères. L'ancienne Philosophie avoit été comme abandonnée depuis longtemps. On s'étoit rempli la tête de fables, d'allégories, de mystagogies: la Poësie s'étoit emparée de la Philosophie; et l'on juge aisément quels ravages elle y avoit faits chez des Peuples d'une imagination naturellement enflamée, et qu'une timidité excessive avoit entièrement tournez vers la superstition. Ainsi l'on employa un grand nombre de caractères figurez ou allégoriques, et qui, sans aucun rapport avec les choses exprimées, en avoient seulement avec quelques contes populaires, et avec les traditions fabuleuses...
  L'Ecriture Chinoise n'est donc pas une Langue philosophique, dans laquelle il n'y ait rien à désirer. On a vu quels obstacles l'ont empêché de demeurer au point de perfection ou elle étoit parvenue il y a près de 3000 ans, à ce que prétendent les Chinois. Je ne sai même s'il faut tout à fait les en croire sur cet article. La construction d'une pareille Langue demande une parfaite connoissance de la nature et de l'ordre des idées qu'il faut exprimer; c'est à dire une bonne Métaphysique, et peut-être même un système complet de Philosophie. Les Chinois n'ont jamais eu rien de pareil; du moins leurs idées sont-elles diametralement opposées à ce que nos Philosophes regardent comme des premiers principes et des maximes d'eternelle vérité en Morale et Métaphysique.[32]

[This irregularity perhaps is the major cause of the difficulty we find in studying

[32] *Mémoires*, IX, pp. 360–1.

these characters. The original philosophy has long since been abandoned. The mind has been filled with fables, allegories and mystifications; poetry has taken philosophy captive, and it is easy to see what ravages it has wrought among peoples whose imaginations are naturally inflamed and whose excessive timidity propels them towards superstition. Thus there have come into use a great number of figurative and allegorical characters, linked not at all with express facts but only with folk-tales and fabulous tradition...

Written Chinese, then, is not a philosophical language which leaves nothing unprovided. We have seen what blockages have prevented its remaining in the condition of perfection it was in three thousand years ago, as the Chinese claim; and I am not sure we should believe them on this point. The construction of such a language would call for a perfect knowledge of nature and of the order of ideas in which it would have to be expounded: that is, for a sound metaphysics and perhaps a complete philosophic system. The Chinese have never had anything of that kind. At least, their ideas are diametrically opposite to those which our philosophers consider the first principles and eternally true maxims of both morals and metaphysics.]

We are getting on to treacherous ground. A perfectly philosophical language, a scheme of notation and expression of the ideas generated by the mind in its successive encounters with the natural world, would furnish a perfect description of that world (whether or not it were a world wholly illusory); but it would necessarily be perfectly coherent and self-sustaining, in short a *système*, and we have seen Freret doubting whether our minds can know nature well enough to furnish us with such a *système* or such a language. Moreover, to construct such a language the mind must be unencumbered by either priestcraft or superstition. Perhaps this is why Freret resorts to the apparently circular argument that the mind cannot construct a language which perfectly describes nature – a *métaphysique* – unless it already possesses *une bonne métaphysique* or *système de philosophie*. What, furthermore, are we to make of Freret's assertion that the Chinese have never had such a *métaphysique* because they differ *in toto* from western philosophers regarding 'les premiers principes et les maximes d'eternelle vérité'? If the hint of irony is at the expense of Christian Aristotelianism, his intentions may be confined to satirising that easy target. On the other hand, conventional deism might well suppose that a naturally philosophical language would lead necessarily to knowledge of a first cause and to a 'natural religion', and there may have been those who credited the Chinese with such a philosophy. Freret insists that they held to no such *système*, and if he is exercising irony at the expense of 'natural religion', there is the possibility that he held to some other – perhaps a 'religion of nature', which was by no means the same thing. At all events, it is not allegory or superstition which accounts for the *métaphysique* he proceeds to attribute to the Chinese; this really is a metaphysics, and the differences which separate it from the philosophies of western Eurasia really are metaphysical. They are based on his understanding of the issues at stake in the recent Rites Controversy,[33] which turned less on the question whether Confucian ancestor rituals were superstitious than on the starker question whether Chinese philosophy had any room for the concept of God. Freret acknowledges the help he and others have received from the Jesuit translators, and adds those sentences already quoted[34] which make the history of opinions the enterprise the Académie is to carry out in the face of its critics. Unlike the Greeks, the Latins and the Arabs, he proceeds:

Les Philosophes Chinois ne mettent aucune distinction réelle entre les differentes substances dont l'assemblage compose l'Univers; ainsi, à prendre ce mot de substance à la rigueur, et au sens que lui donne notre Philosophie, ils ne reconnoissent aucune substance: selon eux, tous les Etres particuliers n'ont qu'une même existence, à laquelle ils participent tous également, et qui est incapable d'augmentation et de diminution, c'est-à-dire, infinie et inaltérable. La force par laquelle chaque Etre existe, ne lui est point propre; il n'existe point independamment des autres; mais son existence est nécessaire, et il ne peut jamais être ni détruit ni produit. Dans le système Chinois, tout est éternel, rien ne commence ni ne cesse d'exister.[35]

[Chinese philosophers make no real distinction between the different substances that collectively compose the universe. If therefore we take the word substance rigorously, as defined in our philosophy, they recognise no substance at all; in their view, all particular entities have but one existence, in which they all participate alike, and which is incapable of enlargement or diminution – infinite, that is to say, and unalterable. The force by which each entity exists is no property of it, and has no being independently of that of others; but its existence is necessary, and can be neither destroyed nor generated. In the Chinese system, all is eternal; nothing either begins or ceases to exist.]

This radically eternal universe – in the most literal meaning of that noun – was not unknown to ancient Greek cosmology, and the *aeternitas mundi* was recognised as the antithesis of the idea of a Creator. What set Chinese apart from Greek metaphysics, however, was the former's refusal to use the concept of substance as instrumental. Scholastics believed that an entity might be known by studying its properties, which

---

[33] *Mémoires*, IX, p. 362. The Rites Controversy, subject of an immense literature, is conveniently summarised in Rule, 1986.   [34] Above, pp. 161–2.   [35] *Mémoires*, IX, pp. 362–3.

were perceived as its essence. In Chinese monism, however, all things
were of the same substance (*ch'i*), but this substance displayed an infinite
diversity of properties (*li*), which combined and recombined in patterns
apparent to the intellect, so that one said that a thing had come into
being when one could see a pattern defining it, had ceased to be when
one could see its pattern no longer, had changed into or been replaced
by another thing when the pattern had been replaced by another.[36]
Freret's account of neo-Confucian metaphysics appears at this point to
be emphasising its Buddhist component; all things are illusion; but this is
not the conclusion salient for him.

Ce principe une fois posée, on voit aisément que la Philosophie Chinoise
n'admet ni création ni providence; et par conséquent ne reconnoit point de
Dieu, c'est-à-dire, d'Etre distingué de l'Univers, qui ait produit ou crée le
Monde, et qui le gouverne ou le conserve en conséquence des loix qu'il a
établies. La Langue Chinoise n'a même point de terme qui réponde à cette
idée.

[Once this principle is admitted, it is easy to see that Chinese philosophy admits
of neither creation nor providence, and consequently recognises no God: that is
to say, no being distinct from the universe who has produced or created the
world, and governs or conserves it according to laws which he has established.
The Chinese language has actually no term corresponding to this idea.]

The distinction between 'Heaven' (*T'ien*) and 'Heavenly King' (*T'ien
Ch'u*) of so much importance in the Jesuit encounter with Confucian
doctrine, the repudiation of the Jesuits by Rome, and the exploitation of
the Jesuits by Voltaire, furnished only a convenient fiction for the vulgar
mind, and even then is far from expressing the Christian idea of God.

Le Roi du Ciel des Idolatres[37] agit à la vérité avec connoissance, et à la maniere
des hommes; mais ce n'est qu'une substance particulière, c'est comme l'âme du
Ciel, et une âme non distinguée du Ciel materiel, parce que, suivant les idées
des Idolatres, la matière est aussi bien capable de pensée et de sentiment,
comme de mouvement. Mais ces idées sont proscrites par les meilleurs Philosophes Chinois, que rejettent tout ce qui pourroit mener à la connoissance d'un
Etre intelligent distingué de l'Univers, et qui témoignent un grand mépris pour
cette opinion.[38]

[The Heavenly King of the idolators indeed acts with knowledge, as humans
do, but is simply a particular substance, the soul of Heaven; a soul, furthermore,
not distinct from Heaven in a material sense, since according to these idolators,

[36] *Mémoires*, IX, pp. 363–4.
[37] This term, probably of Jesuit origin, seems to denote the followers of non-philosophical Chinese
religions, perhaps Taoist or Buddhist.   [38] *Mémoires*, IX, pp. 364–5.

matter is capable of thought and consciousness as of movement. But these ideas are proscribed by the best Chinese philosophers, who reject all that might lead to knowledge of an intelligent being distinct from the universe, and display the greatest contempt for such an opinion.]

Freret answers the Baylean question of how a society of atheists can be a moral society by observing that, for some Confucians at least, the virtuous man, maintaining the rituals and practices of the moral code, finds the *li*, or principle informing both his moral and his material being, condensed, purified and perfected to the point where he may even become an immortal, and be venerated as such after his apparent death, which may be itself an illusion. Those of the learned who do not follow this vulgar superstition nevertheless lay much stress on the pleasure, the sense of physical as well as moral well-being, which flows from the practice of virtuous actions.[39] They have (though Freret does not say so) become Epicureans: practitioners of a non-theist discipline of harmony, which co-exists with superstition at the philosophic level. Freret is in fact at a critical point in the philosophy of Enlightenment. He was a vigorous polemiciser against Christianity, and may have wished for means of proclaiming himself an atheist (for those who could read between the lines); but atheism for one of his generation was very likely to take a Spinozist form, since only there could be found that refusal to separate creator from creation, or spirit from matter, which Freret made central to Confucian metaphysics (and moved Bayle to wonder if Spinoza had been drawing on Chinese sources).[40] But Confucian holism was the elder sister of allegory, metaphor and popular superstition; and Freret must have been well aware that he was describing a *métaphysique*, a *système*, one of those self-sustaining and self-reinforcing views of the universe from which Enlightenment escaped by the substitution of *méthode*. It was well enough to compliment the Confucians on escaping the Peripatetic and Scholastic error of real substances; but their universe, in which substance was unified and properties were illusions, was even less likely than the Aristotelian to produce experimental method, science and *la vraie philosophie*. The Enlightened repudiation of substance might lead the *philosophes* towards atheism; but could they express any form of theism without constructing a *métaphysique* and a *système*? The question was to be crucial in the relations between scep-

---

[39] *Mémoires*, IX, pp. 366–8.
[40] Bayle, *Dictionnaire*, art. 'Spinoza'. The Chinese teachings he describes appear to have been Buddhist or Taoist, which is not to say that Bayle understood the relations between these and orthodox neo-Confucianism.

ticism and atheism, gentlemen and *gens de lettres*. Freret did not pursue it;
but he fell back on the point that the exploration of opinions, of the
diverse *systèmes* produced by *l'esprit humain*, was the proper business of,
and the history and philosophy most appropriate to, the Académie in
which he spent his life.

Le détail des conséquences que les Philosophes Chinois tirent de leurs principes
pour la Métaphysique particuliere et pour la Physique, me meneroit trop loin:
les bornes proscrites à nos Dissertations ne me permettent pas de m'y engager.
J'en ai dit, je crois, assez, pour donner une idée de la Philosophie Chinoise; et je
ne doute pas que cette esquisse imparfaite ne suffise pour montrer combien
leurs idées sont éloignées des nôtres, et combien un langage philosophique
construits sur de tels fondemens doit nous paroître défectueux; quelles bizarres
combinaisons il a dû produire dans l'assemblage des caracteres, qui sont les
signes de leurs idées simples et primordiales; et quelles difficultez les Européens,
qui ne sont pas instruits des fondemens du système philosophique des Chinois,
doivent rencontrer dans l'étude approfondie de l'Ecriture Chinoise.[41]

[It would take me too far to go into the detailed consequences which Chinese
philosophers draw from their principles as regards both metaphysics and
physics; the prescribed limits of our dissertations do not permit of my embarking on this enquiry. I think I have said enough to give an idea of the philosophy
of China, and I do not doubt that this imperfect sketch will suffice to show how
far their ideas are from ours, and how defective a philosophical language raised
on these foundations must appear in our eyes, what strange combinations must
be generated by association of the characters which express their simple and
primordial ideas, and what difficulties the informed study of written Chinese
must present to Europeans who are not versed in the foundations of the
Chinese philosophic system.]

Freret had carried both Chinese history and philosophy to a point not
reached by Voltaire, who in the *Essai sur les mœurs*, denounced the
suggestion that the Chinese were atheists and signally failed to mention
the Spinozistic monism on which Freret's interpretation is evidently
founded. Freret was a more radical *philosophe* than Voltaire; yet he wrote
from within the citadel of *érudition*, and used it to write both radical
philosophy and comparative history. When he died in 1749, Montesquieu's *Esprit des lois* was a year old, a monumental union of *robe*
erudition and *philosophie*; but the foundations of the *Encyclopédie* were laid
and d'Alembert's *Discours préliminaire* was two years in the future.
D'Alembert aimed both to record and to inflict a defeat upon erudition,
and we shall have to understand the historical moment at which he so
intended as we confront his text with that of Gibbon's *Essai sur l'étude de la
littérature*.

[41] *Mémoires*, IX, pp. 368–9.

CHAPTER 8

D'Alembert's 'Discours préliminaire': the philosophe perception of history

(1)

We have now to consider what d'Alembert intended in the *Discours préliminaire à l'Encyclopédie*: what were the foundations of its critique of erudition, and what had this to do with his desire to stabilise a class of *gens de lettres*? These questions must be explored in the light of a further generalisation: d'Alembert was by no means indifferent to history, but set up a contrast between an ideal and an actual history which led him to some remarkable historical insights. The *Discours* presents both a scheme of 'l'histoire philosophique que nous venons de donner de l'origine de nos idées',[1] and a study of 'l'ordre historique des progrès de l'esprit;'[2] and d'Alembert is clear as to the distinction between a 'natural history' of the human mind and the study of its development in actual or civil history, the product of contingency as well as nature:

nous avons suivi dans le Système encyclopédique l'ordre métaphysique des opérations de l'Esprit, plutôt que l'ordre historique de ses progrès depuis la renaissance des lettres...[3]

[we have followed the metaphysical order of the operations of the mind in the encyclopedic system rather than the historical order of its progress since the renaissance of letters.][4]

The sharp distinction here drawn between scientific model and historical narrative heightens d'Alembert's awareness of the latter and does not tempt him to dismiss it as trivial, and Gibbon probably objected to nothing in d'Alembert's history of the enlightened mind beyond the practical implications of its epistemology. The *Essai*'s response to the *Discours préliminaire* is less an incident in the history of

---

[1] *Discours*, p. xiv. [2] *Discours*, p. xv. [3] *Discours*, p. xxv.
[4] Schwab, 1995, p. 76. The words 'in the encyclopedic system' are not happily placed.

historiography than in what we have come to term the history of historicism; the debate is over the ways in which the human mind is engaged in its own history and should learn to understand it.

D'Alembert's enterprise was to provide an *histoire philosophique* of the workings of the human mind, and by its light to make intelligible an *histoire civile* of how that mind had been shaped – often, of course, how it had been perverted – in the workings of a history to whose course it had contributed essentially but indirectly. He had no utopian vision of the future in which the former history should altogether replace the latter; nevertheless, the *Discours préliminaire* is proleptic of Condorcet's *Esquisse d'un tableau historique des progrès de l'esprit humain*, whereas we are bound to see the *Essai sur l'Etude de la Littérature* as the first step towards the *History of the Decline and Fall of the Roman Empire*. The *Discours* is, first and foremost, an account of how the human mind operates to produce *les sciences, les arts et les métiers*; finally, a programme for educating the *gens de lettres* as a class of *philosophes* who understand how their minds operate to produce a history conceived in those terms. But if history is the product of *l'esprit humain*, it contains much that is not so describable, and is even highly unfavourable to the *progrès* (even in Condorcet the word is plural) of that *esprit*. The intelligence is therefore much engaged with an archive of texts, inscriptions and other documents, laid down in a past when the human mind did not understand its own workings and not yet reduced to the order created by that understanding. This is why d'Alembert, laying down as a first principle that nothing is in the intellect which has not been in the senses, has at once to add that this doctrine was accepted as cardinal by the scholastics, but that as the scholastics did nothing right, when they comprehended a truth it was for the wrong reasons.[5] There are long periods in *histoire civile* which are eras of pure darkness in the eyes of *histoire philosophique*; the question is whether their history should be written, or whether their place in history is not better written by passing them over in silence. Gibbon was to encounter this problem in his own way, as in the well-known case of the history of Byzantium; the *Essai*, however, points to a way of approaching it quite other than d'Alembert's.

The *Discours* proceeds to explain how the senses encounter objects and produce ideas, and how the intelligence comes to reflect on its impressions and its ideas. This cannot proceed, however, without language, and with language we encounter the problem of society, which is

---

[5] *Discours*, p. ii.

that from its appearance a primary encounter of humans is with each other. The passions arise, enriching and complicating the work of reflection; 'les langues, nées avec les sociétés' were originally a mere collection of arbitrary signs, but the reflective intellect gradually reduced them, by the invention and application of *règles*, first to words and then to languages, inventing and rendering applicable 'la Grammaire, que l'on peut regarder comme une des tranches de la Logique [, é]clairée par une Métaphysique fine et deliée'.[6] But grammar, to be sharply distinguished from rhetoric, functions more in *l'ordre philosophique* than in *l'ordre historique*; in the latter, the encounter between humans becomes diachronic, giving rise to memory and anticipation which operate in the perceived past and future of language, and there is born an *amour-propre* which makes humans desire to be better known to one another in the state of history as well as the state of nature.

Ce n'est pas assez pour nous de vivre avec nos contemporains, et de les dominer. Animés par la curiosité et par l'amour-propre, et cherchant par une avidité naturelle à embrasser à la fois le passé, le present et l'avenir, nous desirons en même-tems de vivre avec ceux qui nous suivront, et d'avoir vécu avec ceux qui nous ont précédé. De-là l'origine et l'étude de l'Histoire, qui nous unissant aux siecles passés par le spectacle de leurs vices et leur vertus, de leurs connoissances et de leurs erreurs, transmet les nôtres aux siecles futurs. C'est là qu'on apprend à n'estimer les hommes que par le bien qu'ils font, et non par l'appareil imposant qui les entoure: les Souverains, ces hommes assez mal-heureux pour qui tout conspire à leur cacher la vérité, peuvent eux-mêmes se juger d'avance à ce tribunal integre et terrible; la témoignage que rend l'Histoire à ceux de leurs prédécesseurs qui leur ressemblent, est l'image de ce que la posterité dira d'eux.[7]

[It is not enough for us to live with our contemporaries and to dominate them. Being animated by curiosity and self-esteem, we try, in our natural eagerness, to embrace the past, the present, and the future all at the same time. We wish simultaneously to live with those who will follow us and to have lived with those who have preceded us. From these [desires] come the origin and the study of History, which, while uniting us with past centuries through the spectacle of their vices, their virtues, their knowledge, and their errors, transmits our own to the centuries of the future. It is from History that we learn to hold men in high regard solely for the good that they do and not for the imposing pomp which surrounds them. The sovereigns, those quite wretched men from whom every-thing conspires to hide the truth, can judge themselves ahead of time at this terrible and honest tribunal; the testimony of History toward those of their predecessors who resemble them is the image of posterity's judgement upon themselves.][8]

6 *Discours*, p. x.   7 *Discours*, p. xi.   8 Schwab, 1995, pp. 34–5.

From a thirst for historical knowledge self-centred and hegemonic in its origins, d'Alembert is able – it is not clear how – to move directly to the standard classical-humanist account of its moral and political value. The prince, surrounded as he probably is by evil counsellors and flatterers, finds in the discourse of historiography an impartial counsellor; he can judge himself, and imagine himself judged by others, by reading histories which are narratives of deeds and judgments upon them. The question is how far d'Alembert will confine himself within this image of the literature and discourse of history as primarily a *miroir des princes*; but the three cardinal faculties he will distinguish as powers of the human mind – memory, judgment and imagination – have necessarily appeared at this early point.

It is a further question how far d'Alembert was still in the grip of the paradigm which identified the *miroir des princes* with historiography itself. The assumption that to write history was to narrate and pass judgment on the deeds and personalities of princes, statesmen, captains and other noble men was still very strong, and in a world of personal monarchy still very necessary, but the researches of humanists in the vernacular fields had for two centuries been complicating and contextualising 'history' in this sense by adding to it the languages and laws, manners and customs, of peoples. There was a sub-culture of jurists and philologists engaged in this branch of study, and d'Alembert needed to decide whether to include its practitioners among the *érudits* whom the *gens de lettres* were about to leave behind; the more so since d'Alembert was well aware that there existed a great work by Montesquieu *De l'esprit des lois*. Enlightenment had its own need of juristic and philological history, but might have to decide whether to try to wrest it from its specialised exponents. D'Alembert went on almost immediately[9] to speak of its genesis.

Un des principaux fruits de l'étude des Empires et de leurs révolutions, est d'examiner comment les hommes, separés pour ainsi dire en plusieurs grandes familles, ont formé diverses sociétés; comment ces sociétés ont donné naissance aux différentes especes de gouvernemens; comment elles ont cherché à se distinguer les unes des autres, tant par les lois qu'elles se sont donnés, que par les signes particuliers que chacune a imaginées pour que ses membres communiquassent plus facilement entr'eux. Telle est la source de cette diversité de langues et de lois, qui est devenue pour notre malheur un objet considerable d'étude. Telle est encore l'origine de la politique, espece de morale d'un genre particulier et supérieur, à laquelle les principes de la morale ordinaire ne

---

[9] A short paragraph on geography and chronology is omitted.

peuvent quelquefois s'accommoder qu'avec beaucoup de finesse, et qui péné-
trant dans les ressorts principaux du gouvernement des Etats, démèle ce qui
peut les conserver, les affoiblir ou les détruire. Etude peut-être la plus difficile de
toutes, par les connoissances profondes des peuples et des hommes qu'elle
exige, et par l'étendue et la variété des talens qu'elle suppose; sur-tout quand le
Politique ne veut point oublier que la loi naturelle, antérieure à toutes les
conventions particuliers, est aussi la premiere loi des Peuples, et que pour être
homme d'Etat, on ne doit point cesser d'être homme.[10]

[One of the principal rewards of the study of empires and their revolutions lies
in the examination of how men, having been separated into various great
families, so to speak, have formed diverse societies, how these different societies
have given birth to different types of governments, and how they have tried to
distinguish themselves, both by the laws that they have given themselves and by
the particular signs that each has created in order that its members might
communicate more easily with one another. Such is the source of that diversity
of languages and laws which has become an object of considerable study, to our
misfortune. Such is also the origin of Politics, a sort of ethics of a particular and
superior kind, to which the principles of ordinary ethics can on occasion be
accommodated only with much subtlety. Penetrating into the essentials of the
government of states, Politics distinguishes what can preserve, enfeeble, or
destroy them. Perhaps this is the most difficult study of all, by virtue of the
profound knowledge of peoples and men it demands and because of the extent
and the variety of the talents that it presupposes. Such is the case especially
when the man of politics endeavors not to forget that natural law, being
anterior to all particular conventions, is thus the first law of peoples, and that to
be a statesman one must not cease to be a man.][11]

D'Alembert is writing simultaneously in an ancient and a modern
mode. It is 'notre malheur' that the human race has become separated
into 'grandes familles', practising a 'diversité de langues et de lois'.
Something (other than a divine displeasure) has done the work of the
Fall of the Tower of Babel, the Confusion of Tongues and the Dispersal
of the Peoples, that sequence among the successive Falls of Man which
peculiarly concerns the jurist and the historian of society. It was bib-
lically the punishment of the pride of Nimrod, the first aspirant after
universal monarchy and possibly the progenitor of monarchy itself; and
from the doings of kings, so often disastrous, springs 'l'étude des Empires
et de leurs révolutions', so far the sole recognised object of historical
study. The 'diversité de langues et de lois' complicates this study,
because Nimrod (here unmentioned), pursuing his ambitions and per-
forming his exemplary good or evil deeds, might be said to limit his
powers – even to confine them to the maintenance of an ancient con-

---

[10] *Discours*, p. xi.   [11] Schwab, 1995, pp. 35–6.

stitution; but in this passage d'Alembert seems instead to be regarding national peculiarity as the chief source of those *arcana imperii* and that *raison d'état* which render the prince's actions almost impenetrable and oblige the historian to assume the mantle of Tacitus in the endeavour to penetrate them. *Diversité*, then, is 'l'origine de la politique', a superior branch of the science of morality precisely because it is so difficult for morality to inform it; the highest development of the science of casuistry. Is the history of legal and linguistic diversity, therefore, an ancillary of the neo-classical history of reason of state, or a humane discipline in its own right? D'Alembert concedes that it penetrates 'les ressorts principaux du gouvernement des Etats', and *ressort*, so used, is a key term in the vocabulary of Montesquieu; but he warns the 'Politique' – who may be the historian, the counsellor, the statesman or the prince – that natural law is 'antérieure à toutes les conventions particuliers', and that it is in nature, not nationality, that one is truly and ultimately *l'homme*. It is a question, therefore, in the organisation of the *Encyclopédie* and the constitution of the *gens de lettres*, whether the *philosophe* is not anterior or superior to the ancient or the modern historian.

'History', observed the neo-Confucian philosopher Chu Hsi, 'is like looking at a fight; what value is there in looking at a fight?'[12] D'Alembert has reached the point of admitting that there is more to it than the recorded actions of would-be hegemons; there is the *esprit des lois*, the history of the constitution of nations; but he still seems to regard this as a second-class study, lying under the curse of particularity (in Chinese learning it did not achieve even that status). The *Discours préliminaire* proceeds to set forth its *histoire philosophique*, its image of a great tree formed by the *sciences, arts et métiers* in the order in which they emerge from a model of the workings of the human mind. D'Alembert makes it very clear that this *histoire philosophique* is not an *histoire chronologique*; the order in which the sciences emerge in *histoire naturelle* is not that in which they have emerged in recorded history. Recognition of this truth, he believes, will sharpen our understanding of the second kind of history, and of this he will indeed proceed to give an acute and insightful explanatory narrative; but his objective is to produce not historians but philosophers, and to give the more ambitious of his readers opportunity to play the part of these philosophers. Their understanding of the human mind, and how it works in material nature, will give them intellectual control over all its *sciences, arts et métiers*, including the reflec-

---

[12] Translated, in somewhat different language, by Conrad Schirokauer in Hymes and Schirokauer, 1994, p. 199.

tive activity of historiography, which, since its subject-matter is neither *objets* nor *idées*, must remain a science of a secondary order.

Voilà les branches principales de cette partie de la connoissance humaine, que consiste ou dans les idées directes que nous avons reçues par les sens, ou dans la combinaisons et la comparaison de ces idées; combinaison qu'en général on appelle Philosophie. Ces branches se subdivisent en une infinité d'autres dont l'énumération seroit immense, et appartient plus à cet ouvrage même qu'à sa Préface.[13]

[Such are the principal branches of that part of human knowledge which consists either in the direct ideas which we have received through our senses, or in the combination or comparison of these ideas – a combination which in general we call Philosophy. These branches are subdivided into an infinite number of others, the enumeration of which would be enormously long, and belongs more to this work itself than to its preface.][14]

Human minds encounter objects, form ideas, reflect on their formation, and are moved to passions. D'Alembert has already explained the impulse to historiography as arising from certain passions, that to associate oneself with other humans, and that to dominate them by achieving control over the ideas one has of them. But since this association takes place in the order of time rather than the order of nature – with our memories or *idées reçues* of humans in the past, with our imaginations or *idées conçues* of humans in the future – it is hard to systematise it in the way in which the *philosophe* systematises any science constructed by minds encountering objects and forming ideas in the order of nature. D'Alembert's considerable powers of historical insight and synthesis may therefore all be exercised by way of prelude to a dismissal of history from a further role in the enterprise of *philosophie* and the *Encyclopédie*.

Minds encounter objects, form ideas of them, and very early become conscious of their power to do this; imagination is that capacity dynamically exercised and *le génie* is creative capacity exercised beyond any limits that can be set to it. However, aesthetics, *les beaux arts*, originate in *l'imitation de la belle Nature*; in constructing imitations of the objects we encounter, we obtain knowledge of them, power over them, and pleasure from them – or from the activity of constructing and communicating the images of them. There is a crucial step as we pass from painting and sculpture, which mobilise imitations pleasing to the eye, to poetry, which mobilises the names of objects and ideas as sounds

---

[13] *Discours*, p. xi.   [14] Schwab, 1995, p. 36.

pleasing to the ear; it therefore 'parle plûtôt à l'imagination qu'aux sens'. But music, precisely because it deals with sounds so pure as not to be words, 'est devenue peu-à-peu une espece de discours ou même une langue, par laquelle on exprime les differens sentiments de l'âme, ou plûtôt ses différentes passions', and therefore 'parle à la fois à l'imagination et aux sens'.[15] Words and names are recalcitrant to the simple relationship between *les sens* and *les idées*; *l'imagination*, even though it 'ne travaille que d'après les êtres purement matériels'[16] imports the confusing powers of language and gives fresh play to the unlimited creativity of *le génie*. It is not only because the world of material objects in which we live is infinitely diverse, but because we have an unlimited capacity for naming and imagining both them and ourselves in our responses to them that:

Le système général des Sciences et des Arts est une espece de labyrinthe, de chemin tortueux où l'esprit s'engage sans trop connoître la route qu'il doit tenir...[17]

[The general system of the sciences and the arts is a sort of labyrinth, a tortuous road which the intellect enters without quite knowing what direction to take.][18]

L'Univers n'est qu'un vaste Océan, sur la surface duquel nous appercevons quelques îles plus ou moins grandes, dont la liaison avec le continent nous est cachée.[19]

[The universe is but a vast ocean, on the surface of which we perceive a few islands of various sizes, whose connection with the continent is hidden from us.][20]

The intellect has to contend both with the vast tracklessness of the universe and with the tortuous labyrinth of its own proceedings. The first of the two sentences just quoted continues:

Pressé par ses besoins, et par ceux du corps auquel il est uni, il étudie d'abord les premiers objets que se presentent à lui; pénetre le plus avant qu'il peut dans la connoissance de ces objets; rencontre bien des difficultés qui l'arrêtent, et soit par l'espérance ou même par le desespoir de les vaincre, se jette dans une nouvelle route; revient ensuite sur ses pas; franchit quelquefois les premieres barrieres pour en rencontrer des nouvelles; et passant rapidement d'un objet à un autre, fait sur chacun de ses objets à différens intervalles et comme par secousses, une suite d'operations dont la génération même de ses idées rend la

---

[15] *Discours*, p. xii. 'Little by little it has become a kind of discourse, or even language, through which the different sentiments of the soul, or rather its different passions, are expressed...speaks simultaneously to the imagination and to the senses' (Schwab, 1995, p. 38).

[16] *Discours*, p. xiii.   [17] *Discours*, p. xiv.   [18] Schwab, 1995, p. 46.   [19] *Discours*, p. xv.

[20] Schwab, 1995, p. 49.

discontinuité nécessaire. Mais ce désordre, tout philosophique qu'il est à la part de l'ame, défigureroit, ou plûtôt anéantiroit entierement un Arbre ency-clopédique dans lequel on voudroit le représenter.[21]

[Impelled, first of all, by its needs and by those of the body to which it is united, the intelligence studies the first objects that present themselves to it. It delves as far as it can into the knowledge of these objects, soon meets difficulties that obstruct it, and whether through hope or even through despair of surmounting them, plunges on to a new route; now it retraces its footsteps, sometimes crosses the first barriers only to meet new ones; and passing rapidly from one object to another, it carries through a sequence of operations on each of them at different intervals, as if by jumps. The discontinuity of these operations is a necessary effect of the very generation of ideas. However philosophic this disorder may be on the part of the soul, an encyclopedic tree which attempted to portray it would be disfigured, indeed utterly destroyed.][22]

The *arbre* or *histoire naturelle* of how the mind generates the sciences and arts in their conceptual order can never be identical with the sensory and experimental history of how it does so in an experienced and recorded historical actuality. Because d'Alembert is acutely aware of this difference, he is well situated and quite well motivated to write history of science in the latter sense; but doing so must be secondary to the construction of the *arbre encyclopédique* which is, within its limits, his primary commitment. Is it then the case that history can never be philosophy, or that *histoire civile* can never be identical with *histoire naturelle* or *philosophique*? Can philosophy only be the self-understanding of the human mind according to its inbuilt laws, standing apart from, reflect-ing upon, and seeking (perhaps vainly) control over, the history of its workings in recalcitrant reality? This conclusion would explain the paradox that d'Alembert recognises the autonomy of history from philosophy, but at the same time reduces the former to the status of mere stored information for the latter's use. There might even be a latent admission that the *philosophe* is limited to using history in this way and can see it in no other light. At all events, this is the point at which d'Alembert introduces a basic distinction between the human faculties; that to which Gibbon principally objected.

Les objets dont notre ame s'occupe, sont ou spirituels ou matériels, et notre ame s'occupe de ces objets ou par des idées directes ou par des idées réfléchies. Le système des connoissances directes ne peut consister que dans la collection purement passive et comme machinale de ces mêmes connoissances; c'est ce qu'on appelle mémoire. La réflexion est de deux sortes, nous l'avons déjà

---

[21] *Discours*, p. xiv.   [22] Schwab, 1995, p. 46.

observé; ou elle raisonne sur les objets des idées directes, ou elle les imite. Ainsi la mémoire, la raison proprement dite, et l'imagination, sont les trois manieres différentes dont notre ame opere sur les objets de ses pensées. Nous ne prenons point ici l'imagination pour la faculté qu'on a de se représenter les objets; parce que cette faculté n'est autre chose que la mémoire même des objet sensibles, mémoire que seroit dans un continuel exercise, si elle n'etoit soulagée par l'invention des signes. Nous prenons l'imagination dans un sense plus noble et plus precis pour le talent de créer en imitant.

   Ces trois facultés forment d'abord les trois divisions générales de notre système, et les trois objets généraux des connoissances humaines; l'Histoire, qui se rapporte à la mémoire; la Philosophie qui est le fruit de la raison; et les Beaux-Arts, que l'imagination fait naître. Si nous plaçons la raison avant l'imagination, cet ordre nous paraît bien fondé, et conforme au progrès naturel des operations de l'esprit: l'imagination est une faculté creatrice, et l'esprit, avant de songer à créer, commence par raisonner sur ce qu'il voit et ce qu'il connoît. Un autre motif qui doit determiner à placer la raison avant l'imagination, c'est que dans cette dernière faculté de l'ame, les deux autres se trouvent réunies jusqu'à un certain point, et que la raison s'y joint à la mémoire. L'esprit ne crée et n'imagine des objets qu'en tant qu'ils sont semblables à ceux qu'il a connus par des idées directes et par des sensations; plus il s'eloigne de ces objets, plus les êtres qu'il forme sont bizarres et peu assujettie à certaines regles; et ce sont ces regles qui forment principalement la partie philosophique des Beaux-arts, jusqu'à présent assez imparfaite, parce qu'elle ne peut être l'ouvrage que du génie, et que le génie aime mieux créer que discuter.[23]

[The objects to which our soul applies itself are either spiritual or material, and our souls are occupied with these objects either through direct ideas or through reflective ideas. The system of direct knowledge consists simply in the purely passive and almost mechanical collection of this same knowledge; this is what we call memory. Reflection is of two kinds (as we have already observed): either it reasons on the objects of direct ideas, or it imitates them. Thus memory, reason (strictly speaking), and imagination are the three different manners in which our soul operates on the objects of its thoughts. We do not take imagination here to be the ability to represent objects to oneself, since that faculty is simply the memory itself of sensible objects, a memory which would be continually in action if it were not assisted and relieved by the invention of signs. We take imagination in the more noble and precise sense, as the talent of creating by imitating.

   These three faculties form at the outset the three general divisions of our system of human knowledge: History, which is related to memory; Philosophy, which is the fruit of reason; and the Fine Arts, which are born of imagination. Placing reason ahead of imagination appears to us to be a well-founded arrangement and one which is in conformity with the natural progress of the operations of the mind. Imagination is a creative faculty, and the mind, before

---

[23] *Discours*, p. xvi.

it considers creating, begins by reasoning upon what it sees and knows. Another motive which should decide us to place reason ahead of imagination is that in the latter faculty the other two are to some extent brought together. The mind creates and imagines objects only insofar as they are similar to those which it has known by direct ideas and by sensations. The more it departs from these objects, the more bizarre and unpleasant are the beings which it forms. Thus, in the imitation of Nature, invention itself is subjected to certain rules. It is principally these rules which form the philosophical part of the Fine Arts, which is still rather imperfect because it can be the work only of genius, and genius prefers creation to discussion.][24]

The neo-classical intellect was obliged to insist both that it was the nature of art to regulate itself and that it was of the nature of the artist to resist regulation; there arose some historical scenarios in which this became the question whether the creative impulse was not as much barbaric as polite. Gibbon's quarrel with d'Alembert, however, lay in another kind of disagreement over the role of imagination; he wished to clarify the involvement of the mind in historical study, not necessarily to advance the philosophical counter-thesis that the mind imagined first and reasoned afterwards on what it had created. He came to insist, as we have already seen, that 'the nobler faculties of the imagination and the judgment' – the latter term creatively exercised where d'Alembert had placed *raison* and *philosophie* – were significantly deployed in 'the study of ancient literature', the *belles-lettres* which ranked among the *beaux-arts*, and that important discoveries were to be made by employing them there. He objected vigorously to d'Alembert's relegation of both history and erudition to the domain of memory, to the passive and mechanical accumulation of mere facts (or *connoissances directes*) on which the philosopher and the poet were to reflect, shaping and consuming the raw materials piled up for them by laborious drudges. He knew of other ways of exercising reason and imagination; but the argument implies the association by both writers of *histoire* and *érudition*, which were by no means identical terms. *Histoire* might mean no more than the *miroir des princes*, *érudition* the study of the *diversité des langues et des lois*; and d'Alembert had not at this point made it clear that the latter involved the exercise of memory alone. The two were in an advanced stage of interpenetration, which was changing the meaning of the term 'history'; and we cannot pursue Gibbon's disagreement with d'Alembert without first enquiring how the *Encyclopédiste* viewed the character, and the history, of both.

---

[24] Schwab, 1995, pp. 50–1.

It is significant of d'Alembert's mixed feelings on the subject of history that he begins his account of it by positing a divinity, and a revelation, in which he assuredly did not believe.

La distribution générale des êtres en spirituels et en matériels fournit la sous-division des trois branches générales. L'Histoire et la Philosophie s'oc-cupent egalement de ces deux especes d'êtres, et l'imagination ne travaille que d'après les êtres purement matériels; nouvelle raison pour la placer la dernière dans l'ordre de nos facultés.

[The general distribution of beings into spiritual and material provides a subdivision of the three general branches. History and Philosophy are occupied with each of these two kinds of beings, while imagination deals only with purely material beings, which is a new reason for placing it last in the arrangement of our faculties.]

Why spiritual entities cannot be imagined or suggest ideas to the imagination, is not here explained; nor is the imagination's derivation from the material world.

A la tête des êtres spirituels est Dieu, qui doit tenir le premier rang par la nature, et par le besoin que nous avons de le connoitre. Au-dessous de cet être suprème sont les esprits crées, dont la revelation nous apprend l'existence. Ensuite vient l'homme, qui composé de deux principes, tient par son ame aux esprits, et par son corps au monde matériel; et enfin ce vaste Univers que nous appellons le Monde corporel ou la Nature. Nous ignorons pourquoi l'Auteur célebre qui nous sert de guide dans cette distribution, a placé la nature avant l'homme dans son système; il semble au contraire que tout engage à placer l'homme sur le passage que sépare Dieu et les esprits d'avec les corps.

[At the head of the spiritual beings is God, who necessarily holds the first rank by virtue of His nature and of our need to know Him. Below that Supreme Being are the created spiritual beings whose existence is taught us by Revel-ation. Next comes man. Composed of two principles, he belongs by virtue of his soul to the spiritual beings and by virtue of his body to the material world. And finally comes that vast universe which we call the corporeal world, or Nature. We do not know why the celebrated author who serves as our guide in this arrangement has placed Nature before man in his system. It seems, on the contrary, that everything engages us to put man in the passageway that separates God and the spiritual beings from material bodies.]

The celebrated author is Bacon: but if God created man before the material and natural world, the Book of Genesis is mistaken. It is as if a gnostic streak had momentarily showed itself in d'Alembert's thinking.

L'Histoire entant qu'elle se rapporte à Dieu, renferme ou la révélation ou la tradition, et se divise sous ces deux points de vue, en histoire sacrée et en histoire ecclésiastique. L'histoire de l'homme a pour objet, ou ses actions, ou ses connoissances; et elle est par conséquent civile ou littéraire, c'est-à-dire, se partage entre les grandes nations et les grandes génies, entre les Rois et les Gens de Lettres, entre les Conquérans et les Philosophes. Enfin l'histoire de la Nature est celle des productions innombrables qu'on y observe, et forme une quantité de branches presque égales au nombre de ces diverses productions. Parmi ces différentes branches, doit être placée avec distinction l'histoire des Arts, qui n'est autre chose que l'histoire des usages que les hommes ont faits des productions de la nature, pour satisfaire à leurs besoins ou à leur curiosité.

Tels sont les objets principaux de la mémoire. Venons présentement à la faculté qui reflechit, et qui raisonne.[25]

[Insofar as it is related to God, History includes either Revelation or tradition, and according to these two points of view, is divided into sacred history and ecclesiastical history. The history of man has for its object either his actions or his knowledge, and consequently is civil or literary. In other words, it is divided between the great nations and the great geniuses, between the kings and the men of letters, between the conquerors and the philosophers. Finally, the history of Nature is the history of the innumerable productions that we observe therein, forming a quantity of branches almost equal in number to those diverse productions. Among these different branches, a distinguished place should be given to the history of the arts, which is simply the history of the use which men have made of the productions of Nature to satisfy their needs or their curiosity.

Such are the principal objects of memory. Let us turn now to the faculty that reflects and reasons.][26]

Gibbon wanted to know why both reason and imagination were not exercised in the recollection of history, but were assigned by d'Alembert such generically different tasks as theology, metaphysics, physics and criticism. We may note, first, that the actions of both God and man are merely to be remembered, before reason begins its work of reducing them to system. Second, there is a startling confrontation between kings and *gens de lettres*, based on the assumptions that only action and knowledge are worth remembering, and that action is the prerogative of kings as knowledge is that of *gens de lettres*; only conquerors and philosophers are there to be remembered, and the former are as sterile as the latter are productive. Thirdly, the mind is further privileged by the inclusion within natural history – that of the processes of material and organic nature – of the history of the mechanical and liberal arts, which is that of human productions attained by exploiting the productions of nature. History which is the *miroir des princes* is being directly and exclusively confronted with the history recognised by the *Encyclopédie*, that of the

---

[25] The three passages just quoted occur on pp. xvi–xvii. [26] Schwab, 1995, pp. 52–3.

sciences, arts et métiers, and the effect is the exaltation of the *gens de lettres* as the *Encyclopédie* seeks to define and mobilise them. What is at this point excluded is the history arising from the necessary evil of the *diversité des langues et des lois*; there is no hint that the conquerors may also have been lawgivers, or of that *esprit* which produces *les lois*. In terms of the sociology of knowledge, it may prove necessary, or at least possible, to ask whether this amounts to a mobilisation of the *philosophie* of the *gens de lettres* against the *érudition* springing from the *noblesse de la robe*.

D'Alembert's account of erudition, which he considers a kind of hypertrophy of the faculty of memory on which history is founded, begins at the point where he moves from *la division générale de nos connoissances* to

les trois divisions du monde littéraire, en Erudits, Philosophes, et Beaux-Esprits; ensorte qu'après avoir formé l'Arbre des Sciences, on pourrait former sur le même plan celui des Gens de Lettres. La memoire est le talent des premiers, la sagacité appartient aux seconds, et les derniers ont l'agrément en part-age ... Du reste les trois especes de républiques dans lesquelles nous venons de distribuer les Gens de Lettres n'ont pour l'ordinaire rien de commun, que de faire assez peu de cas les unes des autres. Le Poëte et le Philosophe se traitent mutuellement d'insensés, qui se repaissent des chimeres: l'un et l'autre regar-dent l'Erudit comme une espece d'avare, qui ne pense qu'à amasser sans jouir, et qui entasse sans choix les métaux les plus vils avec les plus précieux; et l'Erudit, qui ne voit que des mots par-tout où il ne lit point des faits, méprise le Poëte et le Philosophe, comme des gens qui se croyent riches, parce que leur dépense excede leurs fonds.

[the three divisions of the literary world into Scholars, Philosophers, and *beaux esprits*, so that, after having designed the tree of sciences, one would be able to construct the tree of men of letters on the same pattern. Memory is the talent of the first [group]; wisdom belongs to the second; and the last have pleasure as their portion ... For the rest, the three kinds of republics into which we have just distributed the men of letters ordinarily have nothing in common, except the lack of esteem in which they hold one another. The poet and the philos-opher treat each other as madmen who feed on fancies. Both regard the scholar as a sort of miser who thinks only of amassing without enjoying and who indiscriminately heaps up the basest metals along with the most precious. And the scholar, who considers everything which is not fact to be idle words, holds the poet and the philosopher in contempt as being men who think they are rich because their expenses exceed their resources.][27]

These three republics have little in common with one another, perhaps because there is little dynamic relationship between their sev-

[27] Schwab, 1995, pp. 55–6.

eral faculties. D'Alembert does what he can to exhort them to recognise their *besoin reciproque*, but after assigning *les agrémens* to the *littérateurs* and *les lumières* to the *philosophes*, he can do no more than tell them they need the information which only the labours of the *érudits*, those artisans of memory, can bring them.

Lorsque les Anciens ont appellé les Muses filles de Mémoire, a dit un Auteur moderne, ils sentoient peut-être combien cette faculté de notre ame est necessaire à toutes les autres; et les Romains lui élevoient des temples, comme à la Fortune.[28]

[When the ancients called the Muses the daughters of memory (a modern author has said), they appreciated perhaps how much that faculty or our mind is necessary to all the others. The Romans raised temples to her, just as they did to Fortune.][29]

It is not an encouraging comparison. We may join Gibbon in feeling that if d'Alembert had been able to recognise active faculties of the intellect in scholarship, his three republics would have been less like a Platonic hierarchy and more like equal traders in a mutual commerce of the mind. Between the miser and the spendthrift, it was notorious, there was no sufficient medium of exchange.

(11)

Erudition takes on more three-dimensionality – as, to historians, is not surprising – when d'Alembert turns from 'l'exposition métaphysique de l'origine et de la liaison des Sciences' to 'l'exposition historique de l'ordre dans lequel nos connoissances se sont succedées'. This, he says, will clarify 'la manière dont nous devons transmettre ces connoissances à nos lecteurs'.[30] He was never lacking in awareness of history, or of the moment which his enterprise occupied in it; the question is to what level he was able to develop this awareness, in relation to *l'exposition métaphysique* to which he gave priority. The *exposition historique* begins *à la renaissance des lettres*, of which he gives what was by now the conventional explanation: the flight of scholars from Byzantium, the invention of printing, and (a note more distinctly French) the patronage of the Medici and François I (who in the *Essai sur les gens de lettres* was compared to his disadvantage with Charles V).[31] The *exposition historique* is the more easily confronted with the *exposition métaphysique* because it starts from a

---

[28] Both passages in *Discours*, p. xviii. [29] Schwab, 1995, p. 56. [30] *Discours*, p. xix.
[31] D'Alembert, 1773, pp. 326–8.

point approaching absolute zero; the *renaissance des lettres* was preceded by a long period of darkness and barbarism, in which individual *lumières* were extinguished one by one for the lack of any *république des lettres*:

Les chefs-d'œuvre que les Anciens nous avoient laissés dans presque tous les genres, avoient été oubliés pendant douze siecles. Les principes des Sciences et des Arts étoient perdus, parce que le beau et le vrai qui semblent se montrer de toutes parts aux hommes, ne le frappent guere à moins qu'ils n'en soient avertis. Ce n'est pas que ces tems malheureux ayent été plus steriles que d'autres en génies rares; la nature est toujours la même; mais que pouvoient faire ces grands hommes, semés de loin à loin comme ils le sont toujours, occupés d'objets différens, et abandonnés sans culture à leurs seuls lumieres? Les idées qu'on acquiert par la lecture et la société, sont la germe de presque toutes les découvertes. C'est un air que l'on respire sans y penser, et auquel on doit la vie; et les hommes dont nous parlons étoient privés d'un tel secours. Ils ressembloient aux premieres créateurs des Sciences et des Arts, que leurs illustres successeurs ont fait oublier, et qui précedés par ceux-ci les auroient fait oublier de même. Celui qui trouva le premier les roues et les pignons, eut inventé les montres dans un autre siècle; et Gerbert placé au tems d'Archimede l'auroit peut-être égalé.[32]

[The masterpieces that the ancients left us in almost all genres were forgotten for twelve centuries. The principles of the sciences and the arts were lost, because the beautiful and the true, which seem to show themselves everywhere to men, are hardly noticed unless men are already apprised of them. Not that these unfortunate times were less fertile than others in rare geniuses; Nature is always the same. But what could these great men do, scattered as they always are from place to place, occupied with different purposes, and left to their solitary enlightenment with no cultivation of their abilities? Ideas which are acquired from reading and from association with others are the germ of almost all discoveries. It is like the air one breathes without thinking about it, to which one owes life; and the men of whom we are speaking were deprived of such sustenance. They were like the first creators of the sciences and the arts who have been forgotten because of their illustrious successors, and who, had they but come later, would themselves have caused the memory of the others to fade. The man who first discovered wheels and pinions would have invented watches in another century. Gerbert, situated in the time of Archimedes, would perhaps have equalled him.][33]

D'Alembert does not give technological or sociological reasons why medieval intellects were unable to communicate with one another, though the lack of a printing press, and therefore of a *république des lettres*, or of secular *sociétés de conversation* in court or city, might have been put forward. Instead, we are faced with the standard humanist and *philosophe*

---

[32] *Discours*, pp. xix–xx.   [33] Schwab, 1995, p. 61.

equation of barbarism and religion. If we reckon back twelve centuries from the fall of Constantinople, we come to the beginnings of the Christian empire, and it was during the Christian centuries that classical Greek and Latin were allegedly no longer studied, Europe was submerged by serfdom and superstition, and those who might otherwise have been leaders of intellect 'prenoient pour la véritable Philosophie des Anciens une tradition barbare qui le défiguroit'.[34] D'Alembert proceeds to a conventional invective against scholastic abstraction, and it is uncertain whether he is identifying or distinguishing the neo-Platonist theology of the patristic age and the Aristotelianism of the scholastic middle ages in the Latin west. It is appropriate to put this question, because it is appropriate at this point to remember that, while Gibbon was strongly disposed to share d'Alembert's historiographical conventions, his juvenile reading had been in late antique, Byzantine and Islamic history, and that these were to be the themes of the later volumes of the *Decline and Fall*.

The presumption of a millennium of barbarism enables d'Alembert to describe the difference between the metaphysical and historical accounts of the growth of intellect. Having taken the *renaissance des lettres* as his starting-point, he proceeds:

Quand on considere le progrès de l'esprit depuis cette époque mémorable, on trouve que ces progrès se sont faits dans l'ordre qu'ils devoient naturellement suivre –

but is immediately obliged to diversify the meaning of 'naturellement'.

On a commencé par l'Erudition, continué par les Belles-Lettres, et fini

(how absolute a term is 'fini'?)

par la Philosophie. Cet Ordre differe à la verité de celui que doit observer l'homme abandonné à ses propres lumieres, ou borné au commerce de ses contemporains, tel que nous l'avons principalement considéré dans la premiere Partie de ce Discours: en effet, nous avons fait voir que l'esprit isolé doit rencontrer dans sa route la Philosophie avant les Belles-Lettres. Mais en sortant d'un long intervalle d'ignorance que des siecles de lumiere avoient précédé, la régénération des idées, si on peut parler ainsi, a du nécessairement être différente de leur génération primitive. Nous allons tâcher de la faire sentir.[35]

[When we consider the progress of the mind since that memorable epoch, we find that this progress was made in the sequence it should naturally have followed. It was begun with erudition, continued with *belles-lettres*, and com-

---

[34] *Discours*, p. xx.   [35] *Discours*, pp. xix–xx.

pleted with philosophy. This sequence differs, it is true, from that which a man would necessarily follow if left to his own intelligence or limited to exchanges with his contemporaries – a sequence that we analysed in the first part of this Discourse. For indeed we have demonstrated that a mind left in isolation would of necessity encounter philosophy before it arrived at *belles-lettres*; whereas the regeneration of ideas, if we can speak thus, must necessarily have been different from their original generation, as it involved moving out of a long interval of ignorance that had been preceded by centuries of enlightenment. We are going to try to demonstrate this.][36]

This intellect evolves 'naturellement' in an application of natural law to specific situations. In a 'state of nature' or ideal-type situation, it would discover philosophy before poetry and literature (in part because *les belles-lettres* require the discipline of *règles*; one would like to know whether d'Alembert thought this was what had happened in primitive or pre-classical antiquity). But it illuminates our understanding of Renaissance and Enlightenment to realise that for d'Alembert the barbarism of the Christian middle ages was not a pure state of nature, but a specific situation rendered historical by the *siècles de lumière* (should this be translated as 'Enlightenment'?) which had preceded it; classical antiquity was a precondition of Christian barbarism, and the history of intellect consists specifically in its loss, recovery and (in some respects) supersession. The continued existence through twelve centuries of barbarism and religion of a buried archive of ancient literature (*les belles-lettres*) is the explanation of the historical phenomenon of erudition. Natural man began by developing the art of memory as the record of simple experience, but historic neo-classical man at the *renaissance des lettres* was obliged to apply his intellect to the recovery of a submerged mass of sophisticated and enlightened literature. The case Gibbon sought to state against d'Alembert was that the latter had applied his model so rigorously as to assert that this enterprise had been carried out by means of the faculty of memory alone, and had led to its hypertrophy.

L'étude des Langues et de l'Histoire abandonnée par necessité durant les siecles d'ignorance, fut la premiere à laquelle on se livra. L'esprit humain se trouvait au sortir de la barbarie dans une espece d'enfance, avide d'accumuler des idées, et incapable pourtant d'en acquérir d'abord d'un certain ordre par l'espece d'engourdissement où les facultés de l'ame avoient été si long-tems. De toutes ces facultés, la mémoire fut celle que l'on cultiva d'abord, parce qu'elle est la plus facile à satisfaire, et que les connoissances qu'on obtient par son secours,

---

[36] Schwab, 1995, pp. 60–1.

sont celles qui peuvent le plus aisément être entassées. On ne commença donc point par étudier la Nature, ainsi que les premiers hommes avoient dû faire; on jouissoit d'un secours dont ils étoient depourvus, celui des Ouvrages des Anciens que la générosité des Grands et l'Impression commençoient à rendre communs, on croyait n'avoir qu'à lire pour devenir savant; et il est bien plus aisé de lire que de voir. Ainsi, on devora sans distinction tout ce que les anciens nous avoient laissé dans chaque genre: on les traduisit, on les commenta; et par une espece de reconnoissance on se mit à les adorer sans connoitre à beaucoup pres ce qu'ils valoient.

De-là cette foule d'Erudits, profonds dans les Langues savantes jusqu'à dedaigner la leur, qui, comme l'a dit un Auteur célebre, connoissoit tout dans les Anciens, hors la grace et la finesse, et qu'un vain étalage d'érudition rendoit si orgueilleux, parce que les avantages qui coutent le moins sont assez souvent ceux dont on aime le plus à se parer. C'étoit une espece de grands Seigneurs, qui sans rassembler par le mérite réel à ceux dont ils tenoient la vie, tiroient beaucoup de vanité de croire leur appartenir. D'ailleurs cette vanité n'étoit point sans quelque espece de prétexte. Le pays de l'érudition et des faits est inépuisable; on croit, pour ainsi dire, voir tous les jours augmenter sa substance par les acquisitions que l'on y fait sans peine. Au contraire le pays de la raison et des découvertes est d'une assez petite étendue; et souvent au lieu d'y apprendre ce que l'on ignoroit; on ne parvient à force d'étude qu'à désapprendre ce qu'on croyait savoir. C'est pourquoi, à mérite fort inégal, un Erudit doit être be-aucoup plus vain qu'un Philosophe, et peut-être qu'un Poëte: car l'esprit qu'invente est toujours mécontent de ses progrès, parce qu'il voit au-delà; et les plus grands génies trouvent souvent dans leur amour propre même un juge secret, mais sévere, que l'approbation des autres fait taire pour quelques instans, mais qu'elle ne parvient jamais à corrompre. On ne doit donc pas s'étonner que les Savans dont nous parlons missent tant de gloire à jouir d'une Science herissee, souvent ridicule, et quelquefois barbare.[37]

[People turned first to the study of languages and history, which had perforce been abandoned during the centuries of ignorance. On emerging from barbarism, the human mind found itself in a sort of infancy. It was eager to accumulate ideas, but incapable at first of acquiring those of a higher order because of the kind of sluggishness in which the faculties of the soul had for so long a time been sunk. Of all these faculties, memory was the one which was cultivated first, because it is the easiest to satisfy and because the knowledge that is obtained with its help can be built up most easily. Thus they did not begin by studying Nature as the first men had had to do. They enjoyed an advantage which the earliest men lacked: they had the works of the ancients, which printing and the generosity of men of power and noble birth began to make common. They thought they needed only to read in order to become learned; and it is far easier to read than to understand. And so they devoured indis-criminately everything that the ancients left us in each genre. They translated

---

[37] *Discours*, pp. xx–xxi.

them, commented on them, and out of a kind of gratitude began to worship them, although they were far from knowing their true worth.

   These circumstances gave rise to that multitude of erudite men, immersed in the learned languages to the point of disdaining their own, who knew everything in the ancients except their grace and finesse, as a celebrated author has said, and whose vain show of erudition made them so arrogant because the cheapest advantages are rather often those whose vulgar display gives most satisfaction. They acted like great lords who do not resemble their forefathers in any real merit but who are excessively proud of their ancestry. Moreover, that vanity was not without some degree of plausibility. The realm of erudition and of facts is inexhaustible; the effortless acquisitions made in it lead one to think that one's substance is continually growing, so to speak. On the contrary, the realm of reason and of discoveries is rather small. Through study in that realm, men often succeed only in unlearning what they thought they knew, instead of learning what they did not know. That is why a scholar of most unequal merit must be much more vain than a philosopher or even perhaps a poet. For the inventive mind is always dissatisfied with its progress because it sees beyond, and for the greatest geniuses, even their self-esteem may harbour a secret but severe judge whom flattery may momentarily silence but never corrupt. Thus we should not be surprised that the scholars of whom we speak gloried so proudly in practising a science that was thorny, often ridiculous, and sometimes barbarous.][38]

Gibbon many years later, in one of the concluding chapters of the *Decline and Fall*,[39] gave an account superficially not very different from d'Alembert's of the Renaissance humanists and philologists, some of whom he agreed were just the self-intoxicated and insufferable monsters described in the *Discours préliminaire*. He differed profoundly, however, even in his youth, from d'Alembert's explanation of their character, above all at the point where d'Alembert seems to suggest that they could not be other than what they were and that a separate caste of philosophers and critics, whose personalities were shaped by the development of a different faculty of the mind, was needed if their errors were to be corrected. Gibbon had known from childhood what it might be to read a text, and had continued at Lausanne to develop the critical capacity to do so; he believed that *érudition* (a term he distrusted) possessed its own means of self-direction. It was not that the philological appetite did not need to be regulated; the question was where, in whom and in what capacities of the mind the regulating intelligence was

[38] Schwab, 1995, pp. 63–4.
[39] Chapter 66; Womersley, III, pp. 908–9; Bury, VII, pp. 131–7. The passage characteristically combines the Modern dictum that 'the spirit of imitation is of a servile class' with the Ancient 'nor can the artist hope to equal or surpass, till he has learned to imitate, the works of his predecessors'. Renaissance critics were still 'the slaves of Aristotle'.

located. D'Alembert's three republics, each dominated by a single faculty, may have looked to him, as they may to us, altogether too much like Plato's Republic or Bacon's Solomon's House; the *république des lettres* for Gibbon was a commerce and conversation between many-sided, not single-track personalities.

In the *querelle des anciens et modernes*, the term *anciens* could mean either the ancients themselves, the paragons of Hellas and Rome, or those moderns who adopted certain attitudes towards the study of the ancients which other *modernes* took leave to criticise. In consequence, the *querelle* involved much role-playing and competitive appropriation and ascription of roles. The ancients might initially be those polite gentlemen (in England) or neo-classical poets and orators (in France) who held that the ancients could only be imitated and that they themselves possessed the secret of doing so; in France, but scarcely in England, it was conceivable that one might imitate the ancients so successfully as actually to surpass them (though this might entail the invention of *règles* of classical art, and a further dispute as to whether *philosophes* or *poètes* were the better qualified to invent them). But when philologists and scholars in the Renaissance tradition took issue with the ancients, claiming that a text must be minutely examined and reconstituted before it could be imitated, that this might end by reconstituting it in its historicity to the point where it could not be imitated, and that the activity of the modern scholar differed from that of the ancient poet or orator, the ancients shifted ground. They claimed in an important sense to be more 'modern' than the moderns themselves, stigmatising as Gothic, scholastic and barbarous the philological and textual scholarship which d'Alembert associates with the feeding frenzy of intellects starved for twelve centuries and not yet emancipated from the medieval prison-house. The activity of imitation was now 'modernised' and rendered 'polite'; it became the discovery of the *règles* according to which a classical or neo-classical work of art must be constructed, and this in the hands of *philosophes* and *encyclopédistes* became the discovery of the laws which constituted the workings of the human mind itself. The *exposition historique* in the *Discours préliminaire* is the history of how these laws, previously set forth in the *exposition métaphysique*, were discovered, rather than rediscovered, in a post-Renaissance enlightenment which made them a province of a neo-classical modernity even more than of classical antiquity itself. The former *anciens* now claimed to be more 'modern' than the former *modernes* and even than the formerly inimitable ancients themselves; and if they could claim to have imitated the ancients to the point of surpassing them, they could even claim to be more 'ancient' – that is, more classically perfect than their exemplars. In this way the vocabulary of *anciens et modernes* became deeply ambivalent; and Joseph Levine's case for regarding Gibbon as a moderate *ancien*[40] can be matched, but not refuted, by the present argument for considering him a moderate *moderne*, who agreed with d'Alembert that something more than uncritical *érudition* was called for, but differed from him altogether in holding that the scholars and philologists were not Gothic plunderers or parasitic *grands seigneurs*, but possessed their own capacity for self-improvement. This might in the end modify Gibbon's attitude towards the middle ages, and may help to explain why the *Decline and Fall* is a history, not a dismissal, of the twelve centuries of barbarism and religion which preceded the fall of Constantinople.

D'Alembert proceeded in the *Discours préliminaire* to develop the thesis that what we call Enlightenment – he uses no word equivalent to it – could take shape only as an emancipation from the excesses of Renaissance.

Les Gens de Lettres sont enfins revenues peu-à-peu de cette espece de manie. Il y a apparence qu'on doit leur changement, du moins en partie, à la protection des Grands, qui sont bien-aisés d'être savans, à condition de le devenir sans peine, et qui veulent pouvoir juger sans étude d'un Ouvrage d'esprit, par prix des bienfaits qu'ils promettent à l'Auteur, ou de l'amité dont ils croyent l'honorer.

[Little by little men of letters at last recovered from this kind of mania. It seems that we owe their change, at least in part, to the patronage of the great, who are quite happy to be learned on the condition that they can become so without trouble, and who wish to be able to judge a work of intelligence without hard study, in exchange for the benefits they promise to the author or for the friendship with which they think they honour him.][41]

Young Edward Gibbon, gentleman of letters, had little need of d'Alembert's campaign to emancipate the *gens de lettres* from the condescending *sprezzatura* of noble patrons; there were *grands* in his world, but he could respect them or do without them; so at least his manner of living declared. D'Alembert continues:

On commença à sentir que le beau, pour être en Langue vulgaire, ne perdoit rien de ses avantages; qu'il acquèroit même celui d'être plus facilement saisi du commun des hommes, et qu'il n'y avoit aucun mérite à dire des choses communes ou ridicules dans quelque Langue que ce fût, et à plus forte raison

---

[40] Levine, 1991, ch. 7. [41] Schwab, 1995, p. 66.

dans celles qu'on devoit parler le plus mal. Les *Gens de Lettres* penserent donc à perfectionner les Langues vulgaires; ils chercherent d'abord à dire dans ces Langues ce que les *Anciens* avoient dit dans les leurs.

[Men began to understand that beauty lost none of its advantages for being expressed in the common tongue, that it even gained by becoming more accessible to the generality of men, and that there was no merit in saying common or ridiculous things in any language whatever, especially in those languages which of necessity were spoken the worst. Therefore, men of letters turned their thoughts to perfecting the vulgar tongues. They tried first to say in these languages what the ancients had said in theirs.][42]

But this initially poetic activity could not proceed without a measure of self-emancipation from the ancients themselves. Two paragraphs above he had written:

En effet, il ne fallut pas se livrer long-tems à la lecture des Anciens, pour se convaincre que dans ces Ouvrages mêmes où l'on ne cherchoit que des faits et des mots, il y avoit mieux à apprendre. On apperçut bientôt les beautés que les Auteurs y avoient répandus; car si les hommes, comme nous l'avons dit plus haut, ont besoin d'être avertis du vrai, en récompense ils n'ont besoin que de l'être. L'admiration qu'on avoit eu jusqu'alors pour les Anciens ne pouvoit être plus vive; mais elle commença à devenir plus juste. Cependant elle étoit encore bien loin d'être raisonnable. On crut qu'on ne pouvoit les imiter qu'en les copiant servilement, et qu'il n'étoit possible de bien dire que dans leur Langue. On ne pensoit pas que l'étude des mots est une espèce d'inconvénient passager, nécessaire pour faciliter l'étude des choses, mais qu'elle devient un mal réel, quand elle la retarde;[43]

[Indeed, it was not necessary to read the writings of the ancients for long to be convinced that there were better things to learn in those very works in which formerly only facts or words were sought. Men soon perceived the beauties that the ancients had lavished upon them; for, if men need to be apprised of what is true, as we have stated above, in compensation, that is all they need. Their former admiration for the ancients could not have been livelier; now it became more judicious. However, it was still far from being wise. They believed that the only way to imitate the ancients was to copy them slavishly and that it was possible to speak well only in an ancient tongue. They did not realise that the study of words is a kind of passing inconvenience, necessary insofar as it facilitates the study of things, but becoming a real evil whenever it retards that study;][44]

with the result that philological study shared the characteristic fault of scholasticism, and that the humanist study of ancient literature resulted

---

[42] *Ibid.*, p. 66. [43] This and the two preceding passages are from *Discours*, p. xxi.
[44] Schwab, 1995, pp. 64–5.

in the writing of an absurd and still barbaric pastiche of ancient styles. Even the first vernacular humanists – Ronsard is blamed here – shared this fault, distorting the French language into a barbarous Latinity. D'Alembert's complaint is as old as Erasmus's indictment of the 'Ciceronians', but contains a philosophical as well as a historical dimension; the Renaissance error is less that of attempting to be Romans instead of Frenchmen, than that of mistaking words for things. In perfecting French along classical lines, the *gens de lettres* passed from attempting to say in the vernacular what had already been said in Latin to the discovery that there were things to say which could only be said in French; but this was less a discovery of historicity than a rediscovery of *le génie*. In this way the neo-classical became the equal of the classical, and the heroic age of the seventeenth century began.

MALHERBE, nourri de la lecture des excellens Poëtes de l'antiquité, et prenant comme eux la Nature pour modele, répandit le premier dans notre Poësie une harmonie et des beautés auparavant inconnues. BALZAC, aujourd'hui trop méprisé, donna à notre Prose de la noblesse et du nombre. Les Ecrivains de PORT ROYAL continuerent ce que Balzac avoit commencé; ils y ajouterent cette précision, cet heureux choix de termes, et cette pureté qui ont conservé jusqu'à présent la plûpart de leurs Ouvrages un aire moderne,

(it is *pureté* which qualifies work to be considered *moderne*)

et qui les distinguent d'un grand nombre de Livres surannés, écrits dans le même tems. CORNEILLE, après avoir sacrifié pendant quelques années au mauvais goût dans la carriere dramatique, s'en affranchait enfin; découvrit par la force de son génie, bien plus que par la lecture, les lois du Théatre, et les exposa dans ses Discours admirables sur la Tragédie, dans ses réflexions sur chacune de ses pieces, mais principalement dans ses pieces mêmes. RACINE s'ouvrant une autre route, fit paroître sur le Théatre une passion que les Anciens n'y avoient guere connue; et développant les ressorts du cœur humain, joignit à une élégance et une verité continues quelques traits de sublime. DESPREAUX dans son art poëtique se rendit l'égal d'Horace en l'imitant; MOLIERE par la peinture fine des ridicules et des mœurs de son tems, laissa bien loin derriere lui la Comédie ancienne; LA FONTAINE fit presque oublier Esope et Phedre, et BOSSUET alla se placer à coté de Démosthene.[45]

[Malherbe, nurtured by the reading of the excellent poets of antiquity and taking nature as a model as they had done, was the first to enhance our poetry with a harmony and beauty which it had never known before. Balzac, who is today held too much in contempt, gave nobility and balance to our prose. The writers of Port-Royal continued what Balzac had begun. They added that

[45] *Discours*, p. xxii.

precision, that happy choice of terms, and that purity which makes most of their works seem almost modern even now and which set them apart from a great many antiquated books written at the same time. Corneille, after having for several years made concessions to poor taste in his career as a dramatist, finally freed himself of it; by the strength of his genius more than by reading he discovered the laws of the theatre and set them forth in his admirable Discourses on tragedy, in his Reflections upon each of his plays, but principally in his plays themselves. Racine, opening another route, brought to the stage a passion that the ancients had hardly known. Unfolding the motives of the human heart, he joined a consistent elegance and truth with certain traits of the sublime. In his *Art poétique*, Despréaux made himself the equal of Horace at the same time that he modelled his work after him. Molière left ancient comedy far behind him in the subtle portrayal of the absurdities and the mores of his time. La Fontaine almost caused Aesop and Phaedrus to be forgotten, and Bossuet succeeded in putting himself in the same rank with Demosthenes.][46]

It is not surprising, d'Alembert continues, that the neo-classical objective of equalling or surpassing the ancients was achieved in the *belles-lettres* more rapidly than in philosophy, once the obstacle of undiscriminating erudition was cleared out of the way. The beauties of literature are self-declaratory if not self-evident, and once the mind recovers control of itself it cannot take long to recognise them. But the ancients were less skilled at philosophy, and it was no light task to digest and rearrange their writings. D'Alembert here offers nothing similar to Hobbes's indictment of the whole tradition of Greek philosophy, and merely ridicules the scholastics for supposing that the corrupt texts they had acquired from the Arabs were the true doctrine of Aristotle. The ancients, furthermore, were polytheists, and by an elaborate circumlocution about the essential compatibility of philosophy and theology d'Alembert indicates that the single universal God of the Christians is more readily harmonised with a rational understanding of nature.[47] Problems of mystery, authority and priestcraft none the less had to be overcome, and the *Discours préliminaire* moves into the high gear of grand historical narrative as d'Alembert narrates the works of the giants – Bacon, Descartes, Newton and Locke – who had brought the mind to the point where it understood the workings of nature by understanding how it worked itself.

Tels sont les principaux genies que l'esprit doit regarder comme ses maîtres, et à qui la Grece eut élevé des statues, quand même elle eut été obligée pour leur faire place, d'abattre celles de quelques Conquérans.[48]

[Such are the principal geniuses that the human mind ought to regard as its

---

[46] Schwab, 1995, pp. 66–8.   [47] *Discours*, p. xxiii.   [48] *Discours*, pp. xxiv–xxviii.

masters. Greece would have raised statues to them, even if she had been obliged to tear down a few conquerors in order to give them room.] [49]

A full study of the *Discours* as a history of Enlightenment would analyse these pages in depth, noting how Descartes is the most recalcitrant of the four heroes, both as a creative genius who made many false starts and as the only Frenchman in what is otherwise a French history.

On peut le regarder comme un chef de conjurés, qui a eu le courage de s'élever le premier contre une puissance despotique et arbitraire, et qui en préparant une révolution éclatante, a jetté les fondemens d'un gouvernement plus juste et plus heureux qu'il n'a pû voir etabli. S'il a fini par croire tout expliquer, il a du moins commencé par douter de tout; et les armes dont nous servons pour le combattre ne lui en appartiennent pas moins, parce que nous les tournons contre lui.[50]

[He can be thought of as a leader of conspirators who, before anyone else, had the courage to arise against a despotic and arbitrary power and who, in preparing a resounding revolution, laid the foundations of a more just and happier government, which he himself was not able to see established. If he concluded by believing he could explain everything, he at least began by doubting everything, and the arms which we use to combat him belong to him no less because we turn them against him.][51]

Descartes must play Hamlet to Newton's Fortinbras, if d'Alembert is to conduct his tortuous narrative to a satisfactory denouement.

Concluons de toute cette histoire, que l'Angleterre nous doit la naissance de cette philosophie que nous avons reçue d'elle.[52]

[We may conclude from all this history that England is indebted to us for the origins of that philosophy which we have since received back from her.][53]

This history of natural philosophy is the guiding thread and central pattern of d'Alembert's *exposition historique*. It can be abbreviated here only because it was not this to which the young Gibbon took exception. He objected only to the extrusion of textual scholarship from the story, and d'Alembert, striving to be fair to all parties, was still unable to find for *érudition* any role higher than the menial.

La Philosophie, qui forme le goût dominant de notre siecle, semble par les progrès qu'elle ait parmi nous, vouloir reparer le tems qu'elle a perdu, et se venger de l'espece de mépris que lui avoient marqué nos Peres. Ce mépris est aujourd'hui retombé sur l'Erudition, et n'en est pas plus juste pour avoir changé d'objet. On s'imagine que nous avons tiré des Ouvrages des Anciens

[49] Schwab, 1995, p. 85.   [50] *Discours*, p. xxvi.   [51] Schwab, 1995, p. 80.
[52] *Discours*, p. xxviii.   [53] Schwab, 1995, p. 85.

tout ce qu'il nous importoit de savoir; et sur ce fondement on dispenseroit volontiers de leur peine ceux qui vont encore les consulter. Il semble qu'on regarde l'antiquité comme un oracle qui a tout dit, et qu'il est inutile d'interroger; et l'on ne fait guere plus de cas aujourd'hui de la restitution d'un passage, que de la découverte d'un petit rameau de veine dans le corps humain. Mais comme il seroit ridicule de croire qu'il n'y a plus rien de decouvrir dans l'Anatomie, parce que les Anatomistes se livrent quelquefois à des recherches, inutiles en apparence, et souvent utiles par leurs suites; il seroit pas moins absurde de vouloir interdire l'Erudition, sous prétexte des recherches peu importantes auxquelles nos Savans peuvent s'abandonner. C'est être ignorant ou présomptueux de croire que tout soit vû dans quelque matiere que ce puisse être, et que nous n'ayons plus aucun avantage à tirer de l'etude et de la lecture des Anciens.[54]

[By the progress that it is making among us, philosophy, which constitutes the dominant taste of our century, seems to be trying to make up for the time that it has lost and to avenge itself for the sort of contempt our fathers showed for it. Today this disdain has fallen on erudition, and is no more just for having changed its object. Men imagine that we have already drawn everything worth knowing from the works of the ancients, and on this basis they would willingly spare those who still wish to consult them the trouble. It seems that antiquity is regarded as an oracle that it is useless to consult because it has said everything it is going to say. Nowadays men have hardly more regard for the restitution of a lost passage than for the discovery of a small subdivision of a vein in the human body. But just as it would be ridiculous to believe that there is no more to be discovered in anatomy because the anatomists sometimes give themselves over to apparently useless researches (which are often useful by their consequences), it would be no less absurd to try to forbid erudition because of the rather unimportant researches our scholars may engage in. It would be ignorant and presumptuous to believe that everything is known concerning any subject whatsoever, and that we no longer have an advantage to draw from the study and reading of the ancients.][55]

It was judicious and fair-minded, but did it mean more than that the masters still had need of the labours of their servants, or their research assistants? Gibbon, who knew what was going on in the world of study, was determined to claim for scholars the rank of equal citizens in the *république des lettres*, and must have found increasingly annoying d'Alembert's well-intentioned inability to escape the consequences of his initial decision to permit them the exercise of no faculty higher than that of memory. These consequences include the ascendancy of *raison* over the other faculties, and of the *république des philosophes* over its sisters, and d'Alembert is not altogether happy with them. He doubts even the

[54] *Discours*, p. xxx.   [55] Schwab, 1995, p. 92.

wisdom of attempting to make French rather than Latin the universal
language of culture, since it will provoke competition from the other
vernaculars, though he concedes – citing Buffon as 'rival de Platon et
Lucrece'[56] – that French has made the language of science noble and
polite. Yet:

On abuse des meilleures choses. Cet esprit philosophique, si à la mode
aujourd'hui, qui veut tout voir et ne rien supposer, s'est répandu jusques dans
les Belles-Lettres; on prétend même qu'il est nuisible à leurs progrès, et il est
difficile de se le dissimuler. Notre siècle porté à la combinaison et à l'analyse,
semble vouloir introduire les discussions froides et didactiques dans les choses
du sentiment. Ce n'est pas que les passions et le goût n'ayent une Logique qui
leur appartient: mais cette Logique a des principes tout différens de ceux de la
Logique ordinaire: ce sont des principes qu'il faut démêler en nous, et c'est, il
faut l'avouer, de quoi une Philosophie commune est peu capable... Il faut
pourtant convenir que cet esprit de discussion a contribué à affranchir notre
littérature de l'admiration aveugle des Anciens; il nous a appris à n'estimer en
eux que les beautés que nous serions contraints d'admirer dans les Modernes.
Mais c'est peut-être aussi à la même source que nous devons je ne sais quelle
Métaphysique du cœur, qui s'est emparée de nos théâtres; s'il ne falloit pas l'en
bannir entièrement, encore moins falloit-il l'y laisser régner. Cette anatomie de
l'ame s'est glissée jusque dans nos conversations; on y disserte, on n'y parle plus;
et nos sociétés ont perdu leurs principaux agrémens, la chaleur et la gaieté.[57]

[Men abuse the best things. That philosophic spirit so much in fashion today
which tries to comprehend everything and to take nothing for granted extends
even into belles-lettres. Some claim that it is even harmful to their progress, and
indeed it is difficult to conceal the fact. Our century, which is inclined toward
combination and analysis, seems to desire to introduce frigid and didactic
discussions into things of sentiment. It is not that the passions and tastes do not
have their own sort of logic, but their logic has principles completely different
from those of ordinary logic; these principles must be unravelled within us, and
it must be confessed that ordinary philosophy is quite unsuited to the task... It
must be admitted, however, that this spirit of discussion has contributed to
freeing our literature from blind admiration for the ancients; it has taught us to
value in them only the beauties that we would be compelled to admire in the
moderns. But it is perhaps also to the same source that we owe that species of
metaphysics of the heart which has seized hold of our theatres. While we do not
have to banish it entirely, still less are we obliged to let it thus hold sway. This
anatomy of the soul has even slipped into our conversations; people make
dissertations, they no longer converse; and our societies have lost their principal
ornaments – warmth and gaiety.][58]

In admitting that philosophy is not good at the language of the heart,

---

[56] *Discours*, p. xxxi.   [57] *Discours*, p. xxxi.   [58] Schwab, 1995, pp. 96–7.

and that even polite conversation might suffer because this is so, d'Alembert may be aware – as he is elsewhere[59] – of the accusing presence of Rousseau. Gibbon was never a spokesman of the heart, though he did come to share the widespread concern with a frigidity at the core of modern literature; he was dissatisfied with d'Alembert's exclusion of scholarship from the exercise of reason and imagination, and this placed him at a distance from Rousseau. There was a life of the mind, he thought, of which d'Alembert knew nothing. The lawyer, the divine, the polite genius and the gentleman of letters might find satisfaction in the encounter with texts and documents, and this was a social as well as a philosophical phenomenon which d'Alembert had overlooked, or was deliberately suppressing in his efforts to create an intellectual hegemony of the *gens de lettres*. Learning of this kind was better organised in France than the *Discours préliminaire* seems prepared to admit, and in the next chapters we shall be shown Gibbon making a choice of a kind between the *sociétés de conversation* and the Académie des Inscriptions.

D'Alembert, it may very well be, was less committed to repressing his awareness of an active presence of l'*érudition* than impeded in recognising it by his systematic separation of the three faculties of the mind. It slips into the text of the *Discours préliminaire* at one point only, late in the *exposition historique*, where d'Alembert is seeking to mitigate his admission that he is living in a silver age of the French intellect, and that the glories of the *siècle de Louis XIV* are not to be repeated. This is not to be wondered at, he says; after an era in which many great classics were rapidly created, there may be nothing to do but imitate the critical philosophy that appreciates them. After Demosthenes came Demetrius of Phalerum, after Cicero and Virgil came Lucan and Seneca, and after the *siècle de Louis XIV* came 'le nôtre', the age of the *Encyclopédie*. Yet this does not mean that the neo-classical enterprise of overtaking the exemplars is at an end.

Un Poëte célebre par ses talens et par ses malheurs a effacé Malherbe dans ses Odes, et Marot dans ses Epigrammes et dans ses Epitres.[60] Nous avons vu naître le seul Poëme épique que la France puisse opposer à ceux des Grecs, des Romains, des Italiens, des Anglais et des Espagnols.

[A poet, famous for his talents and his misfortunes, has overshadowed Malherbe in his odes and Marot in his epigrams and epistolary verses. We have

---

[59] *Discours*, p. xxiii.
[60] I am told on good authority that this is Voltaire, who is certainly the epic poet of the following sentence. Schwab, 1995, thought it was J. B. Rousseau.

seen the birth of the sole epic poem which France can set over against those of the Greeks, the Romans, the Italians, the English and the Spanish.][61]

It is noteworthy that the *Henriade* is presented as the equal of the *Faerie Queene* or *Paradise Lost* (almost certainly the latter) at the very time when the English were wondering if they possessed a historian the equal of Tacitus, Guicciardini or de Thou. The *ars historica* pushes its way to the surface of d'Alembert's text after he has observed that

Deux hommes illustres, entre lesquels notre nation semble partagée, et que la postérité saura mettre chacun à sa place, se disputent la gloire du cothurne, et l'on voit encore avec un extrème plaisir leurs Tragédies après celles de Corneille et de Racine.

[Two illustrious men, among whom our nation seems divided and whom posterity will know how to rank in their proper places, compete for the glory of the buskin, and we see their tragedies with an extreme pleasure even after those of Corneille and of Racine.]

No doubt we should know the name of Voltaire's equal as a tragedian,[62] but a mounting and complex *éloge* prevents our being told.

L'un de ces deux hommes, le même à qui nous devons la HENRIADE, sûr d'obtenir parmi les très-petit nombre de grands Poëtes une place distinguée et qui n'est qu'à lui, posséde en même tems au plus haut dégré un talent que n'a eu presque aucun Poëte même dans un dégré mediocre, celui, d'écrire en prose... Son essai sur le siècle de Louis XIV est un morceau d'autant plus précieux que l'Auteur n'avoit en ce genre aucun modéle ni parmi les *Anciens*, ni parmi nous. Son histoire de Charles XII par la rapidité et la noblesse de style est digne du Héros qu'il avoit à peindre; ses pieces fugitives supérieurs à toutes celles que nous estimons le plus, suffiroient par leur nombre et par leur mérite pour immortaliser plusieurs Ecrivains.

[One of the two men, to whom we owe the *Henriade*, is sure of obtaining a distinguished and most particular place among the very small number of great poets, and at the same time he possesses to the highest degree a talent which hardly any poet has had even to a mediocre degree: that of writing in prose... His essay on the *Century of Louis XIV* is all the more precious because the author had no model for this type of writing, either from among the ancients or ourselves. By the swiftness and nobility of its style his *History of Charles XII* is worthy of the hero that he was to portray. His occasional writings,

---

[61] Schwab, 1995, p. 98.
[62] It was probably Crebillon *père*. Schwab, 1995, concurs. I am indebted to Wilda Anderson for this and the preceding identification.

which are superior to all those we hold in highest regard, would be sufficient in their number and their merit to immortalize several writers.]

After a final exclamatory tribute to the glory of Voltaire, d'Alembert continues:

Ce ne sont pas là nos seules richesses. Un Ecrivain judicieux, aussi bon citoyen que grand Philosophe, nous a donné sur les principes des Lois un ouvrage décrié par quelques François, et estimé de toute l'Europe. D'excellens auteurs ont écrit l'histoire; des esprits justes et éclairés l'ont approfondie; la Comédie a acquis un nouveau genre, qu'on auroit tort de rejetter, puisqu'il en résulte un plaisir de plus, et qui n'a pas été aussi inconnu des anciens qu'on voudroit nous en persuader; enfin nous avons plusieurs Romans qui nous empêchent de regretter ceux du dernier siècle.[63]

[These are not our only riches. A judicious writer who is as good a citizen as he is a great philosopher, has given us a work on the principles of the laws which is disparaged by a few Frenchmen and honored by all of Europe. Excellent authors have written history; precise and enlightened minds have probed its meaning. Comedy has acquired a new form which we would be mistaken to reject, since it has added one more pleasure to our lives; and this form of literature was not as unknown to the ancients as some would like to persuade us is the case. Finally, we have several novels which prevent us from regretting those of the last century.][64]

The allusion to Montesquieu may be significant but seems awkward. D'Alembert is having difficulty in allotting Enlightened *histoire philosophique* a place among the *belles-lettres* and the *beaux-arts*. Voltaire's *Siècle de Louis XIV* is an *essai* without a precedent and there is no hint of the *Essai sur les mœurs* (not published till 1756); the *Histoire de Charles XII* appears as a classic heroic narrative such as we expect from the greatest living tragedian. The *Esprit des lois* and the works of other unnamed historians are grouped with the renovation of comedy and the novel. Gibbon – who we know would have preferred one page of Montesquieu to all the historical entertainments of Voltaire – would see in these paragraphs an admission of inability to deal with a whole world of *érudition de la robe*, in which furthermore he found the kind of Enlightenment he needed.

Gibbon was to align himself, in his own fashion, with the Académie des Inscriptions et Belles-Lettres; the *Encyclopédistes* did not campaign against the Académies, but they are ambivalently present when the *Discours préliminaire* says:

[63] These four passages occur on *Discours*, p. xxxii.
[64] Schwab 1995, pp. 99–100. 'Age' would have been a better rendering of 'Siècle' (de Louis XIV).

Quelle idée ne se formera-t-on pas de nos trésors littéraires, si l'on joint aux Ouvrages de tant de grands Hommes les travaux de toutes les Compagnies savantes, destinées à maintenir le goût des Sciences et des Lettres, et à qui nous devons tant d'excellens Livres! De pareilles Sociétés ne peuvent manquer dans un Etat de grands avantages; pourvû qu'en les multipliant a l'excès, on n'en facilite point l'entrée à un trop grand nombre de gens médiocres... Car il ne faut pas s'y tromper: on nuit plus aux progrès de l'esprit, en plaçant mal les récompenses qu'en les supprimant. Avouons même à l'honneur des lettres, que les Savans n'ont pas toujours besoin d'être récompensés pour se multiplier. Temoin l'Angleterre, à qui les Sciences doivent tant, sans que le Gouvernement fasse rien pour elles. Il est vrai que la Nation les considère, qu'elle les respecte même: et cette espece de récompense, supérieur à toutes les autres, est sans doute le moyen le plus sûr de fleurir les Sciences et les Arts; parce que c'est le Gouvernement qui donne des places, et le Public qui distribue l'estime. L'amour des Lettres, qui est un mérite chez nos voisins, n'est encore à la vérité qu'une mode parmi nous, et ne sera peut-être jamais autre chose; mais quelque dangereuse que soit cette mode, qui pour un Mécene éclairé produit cent Amateurs ignorans et orgueilleux, peut-être lui sommes-nous redevables de n'être pas encore tombés dans la barbarie ou une foule de circonstances tendent à nous précipiter.][65]

[What an idea of our literary treasures would result if we added to the works of so many great men those of all the scholarly associations which maintain the taste for sciences and letters and to which we owe so many excellent works! Such societies most assuredly are of great advantage in a state, if certain conditions are observed: they should not be multiplied excessively, thus facilitating the entry of an excessive number of mediocre persons... For let us not be mistaken: we do more harm to the progress of the mind by misplacing such rewards than in suppressing them. To the honour of letters, let us confess that even without the promise of compensation, scholars do yet increase in number. Witness England, a country to which the sciences owe so much, although their government does nothing for them. It is true that the English nation is not neglectful of the sciences, that it even respects them, and this kind of reward, superior to all others, is doubtless the surest means of making the sciences and arts flourish; because while the government distributes offices, it is the public which bestows esteem. Love of letters, a virtue among our neighbours, is still, in truth, only a fashion among ourselves, and perhaps it will never be anything else. But however dangerous might be that mode which produces a hundred proud or ignorant amateurs for every enlightened patron of the arts, perhaps we owe to it the fact that we have not returned to the barbarism into which a multitude of circumstances tends to precipitate us.][66]

D'Alembert is troubled once again by the patronage of the *grands* and its corrupting effects; is he also indicating that the mushroom grows in

---

[65] *Discours*, p. xxxiii.   [66] Schwab, 1995, pp. 101–2.

the open, the toadstool under the tree,[67] and that the *république des gens de lettres* should not be organised into academies by the state, but consist in a free market of works and ideas? Samuel Johnson could have told him more than the young gentleman of letters ever knew about life on the Grub Street underbelly of that market, but perhaps he was not thinking of a market of sales and royalties so much as of the organisation of the *république des lettres* as a public and universal *société de conversation* in which the *estime* which was its own reward would justly be distributed. Such a *république* would have its oracles and hierarchies, and Gibbon need only have been claiming for the *érudits* the parity of esteem which d'Alembert seemed to be denying them. The comparison with England has a Montesquieuan flavour, and after a confrontation with Rousseau's *Discours de l'origine des arts et sciences*, hot from the press in 1751, d'Alembert closed his *exposition historique* in language recalling that of the *Esprit des lois*.

Finissons cette histoire des Sciences, en remarquant que les différentes formes de gouvernement qui influent tant sur les esprits et sur la culture des Lettres, déterminent aussi les espèces de connoissances qui doivent principalement y fleurir et dont chacune a son mérite particulier. Il doit y avoir en général dans une République plus d'Orateurs, d'Historiens, et de Philosophes; et dans une Monarchie, plus de Poëtes, de Théologiens, et de Géometres. Cette regle n'est pourtant si absolue, qu'elle ne puisse être altérée et modifiée par une infinité de causes.[68]

[Let us end this history of the sciences by noting that the different forms of government, which have so much influence on men's minds and on the cultivation of letters, also determine the principal types of knowledge which are to flourish under them, each of these types having its particular merits. In general, there should be more orators, historians, and philosophers in a republic and more poets, theologians and geometers in a monarchy. This rule is not, however, so absolute that it cannot be altered and modified by an infinite number of causes.][69]

It could indeed; he did well to be cautious. His *gens de lettres* would be *philosophes*, living in a monarchy. The place of the *érudits* under government was left undescribed, but Gibbon would see in this passage an admission that the *philosophes* needed to know history, and needed the *érudits* to teach it to them.

---

[67] Fairburn, 1966, p. 154.   [68] *Discours*, p. xxxiii.   [69] Schwab, 1995, pp. 104–5.

(III)

Gibbon's *Essai* was directed against the *Discours préliminaire* and its relegation of the scholar's enterprise to the lowest of the three rigorously separated capacities of the mind; yet we have found good reason to believe that d'Alembert was not engaged in a polemic against the *érudits*, and may have been trying to minimise the consequences of his initial rigour. There are other writings, with some of which Gibbon was early acquainted, that show d'Alembert coming near to closing the gap between *érudits* and *philosophes*, so that it is possible to argue that Gibbon may have exaggerated the gap between d'Alembert and him.[70] In the article 'Erudition' in the twelfth volume of the *Encyclopédie* – whose apparent inconsistency with the *Discours préliminaire* is complained of in a footnote to Gibbon's *Essai*[71] – there is the important concession to the *érudits* of the faculty of judgment which Gibbon desired to claim for them.

L' *érudition*, considerée par rapport à l'état présent des lettres, renferme trois branches principales, la connoissance de l'histoire, celle des langues, et celle des livres...

La connoissance des livres suppose, du moins jusqu'à un certain point, celles des matieres qu'ils traitent, et des auteurs; mais elle consiste principalement dans la connoissance du jugement que les savans ont porté de ces ouvrages, de l'espece d'utilité qu'on peut tirer de leur lecture, des anecdotes qui concernent les auteurs et les livres, des différentes éditions et du choix que l'on doit faire entr'elles.[72]

[Erudition, considered in relation to the present state of letters, consists of three principal branches: the knowledge of history, of languages, and of books...

The knowledge of books presupposes, at least to a certain point, that of the subjects they treat of, and of their authors; but it consists primarily of a knowledge of the judgment which the learned have pronounced regarding these works, of the reasons why it may be profitable to read them, of anecdotes regarding the authors and their books, of the different editions and the choice which should be made between them.][73]

Even here the *érudit's jugement* is of the second order, but one can scarcely evaluate the judgments of others without developing one's own, and Gibbon was at a loss to understand why d'Alembert, capable of thus conceding 'qu'un érudit peut avoir du goût, des vues, de la finesse dans l'esprit', could have given the negative portrait which appears in the

---

[70] This is contended by Giarrizzo, 1954, pp. 97–101.   [71] *MW*, IV, pp. 20–1 nn.
[72] *Encyclopédie* (first edn), XII, p. 952.
[73] Translation JGAP, as are other quotations from the article 'Erudition'.

Discours préliminaire. In 'Erudition' d'Alembert held forth at some length on the qualities of the mind necessitated by *la critique*, implicitly conceding that these – *jugement*, at least, if not *imagination* – would be developed in the intelligence of the *érudit*; he still seemed to confine *la critique* to assessing the reliability of the authors studied, and the *utilité* of the information they conveyed. It was perhaps the narrowness of the concept 'utility' which aroused Gibbon's objections; d'Alembert seemed to him preoccupied with deciding whether a thing was worth knowing or not, and even if his mind was broadly, not narrowly open to historical information – which may very well have been the case – this was not the same as exploring the powers and pleasures of a mind engaged in opening up the worlds of experience which a text properly read might reveal. It was not that d'Alembert did not know what the historical intelligence was, but that something else was always deflecting his attention, and his evaluation, from it.

He knew even how it was itself situated in history.

L'érudition est un genre de connoissance où les modernes se sont distingués par deux raisons: plus le monde vieillit, plus la matiere de l'érudition augmente, et plus par conséquent il doit y avoir d'érudits; comme il doit y avoir plus de fortunes lorsqu'il y a plus d'argent. D'ailleurs l'ancienne Grece ne faisoit cas que de son histoire et de sa langue, et les Romains n'étoient qu'orateurs et politiques: ainsi l'érudition, proprement dite n'étoit pas extrêmement cultivée par les anciens.[74]

[Erudition is a kind of knowledge in which the moderns have taken the lead for two reasons. The older the world grows, the more the materials of erudition accumulate, and the more need there is of the erudite; just as there must be more great fortunes when there is more money in circulation. Furthermore, ancient Greece cared only for its own history and language, and the Romans were mere orators and statesmen, so that erudition, in the proper sense, was not much cultivated by the ancients.]

There had been a few *érudits* in imperial Rome, before the fall of the western empire had plunged the Latin lands into the barbarism in which they lay 'jusqu'à la fin du XVe siècle'. The Byzantine world retained some knowledge of Latin as well as Greek antiquities, but the library of Constantinople was destroyed by Leo the Isaurian ('insensé . . . imbécile et furieux') and that of Alexandria by the Arabs; and one should not make too much of the tradition that western letters had been revived by fugitive Greeks in 1454 (*sic*).

---

[74] *Encyclopédie*, XII, p. 954.

cela est vrai jusqu'à un certain point; mais l'arrivée des savans de la Grece avoit été précédé de l'invention de l'imprimerie, faite quelques années auparavant, des ouvrages du Dante, de Petrarque et de Boccace, qui avoient ramené en Italie l'aurore du bon goût; enfin, d'un petit nombre de savans qui avoient commencé à débrouiller et même à cultiver avec succès la littérature Latine, tels que le Pogge, Laurent Valla, Philelphe et quelques autres.[75]

[This is true up to a point; but the arrival of Greek scholars had been preceded by the invention of printing some years earlier; by the works of Dante, Petrarch and Boccaccio, who had heralded the dawn of good taste in Italy; finally, by a limited number of scholars who had begun to bring to light, and even cultivate with some success, literature in Latin, such as Poggio, Lorenzo Valla, Filelfo and others.]

Medicean Florence was no offshoot of Constantinople, but welcomed the Greek scholars for the use it could put them to; the Latin world had possessed after all the means of rescuing itself from its own barbarism. Rediscovering ancient literature, Renaissance scholarship had for two centuries been the instrument by which *le goût, la critique* and one must add *l'imagination*, had been revived in the Occident; and d'Alembert unhesitatingly praises the work of *l'érudition* to the point where he must acknowledge the claim, made in the *Histoire de l'Académie des Inscriptions et Belles Lettres*, that it is still alive and is unjustly slighted by the *philosophes* with their preference for physics and mathematics. 'Leurs plaintes sont raisonnables', he says, 'et dignes d'être appuyées'; nevertheless he undertakes to answer them. Mathematics and physics, whose crucial role in the self-emancipation of *l'esprit philosophique* was set out in the *Discours préliminaire*, offer a foundation for the mind more solid than any *la critique* can supply; and here d'Alembert is led to advance an argument apparently the contradiction, but perhaps only the corollary, of his previous contention that the world of facts is infinite and intoxicating, that of ideas simple, finite and sane.[76] We now hear that mathematics and physics offer 'la champ plus vaste', whereas in the field of 'bel esprit, il est sans doute très difficile, et plus difficile peut-être qu'en aucun autre genre, d'y produire des choses nouvelles'.[77] This language is less denigratory than it sounds. All the faculties of the enquiring mind have need of one another, and the empire of probability is no less extensive than that of certainty.

L'espece de sagacité que demandent certaines branches de l'*érudition*, par exemple la critique, n'est guere moindre que celle qui est nécessaire à l'étude des Sciences, peut-être même y faut-il quelquefois plus de finesse; l'artet l'usage

---

[75] *Encyclopédie*, XII, p. 955.   [76] Above, pp. 187–8.   [77] *Encyclopédie*, XII, p. 956.

des probabilités et des conjectures, suppose en général un esprit plus souple et plus delié, que celui qui ne se rend qu'à la lumiere des démonstrations.[78]

[The species of sagacity called for in certain branches of erudition, for example in criticism, is scarcely less than that necessary in the study of the sciences, and perhaps there is sometimes greater need of finesse. The art and practice of probability and conjecture presuppose an intelligence more subtle and flexible than that which declares itself only in the light of rigorous proof.]

D'Alembert is irresistibly fair-minded, and yet he never goes beyond being fair to the *érudits*, whom he respects without complete sympathy. His strongest argument showing them to be still indispensable rests on the premise that they have almost, though perhaps they will never have quite, completed their task of enlightening the western intellect through the study of Greek and Latin *belles-lettres*.

D'ailleurs, quand on supposeroit (ce qui n'est pas) qu'il n'y a plus absolument de progrès à faire dans l'étude des langues savantes cultivées par nos ancêtres, le Latin, le Grec, et même l'Hébreu;[79] combien ne reste-il pas encore à défricher dans l'étude de plusieurs langues orientales, dont la connaissance approfondie procureroit à notre littérature les plus grandes avantages? On sait avec quel succès les Arabes ont cultivé les sciences; combien l'astronomie, la médecine, la chirurgie, l'arithmétique et l'algebre leur sont redevables; combien ils ont eu d'histoires, de poëtes, enfin d'écrivains en tout genre. La bibliotheque du roi est pleine de manuscrits Arabes, dont la traduction nous voudroit une infinité de connoissances curieuses. Il en est de même de la langue Chinoise. Quel vaste matiere de découvertes pour nos littérateurs!

[Besides, even if we suppose (as is not the case) that there is absolutely no progress to be made in the knowledge of the tongues cultivated by our ancestors – Latin, Greek and even Hebrew – how much is there still to be harvested in the study of several oriental languages, of which a deeper study would bring great benefits to our literature? We know with what success the Arabs cultivated the sciences; how much astronomy, medicine, surgery, arithmetic and algebra are indebted to them; how many historians, poets and writers of every kind there were among them. The royal library is full of Arabic manuscripts, translation of which would bring us an infinity of curious information. It is the same with the Chinese language. What a wealth of discoveries awaits our literary scholars!]

Even if for the present – d'Alembert's words have an ironic ring after two and half centuries – the difficulties of the Arabic and Chinese languages may consume whole lifetimes of non-exploitable study, this will pass in time.

[78] *Encyclopédie*, XII, p. 957.   [79] This field of learning is not often mentioned.

Nos premiers savans ont passé presque toute leur vie à l'étude du Grec; c'est aujourd'hui une affaire de quelques années. Voilà donc une branche d'*érudition*, tout neuve, trop negligée jusqu'à nous, et bien digne d'exercer nos savans. Combien n'y a-t-il pas encore à découvrir dans des branches plus cultivées que celle-là? Qu'on interroge ceux qui ont le plus approfondi la géographie ancienne et moderne, on apprendra d'eux, avec étonnement, combien ils trouvent dans les originaux de choses qu'on n'y a point vues, ou qu'on n'en a point tirées, et combien des erreurs à rectifier dans leurs prédécesseurs. Celui qui défriche le premier une matiere avec succès, est suivi d'une infinité d'auteurs, qui ne font que le copier dans ses fautes mêmes, qui n'ajoutent absolument rien à son travail; et on est surpris, après avoir parcouru un grand nombre d'ouvrages sur le même objet, de voir que les premiers pas y sont à peine encore faits, lorsque la multitude le croit épuisé... Il s'en faut donc beaucoup que l'érudition soit un terrein où nous n'ayions plus de moisson à faire.[80]

[Our earliest scholars passed their whole lives in the study of Greek; today it can be mastered in a few years. Here then is a branch of erudition, quite new, hitherto neglected, and worthy of the attention of our scholars. How much may there be still to discover in the fields which have been more cultivated? When one questions those who have read deepest into geography ancient and modern, one is amazed to learn how much they find in original sources which has never yet been noticed or brought to light, and how many errors there are to correct in their predecessors. He who is the first to explore a field with some success is followed by a crowd of authors who merely copy him even in his faults, and add absolutely nothing to his labours; and when one has read a great number of works on the same subject, one is astonished to realise that the first steps have hardly been taken, though the multitude think the field has been exhausted... It is then far from being the case that erudition is a field where there remains nothing to be harvested.]

The excitement of discovering what Freret and his colleagues had known for thirty years, that there were whole new worlds of human experience waiting to be explored in the Arabic and Chinese sources, leads d'Alembert to realise, and for the first time proclaim, that the Greek and Latin sources – he could have added the vernacular – are themselves inexhaustible, and that the *érudit* is embarked on a limitless voyage. At this point one might say that humanist and scientist have been placed on a footing of full equality, and yet there is the lingering thought that, possibly in both fields, the great discoverers instantly acquire the status of classics, who can only be imitated, misunderstood or refined. It is not quite certain that the doors of discovery are all fully opened. To Gibbon, reading the article 'Erudition' and the *Discours*

---

[80] See p. 205, note 78.

préliminaire side by side, it must have seemed evident that either the former had destroyed the rigid hierarchies of the latter, or it had not; in which case even the explorers of Arabic and Chinese literature remained mere labourers, heaping up facts to be remembered and exploited by philosophers and poets to whose society they could not aspire.

The tension does not quite disappear, even when we suppose that in 'Erudition' d'Alembert was concerned with the *ordre historique*, in which the mind was faced with tasks that called forth new capacities. There remained the *ordre metaphysique*, in which these capacities were not needed and did not appear. Gibbon, responding to the *Discours préliminaire* between the ages of twenty-one and twenty-four, had reason to believe that he was faced with a Platonic intelligence that dismissed both erudition and history to the Cave. Holding as he already did that the mind – the *esprit humain* which was the subject of Enlightenment – functioned only in a world of history, he set out in the *Essai* to show what philosophy was called for by the need to recognise erudition.

CHAPTER 9

The 'Essai sur l'étude de la littérature': imagination, irony and history

There are two ways of reading the *Essai* which Gibbon's *Memoirs* inform us was written as a defence of erudition against such attacks as those of d'Alembert in the *Discours préliminaire*. We possess the manuscript drafts which were written at Lausanne in 1758, just before Gibbon's return to England and at Buriton later that year and in 1761; the earlier drafts include some paragraphs on the rise of Christianity which were replaced in 1761.[1] From these, and their situation among Gibbon's other manuscripts, it is possible to draw inferences about the origin and growth of Gibbon's intentions as he wrote the *Essai*, inferences which may or may not coincide with what he wrote in the *Memoirs* thirty years later.[2] Alternatively, we possess the printed text published in 1761, and reprinted by Lord Sheffield in the posthumous *Miscellaneous Works*;[3] and this it is possible to read in the context of the print culture of the eighteenth century, juxtaposing it with d'Alembert's text and others with which it may be associated, and so arriving at conclusions regarding what Gibbon may have succeeded in saying, or in being read as saying, in the public and cosmopolitan discourse of his time as we now see it. The former reading (that of the manuscripts) leans to the illocutionary, to the study of what Gibbon may have been trying to say; the latter (that of the published text) to the perlocutionary, to the study of what he may have ended by saying, to readers of his time or possibly of ours; and the two readings may be distinguished though they cannot be separated. It is valuable to pursue both.

The manuscript drafts – assigned to moments of composition by

[1] BL Add. MSS 34880, fols. 129r ('Commencées à Lausanne, environ le 20 Mars 1758'), 135 ('Reprises à Beriton 28 Juillet 1758'), 175 ('A Beriton le 28 Avril 1761'); in all fols. 129r–141, 150–5, 156–157r, 175–84. 'Buriton' appears to be the modern spelling of the house and village where Edward Gibbon II resided and the *Essai* was completed. For the composition of the work, see *YEG*, pp. 116–20, 126–31, 133, 135–6, 151–3.
[2] *Memoirs*, pp. 99–107 (*A*, pp. 167–77, Memoir B).   [3] *MW*, IV, pp. 1–93.

annotations in Gibbon's hand – look back to the Lausanne common-place book and forward to the militia journal, both of which we have already studied, and therefore form part of the record of Gibbon's studies and the growth of his intentions in becoming a scholar and historian. They are initially headed 'Reflexions sur l'Etude des Belles-Lettres', and there is an insertion which reads:

Pour éviter toute équivoque, j'avertis une fois pour tout que j'entends par *l'Etude des Belles-Lettres, celle des Anciens, et de l'Antiquité Grecque et Latine.*[4]

Literature is *belles-lettres*, and *belles-lettres* are ancient. Gibbon is not specifying the genres into which literature may fall, and we shall find that he is far from ruling out the possibility that *belles-lettres* may be studied for their archival as well as their aesthetic value. As the *Essai* proceeds, the two values will merge, as the study of antiquity is seen to entail the exercise of 'the nobler faculties of the imagination and the judgment'. Thinking of this kind is recognised by Gibbon and by us as historical; yet the *Essai* is initially about *belles-lettres* and subsequently about *littérature*, and the genre *histoire* is not singled out as that to which all other literary genres are necessarily subject. At Lausanne Gibbon was engaged in scholarship; in the militia journal he is in search of the theme for a history; in the *Memoirs* he depicts himself at Stourhead discovering new worlds of history; but in the *Essai* he set himself to show that the study of antiquities was co-terminous with that of literature. Nevertheless, the Lausanne draft opens with the crucially d'Alembert-ian words:

L'Histoire des Empires est celle de la Misere des hommes: l'Histoire des Sciences est celle de leur Grandeur et de leur bonheur.

[The History of empires is that of the misery of mankind; the history of the sciences that of its greatness and happiness.]

And these words survive in the printed text; while in the margin, and possibly in a later hand, appear the words 'Idée de l'Histoire Littéraire', and a further crucial (and historising) annotation, 'Les sciences sujettes à la mode'.[5] History, in a post-classical and perhaps post-neoclassical and certainly philosophical sense, is present to both author and reader from the start, but is not aiming at the subjection of all other genres (which as we shall see would render it too *sujette à la mode*).

The Lausanne sections of the draft *Essai* do not contain all the footnotes found in the printed text, and those of the latter which support

---

[4] BL Add. MSS 34880, fol. 130r.   [5] Fol. 130.

the *Memoirs* in representing the *Essai* as a response to d'Alembert's *Discours préliminaire* and article on 'Erudition' reach us as footnotes to a footnote.[6] There is reason to be cautious and entertain the possibility that the *Essai* is the fruit of Gibbon's reading at Lausanne and only in part a polemical response to the *Encyclopédie*. On the one hand, the earlier commonplace book contains a marginal note, apparently of an early date, to an entry on 'Montesqiou' reading

V. L'Eloge Historique de M. De Montesqiou par M. D'Alembert à la tete du Vme Tome de l'Encyclopedie, ou dans le Mercure de France Novembre 1755. p. 77–124.[7]

and the entry may summarise parts of this *éloge*. We therefore have Gibbon aware of the *Encyclopédie* while at Lausanne. On the other hand, it is hard to find any other reference to it in the Lausanne manuscripts, which are filled with citations of the *Mémoires de l'Académie des Inscriptions*. These, not the volumes of the *Encyclopédie*, were the pastures in which Gibbon's mind grazed, and the situation may be summed up by saying that, of the six references to the *Encyclopédie* so far identified in his published and unpublished writings, four are to d'Alembert while a fifth alone expresses positive (if qualified) approval.[8] If Gibbon did not care for the 'vast undertaking' and 'immense compilation', he did not care enough to campaign against it. If the *Essai*, however, did not originate as, it nevertheless became, a tract against d'Alembert, and its language owes a great deal to Montesquieu.[9]

There is one major difference between the first draft of the *Essai*, written in two stages during 1758, and that revised for publication in 1761. The former ends with a section on 'La Religion', combining orthodox with Enlightened sentiments in a way characteristic of its age but not of the later Gibbon. It begins:

---

[6] *MW*, IV, pp. 20–1, nn. *, 1 and 2.

[7] BL Add. MSS 34880, fol. 77r. The name is spelt 'Montesqiou' in both note and entry.

[8] There is mention of d'Alembert's *Discours préliminaire* (*Memoirs*, p. 99, *MW*, IV, pp. 20–1) and his articles 'Comete' (*Decline and Fall*, IV, ch. 43, n. 76: 'Astronomers may study Newton and Halley. I draw my humble science from the article . . . by M. d'Alembert'), 'Erudition' (*MW*, IV, pp. 20–1) and 'Montesquieu' (notes 7 and 9 to this chapter). There is a reference to the article 'Concile' in *Decline and Fall*, II, ch. 20, n. 130 ('the editors have reason to be proud of *this* article. Those who consult their immense compilation seldom depart so well satisfied'). For the article 'Goût', attributed to Montesquieu, see next note. The absence of references to letters later than M and volumes later than 1758 may be observed and arouse suspicions. Even the references to the fifth volume may have been culled from the *Mercure de France*, and we may doubt whether Gibbon read much beyond the letter C.

[9] 'M. De Montesqiou avoit beaucoup encouragé l'Encyclopedie, mais il n'y a rien travaillé qu'un article sur le Gout, lequel quoique imparfait se trouve dans le cinquieme Tome de cet Ouvrage'. BL Add. MSS. 34880, fol. 77r.

La Litterature se fait honneur de se ranger sous les drapeaux de la Theologie [;] non de cette Theologie contentieuse qu'on pourroit peindre comme la muse de la Tragedie [,] une masque au visage, un poignard à la main; mais de cette doctrine celeste, assez bienfaisante pour ne precher à ses enfans que la vertu, assez grande pour la recompenser chez ses ennemis. Cette doctrine est un corps de preceptes [,] mais il est fondé sur des faits qui se sont passé chez ces mesmes peuples que sont l'object des travaux du Literateur. Les livres ou nous puisons ces faits [,] sont-ils aussi anciens qu'ils nous paroissent? Ne contiennent-ils rien de contraire aux moeurs connus de ces tems?[10]

[Literature does itself honour when it enlists under the banner of theology; not that contentious theology which one might paint as the Tragic Muse, a mask on her face and a dagger in her hand, but that heavenly doctrine benevolent enough to preach to her children nothing but virtue and great enough to reward it even among her enemies. This doctrine is a body of precepts, but it is founded on actions which took place among the very peoples who are the object of the labours of the student of literature. Are the books from which we draw these facts as ancient as they appear? Do they contain nothing contrary to the known manners of their time?][11]

This is orthodox liberal Christianity; the religion of dogma, debate and persecution is to be abandoned in favour of a religion of morality, capable of recognising the virtue of pagans. *Belles-lettres* and ancient literature offer us the portrait of that virtue, but if the religion that eternises it is to be Christian it must involve the mission of a divine being, and a dilemma makes its appearance. If the *belles-lettres* are pagan they tell us nothing of Christ; if they contain all that he taught his mission was unnecessary; and here is a hint that the Gospels and Acts are to be read critically in the context which pagan literature supplies. To believe in Christ's divine mission – the text continues – we must believe in the moral corruption of the ancient world, and the literature of Roman decay offers copious and horrifying evidence of this. The *étude des belles-lettres* thus offers us a middle way between believing that Christianity is nothing but morality and believing that it was nothing except revelation,[12] while the more benign aspects of ancient culture explain how a few philosophers and men of virtue could devise a worship of the Supreme Being that might substitute itself for the mythologies of polytheism.[13] There is then a theodicy of the Decline and Fall; the wickedness of the Julio-Claudian emperors and the corruption of Roman virtue – surviving only among Academic and Stoic philos-

---

[10] BL Add. MSS 34880, fol. 154.
[11] Trans. JGAP, as are all translations from the *Essai* in this chapter.
[12] Fols. 154–154r; *YEG*, p. 130.   [13] Fols. 154–5.

ophers – supply the context which gave Christ's appearance meaning and necessity. Augustus was not the worst of the line he founded, but his deification was fraudulent and ineffectual.

Dix huit ans un homme obscur perit par le supplice le plus infame. Il sortoit d'une nation meprisée de toute la terre. Les disciples l'annoncent pour Dieu [,] mais dieu d'un nouvel ordre mais destructeur de tous les dieux de la terre. Cependant sa doctrine s'etend. Persecutée partout, partout il renait de ses cendres. Ses ennemis s'acharnent pour la combattre, ils se refutent par leurs propres aveux. On eriga la croix sur les debris du Capitole. Le Mage et le Druide, le Stoicien et l'Epicurien se reunissent à croire une doctrine qui etonne la raison et qui amortit.[14]

[Eighteen years later, an unknown man perished by the most disgraceful of executions. He came of a nation despised by all the world. His disciples proclaimed him God, but a god of a new kind destructive to all the gods of earth. And yet his doctrine spread. Persecuted everywhere, it everywhere arose from its ashes. Its enemies strove to resist it, but condemned themselves out of their own mouths. The Cross was erected on the ruins of the Capitol. The Magian and the Druid, the Stoic and the Epicurean, united in believing a doctrine which astonishes and silences reason.]

This, the first account of Christ which we have from Gibbon, is also the last which declares that there was something astonishing about the life and death of Jesus and the subsequent spread of doctrine concerning him. In the *Decline and Fall* there is little that is directly about him, and what there is tends to reduce him to a humble preacher unjustly punished, while the triumph of his religion is explained by the operation of historical causes. The Gibbon of 1758 is orthodox by comparison, not least in the indication of an intimate if revolutionary relation between Christian monotheism and either the polytheism or the philosophy of classical culture; yet the words 'Les disciples l'annoncent pour Dieu' could be read as hinting that the apostles and the fathers, rather than Jesus himself, were the founders of the Church of Christ's divinity. As for 'the Cross … erected on the ruins of the Capitol', it is not a foretaste of Gibbon's visit to Rome six years later, but an orthodox and common-place recognition that the history of the empire became the history of the church. The real issue raised by the fifteenth and sixteenth chapters of the *Decline and Fall* was their strongly implied message that the spread of Christianity could be explained without reference to the holiness, as distinct from the morality, of its teachings, or to the divinity of its author;

---

[14] BL Add. MSS 34880, fol. 155; *YEG*, pp. 130–1.

and we do not find that implication thrust upon the modern reader –
there were no readers in Gibbon's day – of the text of 1758.

(11)

The only major change which Gibbon made in the manuscript *Essai* of
1758 was to cancel the section on Christianity and substitute the more
philosophical history of religion[15] which stands at the end of the text as
published.[16] Other than this, most of what appears in the manuscripts of
1758 and 1761 made its way into the printed version, and we are at the
appropriate moment to move from considering the *Essai* in composition
to considering it as publication. It is while we are composing a text that
we formulate intentions and write to carry them out; it is when we look
at the text as complete – especially in a form which is the work of other
hands – that we discover, and others begin discovering for us, what it is
we have performed. This chapter now turns from the *Essai* as intention
to the *Essai* as performance.

Gibbon, we know, was dissatisfied with his performance. His introduction is apologetic beyond the calls of convention.[17] He was uneasy
about the perfection of his French, and sought rather unsuccessfully for
a francophone mentor who would reassure him;[18] he was writing and
publishing in French, but in an England at war with France, and at a
moment in his life when he was unsure which was his primary language.
Here he had to do, as we have, with both the ambivalent relationship
between the two cultures and the complex personal history which was to
take him from telling David Hume in 1767 'I write in French because I
think in French',[19] to publishing the first volume of the *Decline and Fall*,
with its mastery of an English style he had largely invented, nine years
later. There is the more immediate question why he chose to publish in
1762 the essay he had begun in Lausanne four years earlier, and here we
are confronted with the *Memoirs*, which indicate that he was pushed into
it by his father, who hoped it might secure him some public employment; whereas Gibbon was a private man, in process of discovering
that he was also a bachelor, who desired to be no more than a gentleman of letters. To publish in French, however, even in London, was

---

[15] BL Add. MSS 34880, fols. 175–83.   [16] *MW*, IV, pp. 70–88.
[17] *MW*, IV, pp. 5–6; cf. *Memoirs*, pp. 99–104 (*A*, pp. 167–74).
[18] This was Mathieu Maty, of Huguenot descent and editor of a French-language literary periodical
in London. For his preface to the *Essai* see *MW*, IV, pp. 7–14, and for his relations with Gibbon
YEG, pp. 132–5, 136.   [19] *Letters*, I, p. 222.

to appeal to the authority of a 'public', either the *république des lettres* as it had been and might still be, or a 'public' in the new sense of the consumers of a commercial product and the 'public opinion' generated on that market. Here Gibbon was soon to discover, with disappointment if without surprise, that the *Essai* was no great publishing success and generated no response or debate. The experience was less traumatic than that undergone by Hume at the complete failure of the *Treatise of Human Nature*;[20] but it both obliges and leaves us free to evaluate the *Essai* as philosophic performance, considering what it says and does, in and to the intellectual climate of its time. This chapter will argue that what it had to say is significant, and that its inexperienced author expressed perceptions more important than his immediate capacity to project them to a public.

The *Essai* begins, as we have seen, with a contrast between the history of empire and that of science.[21] Gibbon was to spend much of his life writing *l'histoire des empires*, and though he never became their panegyrist, and preferred a Europe of commerce to a Europe unified by empire, was to develop the thesis that the history of empire was ambivalent; it did much to promote *l'histoire des sciences*, as well as much to injure and inhibit them. For the present, however, the *Essai* adopts the same position as the *Discours préliminaire*: that the deeds of conquerors form one kind of history, the deeds of *l'esprit* the other, and that a choice must be made between them. We shall have to enquire how Gibbon moved away from this dichotomy, and perhaps the *Essai* shows him instantly beginning to do so. The text continues:

Si mille considerations doivent rendre ce dernier genre d'étude [i.e., that of *l'histoire des sciences*] precieux aux yeux du philosophe, cette réflexion doit le rendre bien cher à tout amateur de l'humanité.

Que je voudrois qu'une vérité aussi consolante ne reçût aucune exception! Mais, hélas! l'homme ne perce que trop souvent dans la cabinet du savant. Dans cet asile de la sagesse, il est encore égaré par les préjugés, déchiré par les passions, avili par les foiblesses.

L'empire de la mode est fondé sur l'inconstance des hommes; empire dont l'origine est si frivole et dont les effets sont si funestes. L'homme de lettres n'ose secouer son joug, et si ses réflexions retardent sa defaite, elles la rendent plus honteuse.[22]

[If there are a thousand reasons why this branch of study should be precious in

[20] Hume, 'My Own Life' (Miller, 1985, p. xxxiv).   [21] *MW*, IV, p. 15; above, p. 209.
[22] *MW*, IV, *ibid*. This is the point at which the Lausanne text of 1758 has the marginalium 'Les sciences sujettes à la mode' (p. 29, n. 5).

the eyes of the philosopher, this reflection alone should endear it to the lover of mankind.

I could wish that this consoling truth were such as knew no exception; but, alas, the man enters but too often into the study of the scholar, and even in this refuge of wisdom, he is still misled by prejudices, distracted by passions, and debased by weaknesses.

The empire of fashion is founded in the inconstancy of men; its origins are as frivolous as its effects are fatal. The man of letters dare not resist its yoke, and if his reflections delay his captivity, they do but render it more shameful.]

D'Alembert would have agreed that the history of intellect was as full of human imperfection as any other branch of history, but he regarded *la philosophie* as the means of emancipating oneself from the intellect's history as far as possible. Gibbon was already proposing to study this history – as itself a species of *l'histoire des empires* – and to suggest that the philosophical organisation of intellect d'Alembert had been proposing was itself part of an *empire de la mode* and had not escaped from it. We may ask whether he regarded such escape as either possible or desirable.

Tous les pays, tous les siècles ont vu quelque science l'objet d'une préférence souvent injuste, pendant que les autres études languissoient dans un mépris tout aussi peu raisonnable. La métaphysique et la dialectique sous les successeurs d'Alexandre, la politique et l'éloquence sous la république Romaine, l'histoire, la poësie dans le siècle d'Auguste, la grammaire et la juri[s]prudence sous le Bas-Empire, la philosophie scholastique dans le treizieme siècle, les Belles-Lettres jusqu'aux jours de nos pères, ont fait, tour-a-tour, l'admiration et le mépris des hommes. La physique et les mathématiques sont à présent sur le trône. Elles voyent toutes les sœurs prosternées devant elles, enchaînées à leur char, ou tout-au plus occupées à orner leur triomphe. Peut-être leur chute n'est pas eloignée.

Il seroit digne d'un habile homme de suivre cette révolution dans les religions, les gouvernemens, les mœurs, qui ont successivement égaré, désolé et corrompu les hommes. Qu'il se gardât bien davantage de l'éviter.[23]

[Every land and every age has seen some science the beneficiary of a preference too often unjust, while other studies suffer from a contempt equally unjustifiable. Metaphysics and dialectic under the successors of Alexander, politics and eloquence under the Roman republic, history and poetry in the Augustan age, grammar and jurisprudence under the later Empire, scholastic philosophy in the thirteenth century, humane letters until the age of our fathers, have enjoyed by turns the admiration and the scorn of men. Physics and mathemat-

---

[23] IV, pp. 15–17. Gibbon would probably not know of Diderot's observation that d'Alembert's mathematics were already out of fashion, the public mind having turned to other subjects. By 1758 d'Alembert was refusing to take part in any but the mathematical sections of the *Encyclopédie*, but there is no indication that Gibbon had heard of this in Lausanne.

ics are now upon the throne. They see all their sisters prostrate before them, chained to their chariot wheels, or otherwise devoted to the adornment of their triumph. Perhaps their fall is not far distant.

It would be worthy of a skilful writer to pursue this revolution in religion, government and manners, whose successive phases have misled, devastated and corrupted humanity. Let him beware taking part in it himself.]

Gibbon at Lausanne had studied mathematics, apparently at parental prompting, and never altogether lost interest in them. But they were not a passion with him, and in the *Memoirs* he congratulated himself on avoiding the temptation to apply geometrical proof to moral reasoning.[24] Here he is attributing to mathematics a present hegemony over history and the other sciences, and by doing so indicating that they are themselves only part of the history they present the illusion of dominating. By depicting them in the role of an antique *triumphator* and conqueror, he is making them riders on the wheel of Fortune, and inviting the *habile homme*, or philosopher, to study mathematics as history, and history itself as the record of that wheel, 'cette revolution dans les religions, les gouvernemens, les mœurs', which turns out to be nothing other than that *histoire des empires* from which *l'histoire des sciences* was supposed to be an escape. From his initial 'Mais, hélas!' he has been moving to insist on the primacy of an ironic and elegiac perception of history which includes philosophy itself. It is easy to present ourselves as involved in the same debate, and to suppose that it has no end; which is to share Gibbon's conservative and non-emancipatory perception, expressed in his youth and not abandoned thereafter.

The notion of *système* here makes a significant appearance. The triumph of Lockean *philosophie* over *la scholastique* was agreed to be a victory for *méthode* over *système*, but needed to be presented in a historical scenario. It was a long stride from *le Bas-Empire* to *le treizième siècle*, and Gibbon here fills in the interval in a way from which d'Alembert had not dissented, but which he bases on another authority.

L'amour des systèmes, (dit M. Freret,) qui s'empara des esprits après Aristote, fit abandonner aux Grecs l'étude de la nature, et arrêta le progrès de leurs découvertes philosophiques; les raisonnemens subtils prirent la place des experiences; les sciences exactes, la géométrie, l'astronomie, la vraie philosophie disparurent presqu'entièrement. On ne s'occupa plus du soin d'acquérir des connoissances nouvelles, mais de celui de ranger, et de lier les unes aux autres, celles que l'on croyoit avoir, pour en former des systèmes.

C'est là ce qui forma toutes les différentes sectes: les meilleurs esprits

[24] *Memoirs*, pp. 77–8 (*A*, pp. 141–2); above, p. 83.

s'évaporerent dans les abstractions d'une métaphysique obscure, où les mots tenoient le plus souvent la place des choses, et la dialectique, nommée par Aristote l'instrument de notre esprit, devint chez ses disciples l'objet principal et presque unique de leur application. La vie entière se passoit a l'étudier l'art du raisonnement, et à ne raisonner jamais, ou du moins à ne raisonner que sur des objets fantastiques.[25]

[The love of system, says M. Freret, which took possession of men's minds after Aristotle, caused the Greeks to abandon the study of nature and arrested the progress of their scientific discoveries. Subtle ratiocination took the place of experiment; the exact sciences, geometry and astronomy, and the true philosophy disappeared almost entirely. They busied themselves no longer with acquiring new knowledge, but with ordering and connecting that which they thought they already possessed, to make into systems.

Thus there arose all the differing schools and sects; the best minds burned themselves out in the abstractions of a dark metaphysics, and dialectic, which Aristotle had called the tool of our intelligence, became for his disciples the principal and almost the sole object of study. The whole of life was passed in studying the art of reasoning, while reasoning not at all, unless on matters wholly imaginary.]

Gibbon is quoting from a *discours* in which Freret made explicit to the Académie[26] a foreshortening of history which we found implicit in the *Discours préliminaire*; he spoke of the schools of the Second Sophistic, in which 'toutes les différentes sectes' arose, as if they had witnessed the triumph of the Peripatetics and the idolisation and systematisation of Aristotle's writings into a canon of scholasticism. This telescoping of a thousand years of intellectual history obscured the role of neo-Platonism, which only the historiography of Christian theology was competent to restore.[27] But it is significant that Gibbon here turns from d'Alembert and the *Encyclopédie* to Freret and the Académie, and an effect of his doing so is to suggest that the present hegemony of mathematics, asserted in the name of *méthode*, is in fact an effect of *système*, and that the wheel of Fortune operates in *l'histoire des sciences* as *méthodes* harden into *systèmes*, asserting empire and suffering overthrow in their turn. D'Alembert might not have dissented; he believed that geometry was the only legitimate *système* known to the human mind, but agreed that there were worlds of experience to which it could not be directly applied. The issue is Gibbon's claim that mathematics are asserting empire and exposing themselves to Fortune in that world already, and this is what gives meaning to his project of affirming the intellectual autonomy of *l'érudition*.

[25] *MW*, IV, p. 16n.   [26] Above, pp. 158–9.   [27] See Howel, above, p. 36.

Like d'Alembert, he looks back to an age of 'Renaissance des Belles-Lettres'[28] – the *litterae humaniores* – when

Le guerrier les lisoit sous sa tente. L'homme d'état les etudioit dans son cabinet. Ce sexe même qui, content des graces, nous laisse les lumières, embellissoit l'exemple d'une Délie, et souhaitoit de trouver un Tibulle dans son amant,[29]

[The warrior read them in his tent. The statesman studied them in his sanctum. That sex, which, content with the graces of life, leaves to us the powers of intellect, improved the example of a Delia and longed to see a Tibullus in every lover,]

and, heroine exceptions to this gracious rule, Elizabeth of England studied history as a prince and Christina of Sweden preferred to be a scholar and a patron. Gibbon does not deny that the great *savants* were sometimes monomaniacs, and sees Enlightenment as an emancipation from the tyranny of letters,[30] but his account of it differs significantly from d'Alembert's.

La lumière alloit paroître. Descartes ne fut pas littérateur, mais les Belles-Lettres lui sont bien redevables. Un philosophe éclairé, [n. M. Le Clerc, dans son excellent *Ars Critica*, et dans plusieurs autres de ses ouvrages][31] heritier de sa méthode, approfondit les vrais principes de la critique. Le Bossu, Boileau, Rapin, Brumoy apprirent aux hommes à connoître mieux le prix des trésors qu'ils possédoient. Une de ces sociétés qui ont mieux immortalisé Louis XIV qu'une ambition souvent pernicieuse aux hommes, commençoit déjà ces recherches qui réunissent la justesse de l'esprit, l'aménité et l'érudition, ou l'on voit tant de découvertes, et quelquefois, ce qui ne cède qu'à peine aux découvertes, une ignorance modeste et savante.[32]

[Light was about to dawn. Descartes was no man of letters, but literature owes him much. An enlightened philosopher (n. M. Le Clerc, in his excellent *Ars Critica* and several other works), inheriting his method, probed the true principles of criticism. Le Bossu, Boileau, Rapin, Brumoy taught men a better knowledge of the value of the treasures they possessed. One of those societies which have done more to immortalise Louis XIV than an ambition often destructive to humanity was beginning those researches which have joined precision of intellect to politeness and erudition, where we observe many discoveries, and at times a learned and modest ignorance, which gives way slowly before discoveries of this kind.]

The first and third instances evoke the two *républiques des lettres*, the two publishing projects, and in an important sense the two Enlightenments,

---

[28] *MW*, IV, p. 17, marginal heading.   [29] *MW*, IV, p. 17.   [30] *MW*, IV, p. 18.
[31] This note significantly appears, in the manuscript of 1758, at the point designated by note 23 on p. 215 (BL Add. MSS 34880, fol. 130r).   [32] *MW*, IV, p. 19.

which meant most to Gibbon as his mind attained maturity: the Remonstrant and Huguenot *bibliothèques* directed from Amsterdam by Jean Le Clerc, and the *Mémoires* and *Histoire de l'Académie des Inscriptions et Belles-Lettres* as founded by Louis XIV. Like d'Alembert, he sees the growth of critical scholarship as owing much to Cartesian *méthode*, but he sees it as kept alive in these enterprises, instead of following the *Discours préliminaire* in tracing from Descartes to Locke and Newton the growth of a *philosophie* to which *la critique* was not more than ancillary.

But the growth of scholarship unhappily coincided with the *querelle des anciens et des modernes*, in which polite *philosophes* like Fontenelle set out to ridicule the ancients themselves, and the defenders of Greek and Roman literature were trapped in the role of pedants. The term *érudition* was invented – it was still considered a neologism in 1721[33] – and employed to separate the study of ancient literature from *les belles-lettres*, which became the property of the moderns.Though in many ways a superficial development, he goes on, the *querelle* has led to the present unfortunate situation, in which we do not seem to know what to do with the written culture we have inherited, and mathematics exercise an empire attained less by the conquest than by the abdication of others.[34]

It is a fictitious situation, because the great mathematicians and physicists – Descartes excepted – were scholars as well as scientists. Newton studied chronology; Gassendi examined the text of Epicurus; Leibniz was both historian and philosopher. After celebrating the qualities of the mind and imagination displayed by the great textual critics from Erasmus to Le Clerc and Freret,[35] Gibbon proceeds to the ways in which a modern study of *belles-lettres* can develop *le bon goût*, and rectify the unsatisfactory situation the *querelle* has left behind it. Literature presents us with images of three kinds: those of 'l'homme, la nature, et l'art'. Under the first heading, exact criticism of the ancients is not in order, since in reading Euripides or Terence, 'le cœur se reconnoît dans leurs tableaux vrais et naifs, et s'y reconnoît avec plaisir'.[36] There are few great poets of nature, which gives them little to describe beyond storms and seasons; here d'Alembert would have placed the philosopher ahead of the poet, but Gibbon is in search of *le goût* and passes on, to say something which opens up the whole field of historical perception. Still speaking of the poets of antiquity, he says:

L'art leur restoit. J'entends par l'art tout ce dont les hommes ont orné ou

[33] *MW*, IV, p. 20, nn.* and 2.   [34] *MW*, IV, pp. 19–20.   [35] *MW*, IV, p. 21.
[36] *MW*, IV, p. 23.

défiguré la nature, les religions, les gouvernemens, les usages. Ils s'en sont tous servis; et il faut convenir qu'ils ont tous eu raison. Leurs concitoyens et leurs contemporains les entendoient sans peine, et les lisoient avec plaisir. Ils aimoient à retrouver dans les ouvrages des grands hommes de leur nation, tout ce qui avoient rendu leurs ancêtres respectables, tout ce qu'ils regardoient comme sacré, tout ce qu'ils practiquoient comme utile.[37]

[Art remained to them. By art I mean everything with which men have adorned or disfigured nature: religions, governments, customs. They made use of them all, and we must allow that they were all right to do so. Their fellow citizens and contemporaries heard them without pain and read them with pleasure. They loved to discover, in the works of the great men of their nation, all which had rendered their ancestors venerable, all they beheld as sacred, all they practised as useful.]

   Once the domain of the human artifice is extended to include the entire fabric of society and culture, the latter becomes both the subject-matter of which poets sing and the historical context which they and their readers inhabit. The ancient poets depicted the past of which the present was an extension, and encouraged the present both to link itself with and to distance itself from that past. The modern reader has before him the poem, the poet and its ancient readers, constituting a past from which the present is far remote, and in which he knows poetry itself to have a function and character it does not have in his present. Gibbon, returning to the language of the *querelle*, begins to develop a historical paradox which will make him, at this point, an *ancien* precisely because ancient poetry would be out of place in modern society.

Les mœurs des anciens étoient plus favorables à la poêsie que les nôtres: c'est une forte présomption qu'ils nous y ont surpassés.
   A mesure que les arts se sont perfectionnés, les ressorts se sont simplifiés. Dans la guerre, dans la politique, dans la religion, de plus grands effets ont été produits par des causes plus simples.[38]

[The manners of the ancients were more favourable to poetry than ours; it is a strong argument that they have surpassed us in this.
   As the arts became perfect, the springs of action were simplified. In war, politics and religion, greater effects were produced by simpler causes.]

   What then is the relationship between imagination and enlightenment? Maurice de Saxe and Cumberland, commanding huge armies at Fontenoy, without doubt knew more about the art of war than Achilles and Hector riding in chariots to single combat before the walls of Troy, but the poet finds nothing to sing about in their impersonal technology.

[37] *MW*, IV, pp. 23–4.   [38] *MW*, IV, p. 24.

The ancient republics of Greece – says Gibbon, citing Hume's *Political Essays*[39] – knew nothing about the principles of good government, but historians could depict their furious and tumultuous factions as the work of men as they are, whereas the serene operations of a modern bureaucracy offer nothing to the imagination and 'n'excitent chez le poête que l'admiration, la plus froide de toutes les passions' [They excite in the poet nothing but admiration, the most frigid of the passions]. As in *la guerre* and *la politique*, so in *la religion*; the poet could depict the gods of antiquity, but 'l'être infini, que la religion et la philosophie nous ont fait connoître, est au-dessus de ses chantes: le sublime à son égard devient puérile' [The infinite being whom religion and philosophy make known to us is far above their songs; the sublime in his presence becomes childish].[40] Milton's attempt to depict the deeds of Omnipotence as heroic combat were in the end ludicrously unsuccessful, not because he lacked genius but because genius itself was out of place.[41]

The problem of ancient and modern has become linked with the problem of virtue and commerce; *le cœur humain* can know itself only in a world of direct actions and encounters, not in one of the specialisation and co-ordination of minute particulars. But the latter world is at hand in mid-eighteenth-century modernity, and is best understood by the method of philosophy, which is to enquire how the greatest diversity of consequences can flow from the smallest possible number of causes. By this method *l'esprit humain* can know itself, by studying the laws of its own workings; but Gibbon is in search of *moyens de sentir les beautés* which are not to be found by encouraging philosopher and poet to join in despising the *érudit*. He proceeds to argue that if *les beautés*, which feed the heart and its affections, are to be found only in the poetry and history of an ancient world of direct encounters, which has become remote from the way in which modern humans live, they can be recovered only if we learn to think historically.

Mais nous, placés sous un autre ciel, nés dans un autre siècle, nous perdrions nécessairement toutes ces beautés, faute de pouvoir nous placer au même point de vue ou se trouvoient les Grecs et les Romains.[42]

[But we, born under other skies and in another age, must necessarily lose all these beauties, unless we can place ourselves at the same point of vantage as the Greeks and Romans.]

[39] Gibbon's library included the 1760 edition of Hume's *Essays and Treatises on Several Subjects* (*Library*, p. 156), in which the Political Essays formed a separate section.   [40] *MW*, IV, pp. 24–5.

[41] *MW*, IV, p. 26.

[42] *Ibid.*

This is not just a necessary technique of reconstruction, but an effort of imagination undertaken for the imagination's sake; Gibbon is not far from saying that so much has happened with the advent of modernity that *le cœur* can know and satisfy itself only by studying itself as it was in antiquity.

La connoissance de l'antiquité, voilà notre vrai commentaire: mais ce qui est plus nécessaire encore, c'est un certain esprit qui en est le résultat; esprit qui non seulement nous fait connoître les choses, mais qui nous familiarise avec elles, et nous donne à leur égard les yeux des anciens. Le fameux exemple de Perrault peut faire sentir ce que je veux dire: la grossièreté des siècles héroiques choquoit le Parisien. En vain Boileau lui remontroit-il qu'Homère voulait et devoit peindre les Grecs, et non point les François; son esprit demeuroit convaincu, sans être persuadé. Un goût antique (j'entends pour les idées de convention) l'eut éclairé plus que toutes les leçons de son adversaire.[43]

[The knowledge of antiquity is our true commentary, but more necessary still is a certain knowledge arising from it: one which not only teaches us to know things but to grow familiar with them and see them through the eyes of the ancients. The famous example of Perrault makes my point for me. The brutality of the heroic age shocked him as a Parisian. It was in vain that Boileau reminded him that Homer wished and was obliged to depict Greeks, not Frenchmen; in spirit he remained convinced but not persuaded. An ancient taste – I mean a taste for the conventions of antiquity – would have done more to enlighten him than all the lessons read him by his adversary.]

Here of course is the great advantage of including *les religions, les gouvernements et les mœurs* in the domain of human artifice; it supplies the broadest possible context within which the actions and values of the past can be reconstructed. It had been necessary, but impossible, to convince Perrault that if he would have found it repulsive to imitate the actions of Homeric heroes, he could have learned far more about them and himself by examining the differences between their *mœurs*, their moral world, and his own. This was the point at which the *moderne* – an 'ancient' in his subject-matter, a 'modern' in his critical insights, and increasingly what we should mean by a 'historian' – had something to offer to *l'esprit* of which neither philosopher nor poet had the secret.

Roman poets had known something about it. Gibbon insists that one cannot read the *Aeneid* without some knowledge that the poem was written in the time of Augustus, for an imperial city remembering its primitive beginnings. Virgil had responded to the gap between the past and the present in two ways: first by investing the rustic combats

---

[43] *MW*, IV, p. 27.

between Trojans and Latins with the Homeric grandeur of a war among
gods and heroes; second, by making Evander conduct his guest Aeneas
through an unimproved village landscape whose every feature Virgil's
audience recognises as a sacred place in what is now their city. They see
cattle grazing in what will be the Forum;[44] a few years after writing this
Gibbon went there and found it a pasture again.The changing landscape of urban Rome – here mentioned for the first time – was to seize
his imagination and guide it towards the moment when 'the idea of
writing the decline and fall of the city started to my mind'.

Que ce tableau est vif! Que ce contraste est parlant pour un homme instruit
dans l'antiquité! Qu'il est fade aux yeux de celui qui n'apporte à la lecture de
Virgile, d'autre préparation qu'un goût naturel, et quelque connoissance de la
langue Latine![45]

[How vivid is this picture! How this contrast speaks to a reader instructed in
antiquity! How dim must it seem to one who brings to the reading of Virgil
nothing but a natural taste and some knowledge of the Latin language!]

Virgil and the history of Rome cannot be separated, but if in the
Aeneid he speaks out of his own historic sensibility, to read the *Georgics* we
must develop our own. These poems form part of the history of the
legions, whose evolution from militia to professionals was the key to the
history of the republic and empire for ancients and moderns and for
Gibbon himself. Where we expect him to cite Montesquieu's *Considérations sur la grandeur des Romains et de leur décadence* he appears to cite only
William Wotton's *History of Rome*;[46] but key points in Montesquieu's
narrative recur – the siege of Veii, at which the troops first received a
stipend, the need Sulla was under to pay off three hundred thousand
lawless men of no loyalties – 'sans biens, sans patrie, sans principes'[47] –
with confiscated lands instead of money. Could they be settled on the
land, or would they leave it to seek adventure in new civil wars?
Augustus confronted the same difficulty, and Gibbon seriously suggested that Virgil wrote the *Georgics* at his suggestion, with the purpose of
inculcating agrarian values and virtues into the same unmanageable
swordsmen.

Si l'on adopte mes idées, Virgile n'est plus un simple écrivain, qui décrit les
travaux rustiques. C'est un nouvel Orphée, qui ne manie sa lyre,que pour faire
déposer aux sauvages leur férocité, et pour les réunir par les liens des mœurs et
des loix.
    Ses chants produissirent cette merveille. Les veterans s'accoutumèrent insen-

[44] *MW*, IV, p. 30n.   [45] *MW*, IV, pp. 30–1.   [46] *MW*, IV, p. 33n.   [47] *MW*, IV, p. 33.

siblement au répos. Ils passèrent en paix les trente ans qui s'écoulèrent avant qu'Auguste eût établi, non sans beaucoup de difficulté, un trésor militaire pour les payer en argent.[48]

[If you follow me in this, Virgil is no longer a mere writer describing country labour. He is a new Orpheus, who takes up his lyre to persuade savages to lay aside their ferocity and bring them together in the ties of manners and laws.

His songs worked this marvel. The veterans grew insensibly accustomed to repose. They lived peaceably for the thirty years which passed before Augustus established, not without much difficulty, a military treasury to pay them in specie.]

This edifying tale may not have altogether convinced its author, but it could have been written in no age but that of the standing army, and of the heightened historical sensibility which enabled Gibbon to situate all literature in the context of *les mœurs* and to intensify its meaning by treating it as part of the *histoire des mœurs*. It was the capacity to enrich *les belles-lettres* by reading them in this way that he thought d'Alembert had insufficiently recognised.

(iii)

The study of literature, of *belles-lettres*, was enlarging itself into the study of contexts, and these in turn were being presented as the products of *l'art*, of human action in all its variety; the study of texts was becoming the study of history, and this in turn was enlarging itself from the study of what men had done into that of what they had made and what they had been. In this respect, the enlightened *érudits* and *philosophes*, although rebelling against the domination of the humanist philologists and chronologists, were continuing their work. Gibbon, though not here vindicating the work of the historian, includes it in his view when he writes:

La critique est, selon moi, l'art de juger des écrits et des écrivains, ce qu'ils ont dit, s'ils l'ont bien dit, s'ils ont dit vrai. [n. Il faut borner ce vrai historique, à la vérité de leurs témoignages, et non de leurs opinions. Cette dernière espèce de vérité est plutôt du ressort de la logique que de celui de la critique.] De la première de ces branches découle la grammaire, la connoissance des langues et des manuscrits, le discernement des ouvrages supposés, le rétablissement des endroits corrompus. Toute la théorie de la poësie et de l'éloquence se tire de la seconde. La troisième ouvre un champ immense, l'examen et la critique des faits. On pourroit donc distinguer la nation des critiques, en critiques gram-

---

mairiens, en critiques rhéteurs et en critiques historiens. Les prétensions ex-
clusives des premiers ont nui non seulement à leur travail, mais à celui de leurs
confrères.[49]

[Criticism for me is the art of judging writings and writers: what they have said,
whether they have said it well, whether they have spoken truth. (n. We must
limit historic truth to the truth of their testimonies, not of their opinions; the
latter is the province of logic rather than of criticism.) From the first of these
enquiries develop grammar, the knowledge of languages and manuscripts, the
establishment of supposed writings, the restoration of corrupt passages. The
theory of poetry and eloquence derives from the second enquiry. The third
leads us into the immense field of the examination and criticism of facts. We
may then distinguish the nation of critics into critics of grammar, critics of
rhetoric and critics of history. The exclusive pretensions of the first have been
damaging not only to their own work, but to that of their colleagues.]

The *érudits*, third estate of d'Alembert's *république des lettres*, were
themselves divided into a triad of which no one order was superior to the
other two. This intensification and specialisation of their work was
possible because *les faits* were no longer the inert data they had been in
the *Discours préliminaire*, but *facta, res gestae*, the creations of human energy,
to be understood only by those who shared in that energy in its many
forms.

Tout ce qu'ont été les hommes, tout ce que le génie a crée, tout ce que la raison
a pesé, tout ce que le travail a recueilli, voilà le département de la critique. La
justesse de l'esprit, la finesse, la pénétration, sont toutes nécessaires pour
l'exercer dignement. Je suis le littérateur dans son cabinet, je le vois entouré des
productions de tous les siècles: sa bibliothèque en est remplie: son esprit en est
éclairé, sans en être chargé.[50]

[All that men have been; all that genius has created, reason weighed, or toil
recovered; this is the department of criticism. Exactness of mind, subtlety,
insight; all are necessary to discharge it worthily. I follow the man of letters into
his study; I see him surrounded by the products of the ages; his library is filled
with them; his intellect is enlightened without being burdened.]

This is the point at which the confrontation with d'Alembert recurs,
and Gibbon invokes his Parisian allies.

On a dit que la géométrie étoit une bonne logique, et l'on a cru lui donner un
grand éloge: il est plus glorieux aux sciences de développer ou de perfectionner
l'homme, que de reculer les bornes de l'univers. Mais la critique ne peut-elle
pas partager ce titre? Elle a même cet avantage: la géométrie s'occupe de
démonstrations qui ne se trouvent que chez elle; la critique balance les différens

de vraisemblance. C'est en les comparant que nous réglons tous les jours nos actions, que nous decidons souvent de notre sort. [n. Il s'agit principalement des élémens de la géométrie et de ceux de la critique.] Balançons des vraisemblances critiques.

[It has been said that geometry is good logic, and it is thought that this is great praise; it is more glorious in the sciences to develop and perfect man than to press back the boundaries of the universe. But may not criticism claim a share in this description? It has even a certain advantage: geometry is concerned with demonstrations arising purely within itself, whereas criticism weighs the differences of probability. It is in comparing these that we regulate our everyday actions, and often decide our very fate. (n. This applies particularly to the elements of geometry and those of criticism.) Let us then weigh critical probabilities.]

Gibbon respected but had no passion for mathematics, which was exactly d'Alembert's response to textual scholarship; the two men did not disagree but would never agree.[51] At this point Gibbon indicates his close engagement with the text of the *Discours préliminaire*, by silently quoting it and adapting its words to express his opposed meaning; it is a form of appropriation we shall find him employing on other occasions. D'Alembert had written that 'notre siècle qui se croit destiné à changer les lois en tout genre' could no longer take a very exalted view of the Renaissance humanists.[52] Gibbon now writes:

Notre siècle, qui se croit destiné à changer les loix en tout genre, a enfanté un Pirrhonisme historique, utile et dangereux. M. de Pouilly, esprit brillant et superficiel, qui citoit plus qu'il ne lisoit, douta de la certitude des cinq premiers siècles de Rome: mais son imagination peu faite pour ces recherches, céda facilement â l'érudition et à la critique de M. Freret et de l'Abbé Sallier. M. de Beaufort fit revivre cette controversie, et l'histoire Romaine souffrit beaucoup des attaques d'un écrivain, qui savoit douter et savoit decider.[53]

[Our age, which believes itself destined to change laws of every kind, has begotten a historical pyrrhonism, alike useful and dangerous. M. de Pouilly, a brilliant and superficial intelligence who cited more than he read, questioned the certainty of the first five centuries of Roman history; but his imagination, not formed for such researches, sank easily before the erudition and critical skill of M. Freret and the Abbé Sallier. M. de Beaufort reawakened this controversy, and Roman history suffered much from the attacks of a writer who knew how to doubt and how to decide.]

We have already seen something of the debate in the Académie des Inscriptions of 1721–2, to which Gibbon is alluding here. Levesque de

---

[51] *MW*, IV, pp. 39–40.   [52] *Discours*, p. xxi.   [53] *MW*, IV, p. 40.

Pouilly may well have stirred the memory of Conyers Middleton in Gibbon's mind. Louis de Beaufort, a Huguenot scholar living in Maastricht with whom Gibbon had dined on his way back to England in 1759, was the author of a *Dissertation sur l'incertitude des cinq premiers siècles de l'histoire Romaine* (1750) and a larger work on the Roman republic which Gibbon was to read and comment on.[54] With this invocation of a scepticism which knew how to reach conclusions instead of dismissing them, Gibbon pitted implicitly against d'Alembert his affinity with the members of the Académie and the Protestant erudition he associated with theirs. They were to be his allies in what he saw as a battle against the *esprit dominateur* of the *Encyclopédie* and the *gens de lettres*. He continues to be troubled by the thought of a hegemony of *philosophes*, or rather of those who have claimed for themselves an exclusive exercise of *l'esprit philosophique*.

Il y a point d'écrivain qui n'y aspire. Il sacrifie de bonne grâce la science. Pour peu que vous le pressiez, il conviendra que le jugement sévère embarrasse les opérations du génie: mais il vous assurera toujours que cet esprit philosophique qui brille dans ses écrits, fait le caractère du siècle où nous vivons. L'esprit philosophique d'un petit nombre de grands hommes, a formé, selon lui, celui du siècle. Celui-ci s'est répandu dans tous les ordres de l'état, et leur a preparé à son tour de dignes successeurs.[55]

[Every writer aspires to this. He will readily sacrifice science to his ambitions. If you press him a little, he will agree that so severe a judgment must hamper the workings of genius; but he will assure you still that the philosophic spirit which shines so brightly in his writings forms the character of the age in which we live. The *esprit philosophique* of a handful of great men, he declares, has determined the spirit of an age. It has spread itself through all the orders of the state, and has prepared the way for successors worthy of those who possess it.]

The 'il' of this sentence looks very like d'Alembert, and the *grands hommes* are the men of letters with or without their patrons. The *empire de la mode* is a threat to liberty, especially where intellect has become one of the *ordres de l'état* – as Gibbon was to find and Burke was to remark, this was the case in France but not in England – and the remedy must be to diversify its instruments and distribute them more widely.

Cependant si nous jettions les yeux sur les ouvrages de nos sages, leur diversité nous laisseroit dans l'incertitude sur la nature de ce talent; et celle-ci pourroit nous conduire à douter s'il leur est tombé en partage. Chez les uns il consiste à se frayer des routes nouvelles, et à fronder toute opinion dominante, fut-elle de

---

[54] *Library*, p. 65. There is much about Beaufort in Gibbon's manuscripts, some of it critical. Cf. Womersley, III, p. 1196.   [55] *MW*, IV, p. 57.

Socrate ou d'un inquisiteur Portugais, par la seule raison qu'elle est dominante. Chez les autres cet esprit s'identifie avec la géométrie, cette reine impérieuse qui, non contente de régner, proscrit ses sœurs, et declare tout raisonnement peu digne de ce nom, s'il ne roule pas sur des lignes et sur des nombres. Rendons justice à l'esprit hardi, dont les écarts ont quelquefois conduit à la vérité, et dont les excès mêmes, comme les rébellions des peuples, inspirent une crainte salutaire au despotisme. Penetrons-nous bien de tout ce que nous devons à l'esprit géomètre: mais cherchons pour l'esprit philosophique, un objet plus sage que celui-la, et plus universel que celui-ci.[56]

[And yet, if we cast an eye over the writings of these sages, their diversity will leave us uncertain of the nature of their talent, and we will be led to doubt if it is their joint inheritance. With some it consists in finding themselves new paths and sniping at every dominant opinion, be it that of Socrates or a Portuguese inquisitor, for the sole reason that it is dominant. With others the spirit is identified with geometry, that imperious queen who, not content to reign, proscribes her sisters and decrees all argument unworthy of the name, if it turn not on lines and on numbers. Let us do justice to that intrepid spirit, whose leaps have sometimes led to truth and whose very excesses, like popular rebellions, have struck salutary fears in the heart of the despot. Let our thoughts be filled with all that we owe to the geometric spirit; but let us search for the spirit of philosophy, which is at once wiser than the one and more universal than the other.]

Gibbon is still excusing himself, perhaps to his father, for having studied mathematics less than whole-heartedly while at Lausanne. He is also portraying the politics of intellect in an age of enlightenment, when the men of letters, freed from control by the other clerisies, compete with each other for paradigmatic hegemony, and perhaps for power in the state, and there is danger that the *république des lettres* may become, like Machiavelli's Florence, a succession of the transitory dictatorships of factions – in this case the intellectual *fronde* which seeks power by subverting the paradigms of others. The function of literature is to mitigate this threat by diversifying the single-mindedness of philosophy.

L'esprit philosophique consiste à pouvoir remonter aux idées simples; à saisir et à combiner les premiers principes. Le coup d'œil de son possesseur est juste, mais en même tems étendu. Placé sur une hauteur, il embrasse un grande étendue de païs,

(Gibbon's Capitoline vision, dated by him a few years later, may start to our minds)

dont il se forme une image nette et unique, pendant que des esprits aussi justes,

[56] *MW*, IV, pp. 57–8.

mais plus bornés, n'en découvrent qu'une partie. Il peut être géomètre, an-
tiquaire, musicien, mais il est toujours philosophe, et à force de pénétrer les
premiers principes de son art, il lui devient superieur. Il a place parmi ce petit
nombre de génies qui travaillent de loin en loin à former cette première science
à laquelle, si elle étoit perfectionnée, les autres seroient soumises. En ce sens cet
esprit est bien peu commun.[57]

[The philosophic mind is that which can always reason back to simple ideas,
grasping and combining first principles. The vision of one who possesses it is
exact, but at the same time extensive. Placed on a height, he takes in a great
extent of country, of which he forms a single comprehensive image, while
intellects no less precise, but more limited, can see only in part. He may be a
geometer, an antiquary, a musician, but he is always a philosopher, and by dint
of penetrating the first principles of his art he rises above it. His place is among
that little company of geniuses who labour at great intervals to form that
science of sciences to which, were it ever perfected, all others would be subject.
So defined, this kind of intellect is very uncommon indeed.]

There are not many of these great conquerors of the intellect, who
can see and seize at a stroke all the kingdoms of the mind and the glory
of them; their genius is a 'don du ciel' and no particular discipline can
claim to nurture it. In stating his case for holding that *l'étude de la littérature*
can develop and exercise the *esprit philosophique*, Gibbon begins to de-
prive the latter of its imperial power, both by diversifying and by
historicising it.

je crois l'étude de la littérature, cette habitude de devenir, tour à tour, Grec,
Romain, disciple de Zénon ou d'Epicure, bien propre à le développer et à
l'exercer. A travers cette diversité infinie d'esprits, on remarque une conformité
générale entre ceux à qui leur siècle, leur païs, leur religion ont inspiré une
manière à peu près pareille d'envisager les mêmes objets. Les âmes les plus
exemptes de préjugés, ne sauroient s'en défaire entièrement. Leurs idées ont un
air de paradoxe; et en brisant leurs chaines, vous sentez qu'elles les ont portées.
Je cherche chez les Grecs des fauteurs de la démocratie; des enthousiastes de
l'amour de la patrie chez les Romains; chez les sujets des Commode, des Sevère
ou des Caracalla, des apologistes du pouvoir absolu; et chez l'Epicurien de
l'antiquité la condamnation de sa religion.

[I think the study of literature, this capacity to become by turns Greek or
Roman, disciple of Zeno or of Epicurus, well suited to develop it and exert it.
Among this infinite diversity of minds, one observes a general conformity in
those in whom their era, their country or their religion has induced a highly
uniform way of envisaging the same things. The intelligence most free from
prejudices can never distance themselves from these completely. Their ideas
smack of paradox; in breaking their chains, they make you know that they have

[57] *MW*, IV, p. 58.

worn them. Among the Greeks, I seek out the advocates of democracy; among
the Romans, the enthusiasts of love of country; among the subjects of Com-
modus, Severus and Caracalla the apologists of absolute power; and among the
Epicureans of antiquity the condemnation of its religion.]

The successive empires of method are reduced to moments in history,
each fighting the ghost of its predecessor. The *esprit philosophique* now
ceases to go in search of worlds to conquer, or of an infinity of causes
and effects, and goes instead to history for an education in irony.

Quel spectacle pour un esprit vraiment philosophique de voir les opinions les
plus absurdes reçues chez les nations les plus éclairées, des barbares parvenus à
la connoissance des plus sublimes vérités,[58] des conséquences vraies, mais peu
justes, tirés des principes les plus erronés, des principes admirables qui ap-
prochoient toujours de la vérité sans jamais y conduire, le langage formé sur les
idées, et les idées justifiées par le langage, les sources de la morale partout les
mêmes, les opinions de la contentieuse métaphysique partout variées, d'ordinaire extravagantes, nettes seulement qu'elles furent superficielles, subtiles,
obscures, incertaines, toutes les fois qu'elles pretendirent à la profondeur! Un
ouvrage Iroquois, fut-il rempli d'absurdités, seroit un morceau impayable. Il
offriroit une expérience unique de la nature de l'esprit humain, placé dans des
circonstances que nous n'avons jamais emprouvées, et dominé par des mœurs
et des opinions religieuses totalement contraires aux nôtres.[59]

[What a spectacle for the truly philosophical mind to observe the most absurd
opinions received among the most enlightened nations, barbarians arrived at
the knowledge of sublime truths, consequences true but inappropriate derived
from the most erroneous assumptions, admirable principles which ever point to
the truth but never lead to it, language based upon ideas and ideas fortified by
language, the mainsprings of morality everywhere the same, yet the opinions of
metaphysical contention uncertain, every time varied, usually extravagant,
coherent only where they are superficial, subtle, obscure and uncertain, every
time pretending to profundity! A work of Iroquois letters, were it replete with
absurdities, would be a priceless possession. It would offer a unique encounter
with the human mind, placed in circumstances we have never experienced and
governed by manners and religious opinions utterly contrary to our own.]

The emphasis is falling less on the unvarying principles of human
nature, than on the infinite diversity of the languages, beliefs and actions
which they generate under pressures arising in the context of history
from which they never fully disengage themselves.

Nous y apprendrions non seulement à avouer, mais à sentir la force des

---

[58] Possibly those of religion? This would double the irony.
[59] All three passages occur in *MW*, IV, pp. 59–60.

préjugés, à ne nous étonner jamais de ce qui nous paroît la plus absurde, et à nous défier souvent de ce qui nous semble le mieux établi.

[We should learn there not merely to admit but actually to feel the force of prejudices, and to cease being astonished at that which to us seems most absurd, while mistrusting that which seems the most securely established.]

To insist that prejudices are not only inescapable but also justified by their context may be read as anticipating Burke. There was an *esprit philosophique* which studied the prejudices of others to emancipate itself from its own; another which reminded itself how many, reasonable and unreasonable, it might still entertain.

J'aime à voir les jugemens des hommes prendre une teinture de leurs préventions, à les considérer qui n'osent pas tirer des principes qu'ils sentent être exactes. J'aime à les surprendre qui détestent chez le barbare, ce qu'ils admirent chez le Grec, et qui qualifient la même histoire d'impie chez le Payen, et de sacrée chez le Juif.

Sans cette connoissance philosophique de l'antiquité, nous ferions trop d'honneur à l'espèce humaine. L'empire de la coutume nous seroit peu connu. Nous confondrions à tout moment l'incroyable et l'absurde. Les Romains étoient éclairés, cependant ces mêmes Romains ne furent pas choqués de voir réunir dans la personne de César un Dieu, un prêtre et un Athée.[60]

I like to see how men's judgments are coloured by their prepossessions, to observe those who dare not pursue the principles which they sense to be just. I like to catch off their guard those who detest in the barbarian what they admire in the Greek, and who deem the same story impious in the pagan and sacred in the Jew.

Without such a philosophical knowledge of antiquity, we should pay too much honour to the human species. The empire of custom would be little known. We should constantly confuse the incredible with the merely absurd. The Romans were enlightened; yet the same Romans were in no way shocked to see united in the person of Caesar a god, a priest and an atheist.]

And the *Essai* goes on to a detailed analysis of Caesar, at once pontiff and Epicurean; a figure who will recur in the *Decline and Fall*. If philosophy is the science of relating the maximum diversity of effects to the minimum of simple causes, Gibbon continues to rank history among the sciences; but he is visibly becoming interested in the ironies which arise from the inexhaustible combinations and permutations of the effects, and one wonders how far he is committing himself to research into the simple and invariable causes. The words

L'histoire est la science des causes et des effets

occur as a marginal note to the following:

[60] *MW*, IV, p. 61.

L'histoire est pour un esprit philosophique, ce qu'étoit le jeu pour le Marquis de Dangeau. Il voyoit un système, des rapports, une suite là où les autres ne discernoient que les caprices de la fortune. Cette science est pour lui celle des causes et des effets. Elle mérite bien que j'essaie de poser quelques régles propres, non à faire germer le génie, mais à la garantir des écarts: peut-être que si on les avoit toujours bien pesées, on auroit pris plus rarement la subtilité pour la finesse d'esprit, l'obscurité pour la profondeur, et un air de paradoxe pour un génie créateur.[61]

[History is to a philosophic intellect what games of chance were to the Marquis de Dangeau. He saw a system, relationships, a sequence, where others saw nothing but the caprices of fortune. This science is for him that of causes and effects. It deserves that I should seek to posit for it some general rules, not to engender genius but to guarantee its steps. Perhaps, if these had always been well considered, we should less often have mistaken subtle reasoning for acuteness of insight, obscurity for depth, and an air of paradox for creative genius.]

Since the young and tentative author of this essay was Edward Gibbon, we are entitled to wonder what his attempt 'poser quelques règles propres' did 'à faire germer le génie'; but this is of course precisely the point at which over-interpretation becomes all too possible. His search for general laws is carried on under the aegis of Montesquieu, and he plainly regards the *Esprit des lois* as the greatest attempt at 'une histoire philosophique de l'homme' precisely because its author was 'supérieur à l'amour de ses propres systèmes, dernière passion du sage'.[62] He had lost none of his respect for Montesquieu when he wrote the *Decline and Fall*, though by then he had come to think that Montesquieu's love of pursuing a hypothesis (*imagination*) sometimes outran his attention to the facts (*critique*). He moves in his own way from *belles-lettres* towards *philosophie* when, after observing: 'Si les philosophes ne sont pas toujours historiens, il seroit du moins à souhaiter que les historiens fussent philosophes', he adds – voicing an admiration that was never to leave him – that only Tacitus, and never Livy, has fulfilled his ideal of an author who should be both. Here Gibbon significantly departs from an encomium upon Livy which he had written in Lausanne at the age of nineteen.[63] He was never to lose his admiration for the narrative powers of the Paduan historian, and would probably have said that they were superior to those of Tacitus when it came to the *longue durée*. But soon after 1756, philosophy had reared its demanding head, and the problem

---

[61] *MW*, iv, p. 63.   [62] *MW*, iv, p. 69.   [63] *MW*, iv, pp. 422–34. *YEG*, pp. 93–5.

of reconciling narrative with deep interpretation had come to the fore. Livy,

plus attaché à plaire qu'à instruire, vous conduit pas-à-pas à la suite de ses héros, et vous fait éprouver tour-à-tour, l'horreur, l'admiration, et la pitié. Tacite ne se sert de l'empire que l'éloquence a sur le cœur, que pour lier à vos yeux la chaine des événemens, et remplir votre âme des plus sages leçons. Je gravis sur les Alpes avec Annibal, mais j'assiste au conseil de Tibère. Tite-Live me peint l'abus du pouvoir, une sévérite que la nature approuve en frémissant, la vengeance et l'amour qui s'unissent à la liberté, la tyrannie qui tombe sous leur coups: mais les loix des décemvirs, leur caractère, leurs défauts, leurs rapports enfin avec leurs desseins ambitieux, il les oublie totalement. Je ne vois point chez lui comment ces loix faites pour une république bornée, pauvre, à demi-sauvage, la bouleversèrent, lorsque la force de son institution l'eut portée au faite de la grandeur. Je l'aurois trouvé dans Tacite.[64]

[Livy, more concerned to please than to instruct, leads you step by step in the path of his heroes, and makes you feel by turns horror, admiration and pity. Tacitus makes use of eloquence and its empire over the heart only to forge before your eyes the linked chain of events and to fill the soul with the most sagacious lessons. I climb in the Alps with Hannibal, but I am present in the council of Tiberius. Livy depicts for me the abuse of power, a severity that nature approves while shuddering, the revenge and the love which join to seek liberty, the tyranny which falls before their blows; but the laws of the decemvirs, their character, their faults, in short what led them to their ambitious designs, he altogether neglects. I do not see with him how the laws made for a republic limited, poor and half savage, overthrew it when the energy of its foundation had led it to the pinnacle of greatness. I should have found this in Tacitus.]

At this point d'Alembert emerges once more; 'cet écrivain qui unit, comme Fontenelle, le savoir et le goût', but 'ce juge éclairé, mais sévère', who has proposed that at the end of each century 'tous les faits' – meaning presumably the body of recorded knowledge – should be reviewed, a few preserved and the remainder burned.[65]

Conservons-les tous précieusement. Un Montesquieu démêlera dans les plus chétifs, des rapports inconnus au vulgaire. Imitons les botanistes. Toutes les plantes ne sont pas utiles dans la médecine, cependant ils ne cessent d'en découvrir de nouvelles. Ils espèrent que le génie et les travaux heureux y verront des propriétés jusqù' à présent cachées.[66]

[Let us carefully preserve them all. A Montesquieu will disentangle from the most insignificant of them relationships unknown to the common eye. We

---

[64] *MW*, IV, pp. 66–7.
[65] The reference is to d'Alembert's *Mélanges de philosophie et de littérature*, published in 1760.
[66] *MW*, IV, pp. 67–8.

should imitate the botanists. Not all plants are medicinally useful, yet they never cease to discover new species, hoping that by genius and well-judged researches they will discern properties still unknown.]

And in fact the penultimate sentence of the passage comparing Tacitus and Livy is Montesquieuan rather than Tacitean, and what we find in the Roman is the *arcana imperii*, the hidden moves and motives of statesmen, rather than the general laws of the growth and decline of polities. The shift from Livy to Tacitus is made in a direction Machiavellian and still more Guicciardinian; from the heroic eloquence which depicts the foundations of civic virtue to the serpentine narrative and gnomic maxims which convey the counsels, or disregard of them, of the tyrant; and not so much to the discovery of general laws as to that of anachronism. The truism that good laws work ill effects when circumstances change was a discovery of the Florentine authors. The link between Tacitism and Enlightenment is not clear, but must include the premise that the function of historiography is to find general causes but to see their effects as infinitely and challengingly diverse. If we search Gibbon's references for the sources of that richness of exploitable information which renders the *érudit* the equal of the *philosophe*, we find authors already and prospectively important in his reading: d'Herbelot and Sale, Conyers Middleton, Jean Le Clerc, Isaac de Beausobre, Hume, Montesquieu and Warburton.[67] We also find a large number of acknowledgements to authors found in the *Mémoires de l'Académie*, more than any other to Freret and the Abbé de la Bléterie. It was the latter's life of the Emperor Julian that made him prominent in the *Decline and Fall*, but in the *Essai* Gibbon was anticipating his further studies of Augustus, which he expected to improve his understanding of that great chameleon's bewildering changes of role and personality as well as strategy.[68]

Before reaching this analysis, however, Gibbon invokes Montesquieu's 'théorie de ces causes générales ... une histoire philosophique de l'homme',[69] in order to embark on the newly written history of religion that replaced his earlier sections on the rise of Christianity. That treatment had led him to the figure of Augustus as the near contemporary of Christ, situated at the point where polytheism gave way to a monotheism either philosophic or revealed. This theme is maintained in the published *Essai*, but Christ and Christianity have disappeared from the page – there is no language scornful or dismissive of them – and we

[67] *MW*, IV, pp. 70n., 71n., 72n.   [68] *MW*, IV, pp. 89–91 and n.   [69] *MW*, IV, p. 69.

find instead a philosophic history of primitive religion, designed to explain the persistence of mythology and polytheism among the otherwise philosophical Greeks and Romans. The reader is tempted to detect the presence of Hume's *Natural History of Religion*, later important to Gibbon, which he had had opportunity to read by 1761 – he may even have met the great sceptic[70] – but it does not figure among Gibbon's footnotes, which mention Fontenelle, Voltaire and Freret but are otherwise references to the works of *académiciens* and *érudits*;[71] nor does the *Essai* in this version follow Hume or any other into the origins of monotheism and the problem of revelation. It is concerned only with the problem of ancient polytheism and the problem of historical explanation which arises from the former.

There is a refutation of the ancient *système* of Euhemerus, who had claimed that all gods were deified humans, earning himself the reputation of an atheist, notably among the Christian Fathers who nevertheless accepted his diagnosis of ancient religion. There was, however, enough deification of heroes and rulers to make his system intelligible; Gibbon is to some extent giving a history of ancient attempts to account for their own polytheism, once they had seen it to be philosophically untenable. What the ancient lacked was the modern philosophy which turns from metaphysics to psychology, examining the workings of the mind before those of the universe. There follows an anatomy of the primitive mind, that of the savage – here we meet for the first time that crucial figure in eighteenth-century philosophy – who does not understand the origin of the ideas suggested to him by the objects he encounters, and so supposes them to announce the presence of gods and spirits dwelling in every object and declaring it to his mind. The savage is the original poet, giving tongues to rocks, trees and beasts, and the original enthusiast, supposing his ideas to be divine voices speaking in his mind. The Greeks were savages, 'malheureux inhabitants des forêts', until they learned letters from the Phoenicians and the allegorical interpretation of religion from the Egyptians.[72] Allegory was both the father and the mystifier of philosophy; in making gods the embodiments of principles it made evident

---

[70] There is mention in the *Letters* (i, p. 117, dated 30 December 1758) of a forthcoming meeting with Hume, but no further evidence that it took place. It was to have been at the house of Mme Celesia, a daughter of David Mallet. This is part of what evidence there is of Gibbon's keeping company with infidels at this period.

[71] *MW*, IV, pp. 70–88. For Gibbon's judgment in later life of this part of the *Essai*, see *Memoirs*, pp. 104–5 (*A*, pp. 173–4, Memoir B). He calls it an 'enquiry into the origins and nature of the Gods of Polytheism'.   [72] *MW*, IV, p. 73.

que jamais homme ne peut devenir Dieu, ni jamais Dieu être transformé en simple homme,[73]

[that a man could never become a god, nor a god be changed into a mere man,]

thus isolating euhemerism in all its crudity, and sending Christianity a challenge it might be willing to take up; but at the same time it encouraged a language of mystery, which maintained the superstitions of the populace while permitting the philosophers to deify their own ideas in ways that merely sophisticated the workings of the savage mind.

Mais les Stoïciens, dans leur mélange bizarre du Théisme le plus pur, du Spinosisme et de l'idolâtrie populaire, rapportoient ce paganisme, dont ils étoient les zélateurs, au culte de la nature brisée en autant de dieux qu'elle a de faces différentes. Cicéron, cet académicien, pour qui tout étoit objection et rien n'étoit preuve, ose à peine leur opposer le système d' Ephémère.[74]

[But the Stoics, with their bizarre mingling of the purest theism with Spinozism and popular idolatry, connected the paganism of which they were such zealots with the worship of nature fragmented into as many gods as it has different aspects. Cicero, that Academic for whom everything was objection and nothing was proof, hardly dared to plead the system of Euhemerus against them.]

If Gibbon had been reading Fontenelle and Freret, he had also been reading Banier's *Mythologie expliquée par l'histoire* and Warburton's *Divine Legation of Moses*;[75] the Christian indictment of ancient philosophy as contrary to both revelation and right reason is part of what he is saying here. He does not, however, proceed here to the advent of philosophical monotheism, either in conjunction with the challenge of Christ as he had presented it in the 1758 draft or altogether divorced from it as in Hume's *Natural History of Religion*. The abandonment in this text of the earlier account of Christ and the spread of Christianity shows Gibbon turning from the latter historical problem – to which he was to return in the *Decline and Fall*– to a natural history of religion, and may indicate that he was becoming convinced that only a historical treatment of religion was worth undertaking. This in turn would suggest that he was proceeding deeper into scepticism, but not into either deism or non-theism of a Spinozistic kind.[76]

We may have reached the point at which the young author was unsure how he wanted to bring the various components of the *Essai*

---

[73] *Ibid.*   [74] *MW*, IV, p. 77.
[75] Banier had been prominent in his earlier reading at Lausanne; see BL Add. MSS 34880, *passim*, and *YEG*, pp. 66–7, 69. For Warburton, *MW*, IV, p. 72, n.*.
[76] Cf. Ghosh, 1995; Young, 1998a, pp. 180–1.

together. Certainly, the rather contemptuous reference to the Stoic 'culte de la nature brisée en autant de dieux qu'elle a de faces différentes' is hard to separate from Gibbon's praise of a multi-causal approach to history which he may have seen as Montesquieuan and strongly desired to uphold.

Mélange de causes dans les événements particuliers

Dans les événemens plus particuliers, le procédé de la nature est très différent de celui des philosophes. Chez elle il y a peu d'effets assez simples, pour ne devoir leur origine à une seule cause; au lieu que nos sages s'attachent d'ordinaire à une cause, non seulement universelle, mais unique. Evitons cet écueil; pour peu qu'une action paroisse compliquée, admettons y les causes générales, sans rejetter le dessein et le hasard.[77]

[The mixed causes of particular events

In particular events, the course of nature is quite other than it is for philosophers. There are few effects so simple as to owe their origin to one cause alone, whereas our wise men generally adhere to a single cause, not only universal but unique. Let us steer clear of this rock; as soon as an event appears complicated, let us allow for general causes without rejecting either intention or chance.]

And this leads us to the various causes of the collapse of the Roman republic, and the enigmatic diversity of both the personality of Augustus and the system of government he set up. The Decline and Fall of course begins here, but Gibbon is far from regarding it as anything but a topos, while he has actually moved away from linking it with the advent of Christianity. The study of ancient polytheism is prelude to a study of ancient philosophy, implicitly contrasted with a modern Enlightenment capable of recognising both the operation of general causes and the intractability of the recorded facts of human behaviour. Gibbon's aim is not to convince d'Alembert of falling into the same errors as the ancients, or of subjecting history to the discipline of mathematics, so much as it is to establish the textual study of literature – still defined as ancient – as a kingdom of the mind in which all its faculties are exercised and developed. This is Enlightenment – it is *éclairé* and entails *lumière* – but it is not the dictatorship of any one faculty of the mind over the others. Gibbon is not accusing d'Alembert of seeking to establish such a dictatorship, so much as of writing as if he intended this when he probably did not.

---

[77] *MW*, IV, p. 89.

(IV)

In spite of its shortcomings and immaturities, the *Essai sur l'étude de la littérature* is to be read as serious criticism and serious philosophy of history. Between the ages of twenty-one and twenty-four, Gibbon set out to show how the faculties of the mind were engaged in the study of literature, and to claim that this study was necessary, both to the full development of those faculties and to that conscious and critical engagement of the personality in civil society to which we give the name of Enlightenment and Enlightenment gave the name of philosophy. What had begun as an enquiry into *belles-lettres* became an enquiry into *littérature*, but to us it is abundantly evident that the study it advocated was a study of history. The words *histoire* and *historien* recur in its text; but more importantly, the study of literature becomes more and more a matter of anchoring texts in their historical contexts, as we should say; the contexts of past states of society and culture, recovered by philosophy and erudition, the exercise of the imagination and the judgment. Without this texts can barely be understood; with its aid their understanding is enriched, and the mind knows itself better in its capacity so to understand them. To us this is what 'history' means; but Gibbon was writing at a moment when the word was still restricted to denoting a specific literary genre, which was being transformed by these new forms of study but still retained the old meaning of 'narrative', whether classical or philosophical. Without narrative the word 'history' could hardly be employed, and in the midst of his pursuit of *l'érudition*, which might be ancient, and *le goût*, which was modern but employed in the study of the ancient, Gibbon was engaged in that pursuit of a subject for grand historical narrative, classical and philosophical, which engrossed his mind in camp as he waited for responses to the *Essai*.

The understanding of a text in its historical context was a task for the imagination. It was necessary to situate oneself in the world of Virgil and Augustus – *se donner les yeux des anciens* – in order to understand how the *Aeneid* and the *Georgics* had been written, heard or read by inhabitants of that world. Imagination entailed judgment: the critical judgment needed to authenticate a text, the taste needed to evaluate it, and finally the civil, political and philosophical judgment needed to choose between or combine the various probable explanations of an event, the various causes that could plausibly be assigned to it. Judgment was an education in probability, in the need to choose *méthode* over *système*, and in the last analysis in irony; for Gibbon – who leaves his reader aware that the *événement particulier*, the action or motive of an individual, the action which has taken many actors to perform it, never conforms to though it may be illuminated by the operation of a general law – has already declared that there is no pleasure equal to that of watching, and understanding, behaviour which is anomalous or ambiguous, that of actors behaving as you would not expect them to behave or things happening where you would not expect them to happen. It was irony in this sense – going far beyond the capacity for solemn sneer at the expense of Christianity – which he now put forward as more philosophical, more richly satisfying to the diverse capacities of the human intellect, than what he took to be the mathematical austerities that had cut d'Alembert off from the understanding and enjoyment of *belles-lettres* and *érudition*; and this sort of irony was to suffuse his practice as a historian when at last it developed. That was some way off in 1761. Meanwhile the choices he had declared in the *Essai* were to have consequences, some of them political, which may have affected his experience when he went to Paris in 1763 to meet the *philosophes* and know them better, and certainly affected his recollection of this experience when he wrote his *Memoirs* a quarter of a century later.

CHAPTER 10

Paris and the gens de lettres: *experience and recollection*

Gibbon's journey through various Enlightenments – English and Swiss, now French, with the Scottish yet to come – was associated in every case but the last with the possibility of a self-identification, a decision to settle in a certain country or city,[1] and with a moment in the process of selecting the historical study and writing in which he was going to engage. In the *Memoirs* he wrote of his conviction that he had been in pursuit of this search since childhood,[2] and in the militia journal he had recorded a search for the subject of a history. His philosophical defence of erudition has preoccupied us for several chapters, and we have now to return to his visit to Paris in the early months of 1763, undertaken as soon as his militia service could be ended and before the peace treaty that made it possible was finally signed.[3] There is eagerness here to encounter one of the central cultures of Enlightened Europe, while at the same time his critique of d'Alembert had engaged him in debate with its most recent (and very powerful) intellectual enterprise. The written evidence, contemporary and subsequent to his visit, tells of a continuing concern with his identity as a man or rather a gentleman of letters, and the experience ends with a decisive turn towards erudition which had some surprising results. The narrative, including that written a quarter of a century later, requires and may reward close study.

This is impeded by a paucity of documentary evidence. Gibbon did not succeed in keeping a journal for his time in Paris comparable to those we have for other periods in his early life; his attempts at a day-to-day record, or a retrospective evaluation, of his thoughts and activities are fragmentary and soon abandoned.[4] The most probable explanation is that the other journals were planned and executed as accounts, often self-critical, of his life while engaged in study, and that

---

[1] For the Parisian possibility see below, p. 254.   [2] *Memoirs*, p. 119 (*A*, p. 193, Memoir B).
[3] *Letters*, I, p. 132.   [4] See Bonnard in *MG*, pp. 88–91.

his life in Paris was devoted to society and conversation which he did not
find ways to record. Whatever the reason, the result is that we lack the
contemporary evidence which might be used to check the detailed and
interpretative narrative of this visit which he wrote in the *Memoirs* after
the passage of twenty-five years. This is a misfortune, because it was
precisely to experience society and conversation that he went to Paris,
and we wish for a fuller immediate account of it. The fragmentary
journals, and a few surviving letters, support the *Memoirs* in reminding us
that in the processes of Enlightenment, which were intended to substitute civil society for confessional division, the principal achievement
of French culture was held to be that it had carried sociability and
politeness, conversation and hospitality to heights perhaps unequalled
even in antiquity. The *Memoirs* speak of

the national urbanity which from the court has diffused its gentle influence to
the shop, the cottage, and the schools[5]

(the last a significant addition), and the *Decline and Fall* of

the perfection of that inestimable art, which softens and refines and embellishes
the intercourse of social life.[6]

These are not conventional flourishes. French politeness and hospitality,
inscribed in the national character by the court of Versailles – readers of
Saint-Simon may wish to add a note of exclamation – were seriously
considered a contribution to the civilising process in Europe only
equalled by English liberty and philosophy. What the *Memoirs* have told
us concerning the anglomania of the French and the gallomania of the
English[7] is endorsed by a letter of March 1763, which runs:

The name of Englishman inspires as great an idea at Paris, as that of Roman
could at Carthage, after the defeat of Hannibal. Indeed, the French are almost
excessive. From being very unjustly esteemed a set of pirates[8] and Barbarians,
we are now by a more agreeable injustice, looked upon as a nation of Philosophers and Patriots. I wish we would consider this opinion, as an encouragement to deserve a Character, which I am afraid, we have not yet deserved.[9]

This passage indeed follows a complaint against the 'stately' but un-
seemly lack of hospitality which has made the British ambassador, the
Duke of Bedford, the inferior of his Spanish rival. Gibbon's immersion

---

[5] *Memoirs*, p. 126 (*A*, p. 201, Memoir B).
[6] *Decline and Fall*, II, ch. 19, the concluding sentence; Womersley II, p. 724; Bury, II, p. 305.
[7] Above, p. 133.   [8] Given to seizing ships without a declaration of war?
[9] *Letters*, I, pp. 139–40.

in French sociability, however, was not without its problems. He knew it was a matter of language:

Ils aiment leur langue, et la preferent sans façon à toutes les autres; pouvoit on leur faire sa Cour, que par un hommage aussi public, qu'il etoit unique? Des Allemands ont souvent negligé leur langue pour ecrire en François. Jamais Anglois [ne] l'a fait à moins qu'on ne veuille compter le Comte Hamilton et le Chevalier Ramsay, Ecossois de Naissance mais qu'un long sejour avoit naturalisès en France.[10]

[They love their language and openly rank it above all others. Could one better pay court to them than by an act of homage as public as it is unprecedented? Germans have neglected their language to write in French, but no speaker of English has done so, unless one includes the Count Hamilton and the Chevalier Ramsay, Scotsmen by birth but naturalised in France by long residence.]

He therefore turned from keeping his militia journal in English to writing his Parisian notes in French; but though his French, learned in Lausanne, was fluent in conversation and writing, he feared that it might be provincial and while writing the *Essai* had looked for a guide who would give it Parisian polish. He had found only the Huguenot exile Mathieu Maty, and justly complained that the latter's introductory epistle, prefixed to the *Essai*,[11] was ambiguous in its praise. The journals, the *Letters* and the *Memoirs* contain much about this unsatisfactory association,[12] and the latter concludes:

My friends at Paris have been more indulgent: they received me as a countryman, or at least as a provincial; but they were friends and Parisians.

The operative word is of course 'provincial'; Parisian politeness had a double edge.

The defects which Maty insinuates – 'ces traits saillans, ces figures hardies, ce sacrifice de la règle au sentiment, et de la cadence à la force' – are the faults of the youth rather than of the stranger: and after the long and laborious exercise of my own language, I am conscious that my French style has been ripened and improved.[13]

The evident uneasiness of this passage – 'the long and laborious exercise' is of course the writing of the whole *Decline and Fall* – tells us that even at the summit of his career, and even when composing his *Memoirs*

---

[10] *MG*, p. 105. The 'hommage' is Gibbon's publication of his *Essai* in French. Was it, as he suggests, the only philosophic work so published by an Englishman? 'Count Hamilton' is Anthony Hamilton, writing as the Comte de Grammont.   [11] *MW*, iv, pp. 7–14.
[12] Reviewed by Craddock, *YEG*, pp. 132–5.   [13] *Memoirs*, p. 107 (*A*, p. 177, Memoir B).

after the outbreak of revolution in France, Gibbon was troubled by the cultural hegemony of Parisian French and was looking back on a period in which he had had to situate himself in the complex patterns of the western Enlightenments, between French politeness, English *imperium et libertas*, and Swiss and Huguenot critical literature. This had been a problem in 1763, when he had had to collect, and perhaps select, his letters of introduction to Parisian notables whose hospitality he hoped to enjoy. Should these be addressed to the *érudits* he had defended in the *Essai sur l'étude de la littérature* or to the *gens de lettres* whose attention he had hoped to catch by publishing it?

The journal fragments inform us that, before Gibbon left London, Lady Hervey gave him letters to the Comte de Caylus and Madame Geoffrin, Mrs Mallet letters to Madame Bontemps and a certain M. de la Motte. The bulk of his introductions, however, were obtained with Maty's help from the French envoy, the Duc de Nivernois, and may represent Gibbon's own selection:

savoir pour ce meme Comte de Caylus, et pour MM. Duclos[,] d'Alembert, de la Blèterie, de Foncemagne, de Ste Palaye, et Caperonier. Le Docteur Maty lui-mème m'en donna deux, pour M. de la Condamine et l'Abbé Raynal.[14]

Of these all except d'Alembert and perhaps Condamine – and not excluding the *philosophe* Raynal – were *académiciens* and *érudits* of the kind Gibbon had defended against d'Alembert. Gibbon may well have wished, rather apprehensively, to learn from the last-named how he responded to the *Essai*, but Gibbon's papers contain no hint that they ever met or that d'Alembert commented on his criticisms. Caylus was a grandee of the intellect to whom Gibbon had sent a copy of his work, but he proved inhospitable:

je l'attribue moins à son Caractère qu'à son genre de vie. Il se lève de grand matin, court les atteliers des artistes pendant tout le jour, et rentre chez lui a six heures du soir, pour se mettre en Robe de Chambre, et s'enfermer dans son Cabinet. Le Moyen de voir ses amis![15]

[I think this is due less to his character than to his way of life. He rises well into the morning, spends the day in workshops and studies (*n.* it is not quite clear whether 'artists' or 'artisans' are intended here), returns home at six in the evening, changes into a dressing-gown and shuts himself up in his study. What a way of seeing his friends!]

---

[14] *MG*, p. 102 (see footnotes). The same names are listed as furnished by Hervey and Nivernois in *Journal A*, p. 202.   [15] *MG*, p. 104.

Caylus's dedicated life was a problem[16] in an age when the function of learning was to promote politeness. Gibbon goes on from this point to celebrate Parisian hospitality

qui a etabli dans Paris une douceur et une liberté dans la societè inconnues à l'antiquité, et encore ignoreés des autres nations,

[which has established at Paris a moderation and freedom in society unknown to antiquity and to most other nations even now,]

and to make the probably inflated claim that the reception of his *Essai* was enough to make him a man of position.

Il decida de mon Etat; J'etois homme de lettres reconnû, et ce n'est qu'à Paris que cette qualité forme un Etat.[17]

[It determined my status; I was recognised as a man of letters, and only at Paris does this description of men constitute an estate.]

If the first 'Etat' may be translated 'status' the second must be rendered 'estate'. It is an observation of significance; we are being told that the monarchy's institution of the academies, followed by the growth of a literary culture around and beyond them, had made men of letters – *hommes* or *gens* – an estate of the realm. Gibbon enjoyed the standing of a corresponding member of this estate which his command of French opened up to him; he knew that English high culture was incapable of organising itself around the public practice of polite letters; yet he did not altogether desire this kind of 'estate' or 'status' as defining his social being. To his stepmother he wrote at this time:

Paris is divided into two Species who have but little communication with each other. The one who [*sic*] is chiefly connected with the men of letters dine very much at home, are glad to see their friends, & pass the evenings till about nine in agreeable & rational conversation. The others are the most fashionable, sup in numerous parties, and always play or rather game both before and after supper. You may easily guess which sort suits me best.[18]

Gibbon was of course reassuring his family that he was not gambling, but the image of Paris thus divided is in contrast with that later painted in the *Memoirs*, and he was not quite comfortable with his own position in it. In the more retrospective of the two journal fragments he noted:

---

[16] Haskell, 1993, p. 180, notes that, perhaps undeservedly, he was 'heartily disliked by almost every contemporary who wrote about him', and goes on (pp. 180–6) to consider his antiquarian learning in relation to that of Gibbon (pp. 186–93).   [17] *MG*, p. 105.   [18] *Letters*, I, p. 133.

Cette reputation me produisit cependant un petit desagrèment. Elle me fit considerer uniquement comme homme de lettres; ce n'est pas que cette qualité ne soit peut-etre en elle-meme la premiere de la societe, mais j'aurois voulû y joindre celle d'homme de condition à laquelle j'avois des droits si legitimes. Je ne voulois pas que l'ecrivain fit totalement disparoitre le Gentilhomme. Cette vanité ne me fait peut-etre point d'honneur mais je n'ecris pas un Panegyrique. Peut-etre que l'orgueil me faisoit illusion, et que je crûs voir des procèdès à mon egard qui n'existoient que dans mon imagination jalouse. En ce cas la, c'est l'aveu d'un defaut de plus.[19]

[This reputation, however, is causing me some little discomfort. It means that I am regarded simply as a man of letters. It is not that this is not a rank perhaps foremost in this society, but I would have preferred to join with it that of a man of quality, to which I have a legitimate claim. I do not want the gentleman to be lost altogether in the author. This vanity perhaps does me no credit, but I am not writing a panegyric. Perhaps I am deceived by pride, and imagine that I see behaviour towards me that exists only in my jealous imagination. If so, I must acknowledge one more fault in myself.]

Gibbon was engaged in self-examination and self-criticism, but he was also pointing to a fault-line in the social structure of English Enlightenment. The gentlemen had taken over letters and were practising them in order to demonstrate their independence of the clerisies, but there were many ways of being a 'man of quality' or 'fine gentleman' which had nothing to do with letters. And erudition was a severe paideia which demanded a harsh, and therefore perhaps impolite, self-discipline of those self-dedicated to it. Gibbon was and wanted to be a gentleman, but knew his vocation to be that of a scholar; he may have seen the donnish or even monastic life-style of Caylus as a threat, a warning of what he himself might become. At another point on his imaginative horizon appeared the alternative threat of d'Alembert, who in presenting the *gens de lettres* as an *état* or a *société* had seemed to subject erudition to the dictatorship of philosophy in a form alien to Gibbon. There is no mention of the *Encyclopédistes* in these fragments, unless they are hinted at in a note concerning a visit to Jean-Pierre de Bougainville, elder brother of the navigator and a former secretary of the Académie des Inscriptions:

La Conversation rouloit principalement sur les gens de lettres de ce pays. En general il les regarde comme des hommes peu estimable et très dangereux.[20]

[The conversation turned chiefly on the men of letters in this country. In general he thinks them little to be admired and very dangerous.]

---

[19] *MG*, p. 106.   [20] *MG*, p. 100.

Are the *gens de lettres* separating themselves from the *hommes de lettres*, as a *société* aiming to be something more than *un état reconnu*? Bougainville, who died that year, may have been merely grumbling, but the perception was to arise in a future not to be foreseen.

The fragmentary journal, reinforced by an uncompleted 'idée générale', covers only a few days of the more than three months Gibbon spent in Paris, and the account we have of his life there is anything but exhaustive. In February 1763 we find him studying prominent buildings as a traveller should and even listening to sermons and reporting critically on their content and elocution. This he did in the company of Madame Bontemps, to whom he had been recommended by Lucy Mallet and with whom he enjoyed an *amitié amoureuse* a good deal less intense than Hume's with Madame Boufflers, but like it in forming part of the education of a philosopher at Paris; he was intrigued to find her at once *libertine*, *dévote*, tolerant and the author of a prose translation of James Thomson's *The Seasons*.[21] He dined regularly at the tables of Helvetius and Holbach – whose *De l'esprit* he did not mind mentioning in a letter to his stepmother – but says nothing of the conversation he heard there.[22] Here we find him in *philosophe* and in no small degree infidel company[23] – there is nothing to indicate to whom he owed the *entrée* to it – but there is no sign in these scanty documents of any intellectual or social tensions occurring, though the *Memoirs* have much to say on this subject. For the rest, Gibbon's activities associate him with the *érudits*; he examines medals and reflects on their study,[24] embarks on the reading of Mabillon and Montfaucon,[25] and spends time in the society and conversation of Foncemagne, Barthélemy, La Bléterie (the biographer of Julian the Apostate, whom he had read much at Lausanne), La Curne de Sainte Palaye the medievalist, Bougainville and Caylus.[26] All were leading figures in the Académie des Inscriptions, and therefore in the *érudition* which he had defended against d'Alembert, but neither in these fragments nor in what we know of the reception, such as it was, of Gibbon's *Essai* is there much sign (Bougainville excepted) of a *défaite de l'érudition* going on, or of a social distance between *érudits* and *philosophes*.

---

[21] *MG*, p. 96, n. 3. For Gibbon's accounts of their relationship see *MG*, pp. 96–7, 106–7; *Letters*, I, p. 139; *Memoirs*, pp. 127–8 (*A*, pp. 204–5, Memoir B).

[22] *MG*, pp. 96, 98, 99; *Letters*, pp. 133, 136. He tells his father that he met Helvetius through Madame Geoffrin, and Holbach through Helvetius; there is no hint that these might be dangerous company.   [23] Kors, 1976, is an exhaustive study of the extent of atheism in Holbach's circle.

[24] *MG*, p. 98. *Memoirs*, p. 131 (*A*, p. 209).   [25] *MG*, p. 99 and n. 1 (cf. *A*, p. 209).

[26] *MG*, pp. 97–8 (Caylus, Foncemagne), 98 (La Bléterie), 98–9 (Barthélemy), 100 (Bougainville, Sainte-Palaye). These contacts do not appear in the *Letters*.

A very different account of these matters occurs in the *Memoirs*, where Gibbon looked back on his encounter with Paris over the space of twenty-five years.

Recalling his anxiety in 1763 to ensure his amateur status, he then wrote:

> For myself I carried a personal recommendation: my name and my Essay were already known; the compliment of writing in the French language entitled me to some returns of civility and gratitude. I was considered as a man of letters, or rather as a gentleman who wrote for his amusement: my appearance, dress and equipage distinguished me from the tribe of authors who even at Paris are secretly envied and despised by those who possess the advantages of birth and fortune.[27]

This is some distance removed from the portrait of two non-interacting worlds, one of sober men of letters and one of careless high society, presented to Dorothea Gibbon long ago. The former have become the dependants and rivals of the latter, whose feelings towards them are correspondingly ambivalent. By the time he wrote these words Gibbon had completed three brief sojourns at Paris, in 1763, 1765 and 1777, the two latter as a guest of Jacques and Suzanne Necker (*née* Curchod), and the perspective of Madame Necker's *salon* may have something to do with what he wrote in the *Memoirs*. His language also brings to mind a work he never cites: d'Alembert's *Essai sur la société des gens de lettres et des grands, sur la réputation, sur les Mécénes, et sur les recompenses littéraires*,[28] in which the *philosophe* had gently and exhaustively explained to the *gens de lettres* their need for reassurance, their need to seek it from one another, and their need to resist the impulse to seek it from lordly patrons who could never fully grant it. As a gentleman Gibbon should be immune from these insecurities; 'amusement' denotes no lightweight frivolity, but the *sprezzatura* which is essential to the cultivated mind's sociability.[29] But it might also be possible to read d'Alembert's *Essai* as an incitement to the *gens de lettres* to make their *société* an independent *état*,[30] or in Burke's

---

[27] *Memoirs*, p. 126 (*A*, pp. 200, Memoir B; 261, Memoir C).

[28] First published in 1753, and found in successive editions of d'Alembert's *Melánges de littérature, d'histoire et de philosophie* (1753, 1760, 1767, 1770, 1773). Gibbon owned the 1760 edition, dated 1759 in *Letters*, p. 47; citation in *MW*, IV, p. 68. It is certain that he had access to this *Essai*, probable that he read it, but certain that he does not cite it.

[29] The English authority on this is Shaftesbury; cf. Klein, 1994.

[30] He urges them 'de vivre unis (s'il leur est possible) et presque renfermées entr'eux ... Par cette union ils parviendront sans peine à donner la loi au reste de la nation sur les matieres de goût et de Philosophie' (d'Alembert, 1773, I, p. 410). This falls well short of Burke's accusation, but might well appear different to the author of the *Essai sur l'étude de la littérature* when he had read the *Reflections on the Revolution in France*.

language 'a faction known in the state', and there is even more here than the polite man's need to make it clear that he is a gentleman of letters and neither a cleric nor a mercenary. Gibbon continued drafting the *Memoirs* after the outbreak of the Revolution, which Burke in the *Reflections* published in 1790 laid at the door of the men of letters, no longer organised in academies but brigaded under the leadership of the *Encyclopédistes* in an anti-Christian crusade.[31] He may be letting us know that, as far back as 1763, he was not one of the *gens de lettres* whose social position in relation to *les grands* d'Alembert had sought to assert and in whom Burke was to detect the revolt of intelligence against property. He had gone to France in search of the enlightenment of manners,

which from the court has diffused its gentle influence to the shop, the cottage and the schools. Of the men of genius of the age, Montesquieu and Fontenelle were no more; Voltaire resided on his own estate near Geneva; Rousseau in the preceding year had been driven from his hermitage of Montmorency, and I blush at my neglecting to seek, in this journey, the acquaintance of Buffon. Among the men of letters whom I saw, d'Alembert and Diderot held the foremost rank, in merit or at least in fame; these two associates were the elements of water and fire; but the eruption was clouded in smoke, and the stream though devoid of grace was limpid and copious. I shall content myself with enumerating the well-known names of the Count de Caylus, of the Abbés de la Bléterie, Barthélemy, Raynal, Arnaud, of Messieurs de la Condamine, Duclos, de Ste Palaye, de Bougainville, Caperonnier, de Guignes, Suard, etc., without attempting to discriminate the shades of their characters, or the degrees of our connection.[32] Alone in a morning visit I commonly found the wits and authors of Paris less vain and more reasonable than in the circles of their equals, with whom they mingle in the houses of the rich. Four days in the week I had a place without invitation at the hospitable tables of Mesdames Geoffrin and du Bocage, of the celebrated Helvetius and of the Baron d'Olbach . . . Yet I was often disgusted with the capricious tyranny of Madame Geoffrin, nor could I approve the intolerant zeal of the philosophers and Encyclopedists, the friends of d'Olbach and Helvetius: they laughed at the scepticism of Hume, preached the tenets of Atheism with the bigotry of dogmatists, and damned all believers with ridicule and contempt. The society of Madame du Bocage was more soft and moderate than that of her rivals; and the evening conversations of Mr de Foncemagne were supported by the principal members of the Academy of Inscriptions.[33]

---

[31] Burke 1791, pp. 97–8; written partly by his son Richard.

[32] This list largely coincides with that given in the Paris fragments. Raynal he had evidently met by the end of his stay (*Journal B*, p. 224); de Guignes and Suard perhaps later.

[33] *Memoirs*, pp. 126–7 (*A*, pp. 201–4, Memoir B). The plural 'rivals' in the last sentence seems to make them both male and female. Of Foncemagne he had written in 1763, 'Cette maison ne respire que l'Esprit sensé et eclairè, l'aisance, et l'honnètetè' (*MG*, p. 98).

This is a complex if uncompleted portrayal of Parisian Enlightenment as Gibbon claims to have seen it in 1763. The giants are departed; Voltaire and Rousseau – the latter making the first of not many appearances in Gibbon's writings – are present chiefly by their absence; and Gibbon did not meet Buffon until 1777. As for 'the men of letters whom I saw', this verb normally meant that one had been in company but not in society with those of whom it is used (though Gibbon does employ the tag *Virgilium vidi tantum* when writing of Voltaire at *Les Délices*, with whom he elsewhere claims acquaintance by calling him 'my friend').[34] It implies here that he heard d'Alembert and Diderot hold forth in *salons*, but did not meet them in conversation;[35] the language is that in which one evaluates the performance of lions at the dinner table; and we may draw the further implication that Gibbon – who disliked public and competitive speech – means us to infer that he turned away from the pyrotechnics of *philosophes* in *salons* to seek the 'less vain and more reasonable' conversation of the *érudits* and *académiciens* whose names he here enumerates and whose chosen pursuit he had defended against d'Alembert in the *Essai*. 'Alone in a morning visit', we imagine him finding that the *savants* fetched the books from the shelves and sat down to discuss them with him; but the same individuals might be less sociable at dinner, in the d'Alembertian situation of 'mingling with their equals in the houses of the rich'. It is possible to feel that the *république des lettres* is being upheld against the *sociétés de conversation*, and the study of the *belles-lettres* against the philosophy that might look down on it; especially if *salon* conversation is being dismissed as vainly and unreasonably competitive, as it is depicted in the *Essai sur la société des gens de lettres*.

The possibilities darken when we read that 'the philosophers and Encyclopedists', forming the company at 'the hospitable tables' of Helvetius and Holbach, 'laughed at the scepticism of Hume [and] preached the tenets of atheism with the bigotry of dogmatists'. Nothing of this is mentioned in the 1763 fragments, and since Hume was not in Paris at the time of Gibbon's visit, the *Memoirs* do not tell us that anything like the episode reported by Diderot, when Holbach offered to show Hume fifteen atheists sitting down together, occurred under Gibbon's eye at that time. This is not to say that Gibbon did not encounter

---

[34] *Memoirs*, p. 83 (*A*, p. 148); *Journal A*, p. 122.
[35] Bonnard (*Memoirs*, p. 301) thought it possible that Gibbon knew them only by reputation. The question is why they are mentioned here at all. Cf. *A*, p. 261, Memoir C: 'I listened to the oracles of d'Alembert and Diderot, who reigned at the head of the *Encyclopédie* and the philosophic sect.'

Parisian atheism, then or at a later date; it certainly existed, though we are warned not to over-estimate it.[36] Here it is important, as in all matters touching Gibbon's unbelief, to distinguish between deism, scepticism and atheism. Given that these mentalities overlapped, it remains the case that the deist rationally accepted a God who was not the God of the Bible; the sceptic doubted the possibility of knowing how the universe was constituted; while the atheist was certain that he did know, and that its constitution precluded the existence of a God. Since it was an overall purpose of Enlightenment to discourage all forms of metaphysical certainty, the philosopher had every reason to be a sceptic and to distrust the atheist as a potential dogmatist and even fanatic; while in an age when atheism frequently occurred in the shape of a Lucretian or Spinozistic materialism, the atheist could further be suspected of believing that his mind was the substance of the universe grown conscious of itself, and therefore of a species of enthusiasm (a term Diderot did not mind using of himself).[37] Writing his *Memoirs* at the time of the Revolution, therefore, Gibbon had good cause to represent Hume, and by implication himself, as sceptics whose philosophic doubt upheld the existing order and was the antithesis of revolutionary fanaticism. This would not save either from the wrath of those whose horror at the events in France made them unwilling to discriminate between various forms of unbelief, but it may not have been untrue as self-description. Hume, who died in 1776, has been called a 'prophet of the counter-revolution',[38] and what Gibbon set down in his *Memoirs* concerning the *philosophes* at dinner aligns him with Burke's assertation that an organised campaign against the Christian religion took shape, to which

the vast undertaking of the *Encyclopedia*, carried on by a society of these gentlemen, did not a little contribute . . . These atheistical fathers have a bigotry of their own, and they have learned to talk against monks with the spirit of a monk.[39]

Gibbon had found himself in 1763 at what much later came to be seen

[36] Kors, 1976; for Diderot's anecdote, pp. 41–2, and for Gibbon's evidence, pp. 104–5. Holbach's *Système de la Nature*, which is atheist, was published in 1770 (Gibbon acquired a copy), but remained anonymous. Kors says that those who knew of his authorship remained silent, and seems to suggest that those who did not know did not suspect. Kors (pp. 88–91) can find no evidence that the members of this coterie were engaged in any collaborative organised enterprise or collaborated in the production of the *Encyclopédie*. For further study of the character of atheism in France, see Kors, 1990.
[37] On Spinoza I have learned much from Yovel, 1989; on Diderot from Anderson, 1990.
[38] Bongie, 1965.   [39] Burke, 1791; Pocock, 1987, p. 97, and n. 11.

(perhaps by him) as a turning-point in the history of *philosophe* Enlightenment: the point at which the *Encyclopédie* has been held to have inaugurated what some call 'the Enlightenment project', which in turn some hold, and others forcibly deny, to have become a revolutionary militancy exploding into dechristianisation and the fall of regimes. Burke is among the originators of the latter perception. He did not desire to return to a medieval past, but saw modernity – indeed, enlightenment as he understood it – as rooted in Christian and medieval history and unable to deny its roots without destroying itself. He therefore made himself the defender of Europe as a republic of states held together by civilised manners against a rootless intellect bent on subversion,[40] and English opinion in the counter-revolutionary period[41] followed him in differentiating between the Enlightenment which was to be defended and the Enlightenment which assaulted itself. By the time Gibbon wrote his *Memoirs* he was coming to share Burke's instant repudiation of what was being done in France,[42] and to fear the Revolution's spread to Lausanne and even England; and strong echoes of Burke's language regarding the *gens de lettres* and their supposed atheism are to be found in the text of the *Memoirs*. Of his third visit to Paris, in 1777, he significantly remarks: 'The society of men of letters I neither courted nor declined.'[43] It is a long way from 1763, when he was carefully delimiting the sense in which he was one.

There is then evidence that Gibbon in writing the *Memoirs* distanced himself from those variously described as *philosophes*, Encyclopedists and *gens de lettres*; that he emphasised the gap between their atheism and Hume's scepticism, which was also his own; and that he depicted himself, as far back as 1763, turning away from the conversation of the *salons* and the dinner tables to seek the more private and rewarding company of the members of the Académie des Inscriptions. What little evidence we have dating from the 1763 visit cannot be said to support the *Memoirs*, though it does not permit us to reject them altogether; and we have not found reason to suppose that Parisian intellectual society was divided into *philosophes* and *érudits*, or that the contributors to the *Encylopédie* were campaigning to inflict a *défaite* on the latter. The *Mem-*

---

[40] Burke's developing views on the French Revolution may be traced in the following modern editions: Pocock, 1987a; Mitchell, 1989; Ritchie, 1992. See further Pocock, 1985 (ch. 10), 1989a and b.   [41] Deane, 1989.

[42] *Letters*, III, pp. 161, 167, 176, 184, 216 (Burke), 227, 229–30 (Burke), 239, 254, 260 ('Gallic cannibals'), 261 ('wolves', 'savages'), 265 ('tyrants and cannibals'), 268–9 ('cannibals'), 273 ('cannibals'), 275 ('cannibals'), 280–3, 284–5, 290–2, 302–4, 306–8, 324–5, 337.

[43] *Memoirs*, p. 158 (*A*, p. 314, Memoir E).

oirs, then, do not tell us what Gibbon experienced on his first visit to Paris; but it does not necessarily follow that they are fictitious accounts fabricated or imagined in 1789–91. Gibbon was by the latter date a deeply reflective historian, and we may think of him as assessing in the *Memoirs* experiences which had befallen him in earlier life. Here we are possessed of one well-authenticated historical fact. In the *Essai sur l'étude de la littérature*, written between 1758 and 1761, he had charged d'Alembert's *Discours préliminaire* with tending to the dictatorship of one faculty of the mind over all the others. It is a charge which has been brought against the *philosophes* and their Enlightened projects ever since. Gibbon was strongly attracted to Parisian and French culture, and did not identify it with the *esprit philosophique*; he went to Paris in the expectation of experiencing the sovereignty of politeness, and remained to enjoy – however cautiously – a culture which gave extraordinary recognition to men of letters; he did not expect to find, and it does not seem that he did find, a deep cleavage between philosophy and erudition. Looking back, however, from the outbreak of the Revolution and the publication of Burke's *Reflections*, it was possible for him to telescope the dictatorship of the faculties he had perceived in 1758 and 1761 with the image, supplied by Burke, of the *gens de lettres* as aiming at an atheist seizure of power, and to condemn atheism less because it was irreligious than because it was fanatical. Independently of Burke, and indeed echoed by him,[44] Gibbon had by 1788 condemned Joseph Priestley's apocalyptic call for the downfall of the civil powers as a prelude to that of established religion.[45] He had perceived the enthusiastic potential in Rational Dissent, and might share Burke's fear of this movement's sympathy with American and French revolutions.

In this light, Gibbon might and we may re-assess the significance of the *Essai sur l'étude de la littérature*. He had condemned the dictatorship of one faculty over another which seemed to follow from d'Alembert's rigorous separation between them, and had argued instead for their close partnership and equality in a study of *belles-lettres* which became as he analysed it a study of history. This study was philosophical and at the same time counter-*philosophe*; it did not lead to the intellect's sovereignty over its environment, but rather to its immersion in it, perpetually exercising imagination and judgment in a pursuit less of general laws and causes than of the ironies and anomalies that followed the attempt to apply them to the crooked timber of humanity. Such a perception

---

[44] Burke, 1791, p. 50.
[45] Priestley, 1782, vol. II, p. 484; *Decline and Fall*, V, ch. 54, n. 42 (Womersley, III, p. 439; Bury, VI, p. 137, note numbered 49).

was Enlightened, but at the same time humanist and classical. It could exalt Tacitus as the greatest of philosophical historians; it was Lockean in its insistence that the mind lived among probabilities, Humean in its sceptical account of the processes by which the mind arrived at general laws, and left d'Alembert – who understood the issues very well – with no option other than the preference he often expressed for geometry over history. It was also Burkean; though Burke was no ironist he had the religious mind's understanding of scepticism,[46] and an irony like Gibbon's shared his conviction that the mind acted within the immense diversities of history and had no way of acting outside them, or of imposing on history any order beyond that it imposed on itself. Gibbon's Enlightenment, like that of many others, had nothing about it of the *riformatore*.

It is in this light that Gibbon might assess the twenty-five years separating his first visit to Paris from his completion of the *Decline and Fall*, which would appear to him a history deeply Enlightened and deeply hostile to Revolution. He does not supply such an auto-history in the *Memoirs*, and we are driven to mine the language of the several drafts in search of it. Nor is it easy to extract from the evidence any coherent account of the stages by which he may have arrived at the position stated in the *Memoirs*, or to decide whether his final rejection of the *gens de lettres* took an early shape in 1763. We have his account, which we may well find questionable, of how he separated himself from the atheism of Holbach's dinner table; there is also his blow in passing at the 'capricious tyranny' of Madame Geoffrin. He may not have been the only habitué to find her control of conversation at times too close; but the issue is that of *salonnière* hostesses in a polity of conversation.[47] When Gibbon says that Madame du Bocage exercised a 'softer and more moderate' role, the adjectives precisely indicate the function assigned to women in Enlightened culture; like that assigned to conversation, to manners, to property and to culture, it was that of tempering, refining and mediating between the passions, the interests and the ideas of men in action, and when Gibbon speaks or writes of women as confining themselves to the graces of life and leaving thought and action to the males,[48] he does not mean to marginalise them but to invest them with a centrally important function. The feminist case to be brought against

---

[46] Hampsher-Monk, 1998.   [47] Goodman, 1994, pp. 99–111; Kors, 1976, pp. 95–7, 99–100.

[48] E.g., *MW*, IV, p. 17 (*Essai*: 'content des graces, nous laisse les lumières'); *Letters*, II, p. 127 (to Suzanne Necker: 'destiné à consoler le genre humain, à lui plaire toujours, quelquefois à l'instruire, jamais à le faire trembler'; the identification of 'le genre humain' with the male sex cannot pass unnoted).

what he is saying is parallel to that he brings against d'Alembert; he can be charged with too rigorous a separation between the faculties and between those who severally exercise them.

The passage about Geoffrin and du Bocage – Madame Bontemps kept no table, preferring smaller and more intimate gatherings[49] – was written after Gibbon's second and third visits to Paris. On each of these occasions he was the guest of Jacques and Suzanne Necker – her marriage was the occasion of a reconciliation with Gibbon after their angry and reproachful parting in the preceding year – and in 1777 he was responding to her invitation to enjoy the *salon* conversation which would enable him to understand women better.[50] Suzanne Necker took the role of *salonnière* very seriously indeed,[51] and the passage from the *Memoirs*, though it does not mention her, may have much to do with her practice and example. It is important to remember, however, that Gibbon's views on Parisian society are those of an occasional visitor. His first sojourn ended after fourteen weeks, and he moved to Lausanne where he spent the winter and spring, before visiting Italy in 1764. Two years passed between his first and second stays in Paris, twelve between the second and third. We return to the question raised by Venturi; was Gibbon isolated by his separation from the universe of the *philosophes*?

At the end of an account of his friendship with Madame Bontemps, Gibbon in the *Memoirs* says of his departure in May 1763: 'had I been rich and independent I should have prolonged and perhaps have fixed my residence at Paris'.[52] The words possess a face value; he was dependent on the money his father allowed him, was finding Paris expensive, and moved to Lausanne to economise before going on to Italy. The language nevertheless expresses the allure of Paris, in which the society both of women and of men of letters was important; we think of Hume's more vigorous statement that only the outbreak of war in 1756 had prevented his removal to France – to some provincial town since he too found Paris beyond his means – after the apparent failure of his *History* following that of the *Treatise*;[53] but there is the counter-fact that Gibbon never settled in Paris, but in the end at Lausanne. He was in certain ways at odds with the *société des gens de lettres*; does the remark in the *Memoirs* express the thought that these difficulties might have been

---

[49] *MG*, p. 107; *Memoirs*, p. 128 (*A*, p. 205).
[50] *MW*, II, pp. 176–80. The names in the text complete his mention of *salonnières*. A study of Gibbon's relations with women of intellect would probably give most prominence to Lucy Mallet and Suzanne Necker.   [51] Goodman, 1994, pp. 79–82.   [52] *Memoirs*, p. 128 (*A*, p. 205).
[53] Miller, 1985, p. xxxvii.

overcome? Is there any resonance between the words 'rich and independent' and the image of the men of letters 'mingling with their equals in the houses of the rich'?

Gibbon's early encounter with intellectual and social Paris had begun with a defence of erudition against the *Encyclopédie*; it ended with a year spent at Lausanne in very rigorous study of Roman antiquities, and then with the visit to Rome which he says revealed to him the subject of his history. He then returned to England, and the *Decline and Fall* took shape over the next ten years. The *Memoirs* present the months at Paris as a turning away from the *philosophes* and the *gens de lettres* towards erudition and the *académiciens*; and though we have found reason to mistrust this account, there is no mistaking the trajectory which Gibbon's life pursued. He was never a *philosophe*, if by that term be meant one committed to the enterprise of the *Encyclopédie*; there can be no better proof of this than the absence of any sign that he was disturbed by, or even much interested in, the figure of Rousseau, whom Voltaire, d'Alembert, Diderot and Hume all found cause to regard as an accuser and a traitor.[54] He preferred history to philosophy, and had mounted a philosophic defence of it against the *philosophes*. Yet he could not be a Parisian *érudit* either, since the Académie des Inscriptions was closed to him as an Englishman and did not offer him corresponding membership; his deep loyalty to the kind of scholarship it represented was balanced by a parallel loyalty to the memory of the older *république des lettres*. The *académiciens* he met at Paris – some of whom, notably Raynal, were *philosophes* in every sense of the term – were part, and helped shape his image, of the *société des gens de lettres* to which he was strongly attracted but which he seems to have decided was not for him; he chose, and came to believe that he had already chosen, to be a historian in the grand narrative manner as well as an *érudit*, and this was a choice of life-style and of personal and national identity. We have to consider the tensions between him and the *société* he found at Paris if we are to understand the outcomes as well as the causes of his departure for Lausanne.

In the fragmentary 'idée générale de mon sejour à Paris' Gibbon had contemplated the *société de gens de lettres* as an *état*, an estate of a realm not quite identical with a *république des lettres*. It was not his realm and he had no need to belong to an estate; unlike Swift but like Addison, he was a

---

54 Gibbon owned several collections of Rousseau's works, and there are allusions to *Emile* in footnotes to the *Decline and Fall* (Womersley, III, p. 1257). For an indirect encounter with Rousseau in 1763, and a characterisation of him as 'that extraordinary man whom I both admire and pity', see Draft E of the *Memoirs* (*A*, p. 298).

gentleman of a kind now annexing English letters, and enjoying a property and magistracy which – however confused and insecure his own not yet Whig family – carried with it a public position and occupancy of a public space that made them members of a class that did not need an organised corporate existence. Confronted by the *hommes de lettres* in the character of an *état*, he became aware that the danger for such as he – real if not very grave, 'un petit disagrément' – was that the gentleman might be lost in the scholar, while the latter could be neither a cleric in the neo-Latin sense nor an *homme de lettres* in the French. What he saw at Paris was learning formerly organised into an academy by monarchical power – an organisation never carried out in England – and now being transformed by politeness, philosophy, sociability and the other motor forces of Enlightenment into an estate of a realm which had limited room for estates of any kind. When we read Burke's allusion to the Encyclopédistes as 'a society of these gentlemen', we should be aware that they were not 'gentlemen' in the English sense, representatives of an intimate union between country, city and court; Montesquieu, the grandee of a provincial *noblesse de la robe*, could not accurately be described as a 'country gentleman'. When the *Memoirs* speak of 'the wits of Paris' as 'a tribe of authors', 'vain and unreasonable' when 'mingling with their equals' in 'the houses of the rich' who 'envy and despise them', Gibbon is characterising them as an upwardly mobile intelligentsia rendered insecure by their continued dependance on patronage. This is Gibbon's perception, shared by d'Alembert, who in the *Essai sur la société des gens de lettres* had explained to the latter how enlightened monarchy had interested the nobility in letters without educating them sufficiently in their value, and at the same time had raised up the *gens de lettres* without making them secure in their position – 'an aristocracy of talent' perhaps a contradiction in terms – or sufficiently confident of their own values to sustain their own dignity by them. Such a *société* was not one to which an English 'man of letters, or rather a gentleman who wrote for his amusement' was either induced or necessitated to belong.

Burke, whom Gibbon followed, was to see the Revolution as promoted by the men of letters as a discontented *état* organising itself under the banner of dechristianisation; the unchristian Gibbon had no desire to enlist in any such movement of subversion. By 1790 it was open to Gibbon to see the struggle of the faculties for hegemony over one another, which he had suspected in d'Alembert as early as 1758, as the seedbed of later revolution, and to see the *Decline and Fall* as the alternative path for intellect to follow which he had pointed out in the *Essai sur l'étude de la littérature*. In fact, d'Alembert was no revolutionary, but a Tacitean pessimist who doubted if the elites would ever organise themselves to live with dignity; Gibbon, however, could have read the *Essai sur la société des gens de lettres* as the portrayal of a society which was not for him. We lack sufficient evidence to say with certainty that he rejected philosophy and returned to scholarship as a conscious choice made in 1763; but his second stay at Lausanne was an immersion in erudition and his journey to Rome – or so at least he tells us – a redis-covery of history. These choices – and perhaps they were never con-sciously that – amounted to a re-assertion of that informal and non-institutional association between the study of letters and the life of a gentleman, which d'Alembert noted with some envy as peculiarly Eng-lish, but which no one in England thought it necessary to analyse until Coleridge, at the very end of the long eighteenth century, characterised the clerical learning, formerly annexed by the gentlemen and now passing to the control of universities and professions, as a 'national church' distinct from the Christian.[55] Gibbon rejected the *philosophes*, and returned to an England where he was sometimes mistaken for one.

That lay in the future; for the moment he was returning to Lausanne and the erudition he had first discovered there. It is instructive to contrast his Parisian experience of 1763 with that undergone some six years later by the young east German pastor Johann Gottfried Herder, who was amicably received by the *philosophes* but found – unlike Gib-bon – that his conversational French did not allow him to follow what was going on.[56] In consequence – to foreshorten a complex personal history – he returned to his *Heimat* and set about the invention of the *Volk* and of 'yet another philosophy of history', which seems never to have come to Gibbon's attention and of which he would certainly have had little understanding. We see this as a turning-point in the history of Enlightenment and Enlightened historiography,[57] and Herder's bitter rejection of French culture as indicating the depth of its impact upon him. By contrast, Gibbon's departure from Paris happens within the fabric of tensions constituting Anglo-French Enlightenment and is more conservative than romantic in its consequences. Herder departs in search of historicism, Gibbon of history; he writes history, not philos-ophy of history. In a movement leading in some ways towards Burke, he sets about the imagination and the irony of a historiography conceived

---

[55] Coleridge, 1829; Morrow, 1990, 1991.   [56] La Vopa, 1995.   [57] Berlin, 1976.

in classical and neo-classical terms, and already possessing a history which permitted him to admire and practise it as it had been in French, Dutch and Huguenot culture before the time of his birth. To understand where Gibbon went after putting Paris behind him, we must re-examine the relations between erudition and historiography.

PART III

Lausanne and Rome: the journey towards a subject, 1763–1764

CHAPTER 11

The return to Lausanne and the pursuit of erudition

Gibbon's removal from Paris to Lausanne in May 1763 occupies more than one place, and possesses more than one significance, in the frameworks of interpretation we are setting up. It does not complete the tale of his journeys through the Enlightenments, since his encounter with the Scottish variant was still to come; he had read Hume's and Robertson's histories while serving in the militia, but Adam Smith, and perhaps Adam Ferguson, had yet to assume the signal importance he came to ascribe to the former, and to Scottish philosophy in general, in the late sixties and seventies. More immediately, the departure from Paris is of some significance – it is hard to say what, since he was slow to decide himself – in establishing the distance which came to exist between Gibbon and the intellectual politics of French Enlightenment. He had hastened from England to enjoy a polite society, a crown of Enlightenment, in which letters were esteemed and institutionalised; but he had set out after declaring and inscribing his mistrust of the hegemonic tendencies he observed in Encyclopedist philosophy. It is hard to say whether this tension played a significant role in the three weeks of his first Parisian sojourn, but his movements for the rest of his life do not suggest any very strong patterns of attraction or repulsion. He left Paris to re-enter a Europe more certainly his own.

The issue that divided him from d'Alembert and the *Encyclopédie* was the issue of erudition; we have decided to adopt this term, though Gibbon did not favour it. His commitment to a very intense and arduous scholarship, at once clerical, humanist and critical, was extremely strong, and there is not much reason to doubt his word that it dated from what, but for ill health, would have been his schooldays. The need of 'modern' scholarship to emancipate itself from 'ancient' – meaning the impassioned erudition of the Renaissance – must rank high among those aspects of Enlightenment that meant most to him; but he thought d'Alembert had gone too far in that direction and was threatening to destroy scholarship altogether. If we ask what erudition meant to him beyond personal commitments, in the fashioning of himself as a social being that followed the confusions of his childhood and adolescence, we come up with something very English: the need of a swiftly changing gentlemanly class to disarm the clerisies by themselves taking over letters and philosophy, rendering them harmless and even beneficial as the pursuit of a class of polite virtuosos and amateurs. Paradoxically, this had the effect of clericalising gentry and rendering *philosophes* unnecessary; but if Gibbon, in 1761 or later, saw or came to see d'Alembert as threatening a dictatorship by a class of *philosophes* indifferent to erudition, it was a further effect of his stay at Paris that he recognised a tension between erudition and virtuosity, important to his self-establishment as a gentleman. A gentleman could not afford to be too much a man of letters, yet Gibbon's commitment was to erudition.

This tension could not be readily overcome in England, where Gibbon (once out of the militia) was the insecure heir of an unpredictable father and a family thrown off balance less by social mobility than by the deep ideological fissures of post-Revolutionary history. He was in no hurry to return to Hampshire, but moved instead into the role of a curious traveller in search of antiquities; with the difference only that he was not rambling, sketchbook in hand, but settling down in a city made familiar by former exile for a winter, which proved nearly a year, of intensive and dedicated textual scholarship. Here the scenario changes. Gibbon was not merely concerned with fashioning himself as a social type, that of gentleman of letters, important though this fashioning was to him and to our understanding of where he stood in the processes to be termed Enlightenment. He had also a vocation – for such things happen to some people – a vocation to be a historian; and erudition, the theme of his writings so far and of his studies during both the first and the second of his sojourns at Lausanne, was only one part – though for the present by far the most important part – of what was needed to make him the historian he became. We are at a point where we begin turning from the problems posed by Venturi – those of discovering Enlightenments to which Gibbon belonged – to those set up to enrich us by Arnaldo Momigliano. He proposed that Gibbon's supreme achievement, in the context of eighteenth-century historiography, was to effect a synthesis between the erudite or antiquarian scholarship derived from the Renaissance humanists, and the new grand style of philosophical narrative taking shape after Montesquieu in the writings of Hume and

Voltaire.[1] Rightly to understand this hypothesis, however, we have to unpack the concept of philosophical narrative history, and see that beneath it lay a much older stratum of classical and neo-classical narrative, with which also the philosophical had to effect a synthesis. While Gibbon was publishing his *Essai*, a philosophic defence of imagination in erudition, his militia journal shows him in search of a theme for grand narrative. He intended, then, to be a historian as well as an *érudit*, a historian as well as a gentleman of letters. It is in this problematic context that we have to examine the programme of erudition through which he put himself at Lausanne, following his Parisian encounter with men of letters, *érudits* and philosophers, but with no historian in the grand manner. It is to end – as we know in advance – with his Italian journey of the following year and arrival at Rome in October 1764, when, he tells us and there is reason to believe, something occurred which transformed his intentions and restored the primacy of narrative history.

Gibbon arrived in Lausanne in late May 1763, and remained until the middle of the following April. During this year he kept a journal[2] – as he had not in Paris – which resembles his militia journal in being a record both of study and of social life and hard drinking. The company of some rowdy English tourists led him into some instances of riotous behaviour which damaged his reputation, but he endeavoured to reform and was able to resolve his relationship with Suzanne Curchod before her marriage. As a record of research and writing, the Lausanne journal informs us that Gibbon's commitment to the erudite study of Greco-Roman antiquity was stronger than it had been in his militia years, possibly – but possibly not – as a result of his Parisian encounters. When writing the *Essai* he had aligned himself with the *académiciens*; now he had been among them and knew them personally, and one or two – La Blèterie and, ambiguously, Raynal – are mentioned as his 'friends',[3] though this may mean no more than that he had been received by them and might claim their acquaintance. What is noteworthy is that the schemes for Swiss and Florentine histories, in a sense the culmination of Gibbon's self-fashioning in the militia journal,[4] are not to be discerned in that kept at Lausanne. Their place is taken by ambitious schemes for studying and writing the topography of ancient Rome and ancient Italy, programmes entirely produced by Gibbon's involvement in the world of erudition; yet the *Memoirs* assure us that since childhood he had known

---

[1] Momigliano, 1955, 1966.   [2] *Journal B*.   [3] *Journal B*, pp. 14, 224.   [4] Above, pp. 123, 127–8.

his vocation to be that of a historian; and the militia journal shows him preoccupied with the search for a subject for grand narrative history, and choosing as possible themes narratives concerned with the emergence of the states of modern Europe and the republican commentary on that process. Since it was the writing of grand narrative that was to lead him back past d'Alembert into modes of thinking that could be called 'philosophical', we want to know what had become of his intentions to write it during the year of his second sojourn at Lausanne. Had he decided that he must master erudition before he could presume to write history? Was he still preoccupied by the need to show that critical scholarship involved 'the nobler faculties of the imagination and the judgment'? In pursuit of such questions, we must turn to the text of the Lausanne journal, and the disquisitions – of which Gibbon wrote several – associated with it.

The *Lettre sur le gouvernement de Berne* may have been one of these, though there is no mention of it in the journal;[5] we have seen that it contains Montesquieuan reflections on both Roman imperial government and European post-feudal history. Gibbon never lost touch with the modern; his secondary reading throughout the year at Lausanne was an intensive study of the *Bibliothèque Raisonnée*,[6] a journal in which Barbeyrac and others had carried on the work of Jean Le Clerc, where Gibbon found reviews of many volumes of Protestant erudition in the generation preceding his own. Reviews at this period consisted of detailed summary, paraphrase and extensive quotation; and Gibbon renewed his acquaintance with many works that he knew already – Sale's Koran, Beausobre's *Histoire de Manichéisme*, Du Bos on French monarchy, Heineccius on Roman and German civil law, Johann Lorenz von Mosheim's Latin translation of Cudworth's *True Intellectual System of the Universe*, and even Middleton's *Free Inquiry* into the history of miracles, to which he was certainly no stranger.[7] Time passed otherwise in the eighteenth century than it does today, and Gibbon probably thought of these works as contemporary rather than belonging to the recent past; all were to play roles in the making of the *Decline and Fall*. But the genesis of that work has scarcely begun and is not to be found in his continued study of the *république des lettres*. His primary reading was

---

[5] For its dating, see *YEG*, pp. 187–9; Junod, *MG*, pp. 111–20. Above, pp. 85, 89–92.
[6] *Journal B*, p. 9, n. 2. It appeared quarterly at Amsterdam from 1728 to 1753, and Gibbon's readings appear to have begun with the 1734 volume.
[7] *Journal B*, pp. 9 (Cudworth, Sale, Beausobre, Du Bos, Heineccius), 224 (Middleton's *Enquiry*). Other notes of Gibbon's readings in this journal are numerous.

antiquarian and directed at ancient Rome and Italy. While waiting for some other books to arrive, he made his way through the Roman satirist Juvenal, who interested him both by his persona as a curmudgeonly patriot resenting the corruption of the city by Greeks and other slavish orientals – he found a colony of Jews living in the grove where Numa Pompilius met with the nymph Egeria – and by his detailed and lurid accounts of the street culture of urban Rome.[8] We are looking here at Gibbon's intense preoccupation with the material structure, as well as the culture, of the Roman city itself, which was to be central to the account he gives of the conception of the *Decline and Fall* and to help furnish that work with its last three chapters.[9] This was to carry him from Juvenal to the *Roma antica* or *Roma vetus* of the Italian antiquary Fumiano Nardini (1666), which he read in a Latin translation published in a larger compendium at Utrecht in 1699.[10] He was exploring the world of late humanist erudition, which he did not always find congenial but to which in many ways he belonged; and if Nardini's study of the ancient *urbs Roma* quarter by quarter was present when 'the idea of writing the decline and fall of the city started to my mind', he had embarked on it as part of a planned programme of study a year before. The exploration of the city, however, was part of a larger project, which he described in a letter to his stepmother dated 6 August 1763. Here he hoped that his father would approve his spending the winter at Lausanne to pursue

a considerable work I am engaged in, Which will be a most usefull preparation to my tour of Italy and which I shall not be able to finish sooner. It is a Description of the ancient Geography of Italy, taken from the original writers. If I go into Italy with a work of that kind tolerably executed, I shall carry every where about with me an accurate and lively idea of the Country, and shall have nothing to do but to insert in their proper places my own observations as they tend either to confirm, to confute or to illustrate what I have met with in books. I should not even despair, but that this mixture of study and observation properly digested upon my return to England, might produce something not entirely unworthy the eye of the publick, on a subject, upon which we have no regular or compleat treatise.[11]

This project may have originated in conversations with the *érudits* of Paris, but would not have aroused much interest at Holbach's dinner table; and even the *académiciens* would have thought it an enterprise with little that was philosophical about it. Gibbon still aspired to the role of

---

[8] Juvenal references begin on p. 3 and end with a disquisition on pp. 38–40. The Jews appear on p. 3. [9] *Decline and Fall*, VI, chs. 69–71. [10] *Journal B*, p. 42, n. 2. [11] *Letters*, I, pp. 153–4.

gentleman amateur, a learned traveller writing his own guidebook and returning to England to publish the record of his tour; but the intensity of his reading, and the intensity of erudition in the books he studied, was to carry him into deeper waters, and we recognise that his studies were really a species of archaeology, an enquiry into ancient material culture conducted – in the absence of systematic excavations – through the medium of texts, buildings and monuments, *les inscriptions* as well as *les belles lettres*. He was further becoming involved in the study of ancient geography and topography; his use of the great geographer d'Anville, studied in a recent essay,[12] may be seen beginning in the Lausanne journal;[13] and this was to carry him beyond the confines of the city into the structure of the empire, from whose decline and fall that of the former could not be detached. From the *Roma antica* of Nardini he passed to the *Italia antiqua* of Philip Cluver or Cluverius,[14] another giant of seventeenth-century erudition, which had been published at Leyden in the year of its author's death in 1623 and had formed part of a series on the ancient geography of Germany, Sicily, Sardinia and Corsica, intended (Gibbon noted) to make of its author a modern Strabo.[15] Cluverius, and with him Gibbon, were to appear geographers rather than historians; but the topography of ancient Italy was to be, on the one hand, a topography of its ancient peoples, their archaic origins and their primeval religious customs, sometimes suggesting a pastoral origin;[16] on the other, a topography of the Italian provinces of the Roman empire and the system of communications that held them together. Gibbon read d'Anville's *Mesures itinéraires* and Bergier's *Histoire des grands chemins de l'empire Romain*,[17] works which were later to carry him into the empire beyond the Italian peninsula, and as part of his study of Cluverius he read accounts of travel by Cicero, Horace and the late-Roman poet Rutilius Namatianus, and wrote disquisitions on the distances they traversed, the routes they followed and the speed with which they covered them.[18]

If the study of buildings and monuments was still the gateway to the history of the city, the study of roads opened up the history of the empire, and Gibbon knew this. His eyes were fixed on the topography of Italy,

---

[12] Abbatista, 1996.

[13] *Journal B*, pp. 59, 67 (*Traité des mesures itinéraires*) and *passim* (see *Journal* index).

[14] *Journal B*, p. 89, n.3.   [15] *Journal B*, p. 90.   [16] *Journal B*, p. 53.

[17] Nicolas Bergier (1567–1623), whose work had first appeared in 1622 and been re-edited in 1728 and 1736 (*Journal B*, p. 190, n. 2). Gibbon owned a copy of the last edition (*Library*, p. 68).

[18] *MW*, IV, pp. 335–4: 'A Minute Examination of Horace's Journey to Brundusium, and of Cicero's Journey into Cilicia' (Sheffield's translation).

which was an antiquarian not a narrative subject, but the *belles-lettres*, and history among them, are never absent from the journal. He was still perfecting his taste as a reader of literature, commenting on the *Aeneid* and the *Georgics* and writing a disquisition on how far a catalogue of the armies sent into the field was necessary to the development of an epic poem;[19] but literary criticism is applied to the genre of historiography when the problem of Hannibal's route through the Alps leads to a lengthy comparison between Livy and Polybius – as in the *Essai* Livy had been compared with Tacitus – and the conclusion is reached that 'si le recit de l'historien Latin est plus vraisemblable, celui de l'Ecrivain Grec paroit plus vrai'.[20] There are exercises in historical curiosity: Cluverius's views on the origins of the Roman people, in which he firmly rejects both Aeneas and Romulus, are connected with the pyrrhonist debate in the Académie between Pouilly, Sallier and Freret, and with the related work of Louis de Beaufort.[21] A dissertation by a certain Bargaeus *de eversoribus aedificiorum urbis Romae* leads to the conclusion – much altered in the last chapter of the *Decline and Fall* – that the Goths caused less dilapidation of the great buildings than the Popes, and the observation, at variance with what Gibbon was to write about them as savages in his ninth chapter, that the German and Gothic invaders had lost much of their barbarism through service in the Roman army.[22] In another key altogether, there are several pages debating Vertot's account of the Social War in which the subject allies of Rome took up arms to obtain the full rights of Roman citizenship, or independence of Rome as an alternative. Here Gibbon considers, as he sometimes does, issues of natural law and the law of nations, and concludes that since the right of conquest 'n'est fondé que sur la justice, qualité assez etrangère à ces brigands de l'Univers' – apparently the Romans – pacts between conquerors and conquered are binding on both parties, so that the Italian rebels were claiming more than their just grievances entitled them to. 'J'ecris dans le pays de Vaud', he adds, indicating that the Lausannais should be content with their station as subjects to Berne, but have good cause for

---

[19] *MW*, IV, pp. 327–35, also in translation.

[20] *Journal B*, pp. 105–13, esp. 112–13. Ghosh, 1996 (p. 13), who rightly emphasises that Livy remained Gibbon's model in writing historical narrative, might have said more of the contrasts between Livy and Tacitus (above, pp. 232–4) and Polybius, as here, which reveal the challenges that philosophy and criticism posed to narrative. Henceforth the two must exist together.

[21] *Journal B*, pp. 137–9.

[22] *Journal B*, pp. 82–3. See Angelio, 1596. This work came to Gibbon's attention through Graevius's *Thesaurus antiquitatum Romanarum*, a collection of antiquarian writings which was also his source for Nardini. The passage on the Germans is given in English by Sheffield – together with many other extracts from the Lausanne journal – in *MW*, V, pp. 352–3.

complaints.[23] This is part of the evidence suggesting that the *Lettre sur le gouvernement de Berne* may have been written about this time;[24] but in November 1763 Gibbon would not yet be applying his argument to events in Canada or English America. The passage is of interest as illustrating his willingness to think as a jurist, but scarcely suggests that he wrote history as ancillary to jurisprudence. It may be ranked with others as indicating Gibbon's awareness that the most austerely antiquarian pursuit of topography could not escape involvement in problems of criticism, philosophy and history; and the problem of working these into the patterns of a single treatise was to render him dissatisfied with the work of Cluverius, and perhaps with his own attempt to improve on it.

In summing up the *Italia antiqua* when he had finished reading it, Gibbon indicated his dissatisfaction with the seventeenth-century scholar's critical method and organisation.

> Les details de Cluvier sont immense[s], sa methode est confuse, son style est bigarré par un tissû presque continû de citations de tous les tems.

This was largely the fault of the ancient authors whom he had cited, and he had known this.

> Partout il allègue ses autorités, il les epluche, il les compare, et le resultat de cette comparaison ne leur est toujours favorable. Les anciens citoient beaucoup de memoire; les livres etoient rares, les cartes Geographiques l'etoient encore davantage, et dans une science où l'esprit s'egare facilement s'il n'est arreté par le secours des yeux, il leur etoit difficile d'eviter l'erreur ... Mais les plus grands noms de la Geographie ancienne ne sont pas à l'abri de sa censure: Ptolomée qui connoissoit mieux l'orient que l'occident, Strabon qui est quelquefois historien, politique ou philosophe plutot que Geographe, et Pline qui a voulu decrire l'univers dans trente-sept petits livres ... Apres tant d'experiences du peu d'exactitude des anciens Cluvier moins que personne devoit soutenir leur infaillabilité. Je le vois cependant prevenû de ce respect superstitieux pour les grands noms de l'antiquité qui avoit subjugué l'esprit de tous ses Contemporains. Quand il ne reste à Cluvier aucune ressource ni d'explication ni d'excuse, il a celle du moins de rejetter l'erreur sur le copiste. Ce principe general qu'il ne faut que ramener l'expression à la verité, pour rétablir le texte de l'autheur devient fecond entre ses mains. Le nombre de ses correction[s] n'est egalé que par leur hardiesse. La plupart de ces corrections me paroissent inutiles et hazardées, mais il y en a de très heureuses.[25]

[His materials are immense; his method perplexed, and his style a motley mixture of quotations from authors of all ages ... Throughout, his authorities

---

[23] *Journal B*, pp. 122–30; the words quoted at pp. 130, 127. *MW*, pp. 388–400.
[24] Junod in *MG*, pp. 118–20.   [25] *Journal B*, pp. 163–4.

are produced, and sifted, and compared with each other; and the result of the comparison is not always to their honour. The ancients quoted often from memory. Books were scarce; maps still scarcer; and in a science where the mind is so liable to wander without the direction of the eye, error was unavoidable...But our author's censure spares not the greatest names of ancient geography; Ptolemy, who knew the east better than the west; Strabo, who is sometimes an historian, politician or philosopher, rather than a geographer; and Pliny, who undertakes to describe the world in thirty-seven small books...After so much experience of their inaccuracy, it could hardly be expected that Cluverius should maintain the infallibility of the ancients. But we may perceive in his work the same superstitious veneration for the great names of antiquity, which prevailed among his contemporaries. When no other excuse for them remains, he is sure to throw the blame on transcribers. This principle, that the true text needs only to be restored, in order to restore its propriety, he applies with unwearied diligence. The great number of his corrections is only equalled by their boldness; the greater part are rash or useless; but some of them are extremely happy.][26]

Gibbon was writing here as a Modern,[27] conscious that the ancients and their way of seeing things had to be reconstructed through the eyes of a scientific erudition unknown to them since they did not possess the materials necessary to it: 'ancients' of their own, who had left them a textual archive which both necessitated and permitted the growth of methods for studying it critically. It was therefore a modern sensibility to things ancient which would have to be developed, and this recognition is not the least of the 'Enlightenments' in which Gibbon was becoming involved; yet, since it involved 'the nobler faculties of the imagination and the judgment', he would see it as directed against the project of Enlightenment laid down by d'Alembert in the *Discours préliminaire* (though not in the article 'Erudition'). He would agree, however, that Cluverius, like other giants of baroque scholarship, had been insufficiently critical, for lack of *méthode* and lack also of 'philosophy' – meaning insight into the various historical conditions under which the human mind had operated. There was a paradox here; if it lessened Strabo's standing as an authority that he had been 'quelquefois historien, politique ou philosophe plutot que Geographe', the modern, seeking to be rather a critic than an authority, must set himself precisely the same objectives – even if it meant relegating the ancients to the status of d'Alembert's industrious collectors of bare facts. Only to Polybius and Tacitus, among the ancients, had it been given to assume the dignity of philosophical historians.

---

[26] Sheffield's translation; *MW*, v, pp. 426–7.   [27] Levine, 1991.

What might be required of a Modern seeking to improve on both the ancients and the humanists was set out as his objective by Gibbon, when in December 1763 he redrafted his project for a 'Recueil géographique' of ancient Italy.[28] He hoped that this would prove publishable (evidently in French) on his return to England, as well as serving him as a vade-mecum on his forthcoming tour of Italy; and he observed that Latin (and that of Cluverius had been far from elegant) was no longer the language in which a polished scholar should address his public. As for the progress of learning, Cluverius had not had access to recent work (d'Anville's and Bergier's) on the roads of Roman Italy, or to those 'deux nouveaux genres d'erudition, les monumens Etrusques, et ceux d'Herculaneum'.[29] But Gibbon had something else in mind, more philosophical and more ambitious.

[Je suivrois Strabon plutot que Pline. Dans les divisions generales et les nomenclatures, je tacherois de mettre tout l'ordre et toute la netteté dont je suis capable, mais j'envisagerois d'un oeil philosophe l'interieur de l'habitation et les habitans eux-memes après avoir decrit et partagé la surface. Les productions de la nature et de l'art autant qu'elles nous sont connues par les anciens, les migrations des peuples, leurs loix et leur caractère. Parmi tant d'objets si interessans pour un Philosophe, je saisirois toutes les occasions que mon sujet me fourniroit de rechercher quand et jusqu'à quel point la configuration du pays, le climat, la situation ont influé sur les moeurs des habitans et sur les evenemens qui leur sont arrivés ... Apres avoir etabli quelques preliminaires, Je me placerois sur le mont Palatin avec Romulus, et commencant par le berceau de la nation, et le premier *pomoerium* de la ville j'en parcourrais les quartiers differens. Dans la description de l'Italie je suivrais l'ordre des Conquêtes des Romains et j'observerais la division des Regions d'Auguste. Je derogerais seulement à cette division à l'égard du pays des Sabins que je seroit obligé de detacher du Samnium pour le mettre à la tète du Latium. Au moyen d'un changement aussi leger je concilierais ces deux objets et le lecteur suivrait sans peine les armes des Romains et la narration de Tite Live.][30]

[I would follow Strabo rather than Pliny. To my general divisions and tables I would endeavour to give all the neatness and perspicuity possible; while I examined with the eye of a philosopher the interior of the country and the manners of its inhabitants; the productions of art and nature, as far as they were known to the ancients; the migration of tribes, their laws and character. Amidst so many interesting objects, I would seize every opportunity of investigating how far public transactions and manners were affected by local situation and climate ... I would place myself with Romulus on the Palatine Mount, and thus

[28] *Journal B*, pp. 167–70.
[29] P. 168: 'those two fields of erudition, the Etruscan monuments and those of Herculaneum'.
[30] *Journal B*, p. 169.

proceed to the different quarters of Rome, from the cradle of the nation to the first *pomoerium* of the city. In describing Italy, I would follow the progress of Roman conquests, and pay particular attention to its division by Augustus into regions; with this one exception, that I would separate the territory of the Sabines from Samnium, and put it at the head of Latium. By this small alteration I should reconcile the two principles of my arrangement; and the reader would easily follow the progress of Roman arms, and Livy's history.][31]

Gibbon was imagining a programme more ambitious than he carried out. We know that in the event he was to suppose himself seated not on the Palatine hill with Romulus, but on the Capitol with Poggio Bracciolini, conceiving a history less sociological than nostalgic. Here he was envisaging a history not of decline and fall but of *les progrès de l'esprit humain*, using the material structure of the city's buildings, less public than private – he was interested in the *insula* as the unit of habitation in urban Rome[32] – as the setting for a history of their *mœurs*, formed by climate and geography and profoundly affecting the course of events of which history was the narrative. It is a striking departure from the programme of the humanists in favour of that of the antiquarians, looking beyond even Montesquieu to a point where it parallels but does not follow the programme of the *Encyclopédie*. Gibbon imagines the philosophic eye looking beneath the roofs like Asmodeus to study the material culture of the inhabitants; but the authority of narrative history remains paramount, and in the last sentence the reader will attempt to integrate all this new history with Livy's narrative of the Roman conquest of Italy. The history of the city, even at its most philosophical, is not to be separated from the history of its empire.

Gibbon continued work on his 'Recueil géographique' – he saw his journal as giving rise to a separate *recueil* of his readings[33] – down to the time he left Lausanne for Italy and Rome.[34] It is hard to say whether he found it valuable there as a self-programmed guide-book, or whether he added to it in Italy,[35] or after his return to England. Printed after much editing by Lord Sheffield under the title *Nomina gentesque antiquae Italiae*,[36] the manuscript was plainly never prepared for the publication Gibbon had dreamed of in Lausanne, nor does it attempt anything like the

---

[31] Sheffield's translation; *MW*, v, pp. 430–1. [32] *Journal B*, pp. 47–50.
[33] *Journal B*, pp. 190–1.
[34] *Journal B*, pp. 260–2, shows him reading up to 16 December 1764, and leaving Lausanne on the 18th.
[35] See, however, *MW*, iv, p. 224, for allusions to manuscripts in the Palazzo Ricardi at Florence.
[36] *MW*, iv, pp. 155–326; in French – Sheffield made no attempt to translate it. Craddock, *YEG*, pp. 182–6, considers his editing of this text 'a story in itself'.

philosophic programme he had envisaged in the passage just cited. There are moments of philosophic *histoire des mœurs* – Freret, Giannone and Barthélemy are employed and criticised[37] – but it is still the collection of extracts from and comments on ancient authors he had compiled while writing his Lausanne journal, and the grand synthesis of philosophy and narrative does not emerge and seems not to have been undertaken. It is possible to imagine Gibbon criticising himself for failure to get beyond the methods of Cluverius, but the truth may be rather that he never made the attempt. The question would then be whether he abandoned the enterprise as misconceived or beyond his means, or whether it was overtaken and replaced by other projects. We encounter here the historical problems posed by Gibbon's Italian journey.

There is one more disquisition in the Lausanne journal which may furnish us with a pointer. In December 1763 Gibbon read a Latin poem of the fourth century AD, the *Iter, sive de reditu in patriam*, in which Claudius Rutilius Namatianus had recorded his return journey from Rome to his home in Gaul. By the time of this incident, Rome had already been sacked by Alaric and there were settlements of Christian monks on the islands off the Italian coasts; Rutilius was situated at a picturesque moment in the scenario of Decline and Fall. Gibbon seized the occasion for some Montesquieuan observations.

Ce n'etoit pas sous le regne d'Honorius qu'il falloit peindre la force de l'Empire Romain. Ses forces l'avoient abandonné depuis longtems; Mais son antiquité et son etendue, inspiroient une sorte de veneration et meme de terreur à ses voisins et le soutinrent encore. Cette illusion étoit enfin dissipée. Peu à peu les Barbares le connurent, le mepriserent et le detruisirent...Je conviens que notre poete qui voyoit tous ces malheurs a pris la seule tournure qui lui restoit; Sans le dissimuler il les oppose aux journées de Cannes et d'Allie, pour faire sentir que Rome n'eprouvoit jamais des revers que pour s'en relever encore plûs florissante. Comparaison foible et fausse. Tout etoit changé depuis les guerres puniques. Du tems de Rutilius tous les ressorts du Gouvernement etoient usés; le caractère national, la religion, les principes des loix, la discipline militaire; tout jusqu'au siege de l'Empire et à la langue meme succomboit sous le tems et les revolutions, ou n'existoit deja plus.

[The reign of Honorius was not a proper period for describing the greatness of Rome; a greatness long since fallen to decay. A veneration, and even terror, for her name, had been supported by her antiquity and extent of empire. But the illusion was now over. The barbarians gradually knew, despised, and destroyed

[37] *MW*, IV, pp. 158, 161 (Freret), 169, 226, 260, 301 (Giannone), 211 (Barthélemy). There are many citations of Bergier on the Roman roads.

her...I acknowledge that our poet, who was sensible of these calamities, endeavours ingeniously to dissemble their disgrace; comparing them with the defeats of Allia and Cannae, to show that Rome never suffered a reverse of fortune without rising more vigorous from the shock. But the comparison is feeble and false. Since the Punic wars, circumstances were totally changed. In the time of Rutilius, the springs of government were worn out; the national character, religion, laws, military discipline, even the seat of the empire, and the language itself, had been altered or destroyed, under the impression of time and accident.]

So far there is nothing which had not been said before, or would not be reiterated in the *Decline and Fall* whenever set pieces of this order were called for; but Gibbon goes on to say something else.

Il etoit difficile que cet empire se relevât, mais quand il auroit eu ce bonheur, c'etoit plutot l'Empire de Constantinople ou de Ravenne que celui de Rome. Une chose qui auroit du faire sentir à Rutilius combien ses elogues etoient depourvûs de verité et de vraisemblance, c'est l'image fausse et confuse qu'il se forme de Rome personnalisée. Du tems de Virgile elle auroit eté juste. Rome regardée comme un Deesse qu'on invoquoit dans ses temples existoit pour les peuples aussi bien que pour les poetes. Mere des Citoyens, maitresse des provinces elle representoit cet empire qui lui obeissoit. Mais lorsque l'Empire n'etoit plus qu'un assemblage de pays soumis au meme prince, Rome lui etoit devenue etrangere; et cet ville reduite à son idée Physique ne representeroit plus rien que des murs, des temples et des maisons baties sur sept montagnes et situées sur les bords du Tybre.[38]

[It would have been difficult to revive the empire; but even could that have been affected, it would have been the empire of Constantinople or Ravenna, rather than that of Rome. Rutilius might have felt how destitute his panegyric was of truth or probability, from the false and confused ideas excited by his personification of Rome. In the time of Virgil, this figure would have been natural. Rome, regarded as a goddess, and invoked in temples, had an existence in the opinion of the multitude as well as in the fancy of poets. As the mother of the citizens, and the mistress of the provinces, her name recalled the image of her empire; but when this empire consisted in an assemblage of nations, subject to the same prince, Rome was no longer its sovereign; and this city, reduced to an idea merely physical, represented no longer any thing but walls, temples and houses, built on seven hills and on the banks of the Tiber.][39]

This passage opens by recognising that the history of Decline and Fall is a history of transformation; the empire does not disappear but is recreated as the Christian empire of the Byzantine rulers, a process known to Gibbon from his childhood reading of Howel and Echard, but

---

[38] *Journal B*, pp. 178–9.   [39] Sheffield's translation; *MW*, v, pp. 436–8.

unimaginable to the pagan Rutilius. Before this happens, however, the empire has departed from the city; and Gibbon directly connects Rutilius's inability to evoke a convincing *Dea Roma* with the demystification of the great buildings of Rome – now clearly public rather than private – when despotism has deprived them of empire and they are become no more than a collection of the material structures which their generic names denote. This is at the opposite pole from the philosophic project of using the buildings as the key to the *mœurs* and *esprit* of their inhabitants. It proposes an essentially poetic history of the significance invested in the buildings of Rome by the *mœurs* and *esprit* of the people, and then lost with their withdrawal. Such a history can only be told in narrative, and can only be the history of empire. The buildings, awesome as they might still be, held meaning only when they were the seats of imperial power; without it, as Rutilius saw them, they were, in a phrase of Gibbon's, 'venerable but useless monuments of antiquity on the Capitoline hill'; in a phrase of Hobbes's, 'ghosts of the deceased Roman empire, sitting crowned upon the grave thereof'.[40] Narrative, public, poetic, imperial, and elegiac, had at this moment suddenly re-asserted itself in Gibbon's historical imagination through the symbolism of Decline and Fall; and this had occurred four months before he left Lausanne for Italy and nearly ten before he arrived at Rome.

[40] *Decline and Fall*, I, ch. 13; Womersley, I, p. 387; Bury, I, p. 410. Hobbes, 1651, IV, 47; Tuck, 1991, p. 480.

CHAPTER 12

The journey to Rome and the transformation of intentions

Gibbon's Italian journey of 1764 inaugurates the period which presents the greatest difficulties to his biographers. There are two sets of reasons for this. In the first place, the journal which he had begun to keep in camp with the militia breaks off at his arrival in Rome on 2 October 1764, and is never resumed, so that for the remainder of his life we are without this intermittent daily record of his studies and social activities, though not for some years without the manuscript essays on scholarly and historical subjects which he wrote in the course of the former. In the second place, his *Memoirs*, written many years later, make – and he persisted in making – important claims about his Roman experiences, in which he saw and obliges us to see the moment of conception of the *Decline and Fall*, but which in the absence of the journal are hard to document, validate or interpret. As a result, we face problems in tracing what the *Decline and Fall* began as being, what it became, and consequently what it was and is; and these problems extend beyond the sojourn at Rome, to the whole of the decade before Gibbon's first volume was published in 1776. The *Decline and Fall* is of course more than its author intended it to be at any single moment; but in order to understand how it exceeded his intentions, and how these intentions changed and grew in consequence, it is important to know what these were at the several moments of their formation. It is therefore necessary to enquire whether a moment of conception occurred at Rome, and how this conception stands in relation to the gestation which subsequently occurred; and we are both frustrated and stimulated by the evidence and its deficiencies.

The method being followed here is that of focusing on texts written by Gibbon, and situating them in various contexts, immediate and remote (or deeper in the background) and possessing diverse kinds of explanatory value. The texts currently under study consist of two kinds of manuscripts written at Lausanne in 1763–4: the journal kept at that time, and several disquisitions or dissertations written at the same time, forming part of the same intellectual activity as the journal, but surviving and existing independently of it. These overwhelmingly situate Gibbon in the discursive context of antiquarian scholarship, found to have gone on in the Académie des Inscriptions and the *république des lettres*, for the most part in the generation preceding his own. The most prominent of them is the 'Recueil géographique', subsequently published by Sheffield as *Nomina gentesque antiquae Italiae*, on which Gibbon spent much labour at Lausanne; we have found letters and journal entries indicating that he intended to take it with him to Italy and thought of publishing it on his return to England. It is a topography and archaeology of ancient Italy, in which the city of Rome receives central attention, as both a material structure and a cultural construct; and it can be and has been argued that the intention which Gibbon describes himself as conceiving on the Capitol was in the first instance that of writing a history of the city, and became in consequence that of writing a history of the empire[1] – though we have found evidence that the two themes were already intimately connected in his mind, as of course they had been in the minds of poets, rhetoricians and scholars since time beyond memory. Since the 'Recueil géographique' may in this light be considered an immediate ancestor of Gibbon's first intention to write what became the *Decline and Fall*, it is of interest to know where it stands in the record of Gibbon's journey through Italy as far as Rome.

Here the relevant journal[2] leaves us frustrated though deeply interested. On the one hand there is no indication that Gibbon proceeded through Italy with the 'Recueil géographique' in his carriage – he and a friend travelled by chaise – using it to inform what he saw, or annotating and revising it in that light. On the other, it is hard to find any indication in this journal that it was overtaken or superseded by an enterprise of a different sort, compared with which it seemed no longer adequate. The 'silent abandonment' of the 'geographically conceived Recueil'[3] appears to have occurred; but its origins are not to be found in Gibbon's Italian travels before he reached Rome. This was not a journey through the landscape of the 'Recueil', along the Roman roads linking one ancient city and its subjected people with another. It was a journey through the renaissance and baroque landscape of Piedmont, Lombardy and Tuscany, with its stations at Turin, Genoa, Modena and Florence; and it

---

[1] I begin here an engagement with the series of challenging essays by P. R. Ghosh (1983, 1991, 1995, 1996, 1997a and b). We are not always in agreement, but my debt to them is great.
[2] *Journal C.*   [3] Ghosh, 1996, p. 19; 1997a and b, p. 283.

was not a journey through Roman monuments and Roman history, so much as one through the history of art, as revealed in the palaces, museums and churches where Gibbon viewed collections of Roman statues and medals, renaissance, counter-Reformation and neo-classical paintings and architecture. It is significant that one of the more vividly recorded personal experiences is that of a day spent isolated by rain in the Borromeo palace among the islands of the Lago Maggiore.[4] Gibbon was voyaging through the history of taste, of which his journal is itself a document; he was enlarging his experience of taste as part of his programme of historical self-education; he did not omit data drawn from the fine arts in the histories he wrote subsequently. But there is only limited contact between the programme of travel recorded in the journal and the programme of antiquarian study pursued in the 'Recueil géographique', and it is difficult to find in the former anything which explains the abandonment of the latter. Gibbon was not converted from scholarship to taste – he would probably have found the notion of such a conversion meaningless – and there is evidence that as he approached and entered Rome, the imaginative and intellectual excitement of 'antiquity' re-asserted itself and became paramount. Whatever happened to the 'Recueil' may not have happened till then.

It appears once in the journal, when Gibbon at Florence found in the Palazzo Ricardi some collections by Muratori and other modern scholars which

me seront très utiles pour mes Desseins sur la Geographie d'Italie qui subsistent toujours quoique le plan en soit un peu changé. Elles me fourniront surtout beaucoup pour les mœurs, les usages, des curieuses anecdotes, et toute cette histoire interessante qui est cachée dans l'histoire ordinaire.[5]

[very useful for my plans for an Italian geography, which still remain though the plan is a little altered. Above all they will provide much information regarding manners, customs, curious anecdotes and all that interesting history concealed within history of the ordinary kind.]

His main objective on this visit, however, was to obtain permission to copy Bernardo Rucellai's sixteenth-century manuscript *De urbe Roma*,[6] and here we are in sight both of his continuing interest in the topography of the city, and of the literature of civic humanism which might rekindle a very different interest in public rather than cultural history,

---

[4] *Journal C*, p. 54: 'nous avons eté très bien logés, avec la sensation singuliere de nous trouver seuls en liberté, dans un grand palais, entouré d'un lac très etendû et separés ainsi du reste des humains'. This is an experience of travel, not an experience of antiquity or of history.

[5] *Journal C*, p. 221. [6] *Journal C, ibid.*

including that of the transition from republics to ancient principates and modern monarchies. Here and there in the journal are to be found passages of reflection on history at large, and the eclipse of medieval and recent republican government is a theme recurrent among them. The street races and street theatre of the Corso on the *fiesta di San Giovanni* are the last vestiges of the ancient liberty of Florence,[7] and Genoa, Pisa, Siena and Lucca give him occasion to reflect on the loss of republican freedom, its recently attempted revival at Genoa and its persistence on a small scale at Lucca.[8] The Palazzo Ricardi, however, calls forth more complex reflections. It was the house of the Medici,

Citoyens encore de la Republique de Florence. Ils jouoient un role bien plus beau, lorsque dans leur comptoirs ils etoient les protecteurs des arts et les arbitres de l'Italie, que dans la suite qu'ils s'eleverent au grade de souverains obscurs d'un petit Etat . . . Je n'ai pû entrer sans une reverence secrette dans ce berceau des arts, dans une maison d'où la lumiere s'est repandue dans tout l'occident, où sous les yeux d'un Laurent le Magnifique, un Politien, un Lascaris, un Gaza, un Pic de la Mirandole, un Marsile Ficin faisoient revivre les grands hommes de la Grece et de Rome pour instruire leurs contemporains.[9]

[while still citizens of the republic of Florence. They played a far nobler part when in their counting-houses they were the patrons of the arts and the arbiters of all Italy, than when subsequently they rose to be the obscure sovereigns of a minor state . . . I could not but enter with deeply felt reverence into this cradle of the arts, this house from which light spread to all the west, where beneath the eyes of Lorenzo the Magnificent, Politian, Lascaris, Theodore of Gaza, Pico della Mirandola and Marsilio Ficino brought life back to the great men of Greece and Rome for the instruction of their contemporaries.][10]

This is precisely the ambiguous relationship between the arts, liberty and monarchy, which was to have been the theme of the Florentine history Gibbon had imagined two years previously. He still prefers the Medici as patrons rather than as princes, but there is no sign that this now abandoned project is being revived to compete with the geography of ancient Italy. He diligently studies the sculptured tombs of the Medici and the paintings in the Palazzo Ricardi and the New Sacristy, but ventures to admit that a work by a pupil of Michelangelo pleases him more than its neighbour by the master;[11] to a neo-classical eye, Michelangelo was never really polite. It is noteworthy also that in the passage last quoted, scholars and philosophers have silently replaced the

---

[7] *Journal C*, p. 128.
[8] *Journal C*, pp. 65–6, 72–9 (Genoa), 226–7 (Lucca), 227 (Pisa), 230–2 (reflections on the free port of Livorno), 234 (Siena – the architecture only).   [9] *Journal C*, p. 204.
[10] Translation JGAP; not given by Sheffield.   [11] *Journal C*, p. 207.

giants of the *beaux-arts*. Earlier, in the Uffizi, Gibbon had set down the reasons why the visual arts would never rival the verbal in his understanding of history.

Parmi ces premiers peintres

he had been looking at Fra Angelico and Mantegna –

j'appercois un travail minutieux et timide, et un assujettissement rigoureux à toutes les regles qu'ils connoissoient, sans genie et sans aucune de ces hardiesses heureuses et originales qui font le merite des premiers poetes, et qui rachetent tous les ecarts d'une imagination dereglée qui veut disposer en maitre de la langue, de l'histoire et de la nature. Je trouve la raison de cette différence dans l'origine différente des deux arts, sœurs à la verite, mais dont la fortune a souvent variè. La poesie est descendue du ciel, la peinture s'est elevèe de la terre. Les premiers poetes etoient des prophètes, des hommes inspirès dont la genie etoit echauffè par le Fanatisme, qui faisoit taire la froide et faible raison. Les premiers peintres etoient des artisans: obligès de passer par une Mechanique longue et penible, ils osoient à peine se livrer aux essors d'un talent qu'un siecle ignorant auroit meconnû. Ils copioient servilement parce qu'ils voyoient peu de chose, et mal. Le peintre ne trouve point comme le poète ses originaux au fond de son ame. Qu'il y a loin de ces ouvrages au portrait de Jules II par Raphael. L'ame de ce pape fier et ambitieux est peinte sur la toile. J'y vois toute la brusque violence du protecteur de Michel Ange, et la grandeur inflexible de ce Vieillard qui osa chasser de l'Italie les François victorieux. Je contredis ma maxime, mais je crois voir une exception.[12]

[In these early painters I perceive a laborious minuteness and timidity, a rigorous subordination to all such rules as they knew, a lack of genius and of all those happy and original innovations which are the glory of the first poets and redeem the impulses of an ungoverned imagination which aims at mastery over language, history and nature. I find the reason for this difference in the diverse origins of the two arts, sisters indeed but often of unequal fortune. Poetry descended from heaven, but painting has risen from the earth. The first poets were prophets, inspired men whose genius was heated by that fanaticism which silences our cold and feeble reason. The first painters were artisans; obliged to pass through a long and painful training, they hardly dared to yield to the impulses of a talent ill understood by an ignorant age. They copied slavishly because they saw but little, and that ill. How far are these works from Raphael's portrait of Julius II! The soul of this haughty and ambitious pope is painted on to the canvas. I see there the rough violence of the protector of Michelangelo, and the unbending greatness of the aged man who dared drive the victorious

---

[12] *Journal C*, p. 138. Bonnard (n. 2) suggests that the 'maxim' is that a man's character cannot be guessed from his face; the problem of physiognomy is discussed at length by Haskell, 1993. Gibbon also (p. 137) mentions Bartolomeo della Porta's paintings of Isaiah and Job, but presumably did not see his portrait of Savonarola, which should have interested him.

French from Italy. I contradict my maxim here, but I think I see an exception.][13]

Later, in the Campo Santo at Pisa, Gibbon observes that the paintings of Giotto are certainly bad (*mauvais*), but that we must imagine ourselves in times when paintings were rare and even these valuable.[14] His 'renaissance of the arts', it is clear, was a renaissance of letters, and there was as yet no paradigm obliging him to fit a renaissance of the visual arts into it. For this there are two reasons. A neo-classical taste in painting could admire little that was in the most literal sense pre-Raphaelite; the 'Renaissance' that Ruskin hated had hardly yet been invented. Enlightened culture, like the Enlightened state, was in many ways secularised baroque; the classical baroque modernised at the expense of the Tridentine Catholic. It was only as painting became heroic and historical that it could, paradoxically, be rendered polite, and this achievement had been papal and Venetian rather than Medicean. Perhaps this is a reason why Gibbon did not return to his plan for a Florentine history, in which the Medici should have used 'the arts' to cover the extinction of liberty. But 'the arts' are poetical, philosophical and above all textual; we are looking at the rebirth of letters, and there is a philosophy of history to be built around letters, including their prehistory in the heroism and enthusiasm of primeval oral culture. The poet was once a prophet, whereas Gibbon (with no Lascaux before him) can imagine no time when the painter was anything but the servant of the patron, rising to the gentlemanly status of 'my friend Sir Joshua Reynolds' only in the era of modern monarchy.

It takes the titanism and theatricality of history to elevate painting to that inspiration which poetry enjoyed from the beginning, and if a pope is the titan, the myth of the Renaissance is beginning. Yet the first poets were fanatics as well as prophets, and it is rare to find fanaticism in a positive role. Were Pico and Ficino also fanatics – their neo-Platonism might suggest it – and was it not the role of painters after Raphael to institute a courtly and monarchical (not to say an ecclesiastical) politeness? This passage is an excursion into the realm of philosophical history, to which the history of Italy and Europe was more likely to give access than the rigorously geographical programme of the Recueil; the study of *les mœurs* and *les facultés* was enhanced by a public narrative. It was also at Florence – where he had more leisure for study – that Gib-

---

[13] Translation JGAP. Haskell, 1993, pp. 186–90, discusses Gibbon as a student of the visual antiquities.   [14] *Journal C*, p. 228.

bon read Pierre-Henri Mallet's *Histoire du Danemarc*, and met its author. He wrote several pages of reflections on the mythic imagination of the Eddas and the possible history of Odin as the poet, prophet, legislator and impostor – thus the euhemerised god – of ancient Scandinavia, and on why the Goths, easily converted to Christianity in the lands they invaded, had been stubbornly resistant to its missionaries in their Swedish and Norwegian homelands.[15] The history of barbarism could engage his attention even while he wrote detailed catalogues of the medals of Roman emperors and the works of modern painters in the museums and galleries of Florence, and cannot be irrelevant to his state of mind as he approached Rome and the conception of the *Decline and Fall*. There is no sign, however, that anything, even the richness of cultural encounter on his travels, was replacing the 'Recueil géographique' by any other kind of history in his imagination.

After a journey on which, contrary to Protestant experience, they found the lands of southern Tuscany 'nues' and 'steriles', and those of the Papal states instantly an improvement,[16] Gibbon and his friend Guise entered Rome on 2 October. 'Depuis le Pons Milvius j'ai eté dans un songe d'antiquité', immediately dispelled by those 'gens très modernes' the customs officers, who confiscated their chaise for the night and left them to seek lodgings on foot (there were no inns). This occurred after five in the afternoon. Here the journal breaks off forever; it was never resumed;[17] but the *Memoirs*, all those years later, pick up the story in an English far better remembered.

My temper is not very susceptible of enthusiasm, and the enthusiasm which I do not feel I have ever scorned to affect. But at the distance of twenty-five years I can neither forget nor express the strong emotions which agitated my mind as I first approached and then entered the *eternal City*. After a sleepless night –

did Guise go to pick up the chaise? –

I trod with a lofty step the ruins of the Forum; each memorable spot where Romulus *stood* –

Gibbon was not unaware that Romulus might be a fiction –

or Tully spoke, or Caesar fell was at once present to my eye; and several days of intoxication were lost or enjoyed before I could descend to a cool and minute investigation.[18]

---

[15] *Journal C*, pp. 159–61, 162–5; there is an English translation in *MW*, III, pp. 231–8. This is the beginning of Gibbon's intermittent interest in the historicity of Odin.

[16] *Journal C*, p. 235. Cf. *Memoirs*, p. 135 (*A*, p. 268, Memoir C).

[17] *Ibid.* There follow two blank pages and some notes made in December.

[18] *Memoirs*, p. 134 (*A*, p. 267, Memoir C).

This account of deep imaginative excitement receives some support from the journal's 'songe d'antiquité', and more from a letter which Gibbon wrote to his father – not usually an intimate correspondent – on 9 October.

I have already found such a fund of entertainment for a mind somewhat prepared for it by an acquaintance with the Romans, that I am really almost in a dream. Whatever ideas books may have given us of the greatness of that people, Their accounts of the most flourishing state of Rome fall infinitely short of the picture of its ruins. I am convinced there never never[19] existed such a people and I hope for the happiness of mankind that there never will again. I was this morning upon the top of Trajan's pillar. I shall not attempt a description of it. Only figure to yourself a Column 140 feet high of the purest white marble composed only of about 30 blocks and wrought into bas-reliefs with as much taste and delicacy as any chimney piece in Up-Park.[20]

It is in the character of eighteenth-century studies that we remain uncertain whether the last words are a joke directed at Edward Gibbon II's provincial tastes, or a genuine specimen of the neo-classical belief that the moderns had perfected the art of the ancients. The *Memoirs* record that Gibbon explored Rome for eighteen weeks,

till I was myself qualified in a last review to select and study the capital works of ancient and modern art,[21]

thus completing one enterprise that he had pursued through northern and central Italy. They also remind us in retrospect from 1789 to 1764 that Gibbon visited Rome at a certain moment in the history of Enlightenment.

I departed without kissing the feet of Rezzonico (Clement XIII), who neither possessed the wit of his predecessor Lambertini, nor the virtue of his successor Ganganelli.[22]

The language displays the device, favoured by secular intellectuals to this day, of using the personal rather than the regnal names of Popes to desacralise their office; but the word 'virtue' serves further to single out the figure of Clement XIV (Lorenzo Ganganelli, 1769–74), the Pope who, by suppressing the Jesuits in 1773, presented Enlightenment with what should have been its crowning triumph and the capture of the enemy citadel. New crises were to follow, however, and by the time

---

[19] This repetition may be an emphasis, or a slip of the pen.
[20] *Letters*, i, p. 184.
[21] *Memoirs*, ibid. (*A*, p. 268). For the character of his conducted tour of studies, see Prown, 1997.
[22] *Memoirs*, ibid. (*A*, *ibid*.).

Gibbon completed the *Decline and Fall* in 1787, his attitude towards the Papacy had grown significantly milder, as the *Memoirs* may remind us. Meanwhile, in both the contemporary and the retrospective passage something else is going on. Gibbon affirms that his imagination was possessed by the spectacle of Rome as history, and that the ruins evoked the past and presence of Rome both as republic – with Romulus at its beginning, Cicero and Caesar at its end – and as empire; that people from whom all history derived, as should never happen again. Whatever the role of Piedmont and Tuscany in preparing it, this vision suffused the landscape of Rome with the rhetoric of history; the antithesis of the water-colours of Pierre-Henri Valenciennes a few years later, where the Coliseum is not even a historic ghost but an item in a landscape experienced visually.[23] It is a long way from 'the cool and minute investigation' of ancient and modern art, or of Roman geography. It is a temptation to say that from this moment we never hear of the 'Recueil géographique' again; but there is a sense in which it can be seen as transcended rather than abandoned.[24] The *Memoirs* famously say:

Yet the historian of the decline and fall must not regret his time or expense, since it was the view of Italy and Rome which determined the choice of the subject. In my Journal the place and moment of conception are recorded; the fifteenth of October 1764, in the close of evening, as I sat musing in the Church of the Zoccolanti or Franciscan fryars, while they were singing Vespers in the Temple of Jupiter on the ruins of the Capitol.

Alternatively:

It was at Rome on the fifteenth of October 1764, as I sat musing amidst the ruins of the Capitol, while the barefooted fryars were singing Vespers in the temple of Jupiter that the idea of writing the decline and fall of the City first started to my mind.[25]

Because the journal breaks off on 2 October, and contains no account of this or any other Roman experience, Gibbon's insistence that it does record the 'Capitoline vision' on the 15th has been much debated. Was there once another journal now lost to us?[26] Was Gibbon's memory

---

[23] 'In the Light of Italy: Corot and early open-air painting'; an exhibition at the National Gallery of Art, Washington, May–September 1996.

[24] Ghosh has rightly moved from regarding October 1764 as a false start (1983) to insisting on it as a creative moment (1997a and b). It is central to his thesis (with which I concur) that we must regard the stages of composition of the *Decline and Fall* as a series of leaps rather than the unhurried execution of a plan.

[25] *Memoirs*, p. 136 and n. 7; *A*, pp. 270 (Memoir C), 302 (Memoir E; the version cited above).

[26] *YEG*, p. 222. The difficulty here is the blank pages following the entry for 2 October in the existing journal.

confused?²⁷ was he for some reason fabricating the whole story?²⁸ What seems certain is that the *Memoirs* use the moment on the Capitol to introduce an account of the *Decline and Fall*'s composition which may certainly be accepted, and of which the moment itself may be accepted as part.

But my original plan was circumscribed to the decay of the City, rather than of the Empire: and, though my reading and reflections began to point towards the object, some years elapsed, and several avocations intervened before I was seriously engaged in the execution of that laborious work.²⁹

Something had occurred, of sufficient impact to bring about the silent abandonment of the 'Recueil géographique' – if it be true that we never hear again of this work over which he had taken a great deal of trouble – but Gibbon is warning us against any belief that the *Decline and Fall*, as published twelve years later, yet existed even as embryo in his mind, or that its development was free from setbacks, confusions, and false starts. Indeed, it will concern us to ask whether the work as it emerged possesses a final unity – let alone one derived from the moment of conception.

The decision was visual; 'it was the view of Italy and Rome', and we may ask what is meant by placing Italy before Rome. Cluverius before Nardini? The renaissance and baroque before the ancient and ecclesiastical? The *imperium* before the *senatus populusque*? The order seems to challenge the obvious fact that it was as he entered Rome that Gibbon's imagination became deeply excited. It was the immediate sight of the ruins of republic and empire that transcended the purely textual plan of the 'Recueil', but the argument has been put forward that Gibbon still carried that plan in his head, and that this explains why his original plan was circumscribed to the decay of the city, rather than of the empire. He intended, that is, a history of 'the decline and fall of the city' as the emperors abandoned it and as the empire itself disintegrated; and the urban history, the history of private and public buildings, and the roads leading to them, about which he had been thinking so hard during the previous year in Lausanne, continued strong in his mind and never

---

²⁷ Ghosh, 1983, p. 6. Gibbon when he wrote the *Memoirs* is here described as 'elderly' and 'an old man'; he was about fifty-two, and though the expectancy of life was then lower, the same is not necessarily true of the onset of senescence.

²⁸ Bonnard in *Memoirs*, pp. 304–5. The difficulty here is the absence of any motive for the deliberate construction of a fiction. The remaining (and unsatisfactory) explanation is that Gibbon had repeated the story many times with the date of the 15th, and uncharacteristically did not check a documentation on which he is insistent.   ²⁹ *Memoirs*, pp. 136–7 (*A*, pp. 270–1, Memoir C).

ceased to shape his history,[30] even when it had become *The History of the Decline and Fall of the Roman Empire*. This argument must derive a great deal of weight from a single circumstance. The *Decline and Fall* does in the end revert to being just such a history. After the fall of Constantinople, the three concluding chapters narrate the history of the city, not by this time of imperial Rome in its decay, but of papal Rome in its failure to become either a republic or the capital of a major territorial state. Gibbon announced this as his intention in introducing the first volume of his history, and the relation of these chapters to his overall design, whether as announced in 1776 or as completed in 1788, is problematic and gives rise to many questions. What moved him to enlarge the decline and fall of the city into the decline and fall of the empire is one of these questions, and it seems to have a prehistory in 1763 as well as 1764.

The 'Recueil géographique' was to have embraced all Italy, and in the form in which it survives (Sheffield's edition of the *Nomina gentesque*) the section on 'Urbs Romae' is long but not the longest;[31] it is however this section, which we must think of as 'transcended' as Gibbon envisaged the history of the city, which survives as a component of the *Decline and Fall*. We have found him aware of two ways in which a history of the buildings of Rome might become more than the rigorously topographical and architectural study that was all the antiquarian discipline prescribed. It might become a history of the *mœurs*, *usages* and *climat* of the inhabitants, part of 'toute cette histoire intéressante qui est cachée dans l'histoire ordinaire';[32] or it might, as he had noted in his commentary on Rutilius,[33] become a history of the city in its interaction with the empire, one in which the public buildings – surviving awesomely as the bare stones of the Forum or the columns, arches, baths and circuses of the emperors – nevertheless lost meaning as the empire moved away from the city and the latter ceased to be its centre. It was surely the second kind of history – still containing but not concealing the first – which appealed to Gibbon's imagination as the drama and rhetoric of the Roman cityscape made the austere project of the 'Recueil géographique' no longer satisfying. 'The decline and fall of the city' would have been a history of the buildings of Rome, and necessarily of the senate and people who had inhabited them, gradually losing significance and sinking into decay, as the emperors lost

---

[30] *Decline and Fall*, I, Preface; Womersley I, p. 2; Bury I, p. xl.
[31] *MW*, IV, pp. 206–25; cf. Latium and Campania, pp. 225–65.   [32] Above, p. 277.
[33] Above, pp. 272–4.

interest[34] in the city and defended or governed the empire from capitals of their own at Milan, Sirmium, Nicomedia and finally Constantinople.

There are writings – the historical disquisitions Gibbon regularly drew up as exercises – from the months he spent at Rome, which may exhibit his interest in the history of the city extending itself into the history of decline and fall. A manuscript on the origins, route and rituals of the triumphal procession is full of debates with Nardini and other antiquarians, but is at the same time a disquisition on the manners and morals, the mingled *gravitas* and *crudelitas*, of the Roman people at their imperial height.[35] It does not go further than Augustus, and the last figure named in it is Jugurtha, by the time of whose imprisonment and death the corruption of the republic was at the point described by Sallust. What is missing here, however, is the theme of decline and fall: the gradual decay of the triumph as the emperors abandoned the city and victories grew rarer. The thrust of antiquarian enquiry was towards republican and even archaic Rome, and must be manoeuvred into becoming a search for the origins of the papal city. As against this, however, there is a brief notice of a book *del governo civile di Roma*, of which Gibbon noted: '[il] traite principalement des revolutions qu'à eprouvées cette ville depuis la chute de l'empire Romain, sujet qui m'interesse beaucoup'.[36] The grammatical emphasis is on the fortunes of the city, and the fall of the empire is contextual; but which is to command the narrative?

The history of the city's decay is to be found in the *Decline and Fall*, and its language is profound and moving enough to make the tone of the work as elegiac as it is ironic; but it is not the central spine of the work as a whole, or even in the narrative to AD 476; and the three concluding chapters in which it re-emerges trace the history – not altogether the decay – not of the imperial city, but of the papal city which came to sit crowned upon its grave. Two things have happened to transcend in its turn the history envisaged on the Capitol which transcended the plan for the 'Recueil géographique'. In the first place, the history of the empire, always recognised as inseparable from that of the city, has

[34] Cf. *MW*, IV, p. 311: 'les Empereurs Chrétiens trouvèrent dans leur haine pour Rome une nouvelle raison' to prefer Milan and afterwards Ravenna.

[35] Given in English by Sheffield (*MW*, IV, pp. 359–98) and consisting of two manuscripts dated from Rome on 28 November and 13 December, 1764; coinciding in time, therefore, with the notes on paintings and antiquities dated 'December' in *Journal C*, pp. 170–3. The French text may be found in the 1796 *Miscellaneous Works*.

[36] 'It deals principally with the revolutions suffered by their city since the fall of the Roman empire, a subject I find very interesting.' For bibliographical details, see *YEG*, pp. 227, 353 n. 126.

ceased to be its backdrop or deep background; and as the action moves into the wings, the historian follows it and sets up new scenery among which it takes place. The decline and fall of the city becomes the decline and fall of the empire, and the latter theme comes to command and provide the narrative. This movement enlarges the history in at least three directions. To begin with, the history of empire is seen to be a history of its governing institution: the Augustan principate, whose problems, inherited from the Roman republic, appeared to have been overcome by the Antonines. Here the great theses of Machiavelli and Montesquieu asserted themselves, and Gibbon had need of a history less Livian than Polybian and Tacitean; in a decision of vast importance to his first volume, he chose to begin his narrative not in AD 79, where Tacitus might be said to have left off, but in AD 180 when the Antonine monarchy began to disintegrate. None of this could possibly have been in his mind in the later months of 1764.

Next, as the history of empire ceases to be that of *principes* interacting with the senate and people they have subjugated, and becomes that of *imperatores* situated in the provinces and along the frontiers they are defending, it separates itself decisively from that of Rome and even Italy, and therefore from the history of the city we suppose to have been envisaged on the Capitol. A vast tension opens up in Gibbon's work, one perhaps more profound even than the tension between Roman and Byzantine history inherent in his slow and reluctant decision to go beyond 476 to 1453. From the history of Italy, and of the *urbs Roma* as situated in its conquest and organisation of Italy, he was led to extend his history, not only northwards into Gaul and Britain, but eastwards along the Alpine and Danubian frontier, and from the Black Sea into the Hellenised Asian and African provinces which the empire had inherited from the republic; and in so doing, he moved away from the Latin Europe, papal, Protestant and commercial, in which Enlightenment had its being and whose history since 476 the Enlightened historians considered they understood, into regions which Europe no longer controlled and whose history it was little accustomed to write. This had happened by the time Gibbon wrote the opening chapters of the *Decline and Fall*, in which a Cluverian topography of *Italia antiqua* (and its pre-Roman antiquities; the Etruscan regions almost outweigh the Roman in the *Nomina gentesque*)[37] is replaced by a far more ambitious and less

---

[37] *MW*, IV, pp. 183–206.

antiquarian topography of the provinces constituting the empire as a whole.[38]

As he did this, furthermore, Gibbon encountered the two sets of actors whose presence was to transform his work from a history of 'the decline and fall' of the city and the empire to one of 'the triumph of barbarism and religion'. It is a premise of this book that Gibbon's six volumes are in great measure a product of his concern with these two entities and with the discursive impact of mentioning them in a single bracket; but the barbarians at least are not mentioned and are very hard to discern in his account of the Capitoline vision. In Lausanne the year before, he had noted with approval Bargaeus's suggestion that the destruction of the Roman monuments had been less the work of the Goths than of the Popes[39] – a view he was later to modify in favour of the clergy – and both here and in examining Mallet's history of Denmark, he had stressed to himself that the history of these barbarians was a complex subject in its own right.[40] They are not indicated in the passages from the *Memoirs*, though it is true that the ruins of Rome could scarcely be mentioned without evoking Alaric and Totila; but as his imagination later moved down the Danube and beyond the Black Sea, it encountered non-Roman and non-Hellenic peoples – 'barbarians' in the broad ancient sense – of three kinds. There were the Germanic peoples, Goths and Franks, Burgundians and Angles, Danes and Swedes, who were to enter European history and colonise its ver- naculars; there were the 'orientals', Arabic, Persian, Turkish and Mos- lem, who had excited his imagination as a schoolboy; and beyond them and hardly yet mentioned, there were 'barbarians' and 'orientals' of a third kind: the Huns, Avars, Mongols and Turks of central Asian nomadism, and the civilised empires with which Europeans were inten- sifying contact by sea and Russians by land. As Gibbon's history moved outward it became also a multi-faceted history of barbarism; and it is hard to find even the germ of this on 15 October, 1764.

If the barbarians are not yet to be seen in Gibbon's account of his experience on the Capitol, there is another presence, neither of city nor of empire, which is the second force transforming the history there conceived as replacing the 'Recueil géographique'. This is the presence of the bare-footed friars, the Zoccolanti or *discalzi*, singing vespers in the Temple of Jupiter; and they may well have been really there, or thereabouts, on one or more of Gibbon's visits to the Capitol.[41] The

---

[38] *Decline and Fall*, I, ch.1.   [39] Above, p. 267; *MW*, IV, pp. 223–4.   [40] Above, p. 281.
[41] They occupied the church of Ara Celi, once the temple of Juno, not Jupiter. Guise's diary has Gibbon visiting the Capitol on 6th, 9th, 10th, 12th and 13th October (*Memoirs*, p. 305).

transformation of pagan and imperial into Christian and papal Rome, 'the cross erected on the ruins of the Capitol', the dilapidation and appropriation of ancient structures by ecclesiastics, was already a trope of the literature of Rome, and there is no need to explore its growth or origins. In mentioning the friars in the *Memoirs*, Gibbon may have been indicating in retrospect the need to decide whether the decline and fall of the city was completed, reversed or transformed by the achievement of the papal city; and he had by the time he wrote this passage completed the last three chapters of the *Decline and Fall*. The growth of the papacy and papal power, however, though of enormous importance in Gibbon's completed history, is only one and not the most central of its connecting themes. The movement down the Danube and beyond, into Hellenised heartlands of the Roman empire, means that the ecclesiastical history the *Decline and Fall* necessarily becomes is not centrally a history of the Popes at Rome, but of the Fathers, the Councils and the patriarchs at Nicaea, Antioch, Ephesus, Chalcedon and Constantinople; a history not of Catholic authority but of Orthodox disputation and theology; while the pursuit of Byzantine history to 1453 is either the cause or the effect of Gibbon's decision not to focus upon the history of the medieval West, until the last three chapters. If the history of empire has its centre decreasingly at Rome, the history of the church finds its centre there only after the end of empire in the west.

The more we study the ways in which the *Decline and Fall* departed from what the *Memoirs* depict as the original Capitoline idea – the move from a history of the city to a history of empire, barbarism and religion – and the more we remain conscious of the tug by which the original vision brought the history back to its starting-point at the last, the more we must realise that it was not a simple unfolding of original implications; but proceeded with great difficulty, with many leaps and frustrations,[42] and by the accretion and appropriation of materials not envisaged or intended at first. The unity of Gibbon's style – and when was that achieved? – must not deceive us into believing in the unity of the work's structure; and it has been valuable to be asked whether the structure ultimately succeeds or fails. A great deal had happened to the Capitoline vision by the time the first volume was published in 1776, but it had had nearly twelve years in which to happen. It is a torment to biographers that these years, unlike the two that precede them, are not illustrated by a continuous journal, though there are publications,

---

[42] I would like to quote and applaud Ghosh's observation (1983, pp. 22–3) 'that the writing of his History was a voyage of discovery for Gibbon, and that, from volume to volume, he was never quite sure how it would turn out'.

dissertations and documents of other kinds. This book, which is only in part biographical, will proceed in another manner.

An implication of all that we know about the visit to Rome is that there occurred some kind of turn away from purely antiquarian study. On the one hand, the 'Recueil géographique' was given up; on the other, it has been pointed out,[43] Gibbon continued to write studies of this kind for some years after he left Rome and returned to England, and this may be ground for arguing that the history he intended to write remained a classical history. But a 'decline and fall', no matter what its subject, was necessarily a narrative history, and if he now conceived of one, Gibbon was reverting from the writing of antiquarian *mémoires* to the classical grand narrative for which he had been in search of a theme during the years of his first journal. Such a theme he had in hand, but it was a modern theme: the history of Swiss liberty, which should have narrated the Habsburg and Burgundian wars of the thirteenth through fifteenth centuries, when feudalism was in decay and the European states system in formation. Gibbon did not carry out this project, and we may emphasise either that he gave it up in 1767,[44] or that he did not give it up till then. There was coming to exist by that time a category of grand Enlightened histories, which began with the fall of the western empire, the formation of the Latin church, the barbarian invasions and the growth of feudal tenures, and ended with the emancipation of the European states from the ecclesiastical and feudal orders. To that category the history of Swiss liberty would have belonged if it had been completed. To that category the *Decline and Fall* was rapidly and has continued to be assigned, though there are important senses in which it does not belong there. The major works composing that category are all mentioned in Gibbon's first volume, and played parts of widely varying importance in making it what it was and is. For these reasons the next volume of this project will consist of detailed studies of these great works, from Giannone and Voltaire to Hume, Robertson and Ferguson; not because they were crucial (though some of them were) in determining how the *Decline and Fall* came to be, but because they are crucial in characterising what it came to be and what it is. This study of Enlightenment historiography, ranging far beyond matters of immediate concern to Gibbon, provides one of the most important contexts in which the *Decline and Fall* can be viewed and understood; because it is in its way a great Enlightened narrative, and we need to understand the ways in

---

[43] Ghosh, 1983, p. 4.   [44] His own account is in *Memoirs*, pp. 141–2 (*A*, pp. 276–7, Memoir C).

which it is like and unlike the others, just as we have been considering the ways in which it is and is not a product of the erudition Gibbon sought to practice and defend. At the end of the next volume, we shall consider the formation of the *Decline and Fall* in the light it may have shed.

Gibbon and the rhythm that was different

From Rome – and from excursions to Naples and Venice – Gibbon returned to Hampshire by way of Paris, where he spent a fortnight in the company of both Madame Bontemps and Madame Necker, as Suzanne Curchod had by now become.[1] There is little sign that he renewed his explorations of the *société des gens de lettres*, and he did not visit Paris again until 1777, or Lausanne until 1783. From 1765 begins the middle period of Gibbon's life, during which the *Decline and Fall* took shape and half of it was written. These eighteen years present many problems to the critic, biographer and historian, not least because we are no longer informed by journals in which Gibbon recorded his doings, readings and reflections; there are only a number of historical essays, not always easy to date,[2] what can be learned from his letters, and the *Decline and Fall* itself. The years from 1765 to 1776, when the first volume of his history appeared, have been dubbed 'Gibbon's dark ages',[3] not only because the formation of his project and intentions is ill documented and obscure to us, but because it may – as the *Memoirs* sometimes indicate – have been obscure to Gibbon himself.[4] Some generalisations are, however, permissible. There is a process of self-fashioning, freed of many inhibitions by the death of Edward Gibbon II, in which Gibbon solved his problem of being both gentleman and historian by moving to London, living off the income from leasing his estate, and moving in the circles of the Literary Club and the House of Commons (to which he was elected by a patron in 1774). About this time he jokingly described himself as 'an Englishman, a philosopher, and a Whig',[5] as if his identity were settled; but in 1776, with the publication of his first volume, he

---

[1] *Memoirs*, p. 137 (*A*, p. 271); *Letters*, pp. 199–201; *YEG*, pp. 227–8; Baridon, I, pp. 122–4.
[2] These are to be found, as dated by Lord Sheffield, in *MW*, III–V; Craddock's *English Essays* is a critical edition of those in that language. A complete edition of Gibbon's essays in both French and English is much to be desired.   [3] Ghosh, 1983.
[4] *Memoirs*, pp. 136–7, 140–2 (*A*, pp. 275–6), 146–7 (*A*, pp. 283–5), 155–6 (*A*, p. 308).
[5] *Letters*, II, p. 6 (11 March 1774).

further became, and remained after death, 'the Historian of the Roman Empire'. The fashioning of the self and the persona is inseparable from the fashioning of the text and the history, and the latter has a great deal to tell us besides information about the former; Gibbon had more to attend to in this world than his own identity. The two processes, however, are not to be separated, and a crucial step in both occurs about 1768, when he gave up his projected history of Swiss liberty, thus abandoning both the history of recent modernity – for Gibbon the 'modern' began with the ending of the 'ancient' – and the attempt to write history in that language of which he had just observed to Hume that 'I write in French because I think in French.'[6] About 1768 his manuscript essays became predominantly English,[7] and by 1776 he had achieved that English prose style which many have loved and some hated, and which was to carry him through six volumes of the *Decline and Fall*. The history of its formation eludes us, because it occurred in the privacy of an interior monologue; it accompanies both the history of Gibbon's historiography, erudition and philosophy, and the history of his decisive, if never quite final, acceptance of an English identity. There is a history – one among several – of the *Decline and Fall* situated in the history of English historiography.

It is therefore desirable to re-assess Gibbon's place in that culture to which he now returned, but in which Franco Venturi regarded him as both solitary and something of an exile. When Venturi spoke at Cambridge in 1969, at the outset of his series of works on European Enlightenment, he was preoccupied with liberating the history of that movement from both a narrowly Marxist interpretation stressing the role of 'the bourgeoisie', and a German interpretation which centralised and privileged the processes in that culture collectively known as *die Aufklärung*.[8] From this liberation emerged Venturi's great work on the *Settecento Riformatore*, a study in Enlightenment concerned with concurrent developments in France, the Italian and Iberian peninsulas, and eastern Europe. For this reformation a price was to be paid, and to his few[9] Cambridge hearers Venturi said:

Power and philosophy seek each other, converge and diverge, according to the circumstances. Their struggles and agreements dominated republican Europe, just as they dominated monarchical Europe. They ruled over the Mediterranean, just as they ruled over eastern and central Europe.

---

[6] *Letters*, I, p. 222 (25 October 1767). [7] Sheffield's datings are examined by Ghosh, 1983, 1991.
[8] See Robertson, 1992, for a close consideration of Venturi's achievement.
[9] A personal recollection.

Only one country was absent from this array of 'Enlightened' thinkers in the sixties and seventies, and that was England... The fact remains that no 'parti des philosophes' was formed in London, and so could not claim to guide society. The struggles which did take place (one has only to recall 'Wilkes and liberty') are not those of a nascent intelligentsia. Even the English giant of the Enlightenment, Gibbon, was not only closely linked with continental culture but remained an isolated figure in his own country, a solitary figure... One has to wait until the eighties and nineties to find men such as Bentham, Price, Godwin and Paine. In England the rhythm was different.[10]

As historians know – but do not always remember – the problem with any exceptionalist thesis is less the exception which it claims (since every culture or moment is unique if closely enough examined) than the rule which it establishes: the set of general characteristics, belonging to some class of phenomena, from which some *Sonderweg* is said to depart. In Venturi's case this consisted in the relations between power and philosophy, and was manifest in the presence of a party of *philosophes* claiming to guide society on the roads laid down in the *settecento riformatore*. Their activities, and the responses to them, both constituted Enlightenment and 'dominated' or 'ruled' the history of Europe in general. Venturi made this assumption, and further assumed that Gibbon was a *philosophe* in this sense; and because he could find no class of English *philosophes* whose enterprises and activities had accompanied those ascribed or imputed to Gibbon, he was led – we might say obliged – to conclude that Gibbon was 'solitary' and 'isolated' in his own country, where there was no history of Enlightenment in which he could take part.

Venturi's account of a Europe-wide movement of *philosophes*, their writings and ideas, and their associations with one another, need in no way be challenged; he has left us a great portrait of who they were and what they were doing and attempting. Nor should we challenge his statement that England played no part in this movement till it had almost run its course, and that there were till then no *philosophes* in England. We may even shorten his list of those who finally appeared; perhaps only Bentham and the Philosophical Radicals – atheist, bureaucratic, possessed of an instrumental rationality that made them ready to codify England's laws and reconstruct its institutions – fit his specifications and count as *philosophes*; and even then, the philosophy that regarded the Rights of Man as 'nonsense on stilts' is far enough removed from that preceding 1789. The thesis that in England there were no

---

[10] Venturi, 1971, p. 132.

philosophes, and that to this extent 'the rhythm was different', is not to be overturned; but its presuppositions are to be re-examined. In the chapters composing this book, an attempt has been made to accept Gibbon as 'an English giant of Enlightenment' – the definite article has been dropped – and to reconstruct an Enlightenment into which he may be seen to fit. This has been a pluralist account; it has retained the *philosophes* and their enterprises, the *settecento riformatore* and perhaps even 'the Enlightenment Project',[11] as cosmopolitan and Europe-wide phenomena, while denying them the privilege of defining 'Enlightenment', or 'Europe', by formulae from which either Gibbon or England must be excluded. It has been led to make several claims: first, that Gibbon was not a *philosophe* in the senses that term took on at Paris and were disseminated throughout the *settecento riformatore*; second, that there were forms of Enlightenment, mainly Protestant in origin and character, to which he belonged and in which England's peculiar national institutions led it to take a part, but which did not produce or necessitate the presence of *philosophes* as Venturi defined them; third, that 'Enlightenment' denotes a complex of phenomena, diverse yet associated in their origins, about which general statements may be made but which no one such statement may define to the exclusion of others. There may therefore be 'Enlightenments' – such as an 'Enlightenment' defined by the presence of *philosophes* – in which England exceptionally took no part; but there can be no definition which 'rules' or 'dominates' the history of either 'Enlightenment' or 'Europe' in such a way as to leave England exceptional, or Gibbon isolated, in the context of a holistic construction.

The England which expelled Gibbon in 1753, which he served in the militia between 1759 and 1763, and to which he returned with some finality in 1765, was involved in Enlightenment in a number of ways. Some of these may be traced to the Arminian movements of the preceding century, which had affected all the Calvinist churches of western Protestantism, including that of England to the extent to which it was Calvinist; we have seen how this was capable of leading to Socinian and other conclusions, forming part of an even more general impulse to subordinate spiritual to civil authority by means that could involve a diminution of the divine nature of Christ. This in turn may be set in the context of an impulse to ensure that the wars of religion, seen as destructive of both civil magistracy and civil society, should not

---

[11] For this concept in contemporary political philosophy, see most recently, Gray, 1995, who traces it to MacIntyre, 1981, and for recent Italian comment, Giarrizzo, 1997.

return; and a significant moment in the history of that impulse has been located in the breach between Pierre Jurieu and other leaders of the Huguenot diaspora after 1683. Jean Le Clerc and Pierre Bayle, with their historical erudition tending to reduce theological dispute to civil history, were architects of the *république des lettres* that meant so much to Gibbon seventy years later, and may be linked with Parisian Enlightenment, as presented by Voltaire, by their shared perception that Louis XIV's Gallican monarchy had both defected to the cause of religious persecution and threatened European civil society by the magnitude of its ambitions and its wars.

Before the British kingdoms became involved in the opposition to Louis XIV, their wars of religion, and consequently their history and their brand of Enlightenment, had taken a course distinctively their own, occasioned by the peculiar character of the Church of England, like no other Protestant communion in the complexity of its relations with a sacred monarchy and its consequent commitment to an apostolic priesthood, a Constantinean monarchy, and the Catholic and Nicene theology which Constantine and the Church had engendered between them (and of which Gibbon was to become a historian). Since these elements sought to co-exist with a Calvinist theology and a Puritan account of religious experience, the Arminian reaction had endangered the Stuart monarchy it was designed to support by appearing to move it in a Catholic direction; and the Wars of the Three Kingdoms, in particular the English civil wars that were part of them, had been wars of religion to the extent that these issues had entered, occasioned and characterised them. Since they had involved a brief but unforgettable interlude of rule by armed sectarians who had advanced beyond Calvinism in evangelical and antinomian directions, both Anglican reaction and English Enlightenment displayed a revulsion against 'enthusiasm', in the precise sense of that term, more vivid in its historical memories than is found in the other Enlightenments which shared it.

Reaction and Enlightenment, in the above senses, are hard to separate because both are inherent in the re-establishment of the Church of England which occurred in 1660–2 and is a central theme of the 'long eighteenth century' we see as enduring until 1829–32. Because an apostolic church could be accused of claiming a crypto-papal independence of the monarchy, because the restored Stuart kings could be accused of a design to papalise the church, and because the spectres of presbytery and enthusiasm still haunted the English imagination, it was necessary to insist on the conformity between spiritual and civil authority; and this could lead to a reduction of the church to the status of a civil association, and of Christ to that of a preacher of civil morality, which leaders of the Anglican establishment might pursue, or be suspected of pursuing, to the point where there must occur a re-assertion of the apostolic authority, and conciliar and patristic theology, which both church and monarchy demanded. From this point, however, the pendulum might swing back; for the Church of England was obliged by its history and foundation to be both a Catholic church in the succession to the apostles and an Erastian church as by law established. The crucial distinction between Trinitarian and anti-Trinitarian doctrine was the ultimate though not the invariable hinge on which these alternations turned; and from the days of John Locke and Archbishop Tillotson there existed a Socinian undercurrent within the church itself, and a hierarchy willing to recognise its presence so long as it confined itself to the serious and by no means clandestine sphere of private discussion as distinct from public profession. This fragment sought to emerge from the closet in the petitioning movement of the 1770s, when it was joined by Rational Dissent proper, as we term the unitarianism to which Presbyterian and other Old Dissenting congregations had now and then turned, for reasons akin to those operating within the established church, since the beginning of the century.[12] However moderate its intentions, the movement for relief from subscription to the Thirty-Nine Articles had a strong potential for subversion in the years of the American Revolution; it queried the foundations of the regime and looked as far as the separation of church and state. This was the context in which we must read both the response to the 1776 volume of Gibbon's *Decline and Fall*, and Burke's *Reflections on the Revolution in France*; it is also the context in which three out of four of Venturi's equivalents for *philosophes* – Price, Paine and Godwin – made their appearance.[13]

   Tensions within the established church, between establishment and dissent, and within dissent itself, provide the context in which English Enlightenment must be seen. Because these tensions were widely and diversely experienced, they did not polarise the various confessions into simply opposite groups, and as a result elements of what we term Enlightenment are broadly distributed. The alliance between the higher clergy and post-Aristotelian natural philosophy, of which so much has

[12] Haakonssen, 1996a.
[13] For the view that anti-Trinitarianism was the origin of English and American political radicalism, see J. C. D. Clark, 1986 and 1994. The thesis of the present study does not look beyond the assertion that the two phenomena very often went together.

rightly been made, originated before the Restoration with clerics who must be classed as latitudinarians since they conformed to the post-1660 settlement after holding office under another; but it was carried on by churchmen as 'high' as the redoubtable (and suspect) Samuel Parker.[14] Isaac Newton in his later years kept private his Arian and alchemical views to serve as a pillar of the Revolution order in church and state. The most anti-clerical movement in the politics of culture – the 'polite learning' by which Locke, Shaftesbury and Addison intended to shift letters and philosophy from clerical to gentlemanly control – was one in which clergymen could join and be recognised as themselves gentlemen; the gentleman historian and sceptic Gibbon became a master of ec- clesiastical history. These were certainly circumstances in which he could underestimate the vehemence of clerical reaction to the fifteenth and sixteenth chapters of the *Decline and Fall*; but so to describe the episode implies that he had no programme or 'Enlightenment project' of de-Christianisation. In Gibbon's England there were wide twilight areas in which latitudinarianism could slide towards deism, and beyond it to scepticism, without expecting to be called to account at any particular point; and conversely, those with an avowed programme of replacing Christian belief – miscalled 'the English deists' – arrived at an occultist and quasi-Spinozist materialism considered atheist in the sense that it was also pantheist. When Venturi singled them out as England's chief contribution to continental Enlightenment,[15] he was privileging a definition of the latter term as entailing a clandestine irreligiosity. Such existed, in England as elsewhere, and its importance was considerable; the question is how far Enlightenment was, or is to be, organised around it.

To characterise Enlightenment as the anti-Nicene consequences of a subordination of spiritual to civil authority is to concede that in Eng- land, where the objective was as much reconciliation as subordination, it was pursued in ways strongly involving the churches themselves, and may therefore be described as both clerical and conservative – meaning by the last term not a defence of tradition against criticism, but the maintenance of church and state against the aftershocks of the civil wars. There is the further implication that Enlightenment, even philo- sophic unbelief itself, was in England contained within a context of religious diversity, establishment and dissent, where it was never fully unwelcome to those of any persuasion; and that we have here the

[14] For this figure, see Pocock, 1990b and Schochet, 1993, 1995.
[15] Venturi, 1971, pp. 49–67; cf. Young, 1998b, pp. 181–2.

explanation of the absence of *philosophes* from England. Paradoxically, 'in England the rhythm was different' because the contestations within religion kept it a profoundly ecclesiastical and in some ways clerical society, in which there was neither necessity nor opportunity for secular and irreligious intellectuals – of whom there were plenty – to 'act in corps or as a faction in the state'. Edmund Burke's words express this awareness, while further signalling that the absence of *académies* meant also the absence of a counter-organisation of *philosophes* and *Encyclopédistes*. The public space was occupied by clerisies and laities energetically debating, but as often as not maintaining, the terms of the Anglican supremacy in church and state; it was not occupied by the intellectuals of a new Enlightenment imagining alternative forms of public or cultural order. When such figures appeared at the end of the century, it was at the point where rational dissent and the responses to it merged into forms of romantic idealism. Venturi's choice of Godwin pointed in this direction.

The polity to which Gibbon returned was both England and the Kingdom of Great Britain. Gibbon's encounter with Enlightenment in its Scottish form may be said to have begun when he read the histories by Hume and Robertson during his militia service, but has yet to concern us – partly because he did not at any time visit Glasgow or Edinburgh and expose himself to Scottish culture, but also because it was only when, at a later date, he came in contact with Ferguson and Smith that Scottish philosophy played its full role in the development of his historiography. These figures call for attention here because of their appearance in the thesis of Franco Venturi which this epilogue is seeking to reconstitute. From his account of Gibbon as a *philosophe* left homeless in the rhythm that was different, Venturi went on to greet the Scottish Enlightenment as a member of his great company akin to the Enlightenments of Lombardy or France.

If looked at from Milan or Paris, Scotland in the sixties and seventies seems a familiar land, however great the originality and vitality of its intellectual life. Ferguson and Millar are of the same world as Filangieri and Condorcet. Dr Johnson is a native English god.[16]

In Scotland there was, as in England at this time there was not, a company of philosophers, well known to one another and producing major works in which a common programme may be discerned; and Venturi may be read as saying that Gibbon was a solitary figure because

---

[16] Venturi, 1971, p. 133.

he lacked such a company in England. This, however, is not to say that
the Scottish *literati* occupied a social position so close to that of the
Parisian or Milanese *philosophes* as to qualify them for inclusion in an
Enlightenment conducted by an international consortium of intellectuals bent on the criticism and reform of European society. As
philosophers in an eighteenth-century sense, they were interested in
what other philosophers were doing, and took every opportunity to
inform themselves on the subject; Hume frequented the *salons* of Paris,
at least until his disastrous experiment with Rousseau, and Smith was
caught up in the debate over political economy with the French physio-
crats. It is another thing, however, to claim, in Venturi's terms, that they
stood for philosophy seeking out power as a force independent of it.
Where we think of the *philosophes*, or the *Gelehrten*, as establishing a world
of critical thought looking at power from a standpoint outside it, the
Scottish *literati* – with Hume as a significant and major exception – held
high and legitimate office in church, law and university; they took the
lead in constituting the Moderate party in Scottish affairs, of which
William Robertson was an adroit political leader and which stood for
the interests of lay patrons of ecclesiastical livings as well as for those of
philosophers;[17] and, Unionists and Whigs to a man, they formed part of
the group of elites who conducted Scottish affairs in the interests of the
Kingdom of Great Britain. Their philosophy was neither critical nor
uncritical of established power, and was designed to support it.

In this self-chosen role, they decided that if the Union was to endure,
Scotland immediately, and England less directly, needed instruction in
the character of Enlightened commercial society, and accordingly set
about producing a series of major re-evaluations of moral philosophy,
Scottish, English, European and American history, the theoretical history of civil society, and the new field of political economy. These were
exported to England, where the re-organisation of the London book
market by Scottish publishers was the British equivalent of 'the business
of Enlightenment' – and incidentally, managed the sales of Gibbon's
Decline and Fall – and translated into French and German, following in
the latter case the trail blazed into European readership by English
Enlightenment in the form of Addison's *Spectator* and its many continental imitators. Gibbon both met and corresponded with Hume and
Robertson, may have reviewed Ferguson, and declared that he regarded Smith as a friend; but he did not need to travel to Scotland (we may

[17] Sher, 1985.

regret that he did not) in order to avail himself of Scottish intellectual productivity.

The Moderates produced philosophy (in the Enlightened sense) for Great Britain, and the English rather reluctantly consumed it; Burke served as Lord Rector of Glasgow University, Pitt proclaimed his circle Adam Smith's disciples, and the Foxite aristocracy sent their sons to study with John Millar. As well as a British and European, this was a Scottish enterprise taking place in a Scottish context; and since the latter was strongly Calvinist, Moderatism has some of the characteristics of what in this volume has been termed 'Arminian Enlightenment'. The rhetoric of Calvinist election was watered down – silently, yet against strong vocal opposition – into that of civil society and civil morality, and since Scots law was heavily civilian, the way was open for Pufendorfian natural jurisprudence – German, Dutch and Scandinavian, converging with Lockean (and therefore English) epistemology and pedagogy[18] – to provide a massive matrix through which all major Scottish enterprises passed as they took shape. It is hard to find this happening in England, and Gibbon's *Decline and Fall* seems to us formed in a humanist rather than a jurist setting – he taught himself civil law in order to write his great fifty-fourth chapter. The European problem with which he was most concerned was that of the persistence of the *belles-lettres*. We can say of the Scottish philosophers, therefore, that they shared in a common enterprise, that of substituting civil morality for Calvinist theology and converting it into philosophies and histories for civil society; and that this enterprise linked them with Enlightenment conceived on a grand scale, in its Protestant as well as its Parisian and other west European forms (even the German, of which Gibbon knew very little). We do not say this of Gibbon, or of the England in which he wrote, and we are left still facing Venturi's problem: does this leave England isolated from Enlightenment, or Gibbon isolated in England?

Scottish Enlightenment, it is well to remember, was a British as well as a European enterprise, and therefore operated in some distinctively Scottish contexts. In the first place, Lowland-dominated Scotland alone among the western kingdoms saw itself as possessing a barbarian frontier; north of the Highland line there were held to exist cattle-herding Gaelic warriors, recently defeated but yet to be absorbed into commercial society.[19] (In Ireland, the masses of unassimilated and discontented peasantry presented a problem of a different order, complicated by the

---

[18] Haakonssen, 1996b.
[19] I do not mean to endorse this vision, only to record its presence and some of its effects.

presence of Anglo-Scottish Presbyterians carrying on the discontents of the Wars of the Three Kingdoms.) Awareness of this clash of cultures does much to account for the Scottish concern with the progress through successive stages – hunting, pasture and agriculture – of the history of civil society in Europe but not in America; an interest, though not a concern, in which Gibbon came to share. In the second place, Scottish Unionism, of which Scottish Enlightenment is unmistakably a product, represented a move away from the strong alliance between Calvinist clergy and laity which had led to the Covenants of the middle of the seventeenth century; even the re-establishment of a presbyterian church in 1689 had been sufficiently the work of lay patrons and had pointed to the Moderate ascendancy of the period of Enlightenment. It became a premise of Enlightened thought that not only Union but Anglicisation were necessary to the establishment of a civil society unshaken by religious and civil war; and in consequence the history of England, and of English emergence from the wars of religion, came to appear the history that Scotsmen needed to know. David Hume in the 1750s,[20] John Millar some forty years later,[21] wrote English history, aiming as Unionists to write it better and more philosophically than the English could write it themselves; but while Hume wrote a great history of the English civil wars, neither Robertson nor any other wrote an Enlightened history of the Covenants or the Wars of the Three Kingdoms, in which Scotsmen might have been depicted attempting, even unsuccessfully, to determine the course of British history by their own acts.[22] It has therefore been argued that the great Enlightened histories of civil society in Britain, Europe and the world were achieved at the price of emptying Scottish history of its autonomy;[23] and it may be added that the cosmopolitan histories which the Scots philosophers so successfully wrote[24] were histories of a Britain and a Europe in whose making the English played an increasingly visible role, while continuing to live in a history which was theirs. The Europe of Enlightenment, it should be remembered, was in significant measure an Anglo-French condominium.

In the making of this Anglo-British historiography Gibbon played no

---

[20] Hume, 1754–62, I, pp. xii–xiii.   [21] Millar, 1787–1803.

[22] For recent proposals to present the history of this period with Scottish or Irish action as a moving force, see Russell, 1991; Morrill, 1993; Ohlmeyer, 1993; M. Bennett, 1997.

[23] Kidd, 1993; cf. Allan, 1993, and the bibliographies supplied by both.

[24] O'Brien, 1997; Robertson, 1997b. Both seem to me to suppose too simple an opposition between 'cosmopolitan' and 'national', and to overstate the degree to which the particular context may be identified with the latter.

part. Reading Hume and Robertson had helped him reach an early decision that he would write no English, let alone British, history, both because it was too contentious and because it had been done too well already. He returned in 1765 with a heavy load of neo-Latin erudition and a strong commitment to several contending centres of European learning. He returned also to a powerful imperial state, a major component of that Enlightened Europe which aimed to substitute itself for the wars of religion and the wars of universal monarchy, and which was beginning to need, and to generate, a history of the emergence of a European states system and a history of civil society lying behind it. The next volume in the series of which this is the first is planned as a study of that historiography, and the *Decline and Fall* will appear both as deeply connected with it and as individual to the point of anomaly in the context it provides; the histories of Hume and Robertson are more immediately representative of it. Gibbon's relation to what will be termed 'the Enlightened narrative' is a complex one, and it cannot be said that he ever committed himself to supplying it. The histories of Florence and the Swiss, envisaged as early as 1762, are certainly case studies in the emergence of modern from medieval Europe, but in both the problem of republican liberty in its relation to polite culture is salient, to the point of reminding us that the criticism of commercial society in the name of civic virtue was a constant challenge which Enlightenment was called upon to answer, and which had since Machiavelli if not earlier carried European historians back to consider the decline and fall of Roman virtue, preceding that of empire. It was in the logic of the kind of history Gibbon had begun to consider; before Enlightenment there had been the church; before the church there had been ancient pagan virtue; but between virtue and the church had intervened the empire. The ancient world must be confronted first with itself, then with the Christian, and then with the modern.

It will be found that 'the Enlightened narrative' typically begins with 'barbarism and religion' – the title of this series – that is, with the feudal and ecclesiastical regimes of medieval Europe, and proceeds at what speed it may towards the states system and civil society constituting Enlightenment. Gibbon is unusual in this company, first in going back to ancient virtue and then in proceeding to late antiquity and the history of the church. We have scarcely begun to consider why he did so, and there is the further problem of how and by what stages his early interest in the relations between the city and its empire in their decay expanded into a decision to write the history of empire itself (and its role in the decline of virtue). This was a turning-point in the history of 'barbarism and religion'; from the question of whether Goths or Christians had done more to ruin the buildings of Rome, Gibbon enlarged his vision into a history of barbarian society and its relation to empire, merging with the history of civil society at the point where the barbarians could be identified as belonging to the shepherd stage in conjectural history and political economy.

It was further a turning-point in the relation – identified by Arnaldo Momigliano as crucial to Gibbon's historiography[25] – between the erudition which had led him down the roads to the buildings of Rome and the grander and more philosophical narratives to which he was led by both his humanist excitement at the spectacle of ancient virtue and empire, and his Enlightened concern with the emergence of a post-ecclesiastical Europe. There are philosophical and even political dimensions here; it was his commitment to erudition that had stood between him and the *Encyclopédie,* and ensured that he had not the philosophic commitment to the sovereignty of reason to which he might see Rousseau as a threat. Where the philosopher of anti-history had commanded the individual to seek freedom in the agonising gap between personality and society, Gibbon may be read as enjoining him (and perhaps her) to enter on the crooked ways of history, ironically examining the ways in which the conduct of the individual incessantly departed from the laws of human conduct; an injunction which was to bring him close to Burke in the end.

In the same sequence, moving from the history of city and empire, the history of barbarism and empire became a history of barbarism and religion. Gibbon did not have the impulse to condemn religion and expunge it from the history of civil society; it became his criticism of the Scottish philosophers that they had failed to deal with it adequately; and the two deepest and most enigmatic departures of the *Decline and Fall* from the patterns of the 'Enlightened narrative' – the fruit of decisions probably taken only as his project advanced – were the development of a history of the patristic rather than the papal church, and the subsequent formation of a history of the eastern rather than the western empire. Neither was particularly welcomed by the readers of the *Decline and Fall,* who have always tended to judge the work by its first volume, and the search for their origins must be a complex one. We may conclude this

[25] Momigliano, 1966.

epilogue by considering them in the setting of 'the rhythm that was different'.

The Britain to which Gibbon returned in 1765 had just concluded a triumphant war that enlarged empire beyond the limits of the Treaty of Utrecht, and had witnessed that rally of the country gentlemen to Hanoverian loyalties which put an end to the dynastic uncertainties dating from 1688 and 1714. These things were bought at a price, and the system was moving towards the 'present discontents' (as Burke in opposition called them) with George III, towards the long crisis with the American colonies and Ireland, and towards the ideologically if not materially significant crisis of an anti-Trinitarian movement in both Establishment and Dissent, petitioning against the Thirty-Nine Articles and the limits of toleration. It was to be in this climate that Gibbon wrote and published the *Decline and Fall*, while himself becoming a Whig and a supporter of Lord North. The turbulence of the times caused Hume to die in the conviction (in fact unjustified) that the Hanoverian regime, undergoing *crisi*, was approaching *caduta*, while the last and perhaps the bitterest of Gibbon's quarrels with the clergy was directed against no High Church Trinitarian but against the millennial and revolutionary Unitarian Joseph Priestley. The issue was whether England – in Glasgow and Edinburgh they were less deeply shaken – could remain a regime at once Anglican and Enlightened, and Gibbon had no desire to witness the fall of Establishment. If he detested Priestley, he was on excellent terms with Richard Watson, the crypto-Socinian Bishop of Llandaff.[26] The *Decline and Fall* was written and read, attacked and defended, in the context of a crisis of the Hanoverian regime which included a crisis in the history of the English religious structure, and it is possible as well as necessary to plot Gibbon's place in this study.

He was a child of this regime, and its problems attended him through his exile from Oxford to the reception of the *Decline and Fall* and his successive decisions to follow his class in rallying to its support – a support including that given to an established church which did not much welcome it coming from Hume and Gibbon. If we are to call this the British *ancien régime*, we must keep its ecclesiastical aspect at the centre of our picture, while recollecting that like most other *anciens régimes* it believed itself both modern and Enlightened. The true meaning of *ancien* in this setting is less 'ancient' than 'ci-devant', and we are looking here at a regime that underwent crisis but did not fall in the face

---

[26] *Memoirs*, p. 162, 171 (*A*, pp. 317 n. 35, 322).

of the American and French revolutions. Gibbon's historiography was, in significant measure, shaped in this regime and by its requirements and its problems. From the moment when a crisis in his reading of sacred history drove him to Lausanne, we have been escorting him on a double English and European journey: one through a diversity of Enlightenments, another—which may have meant more to him—through the patterns of European historiography, to which there is little reason to doubt his word that he had felt from childhood an attraction amounting to a vocation. It was the politics of erudition that separated him from the first 'Enlightenment project' that drew his attention, the project of the *Encyclopédie*; behind it lay the critical enterprise of the Remonstrant and Huguenot *république des lettres* and the less combative but still Gallican enterprise of the Académie des Inscriptions. Behind both, as behind much Anglican thinking, lay the diffused enterprise which may be termed Enlightenment in the broadest sense, that of diminishing spiritual authority, or reconciling it with that of civil society, by the conversion of theology into history; a historiography convergent with the 'Enlightened narrative' that traced the emergence of the European states system and the history of civil society. But the defence of erudition against philosophy—whether or not crucial in the history of Enlightenment—ensured that Gibbon was never a *philosophe*, and that 'the English giant of the Enlightenment' had no part in the *petit troupeau des philosophes*, no part in the *settecento riformatore*, and no part whatever in the *Aufklärung*, of which he seems altogether unconscious. It further ensured that he would never be a Rational Dissenter or a Philosophic Radical; in England he could be a silently sceptical conformist to the Church of England, studying the history of a theology that maintained it and it maintained, but in which he did not believe. The problems he encountered were the problems of this posture; the posture, rather than the problems, made him the historian he was.

The defence of erudition has the further effect of moving him from the history of Enlightenment as studied by Venturi, into the history of historiography as studied by Arnaldo Momigliano, who has made us see it in terms of the contests and reconciliations among the three components of erudition, philosophy and narrative. This must be the theme of future study, but we have already watched Gibbon journeying through the landscapes it provides, varying his intentions within its matrix as he moved from Lausanne to Hampshire, and from Paris through Lausanne to Rome. He returned to England, where his intentions completed a new turn that seems to have begun on his Italian journey, bearing with him a commitment to erudition so vast that it is hard to narrate its development, and a commitment to narrative that could be completed only on a global scale. The British imperial state, insular, European and maritime, had its own reasons for being interested in the history of empires both ancient and modern. The history of Roman empire, and the new philosophic history of European civil society and religion, could alike be written only on a scale extending far into the distances of Eurasia, as the giants of Enlightened historiography were in process of discovering. Gibbon took part in this enterprise, from a starting-point defined by his discovery, made during 1764, that the history of Rome as city was the history of its abandonment by Rome as empire; but he made himself unique, in the company of Enlightened if not of ecclesiastical historians, by his decision to write a history of late antiquity as a history of theological culture. It is more important that he took this decision than that he wrote as an unbeliever in the theology in question; and while the decision may be justified by the needs of historiography, its origins were English, Anglican, familial and juvenile. His critical resolutions, that the history of Christian theology was a history of Platonist philosophy, and that the history of imperial Constantinople must take precedence over that of papal Rome and the barbarian kingdoms, were both, as we have seen, foreshadowed and taken for him by the Restoration churchman William Howel, whose *History of the World* he recalls in the *Memoirs* reading at Stourhead when he was fourteen, and whom he mentions in the *Decline and Fall* as 'that learned historian, who is not sufficiently known'.[27] It is a paradox in the study of Edward Gibbon that both his Enlightenment and his historiography had Anglican origins from which there was never any need that his European journeyings or the growth of his unbelief should separate him. English churchmanship and English Enlightenment are part of the history of Europe.

English Enlightenment, and the English churchmanship out of which it partly grew, are part of the history of post-Reformation Europe, as is the history of the Kingdom of Great Britain, formed by Orange and Hanoverian initiatives as well as by the pressures of English and Scottish history. In this volume we have followed Gibbon through the cultural landscapes of southern England, the Pays de Vaud and Paris – or, if we may enlarge the regional into the national, of Britain, Switzerland and France. A fourth, that of Italy, he experienced only *turis-*

---

[27] *Decline and Fall*, II, ch. 17, n. 130 (Wanersley, I, p. 621; Bury, II, p. 189).

ticamente; but of the first three we may say that he was deeply but not finally self-identified with two, and fascinated by the third. The return to England, necessary to his writing and our understanding of the *Decline and Fall*, was a choice but not an exile, and he carried his erudition and philosophy in both directions. Europhiles and Europhobes at present share a bad habit of placing 'England' and 'Europe' in a zero-sum relation, so that any attention to the one entails a diminution of the other. This must be avoided if we are to understand Edward Gibbon's movements in a 'Europe' in some measure an Anglo-French creation and a 'Britain' which was an Anglo-Scottish creation: a cultural scene Protestant as well as Catholic, ecclesiastical as well as civil, regional as well as cosmopolitan, social as well as monarchical, ancient as well as modern, needing and developing diverse forms of Enlightenment and comparably if not correspondingly diverse forms of historiography.

References

ORIGINALLY PUBLISHED BEFORE 1800

Angelio, Pietro (called Il Bargaeo), 1596: *De privatorum publicorumque aedificiorum Romanorum eversoribus: epistola ad Petrum Usimbandum*. Florence

Bayle, Pierre, 1696, 1697: *Dictionnaire Historique et Critique*, vols. I and II. Rotterdam

Beausobre, Isaac de, 1734: *Histoire critique de Manichée et du Manichéisme*. In two volumes. Amsterdam; repr. Leipzig, Zentralantiquariat der Deutschen Demokratischen Republik, 1970

Bossuet, Jacques-Benigne, 1671: *Exposition de la doctrine de l'église catholique sur les matières de controverse*. Paris

1681: *Discours sur l'histoire universelle à monseigneur le Dauphin, pour expliquer la suite de la religion et les changements des empires*. Paris. See Ranum, 1976

1688: *Histoire des variations des églises protestantes*. Paris

Boulainvilliers, Henri Comte de, 1730: *La Vie de Mahomed*. London

Brown, John, 1758: *An Estimate of the Manners and Principles of the Times*. London

Burke, Edmund, 1791: *Reflections on the Revolution in France, and the Proceedings of Certain Societies in London relative to that Event*. London. See Pocock, 1987a; Mitchell, 1989

Carte, Thomas, 1747: *A General History of England, containing an Account of the First Inhabitants of that Country, and the Transactions in it, from the Earliest Times to the Death of King John, AD MCCXVI*. In two volumes. London

Chillingworth, William, 1638: *The Religion of Protestants a Safe way to Salvation*. Oxford

1742: *The Works of William Chillingworth, Master of Arts, of the University of Oxford, containing his Book, entitled the Religion of Protestants a Safe Way to Salvation*... London

Crousaz, Jean Pierre de, 1724: *Système des reflections qui peuvent contribuer à la netteté et à l'étendue de nos connoissances, ou Nouvel essai de logique*. Geneva. First published Amsterdam, 1712

D'Alembert, Jean le Rond, 1751: 'Discours préliminaire des editeurs', 'Erudition' in *Encyclopédie ou dictionnaire raisonnée des sciences, des arts et des métiers, par une société des gens de lettres*. Paris. See Schwab, 1995

1773: *Mélanges de littérature, d'histoire et de philosophie*. Amsterdam

Defoe, Daniel, 1698: *An Argument Shewing that a Standing Army with Consent of Parliament is Not Inconsistent with a Free Government.* London

D'Herbelot, Barthélemy, 1697: *Bibliothèque orientale, ou dictionnaire universelle contenant généralement tout ce qui regarde la connoissance des peuples de l'Orient.* Paris

Echard, Laurence, 1713: *The Roman History, from the Removal of the Imperial Seat by Constantine the Great, to the Taking of Constantinople by the Turks. Revised, with a Recommendatory Preface, by Laurence Echard, A.M. Being a Continuation of his History*, vols. I-V. London

Fletcher, Andrew, 1697, 1698: *A Discourse concerning Militias and Standing Armies.* London; *A Discourse of Government in its Relation to Militias.* Edinburgh
  1704: *An Account of a Conversation Concerning a Right Regulation of Governments for the Common Good of Mankind.* Edinburgh

Gibbon, Edward, 1761: *Essai sur l'étude de la littérature.* London
  1776: *The History of the Decline and Fall of the Roman Empire*, vol. I. London
  1781: *The History of the Decline and Fall of the Roman Empire*, vols. II and III. London
  1788: *The History of the Decline and Fall of the Roman Empire*, vols. IV, V, VI. London. See Bury, 1909; Womersley, 1994

Guichardt, C.T., 1760: *Mémoires militaires sur les Grecs et les Romains.* Lyons
  1774: *Mémoires critiques et historiques sur plusieurs points d'antiquités militaires.* In four volumes. Berlin

Heylyn, Peter, 1652: *A Cosmographie in Foure Bookes*...London
  1657 (1681): *Ecclesia Vindicata*, repr. in *The Historical and Miscellaneous Tracts of the Reverend and Learned Peter Heylyn, D.D.* London

Hobbes, Thomas, 1651 (1991): *Leviathan, or the Matter and Form of a Commonwealth* (ed. Richard Tuck). Cambridge: Cambridge Texts in the History of Political Thought, Cambridge University Press

Howel(l), William, 1680–5: *An Institution of General History; or the History of the World.* (Vol. I) *Being a Complete Body thereof, from the Beginning of the World till the Monarchy of Constantine the Great*...(Vol. II) *That of the Roman Empire, its flourishing Condition, its Middle or Neutral State, and its Ruine and Downfall in the West*...(Vol. III)... *The History of the Ecclesiastical Affairs of the World*...*From the Conversion of Constantine the Great to the Fall of Augustulus, and the Ruine of the Empire in the West*...*The Fourth Part, containing the Original and Kingdoms of the Heruli, Goths, Lombards and Franks in Italy*...*The Monarchy of the English Saxons*...*Down to that of William the Norman*...*And Also That of the Constantinopolitan Roman Empire, from the Promotion of Nicephorus to the Death of Constantine Ducas VII, AD MLXVII, being the Year after the Conquest of this Nation by Duke William the Norman.* London

Hume, David, 1742–(1985): *Essays Moral, Political and Literary* (ed. Eugene F. Miller). Indianapolis: Liberty Press
  1754–62 (1983): *The History of England.* London (ed. William B. Todd). Indianapolis (Liberty Classics)

Macaulay, Catharine, 1763–83: *History of England from the Accession of James I to the Elevation of the House of Hanover.* In eight volumes. London

1778: *History of England from the Revolution to the Present Time, in a Series of Letters to a Friend*. London

Middleton, Conyers, 1749: *A Free Enquiry into the Miraculous Powers which are Supposed to have Subsisted in the Christian Church, from the Earliest Ages through Several Successive Centuries: By which it is Shewn that We Have no Sufficient Reason to Believe, upon the Authority of the Primitive Fathers, that any such Powers were Continued to the Church, after the Days of the Apostles*. London. Reprint (ed. René A. Wellek), New York, Garland Press, 1976

Millar, John, 1787–1803: *An Historical View of the English Government*. London

Ockley, Simon, 1708–18 (repr. 1847): *The History of the Saracens, containing the Lives ... of the Immediate Successors of Mahomet*. London

Pococke, Edward, 1663 (ed.): *Historia compendiosa dynastiarum, authore Gregorio Abul-Pharajio ... A mundo creato, usque ad tempore authoris, res orientalium accuratissime describens*. Arabice edita, et Latine versa, ab Eduardo Pocockio ... Oxford

Priestley, Joseph, 1782: *A History of the Corruptions of Christianity, in Two Volumes*. Birmingham

Smollett, Tobias, 1757: *History of England from the Restoration of 1688 to the death of George II*. London

Stephens, William, 1696 (1990): *An Account of the Growth of Deism in England*; London, 1696; Los Angeles, Augustan Reprint Society, William Andrews Clark Memorial Library

Swift, Jonathan, 1758: *The History of the Four Last Years of the Queen*, by the late Jonathan Swift. London

Trenchard, John, 1697: *An Argument Showing that a Standing Army is Inconsistent with a Free Government*. London

Whitworth, Sir Charles, (ed.), 1771: *The Political and Commercial Works of Charles d'Avenant*. London

MODERN AND SECONDARY SOURCES

Abbatista, Guido, 1981: ' "The Literary Mill": per una storia editoriale della *Universal History* (1736–1765)', *Studi Settecenteschi*, 1, 2, pp. 91–134

1996: 'Alla ricerca dell' "ordine del tempo e dello spazio." Erudizione francese e geografia "razionale" nella cultura storica di Edward Gibbon', in Imbruglia, 1996, pp. 103–88. English translation in Womersley (ed.), 1997, pp. 45–72

Adams, Geoffrey, 1991: *The Huguenots and French Opinion, 1685–1787: The Enlightenment Debate on Toleration*. Waterloo, Ontario: Wilfrid Laurier University Press

Ajello, Raffaele, Firpo, Massimo, Guerci, Luciano and Ricuperati, Giuseppe (eds.), 1985: *L'Età dei Lumi: Studi Storici sul Settecento Europeo in onore di Franco Venturi*. 2 vols. Naples: Jovene

Allan, David. 1993: *Virtue, Learning and the Scottish Enlightenment*. Edinburgh: Edinburgh University Press

Anderson, Wilda, 1990: *Diderot's Dream*. Baltimore: The Johns Hopkins University Press

Armstrong, B. G., 1969: *Calvinism and the Amyraut Heresy; Protestant Scholasticism and Humanism in Seventeenth-Century France*. Madison: University of Wisconsin Press

Ashcraft, Richard L., 1986: *Revolutionary Politics and Locke's Two Treatises of Government*. Princeton: Princeton University Press

Baridon, Michel, 1975: *Edward Gibbon et le mythe de Rome: histoire et idéologie au siècle des lumières*: Lille: Service de Reproduction des Thèses; reprinted Paris: Editions Honoré Champion, 1977

Barnes, Annie, 1938: *Jean Le Clerc (1657–1736) et la république des lettres*. Paris: Librairie E. Droz

Barret-Kriegel, Blandine, 1988–9: *Les historiens et la monarchie*. Vol. I: *Jean Mabillon, 1632–1717*; vol. II: *La défaite de l'erudition*; vol. III: *Les académies de l'histoire;* vol. IV: *La république incertaine*. Paris: Presses Universitaires de France

    1989: *L'état et ses esclaves: refléxions pour l'histoire des états*. Paris: Editions Payot. English translation by Marc A. Le Pain and Jeffrey C. Cohen, *The State and the Rule of Law*. Princeton: Princeton University Press

Beddard, R.A. (ed.), 1991: *The Revolutions of 1688: The Andrew Browning Lectures for 1988*. Oxford: Oxford University Press

Bennett, G.V., 1975: *The Tory Crisis in Church and State: The Career of Francis Atterbury, Bishop of Rochester*. Oxford: The Clarendon Press

Bennett, Martyn, 1997: *The Civil Wars in Britain and Ireland, 1638–1651*. Oxford: Blackwells

Berlin, Isaiah, 1976: *Vico and Herder: Two Studies in the History of Ideas*. London: Hogarth Press

Bloch, Marc, 1952: *Apologie pour l'Histoire, ou Métier d'Historien*. Paris: Librairie Armand Colin, Cahiers des Annales, 3

Bloom, Edward and Bloom, Lilian, 1971: *Joseph Addison's Social Animal: In the Market Place, on the Hustings, in the Pulpit*. Providence, RI: Brown University Press

Bongie, Laurence L., 1965: *David Hume, Prophet of the Counter-Revolution*. Oxford: The Clarendon Press

Bowersock, Glen, Clive, John and Graubard, Stephen, (eds.), 1977: *Edward Gibbon and the Decline and Fall of the Roman Empire*. Cambridge, MA: Harvard University Press. Originally published as *Daedalus*, 105, 3 (1976). Italian translation: Rovigatti, Franca, *Gibbon, Niebuhr, Ferrabino*. Rome: Istituto della Enciclopedia Italiana, 1980

Boynton, Lindsay, 1967: *The Elizabethan Militia, 1558–1658*. London: Routledge and Kegan Paul

Brewer, John, 1989: *The Sinews of Power: War, Money and the English State, 1688–1763*. New York: Alfred A. Knopf

Cerny, Gerald, 1987: *Theology, Politics and Letters at the Crossroads of European Civilisation; Jacques Basnage and the Baylean Huguenot Refugees in the Dutch*

Republic. The Hague: Martinus Nijhoff, International Archives of the History of Ideas, no. 107

Champion, J. A. I., 1992: *The Pillars of Priestcraft Shaken: The Church of England and its Enemies, 1660–1730*. Cambridge: Cambridge University Press

Childs, John, 1976: *The Army of Charles II*. London: Routledge

Clark, J. C. D., 1986: *English Society, 1660–1832; Ideology, Social Structure and Political Practice during the Ancien Regime*. Cambridge: Cambridge University Press

    1994: *The Language of Liberty, 1660–1832: Political Discourse and Social Dynamics in the Anglo-American World*. Cambridge: Cambridge University Press

Clark, Katherine Redwood Penovich, 1998: ' "The Whole Frame of Nature, Time and Providence": Daniel Defoe and the Transition from Rights to Politeness in English Political Discourse', PhD dissertation, The Johns Hopkins University, 1998

Colley, Linda, 1982: *In Defiance of Oligarchy: The Tory Party, 1714–1760*. Cambridge: Cambridge University Press

Cowling, Maurice, 1980: *Religion and Public Doctrine in Modern England*. Cambridge: Cambridge University Press

Cragg, Gerald R., 1968: *The Cambridge Platonists*. Oxford: Oxford University Press; repr., n.d., Lanham, MD: University Press of America

Cranston, Maurice, 1957: *John Locke: A Biography*. London: Longmans, Green

Crimmins, James E., 1983: 'John Brown and the Theological Tradition of Utilitarian Ethics', *History of Political Thought*, 4, 3, pp. 523–50

Cruickshanks, Evelyn, 1979: *Political Untouchables: The Tories and the '45*. London: Duckworth

    (ed.), 1982: *Ideology and Conspiracy: Aspects of Jacobitism, 1689–1759*. Edinburgh: John Donald

Daniel, Stephen, 1985: *John Toland: His Methods, Manners and Mind*. Kingston and Montreal: McGill-Queens University Press

Darnton, Robert, 1979: *The Business of Enlightenment: A Publishing History of the Encyclopédie*. Cambridge, MA: The Belknap Press of Harvard University Press

Davis, Herbert (ed.), 1951: *The Prose Works of Jonathan Swift*, vol. III: *The History of the Four Last Years of the Queen*. Oxford: Oxford University Press

Deane, Seumas, 1989: *The French Revolution and Enlightenment in England, 1789–1832*. Cambridge, MA: Harvard University Press

De Grazia, Sebastian, 1989: *Machiavelli in Hell*. Princeton: Princeton University Press

Diamond, W. Craig, 1982: 'Public Identity in Restoration England: From Prophetic to Economic', PhD dissertation, The Johns Hopkins University

Dibon, Paul (ed.), 1959: *Pierre Bayle, le philosophe de Rotterdam; études et documents*. Amsterdam

Dickinson, H. T. , 1970: *Bolingbroke*. London, Constable

Dickson, P. G. M., 1967: *The Financial Revolution in England: A Study in the Development of Public Credit*. London: Macmillan

Dodge, Guy Howard, 1947: *The Political Theory of the Huguenots of the Dispersion: with Special Reference to the Thought and Influence of Pierre Jurieu*. New York: Columbia University Press

Douglas, D. C., 1943: *English Scholars*. London: Jonathan Cape

Dunn, John, 1990: *The Economic Limits to Modern Politics*. Cambridge: Cambridge University Press

Ealy, Lenore T., 1997: 'Reading the Signatures of the Divine Author; Providence, Nature and History in Ralph Cudworth's Apologetic'', PhD dissertation, The Johns Hopkins University

Evans, A. W., 1932: *Warburton and the Warburtonians: A Study in some Eighteenth-Century Controversies*. Oxford: Oxford University Press

Fairburn, A. R. D., 1966: *Collected Poems*. Christchurch: The Pegasus Press

Fatio, Olivier and Martin-van Berchem, Louise, 1985: 'L'eglise de Genève et la Revocation de l'Edit de Nantes', in *Genève au Temps de la Révocation de l'Edit de Nantes*. Geneva: Mémoires et Documents publiés par la Société d'Histoire et d'Archéologie de Genève

Fix, Andrew C., 1990: *Prophecy and Reason: The Dutch Collegiants in the Early Enlightenment*. Princeton: Princeton University Press

Fletcher, Anthony, 1981: *The Outbreak of the English Civil War*. New York: New York University Press

Fontana, Biancamaria, 1991: *Benjamin Constant and the Post-Revolutionary Mind*. Cambridge: Cambridge University Press

Gascoigne, John, 1990: *Cambridge in the Age of the Enlightenment: Science, Religion and Politics from the Restoration to the French Revolution*. Cambridge: Cambridge University Press

Gentles, Ian, 1992: *The New Model Army in England, Scotland and Ireland, 1645–1655*. New Haven: Yale University Press

Ghosh, P. R., 1983: 'Gibbon's Dark Ages: Some Remarks on the Genesis of the *Decline and Fall*', *Journal of Roman Studies*, 73, pp. 1–23

1991: 'Gibbon Observed', *Journal of Roman Studies*, 81, pp. 132–56

1995: 'Gibbon's First Thoughts: Rome, Christianity and the *Essai sur l'Etude de la Littérature*', *Journal of Roman Studies*, 85, pp. 148–64

1996: 'Gibbon e la concezione del *Decline and Fall*', in Imbruglia, 1996, pp. 5–53

1997a: 'The Conception of Gibbon's *History*', in McKitterick and Quinault, 1997, pp. 271–316

1997b: 'Gibbon's Timeless Verity: Nature and Neo-classicism in the Late Enlightenment', in Womersley, 1997, pp. 121–63

Giarrizzo, Giuseppe, 1954: *Edward Gibbon e la cultura europea del settecento*. Naples: nella Sede del Istituto, Istituto per gli Studi Storici

1997: 'Enlightenment: The Parabola of an Idea', *Proceedings of the American Philosophical Society*, 141, 4, pp. 436–53

Goldgar, Anne, 1995: *Impolite Learning: conduct and community in the Republic of Letters, 1680–1750*. New Haven: Yale University Press

Goldie, Mark, 1980: 'The Roots of True Whiggism', *History of Political Thought*, 1,

2, pp. 195–236

1991: 'The Political Thought of the Anglican Revolution', in Beddard, 1991, pp. 102–36

Goodman, Dena, 1994: *The Republic of Letters: A Social History of the French Enlightenment*. Ithaca, NY: Cornell University Press

Gossman, Lionel, 1968: *Medievalism and the Ideologies of Enlightenment: the world and work of La Curne de Sainte-Palaye*. Baltimore: The Johns Hopkins University Press

  1981: *The Empire Unpossess'd: An Essay upon Gibbon's Decline and Fall*. Cambridge: Cambridge University Press

Gould, Eliga H., 1991: 'To Strengthen the King's Hands: Dynastic Legitimacy, Militia Reform and the Ideas of National Unity in England, 1745–1760', *Historical Journal*, 34, 2, pp. 329–48

  1992: 'War, Empire and the Language of State Formation: British Imperial Culture in the Age of the American Revolution', PhD dissertation, The Johns Hopkins University

  1997: 'American Independence and Britain's Counter-Revolution', *Past and Present*, 154, pp. 107–42

Gray, John, 1995: *Enlightenment's Wake: Politics and Culture at the Close of the Modern Age*. London: Routledge

Grell, Chantal, 1993: *L'histoire entre érudition et philosophie; étude sur la connaissance historique à l'âge des lumières*. Paris: Presses Universitaires de France

Haakonssen, Knud, 1996a: *Natural Law and Moral Philosophy: From Grotius to the Scottish Enlightenment*. Cambridge: Cambridge University Press

  (ed.), 1996b: *Enlightenment and Religion: Rational Dissent in Eighteenth-Century Britain*. Cambridge: Cambridge University Press

Haitsma Mulier, E. O. C., 1980: *The Myth of Venice and Dutch Republican Thought*. Assen: Van Gorcum

Hampsher-Monk, Iain, 1998: 'Burke and the Religious Sources of Skeptical Conservatism', in J. Van der Zande and R. H. Popkin (eds.), *The Skeptical Tradition around 1800*, The Hague: Kluwer Academic Publishers, pp. 235–59

Haskell, Francis, 1993: *History and its Images: Art and the Interpretation of the Past*. New Haven: Yale University Press. Paperback edn 1995

Heyd, Michael, 1982: *Between Orthodoxy and the Enlightenment: Jean-Robert Chouet and the Introduction of Cartesian Science in the Academy of Geneva*. The Hague: Martinus Nijhoff; Jerusalem: The Magnes Press, International Archives of the History of Ideas, no. 96

Hibbard, Caroline, 1983: *Charles I and the Popish Plot*. Chapel Hill: University of North Carolina Press

Hicks, Philip S., 1987: 'Bolingbroke, Clarendon, and the Role of Classical Historian', *Eighteenth-Century Studies*, 20, 4, pp. 445–71

  1988: 'Historical Culture from Clarendon to Hume: The Fortunes of Classic British History, 1671–1757', PhD Dissertation, The Johns Hopkins University

1996: *Neo-classical History and English Culture: from Clarendon to Hume.* New York: St Martins Press

Hill, Bridget, 1992: *The Republican Virago: The Life and Times of Catharine Macaulay, Historian.* Oxford: The Clarendon Press

Hoak, Dale F. and Feingold, Mordechai, (eds.), 1996: *The Revolution of 1688–89: Anglo-Dutch Perspectives on the World of William III and Mary II.* Stanford: Stanford University Press

Holmes, Geoffrey, 1973: *The Trial of Doctor Sacheverell.* London: Eyre Methuen

Hont, Istvan, 1990: 'Free Trade and the Economic Limits to National Politics: Neo-Machiavellian Political Economy Reconsidered', in Dunn, 1990, pp. 41–120

Hymes, Robert P. and Schirokauer, Conrad, (eds.), 1994: *Ordering the World: Approaches to State and Society in Sung Dynasty China.* Berkeley and Los Angeles: University of California Press

Imbruglia, Girolamo (ed.), 1996: *Ragione e Immaginazione: Edward Gibbon e la storiografia europea del Settecento.* Naples: Liguori

Iofrida, Manlio, 1983: *La filosofia di John Toland: Spinozismo, scienza e religione nella cultura europea fra '600 e '700.* Milan: Franco Angeli

Israel, Jonathan I. (ed.), 1991: *The Anglo-Dutch Moment: essays on the Glorious Revolution and its world impact.* Cambridge: Cambridge University Press

Jacob, J. R., 1978: *Robert Boyle and the English Revolution.* New York: Burt Franklin
    1983: *Henry Stubbe: Radical Protestantism and the Early Enlightenment.* Cambridge: Cambridge University Press

Jacob, M. C., 1976: *The Newtonians and the English Revolution.* Ithaca: Cornell University Press
    1981: *The Radical Enlightenment: Pantheists, Freemasons and Republicans.* London: Allen and Unwin
    1985: 'In the Aftermath of Revolution: Rousset de Missy, Freemasonry and Locke's *Two Treatises of Government*', in Ajello, 1985, vol. II, pp. 487–522
    1991: *Living the Enlightenment: Freemasonry and Politics in Eighteenth-Century Europe.* New York: Oxford University Press

Jones, J. R., 1973: *The Revolution of 1688 in England.* New York: W. W. Norton
    (ed.), 1992: *Liberty Secured? Britain before and after 1688.* Stanford, Stanford University Press

Kelley, Donald R., 1990: *The Human Measure: Social Thought in the Western Legal Tradition.* Cambridge, MA: Harvard University Press

Kenyon, John P., 1977: *Revolution Principles. The Politics of Party, 1689–1720.* Cambridge: Cambridge University Press

Kidd, Colin, 1993: *Subverting the Scottish Past: Scottish Whig Historians and the Creation of an Anglo-British Identity, 1689–1830.* Cambridge: Cambridge University Press

Kishlansky, Mark, 1979: *The Rise of the New Model Army.* Cambridge: Cambridge University Press

Klein, Lawrence E., 1994: *Shaftesbury and the Culture of Politeness: Moral Discourse and Cultural Politics in Eighteenth Century England.* Cambridge: Cambridge

University Press

Kors, Alan C., 1976: *D'Holbach's Coterie: An Enlightenment in Paris.* Princeton: Princeton University Press

1990: *Atheism in France, 1650–1729.* Vol. I: *The Orthodox Sources of Disbelief.* Princeton: Princeton University Press

Kroll, Richard, Ashcraft, Richard and Zagorin, Perez (eds.), 1992: *Philosophy, Science and Religion in England, 1640–1700.* Cambridge: Cambridge University Press

Labrousse, Elisabeth, 1963–4: *Pierre Bayle.* Vol. I: *Du pays de Foix à la cité d'Erasme*; Vol. II: *Hetérodoxie et rigorisme.* The Hague: Martinus Nijhoff, International Archives of the History of Ideas, nos. 1, 6

Lamont, William M., 1963: *Marginal Prynne, 1600–1669.* London: Routledge and Kegan Paul

1979: *Richard Baxter and the Millennium.* London: Croom Helm

Langford, Paul, 1989: *A Polite and Commercial People: England, 1727–1783.* Oxford: Oxford University Press

Laslett, Peter (ed.), 1960: *Two Treatises of Government by John Locke.* Cambridge: Cambridge University Press; (1990) Cambridge Texts in the History of Political Thought. First published 1960

Laursen, John Christian, 1992: *The Politics of Scepticism in the Ancients, Montaigne, Hume and Kant.* Leiden: E. J. Brill, Studies in Intellectual History, no. 35

(ed.), 1995: *New Essays on the Political Thought of the Huguenots of the Refuge.* Leiden: E. J. Brill, Studies in Intellectual History, no. 60

La Vopa, Anthony J., 1995: 'Herder's *Publikum*: Language, Print and Sociability in Eighteenth-Century Germany', *Eighteenth-Century Studies*, 29, 1, pp. 5–24

Lenman, Bruce, 1980: *The Jacobite Risings in Britain, 1689–1746.* London: Eyre Methuen

Levine, Joseph M., 1991: *The Battle of the Books: History and Literature in the Augustan Age.* Ithaca: Cornell University Press

1997: 'Erasmus and the Problem of the Johannine Comma', *Journal of the History of Ideas*, 8, 4, pp. 573–96

Litchfield, R. Burr, 1989 (trans.): *Franco Venturi: The End of the Old Regime in Europe (1768–1776): The First Crisis.* Princeton: Princeton University Press

1991 (trans.): *Franco Venturi: The End of the Old Regime in Europe (1776–1789).* Vol. I: The Great States of the West. II: *Republican Patriotism and the Empires of the East.* Two volumes. Princeton: Princeton University Press

Lowenthal, David, 1965 (trans.): *Considerations on the Causes of the Greatness of the Romans and their Decline, by Montesquieu.* New York: The Free Press

MacInnes, Angus, 1970: *Robert Harley: Puritan Politician.* London: Gollancz

MacIntyre, Alasdair, 1981: *After Virtue.* London: Duckworth

McKitterick, R. and Quinault, R. (eds.), 1997: *Gibbon and Empire.* Cambridge: Cambridge University Press

MacLachlan, H. J., 1951: *Socinianism in Seventeenth-Century England.* Oxford: Oxford University Press

McLynn, F. J., 1985: *The Jacobites.* London: Routledge and Kegan Paul

Mansfield, Harvey, 1979: *Machiavelli's New Modes and Orders: A Study of the Discourses on Livy*. Ithaca, Cornell University Press

Manuel, Frank E., 1963: *Isaac Newton, Historian*. Cambridge, MA: Harvard University Press

1974: *The Religion of Isaac Newton*. Oxford: Oxford University Press

Marino, James F., 1998: 'Empire and Commerce: An History of the Modern States-System', PhD dissertation, The Johns Hopkins University

Marshall, John, 1990: 'John Locke in Context: Religion, Ethics and Politics', PhD dissertation, The Johns Hopkins University

1992: 'John Locke and Latitudinarianism', in Kroll, Ashcraft and Zagorin, 1992, pp. 253–82

1994: *John Locke: Resistance, Religion, Responsibility*. Cambridge: Cambridge University Press

forthcoming: 'John Locke and Socinianism', in M. A. Stewart (ed.), *Seventeenth-Century Philosophy in Historical Context*. Oxford: The Clarendon Press

Mastellone, Salvo (ed.), 1988: *Daniel Mazel: Du gouvernement civil, ou l'on traite de l'origine des fondemens de la nature, du pouvoir, et des fins des societes politiques; traduit de l'Anglois*. Florence: Centro Editoriale Toscano; Politica e Storia, Saggi e Testi

Miller, Eugene F. (ed.), 1985: *David Hume: Essays Moral, Political and Literary*. Indianapolis: Liberty Classics

Miller, John, 1973: *Popery and Politics in England, 1660–1688*. Cambridge: Cambridge University Press

1989: *James II: a Study in Kingship*. London: Methuen

Mintz, Samuel, 1962: *The Hunting of Leviathan*. Cambridge: Cambridge University Press

Minuti, Rolando, 1986: 'Il problema storico della libertà inglese nella cultura radicale dell'età di Giorgio III, Catharine Macaulay e la rivoluzione puritana', *Rivista Storica Italiana* 98, 3, pp. 793–860

Mitchell, L. G. (ed.), 1989: *The Writings and Speeches of Edmund Burke*, Vol. VIII: *The French Revolution, 1790–94*. Oxford: The Clarendon Press

Momigliano, Arnaldo, 1955: *Contributo alla Storia degli Studi Classici*. Rome: Edizioni di Storia e Letteratura

1966: *Studies in Historiography*. London: Weidenfeld and Nicolson

Monod, Paul, 1989: *Jacobitism and the English People, 1688–1788*. Cambridge: Cambridge University Press

Moore, James, 1989: 'Natural Law and the Pyrrhonian Controversy', in Peter Jones (ed.), *Philosophy and Science in the Scottish Enlightenment*. Edinburgh: John Donald, pp. 20–38

Morrill, John (ed.), 1990: *Oliver Cromwell and the English Revolution*. London: Longmans

1991: *The Impact of the English Civil War*. London: Collins and Brown

1993: *The Nature of the English Revolution*. London: Longmans

Morrow, John, 1990: *Coleridge's Political Thought: Property, Morality and the Limits of Traditional Discourse*. Houndsmills: Macmillan

(ed.) 1991: *Coleridge's Writings*, Vol. 1: *On Politics and Society*. Princeton: Princeton University Press

Muret, Pierre, 1937: *La Prépondérance Anglaise*. Paris: Alcan; series eds. Louis Halphen and Philippe Sagnac, Peuples et Civilisations: Histoire Générale

Murray, James P., 1986: 'Charity, Zeal and Spiritual Authority in Britain, 1660–1700', PhD dissertation, The Johns Hopkins University

Nenner, Howard, 1991: 'Liberty, Law and Property: the Constitution in Retrospect from 1689', in J. R. Jones, 1992, pp. 88–121

Neveu, Bruno, 1966: *Un Historien à l'Ecole de Port-Royal: Sébastien Le Nain de Tillemont, 1637–1698*. The Hague: Martinus Nijhoff

Newman, Gerald, 1987: *The Rise of English Nationalism: A Cultural History, 1740–1830*. New York: St Martin's Press

O'Brien, Karen, 1997: *Narratives of Enlightenment: Cosmopolitan History from Voltaire to Gibbon*. Cambridge: Cambridge University Press

Ohlmeyer, Jane, 1993: *Civil War and Restoration in the Three British Monarchies: The Career of Randal Macdonnell, Marquis of Antrim, 1609–1683*. Cambridge: Cambridge University Press

Okie, Laird, 1991: *Augustan Historical Writing: Histories of England in the English Enlightenment*. Lanham, MD: University Press of America

Pagden, Anthony (ed.), 1987: *The Languages of Political Theory in Early Modern Europe*. Cambridge: Cambridge University Press

Parel, Anthony, 1992: *The Machiavellian Cosmos*. New Haven: Yale University Press

Parker, Geoffrey, 1988: *The Military Revolution: Military Innovation and the Rise of the West, 1500–1800*. Cambridge: Cambridge University Press

Patrides, C. A., 1969: *The Cambridge Platonists*. Cambridge: Cambridge University Press

Perry, Elisabeth Israels, 1973: *From Theology to History: French Religious Controversy and the Revocation of the Edict of Nantes*. The Hague: Martinus Nijhoff, International Archives of the History of Ideas, no. 67

Phillipson, Nicholas and Skinner, Quentin (eds.), 1993: *Political Discourse in Early Modern Britain*. Cambridge: Cambridge University Press

Pocock, J. G. A., 1975: *The Machiavellian Moment: Florentine Political Thought and the Atlantic Republican Tradition*. Princeton: Princeton University Press

(ed.), 1977a: *The Political Works of James Harrington*. Cambridge: Cambridge University Press

1977b: 'Between Machiavelli and Hume; Gibbon as Civic Humanist and Philosophical Historian', in Bowersock, Clive and Graubard, 1977, pp. 153–69

1981: 'Gibbon and the Shepherds: The Stages of Society in the *Decline and Fall*', *History of European Ideas*, 2, 3, pp. 193–202

1982: 'Superstition and Enthusiasm in Gibbon's History of Religion', *Eighteenth-Century Life*, 8, 1, pp. 83–94

1985a: *Virtue, Commerce and History; Essays on Political Thought and History, chiefly in the Eighteenth Century*. Cambridge: Cambridge University Press

1985b: 'Clergy and Commerce: The Conservative Enlightenment in England', in Ajello, 1985, I, pp. 523–62

(ed.), 1987a: *Edmund Burke: Reflections on the Revolution in France*. Indianapolis: Hackett Publishers

1987b: *The Ancient Constitution and the Feudal Law. English Historical Thought in the Seventeenth Century*, reissued with a retrospect. Cambridge: Cambridge University Press

1988 (1992): 'The Fourth English Civil War: Dissolution, Desertion and Alternative Histories in the Glorious Revolution', *Government and Opposition*, 23, 2, pp. 151–66; partly reprinted in Schwoerer 1992, pp. 52–64

1989a: 'Conservative Enlightenment and Democratic Revolutions: The *Government and Opposition*/Leonard Schapiro Lecture, 1988', in *Government and Opposition*, 24, 1, pp. 81–105

1989b: 'Edmund Burke and the Redefinition of Enthusiasm: The Context as Counter-Revolution', in François Furet and Mona Ozouf (eds.), *The French Revolution and the Creation of Modern Political Culture*, vol. III. Oxford: Pergamon Press

1990a: 'Edward Gibbon in History: Aspects of the Text in *The History of the Decline and Fall of the Roman Empire*', in Grethe B. Peterson (ed.), *The Tanner Lectures on Human Values*, vol. XI. Salt Lake City, The University of Utah Press, pp. 289–364

1990b, 'Thomas Hobbes Atheist or Enthusiast? His Place in a Restoration Debate', *History of Political Thought*, II, 4, pp. 737–49

1994: 'Machiavelli and the Rethinking of History', *Il Pensiero Politico*, 27, 2, pp. 215–30

1995: 'Within the Margins: The Definitions of Orthodoxy', in Roger D. Lund (ed.), *The Margins of Orthodoxy: Heterodox Writing and Cultural Response, 1660–1750*. Cambridge: Cambridge University Press, pp. 33–53

1996: 'Standing Army and Public Credit: the Institutions of Leviathan', in Hoak and Feingold, 1996, pp. 87–103

Popkin, Richard H., 1979: *The History of Scepticism from Erasmus to Spinoza*. Berkeley and Los Angeles: University of California Press

Porter, Roy and Teich, Mikulas (eds.), 1981: *The Enlightenment in National Context*. Cambridge: Cambridge University Press

Prown, Jules David, 1997: 'A Course of Antiquities at Rome, 1764', in *Eighteenth-Century Studies*, 21, 1, pp. 90–100

Pullapilly, Cyriac K., 1975: *Caesar Baronius, Counter-Reformation Historian*. Notre Dame: University of Notre Dame Press

Rahe, Paul A., 1992: *Republics Ancient and Modern*. Ithaca, Cornell University Press

Ranum, Orest (ed.), 1976: *Jacques-Benigne Bossuet: Discourse on Universal History*. Translated by Elborg Forster. Chicago: University of Chicago Press

Rex, Walter E., 1966: *Essays on Pierre Bayle and Religious Controversy*. The Hague: Martinus Nijhoff

Richter, Melvin (ed.), 1990: *Montesquieu: Selected Political Writings*. Indianapolis:

Hackett

Ritchie, Daniel E. (ed.), 1992: *Further Reflections on the Revolution in France: Edmund Burke*. Indianapolis: Liberty Fund

Robbins, Caroline, 1959: *The Eighteenth Century Commonwealthman: Studies in the Transmission, Development and Circumstances of English Liberal Thought from the Restoration of Charles II until the War with the Thirteen Colonies*. Cambridge, MA: Harvard University Press

Robertson, John, 1985: *The Scottish Enlightenment and the Militia Issue*. Edinburgh: John Donald

   1992: 'Franco Venturi's Enlightenment', *Past and Present*, 137, pp. 183–206

   (ed.) 1993a: *A Union for Empire: The Union of 1707 in the History of British Political Thought*. Cambridge: Cambridge University Press

   1993b: 'Universal Monarchy and the Liberties of Europe; David Hume's critique of an English Whig doctrine', in Phillipson and Skinner, 1993, pp. 349–73

   (ed.), 1997a: *Andrew Fletcher: Political Works*. Cambridge: Cambridge University Press

   1997b: 'The Enlightenment above National Context: Political Economy in Eighteenth-Century Scotland and Naples', *Historical Journal*, 40, 3, pp. 667–98

Rossini, Gigliola, 1987: 'The Criticism of Rhetorical Historiography and the Ideal of Scientific Method: History, Nature and Science in the Political Language of Thomas Hobbes', in Pagden, 1987, pp. 303–24

Rule, Paul A., 1986: *K'ung-tzu or Confucius? The Jesuit Interpretation of Confucianism*. Sydney: Allen and Unwin

Rupp, Ernest Gordon, 1986: *Religion in England, 1688–1791*. Oxford: The Clarendon Press

Russell, Conrad, 1991: *The Fall of the British Monarchies, 1637–1642*. Oxford: The Clarendon Press

Schochet, Gordon J., 1993: 'Between Lambeth and Leviathan: Samuel Parker on the Church of England and Political Order', in Phillipson and Skinner, 1993, pp. 189–208

   1995: 'Samuel Parker, Religious Diversity and the Ideology of Persecution', in Roger D. Lund (ed.), *The Margins of Orthodoxy: Heterodox Writing and Cultural Response, 1660–1750*. Cambridge: Cambridge University Press, pp. 119–48

Schwab, Richard N. (ed. and trans.), 1995: *D'Alembert: Preliminary Discourse to the Encyclopedia of Diderot*. Originally published Indianapolis and New York: Bobbs Merrill, Library of Liberal Arts, 1963; republished Chicago: University of Chicago Press

Schwartz, Hillel, 1980: *The French Prophets: The History of a Millenarian Group in Eighteenth-Century England*. Berkeley and Los Angeles: University of California Press

Schwoerer, Lois G., 1975: *No Standing Armies! The Anti-Army Controversy in Seventeenth-Century England*. Baltimore: The Johns Hopkins University Press

(ed.), 1992: *The Revolution of 1688–1689: Changing Perspectives.* Cambridge: Cambridge University Press

Shapin, Steven and Schaffer, Simon, 1985: *Leviathan and the Air-Pump: Hobbes, Boyle, and the Experimental Life.* Princeton: Princeton University Press

Sher, Richard B., 1985: *Church and University in the Scottish Enlightenment: The Moderate literati of Edinburgh.* Princeton: Princeton University Press

Siedentop, Larry (ed.), 1997: *Francois Guizot: the History of Civilization in Europe.* Harmondsworth: Penguin Books

Speck, W. A., 1989: *Reluctant Revolutionaries: Englishmen and the Revolution of 1688.* Oxford: Oxford University Press

Spurr, John, 1991: *The Restoration Church of England, 1646–1689.* New Haven, Yale University Press

Stephan, Deborah, 1986: 'Eighteenth-Century England Reviews its Seventeenth-Century Past', PhD dissertation, University of Sydney

   1989: 'Laurence Echard, Whig Historian', *The Historical Journal,* 33, 4, pp. 843–66

Strauss, Leo, 1969: *Thoughts on Machiavelli.* Seattle: University of Washington Press

Sullivan, Robert, 1982: *John Toland and the Deist Controversy.* Cambridge, MA: Harvard University Press

Szechi, Daniel, 1984: *Jacobitism and Tory Politics, 1710–14.* Edinburgh: John Donald

Thom, Martin, 1995: *Republics, Nations and Tribes.* London: Verso

Toomer, G. J., 1996: *Eastern Wisedome and Learning: The Study of Arabic in Seventeenth-Century England.* Oxford: The Clarendon Press

Trevor-Roper, H. R., 1968: *The Crisis of the Seventeenth Century: Religion, the Reformation and Social Change.* New York: Harper and Row

   1988: *Catholics, Anglicans and Puritans.* Chicago: University of Chicago Press

   1992: *From Counter-Reformation to Glorious Revolution.* Chicago: University of Chicago Press

Tuck, Richard, 1988: *Hobbes.* Oxford: Oxford Past Masters Series

   (ed.), 1991: *Thomas Hobbes: Leviathan.* Cambridge: Cambridge Texts in the History of Political Thought

Turnbull, Paul, 1982: 'The Supposed Infidelity of Edward Gibbon', *The Historical Journal,* 25, 1, pp. 23–42

   1987: ' "Buffeted for Ancestral Sins": Some Neglected Aspects of Gibbon's Roman Conversion', *Eighteenth-Century Life,* 11, n.s. 1 (Studies in the Eighteenth Century 6: *Papers presented at the Sixth David Nicol Smith Memorial Seminar,* Melbourne, 1983), pp. 18–37

   1991: 'Gibbon and Pastor Allamand', *Journal of Religious History,* 16, 3, pp. 280–91

Tyacke, Nicholas, 1987: *Anti-Calvinists: The Rise of English Arminianism, c. 1590–1640.* Oxford: The Clarendon Press. Paperback edition 1990

Velema, W. R. E., 1993: *Enlightenment and Conservatism in the Dutch Republic: the political thought of Elie Luzac (1721–1796).* Assen: Van Gorcum

Venn, A. W., 1922: *Alumni Cantabrigienses*. 2 vols. Cambridge: Cambridge University Press

Venturi, Franco, 1969: *Settecento Riformatore: da Muratori a Beccaria*. Turin: Einaudi

  1971: *Utopia and Reform in the Enlightenment*. Cambridge: Cambridge University Press

  1976: *Settecento Riformatore*, vol. II: *La chiesa e la repubblica dentro i loro limiti*. Turin: Einaudi

  1979: *Settecento Riformatore*, III: *la prima crisi dell'Antico Regime (1768–1776)*. Turin: Einaudi

  1984: *Settecento Riformatore*, IV (1) and IV (2): *la caduta dell'Antico Regime (1776–1789)*. (1) *I grandi stati dell'Occidente*; (2) *il patriottismo repubblicano e gli imperi dell'Est*. Turin: Einaudi. See Litchfield, 1989, 1991

Vuilleumier, Henri, 1927–33: *Histoire de l'Eglise Reformée du Pays de Vaud sous le Régime Bernois*. In four volumes. Lausanne: Editions La Concorde

Waquet, Françoise, 1989: 'Qu'est-ce que c'est la République des Lettres? Essai de sémantique historique.' *Bibliothèque de l'Ecole des Chartes*, 147, pp. 473–502

Webb, Stephen Saunders, 1979: *The Governors General: The English Army and the Definition of Empire*. Chapel Hill: University of North Carolina Press

Western, J. R., 1965: *The English Militia in the Eighteenth Century: The Story of a Political Issue, 1660–1802*. London: Routledge and Kegan Paul

Williamson, Arthur H., 1979: *Scottish National Consciousness in the Age of James VI: The Apocalypse, the Union and the shaping of Scotland's public culture*. Edinburgh: John Donald

Womersley, David, 1988: *The Transformation of the Decline and Fall of the Roman Empire*. Cambridge: Cambridge University Press

  (ed.), 1994: *Edward Gibbon: The History of the Decline and Fall of the Roman Empire*. In three volumes. London: Allen Lane, The Penguin Press

  (ed.), 1997: *Gibbon: Bicentenary Essays*. Oxford: The Voltaire Foundation

Woolrych, Arnold, 1987: *Soldiers and Statesmen: The Army Council and its debates*. Oxford: The Clarendon Press

Wootton, David, 1983: *Paolo Sarpi: Between Reason and Enlightenment*. Cambridge: Cambridge University Press

Yolton, John, 1983: *Thinking Matter: Materialism in Eighteenth-Century Britain*. Minneapolis: University of Minnesota Press

Young, B. W., 1998a: ' "Scepticism in excess": Gibbon and Eighteenth-Century Christianity', *Historical Journal*, 41, 1, pp. 179–200

  1998b: *Religion and Enlightenment in Eighteenth-Century England: Theological Debates from Locke to Burke*. Oxford: The Clarendon Press

Yovel, Yirmiyahu, 1989: *Spinoza and Other Heretics: The Marrano of Reason*. Princeton: Princeton University Press

Index